# TERRORISM IN PUNJAB

# TERRORISM IN PUNJAB

Satya Pal Dang

Edited by
V.D. Chopra and Ravi M. Bakaya

GYAN PUBLISHING HOUSE
NEW DELHI-110002

TERRORISM IN PUNJAB
*CRIME*

ISBN: 81-212-0659-6



Published in 2000 in India by
Gyan Publishing House
5, Ansari Road,
New Delhi-110 002

*Laser Typesetting at:* Power Photocomposers, New Delhi-110 002
*Printed at:* Mehra Offset Press

## Contents

## From the Editors

No one is in a better position to write on the subject of this book than its author who was not only an eye-witness to many events described here, but also an active participant in the grim struggle against terrorism and secessionism in Punjab.

Most of these articles were published in various newspapers and periodicals of the country, too numerous to be enumerated individually. This book is not only a unique record of what happened, but also a brilliant analysis of why it happened, and provides an answer to what must be done to overcome the menace of terrorism and secessionism to preserve the unity and integrity of our country.

Born on October 4, 1920 in Gujranwala district (now in Pakistan), Satya Pal Dang had a brilliant academic career, graduating from Government College, Lahore. He took an active part in the pre-independence student movement and rose to be the General Secretary of the All-India Students Federation. He was also elected a Vice-President of the World Youth Federation. He and his future wife Vimla Bakaya met as activists of the Lahore Students Union. In 1943 both of them went to Bengal to campaign for aid to the victims of the great famine of 1943, which claimed over three million lives. They got married in Bombay in 1952 after Vimla had returned from Prague, where she represented India in the International Union of Students.

In early fifties the Dangs settled down in Chheharta, a small industrial suburb of Amritsar. Living in the working class area, Satya Pal along with other trade union leaders built up a strong trade union movement in Punjab. He was also the leading figure in the Chheharta Municipal Committee since 1953 and its president until 1967, when he joined the United Front Government as a minister. They built up the municipal committee as a model municipality in which all parties worked together to improve civic conditions and build roads, provide hand pumps and street lights, a hospital and several dispensaries, a citizen's hall and other amenities. Later Vimla Dang took over as president. In 1967,

Satya Pal entered the Punjab Legislative Assembly by defeating the then Chief Minister Gurmukh Singh Musafir in the Amritsar West constituency, a seat he held continuously until 1980, when he was defeated by Sewa Ram Arora of the Congress. The seat was won back by Vimla Dang in the 1992 elections.

For Satya Pal and Vimla Dang politics has never been a matter of power and pelf. Some years ago both retired from the National Council of the CPI, and in 1997 declined to stand for assembly elections as they feel that there should be an age limit also for holding political office. However, notwithstanding old age and health problems, they continue to work amongst the people as before. The Punjab Istri Sabha, of which Vimla Dang has been a founder member and leading light, has helped thousands of children who lost their parents during the years of terrorism, to get education, by providing monthly stipends and other facilities without consideration of party and political affiliations and religious background of their families. For outstanding social work Vimla Dang was honoured with a Padma Shri several years ago. A greater honour, Padma Bhushan, came to Satya Pal Dang belatedly in 1997.

The Dangs never left Chheharta, a few miles away from the Golden Temple, throughout the long years of terrorism and threat to their lives. Being in the thick of the struggle, Satya Pal Dang studied the problem from all angles—social, political and religious, its national and international ramifications—and wrote illuminating articles which were in great demand by the Punjabi, Urdu and English-language press.

A universally respected elder leader of the CPI, Satya Pal Dang continues to work and write on various problems affecting Punjab, the left movement and the country. Apart from scores of articles and some pamphlets, he has written two books on Punjab and terrorism.

# Brief Chronology

| | |
|---|---|
| NOVEMBER 1, 1966 | Punjab State formed. |
| 1972-77 | Giani Zail Singh's tenure as Chief Minister of Punjab. |
| OCTOBER 16-17, 1973 | Anandpur Sahib Resolution adopted by Working Committee of Shiromani Akali Dal. |
| JUNE 25, 1975 | Centre declares Emergency. Akalis actively oppose. |
| MARCH, 1977 | Congress loses Parliamentary elections. Janata Party with Morarji Desai forms government. In Punjab Congress loses assembly elections and Akalis form coalition with Janata Party. |
| APRIL 13, 1978 | Akhand Kirtani Jatha clashes in Amritsar with Nirankaris at their convention. 12 Sikhs and 3 Nirankaris killed. Formation of Dal Khalsa announced. |
| OCTOBER 28-29, 1978 | The 18th All-India Akali Conference at Ludhiana endorses the 1973 Anandpur Sahib Resolution and also adopts its own 12 detailed resolutions. (The 1973 resolution has invariably been considered the authentic version.) |
| JULY, 1979 | Morarji Desai resigns as Prime Minister after Lok Sabha passes a no-confidence motion against his government. Charan Singh sworn in as PM. He continues as Prime Minister until the return of Congress-I to power after the January 1980 mid-term elections. |
| JANUARY 14, 1980 | Congress wins general elections. Indira Gandhi returns as PM. Giani Zail Singh becomes Home Minister. After mid-term polls Congress returns to power in Punjab. Darbara Singh becomes Chief Minister. |
| APRIL 24, 1980 | Nirankari Guru Gurbachan Singh assassinated in Delhi by Ranjit Singh of Akhand Kirtani Jatha. |
| APRIL 9, 1981 | Lala Jagat Narain, proprietor of *Hind Samachar* group of papers, shot dead by Khalistani terrorists. |
| SEPTEMBER 20, 1981 | Bhindranwale arrested. |
| SEPTEMBER 29, 1981 | Khalistani terrorists highjack IA plane to Lahore. |
| OCTOBER 15, 1981 | Bhindranwale released. |
| JUNE 19, 1982 | Bhindranwale shifts to Akal Takht inside Golden Temple premises. |
| JULY 25, 1982 | Zail Singh sworm in as President of India. |
| MARCH, 1983 | Prime Minister announces formation of Sarkaria Commission. |
| APRIL 23, 1983 | DIG A.S. Atwal gunned down when coming out of Golden Temple. |
| OCTOBER 6, 1983 | Darbara Singh ministry made to quit and President's rule imposed on Punjab. |

| | |
|---|---|
| JUNE 5-7, 1984 | Operation Blue Star. Indian Army enters Golden Temple. Bhindranwale, Shahbeg Singh and many others killed. |
| OCTOBER 31, 1984 | Indira Gandhi assassinated by two Sikh members of her bodyguard. Rajiv Gandhi sworn in as PM by President Zail Singh. Widespread anti-Sikh riots break out in which over 2500 Sikhs are killed in Delhi alone. |
| DECEMBER 24-27, 1984 | Rajiv Gandhi wins parliamentary elections with 401 seats for the Congress, the highest ever figure. |
| JULY 24, 1985 | Rajiv-Longowal Accord signed. |
| AUGUST 20, 1985 | Sant Harchand Singh Longowal assassinated. |
| SEPTEMBER, 1985 | In Punjab Assembly elections Akalis win 73 out of 117 seats. Surjit Singh Barnala becomes Chief Minister. |
| JANUARY 26, 1986 | "Sarbat Khalsa" convened at the site of Akal Takht. Panthic Committee formed. |
| APRIL 13, 1986 | Second "Sarbat Khalsa" convened. |
| APRIL 27-28, 1986 | Panthic Committee declares formation of Khalistan from within the precincts of Golden Temple. |
| MAY 12,1987 | Barnala government dismissed. Punjab once again comes under President's rule. |
| MAY 15-17, 1988 | Operation Black Thunder results in flushing out terrorists from Golden Temple. 200 armed terrorists surrender. |
| NOVEMBER, 1989 | Janata Dal wins 143 seats in parliamentary elections. V.P. Singh becomes Prime Minister with support from outside by BJP and Left parties. |
| NOVEMBER 10, 1990 | After V.P. Singh loses the vote of confidence in Parliament consequent on withdrawal of support by the BJP, Chandra Shekhar is sworn in as Prime Minister with tacit support of the Congress. (When he lost Congress support in March 1991, Chandra Shekhar resigned, but continued to lead a care-taker government until June 21.) |
| MAY 21, 1991 | Rajiv Gandhi assassinated during election campaign. |
| JUNE 21, 1991 | Chandra Shekhar's care-taker government resigns. P.V. Narsimha Rao forms Congress government though Congress failed to get absolute majority in the May-June 1991 mid-term elections. |
| FEBRUARY, 1992 | Elections held in Punjab with Akalis declaring a boycott. Congress wins overwhelmingly with record low assembly vote. Beant Singh becomes Chief Minister. |
| DECEMBER 6, 1992 | Babri Masjid demolished by Hindu communalists. |
| AUGUST 31, 1995 | Chief Minister Beant Singh shot dead. |
| MAY-JUNE, 1996 | United Front Government of H.D. Deve Gowda sworn in with outside support of Congress after BJP's failure to get a vote of confidence in the Parliament. |
| FEBRUARY, 1997 | Elections to Punjab Assembly won by Akali-BJP alliance. Parkash Singh Badal becomes Chief Minister. |

# Preface

Amritsar district was the worst affected by Khalistani terrorism in Punjab. Living in Amritsar, I joined hands with innumerable comrades—leaders and activists in the field—in the fight against it. A large number, especially those living in rural areas, became victims of the bullets of the terrorists. I was amongst the lucky ones to survive and to fight on to the best of my capacity.

Our main activities were to address meetings, big and small, in Amritsar as also in rural areas, including villages considered to be terrorist strongholds, arguing and rousing the people against terrorism; to participate in demonstrations against terrorism; to visit sites of gruesome incidents; to call on families of victims of terrorism to offer condolences and to express our sympathy and solidarity, and to help them so that they actually got the relief promised by our government. We also tried to assist the Punjab Istri Sabha—and later, the Punjab Istri Sabha Relief Trust—in its work to help these families out of the funds raised for the purpose, especially by giving stipends to children of victims of terrorism who were studying. At the same time we struggled for justice to victims of police excesses, quite a number of which were avoidable.

Besides all this and such other activities organised by the CPI, and the CPI-M jointly, by all parties together and by trade unions and other Left-led organisations, I managed to write a number of articles in the English, Urdu and Punjabi press about terrorism and about how to fight it.

Now that there is apprehension about the revival of terrorism, though in a different form, some friends suggested that I should write a book on the subject. I did not think I could manage it. Dr. Amrik Singh* then advised me that I should consider publishing a book consisting of articles out of the many that I had written, with explanatory footnotes added, where necessary. This book is the result of Dr. Amrik Singh's advice,

*Dr. Amrik Singh is a well-known educationist and writer and former Vice-Chancellor of Punjabi University, Patiala.—*Editor.*

which he was kind enough to give me, though I decided to skip the part of it about footnotes. I am grateful to him.

In formulating my own ideas, reflected in my articles, I was helped by what I had read about terrorism in the writings of Lenin and of Indian Marxists, on the one hand, and books by Indian authors about Nagaland and Kashmir, on the other.

I hope this book will be of some use to those who are keen that India should be rid of the menace of terrorism, which—besides region-specific features—has some common basic features as well.

I have to sincerely thank Shri V.D. Chopra and Dr. Ravi M. Bakaya, but for whose immense help the publication of this book would not have been possible. I am grateful to Shri Chopra for agreeing to write an introduction to this book.

May, 2000
Ekta Bhavan
Chheharta
Amritsar-143 105

**Satya Pal Dang**

# Introduction

## HISTORICAL ROOTS OF TERRORISM IN KASHMIR AND PUNJAB

### V.D. Chopra

Recent events in Kargil, intrusion by Pakistan on the Line of Control under a well-conceived and thoroughly planned invasion, have shaken the Indian nation, for that matter, the entire international community. This book by an outstanding political personality of India was written before this aggression on India. It is of relevance to contemporary developments in South Asia, to Indo-Pak relations in particular, because on the basis of concrete evidence, the author has analysed the rise of secessionism and terrorism in Punjab since the early eighties. The unique feature of this book is that the author, who himself has played a leading role in the movement against terrorism, has interpreted the events with remarkable objectivity and has conclusively shown that terrorism in Punjab has not exhausted its potentialities of challenging the secular edifice of this border state of India.

The developments in Punjab and in Jammu and Kashmir, especially the recent developments in Kargil, should not be seen in isolation from each other. India as a multi-religious, multi-cultural multi-ethnic country and the second most populated country of our planet, has already emerged as a major factor in the politics and economy of the world. That being the position, its integrity and unity is facing new challenges. These challenges have always been there and we have been grappling with them since we won our independence. However, during the last two decades certain alarming developments have taken place in the world, and particularly in our region. Almost simultaneously, forces of internal subversion, wrapped in all types of packages of communalism, parochialism, casteism, regionalism and fanaticism, have intensified their activities. It is important to note in this context that in the most sensitive areas of the country's borders, both the north-east and the west, a handful of people have started raising secessionist slogans, and some among them have taken resort to terrorism. Organised political terrorism is a new feature in our polity.

Thus, if one looks at India from any angle, the conclusion is inevitable that the freedom and unity of the country are really in peril. India, of course, is the world's largest multi-party democracy, larger than the oldest democracies of Europe and America. We are also the biggest non-aligned country and have the proud privilege of being one of the founders of non-aligned movement. It is important to stress this at a time when mankind is facing the threat of the emergence of a unipolar world. Again, India is the most developed among the developing countries and has set an example of independent economic development for many of them. In this sense, what happens to India will go a long way in shaping the course of events in other countries.

It will not be chauvinistic to say that a strong, united and economically independent India can be a pace-setter for a large number of young and dynamic states which have come into their own after the Second World War, despite intense political and economic pressures. In fact, economic viability and political independence of most of the countries which won their independence after the Second World War are threatened both overtly and covertly by their former colonisers. Countries in Asia, Africa and Latin America have been subjected to different kinds of intervention. According to a study conducted by the Italian historian Angelo Colleoni, America intervened in as many as 40 newly-independent countries in one way or the other to change the course of their history. *Newsweek*, on October 10, 1983, disclosed that covert operations of the CIA had increased five-fold under the Reagan administration. But in the recent years the United States too has begun to exhibit its anxiety over the rise of religious fundamentalism and state-sponsored terrorism. This shift should not be ignored. This was evident on the stand it took on Kargil.

It needs determination and, above all, the unity of the people in these regions, to resist these threats. A weak and disunited India will be easily vulnerable to these pressures. Thus, a stage has come for every patriotic Indian to take a forthright stand on the growing threats to India's independence. The time has also come to assess to what extent internal pressures are building up for the disintegration of the country. What are the social forces which constitute the main base for communalism, parochialism and regionalism? We have to objectively assess how, and through what instruments, foreign forces are pressuring us to change our policies in directions which are against our national interests. Satyapal Dang has made a study of this problem on the basis of concrete realities in Punjab.

The problem has to be examined from yet another angle. Defence of independence and unity of the country is closely related to economic development. Let us leave this question at that, and examine the rise of religious fundamentalism and terrorism in the sensitive areas of the country.

It is relevant to ask: why were Punjab and Kashmir selected both by the colonial powers and the local vested interests to make these who border states springboards for religious fundamentalism and terrorism?

The Jammu and Kashmir State, to give its full name, is the northernmost part of India and many of the difficulties facing its peple are the result of its extremely important strategic location. The Kashmir Valley is surrounded by hilly and mountainous terrain. The areas of Jammu, Poonch, Muzaffarabad, Gilgit, Baltistan and Ladakh constitute the ring of highlands that stands sentinel over the Valley. They border on India, Pakistan, Afghanistan, and the Sinkiang and Tibet part of China, and only a kilometres separate Kashmir from the Central Asian Republics of Tajikistan, Turkmenistan and Uzbekistan.

There is enough historical evidence to prove that even long before the Russian Revolution, the British rulers viewed Jammu and Kashmir and Afghanistan as integral parts of what they called their "forward policy". British colonial rulers always kept Jammu and Kashmir under their hold because of its contiguity with Central Asia, against which British imperialists always harboured expansionist designs. After the Russian Revolution and the formation of the USSR, Kashmir assumed still greater strategic importance in imperialist plans. Following World War I, as the Russian Revolution spread over Central Asia, British military missions were established in Kashmir to carry out flagrant subversive activities in the Central Asian Republics of the USSR.

Gilgit was "acquired" from the Maharaja of Jammu & Kashmir under a 60-year lease and used for the construction of airfields and a wireless station. The new developing situation created by the success of the Russian Revolution inevitably stimulated fresh British interest, both in Afghanistan and Kashmir. This fact is being recalled to stress the geostrategic and economic importance of this region—Kashmir in particular. Even, after the disintegration of the Soviet Union, the importance of this region has in no way been reduced. On the contrary, the geo-economic importance of this region has increased manifold. For instance, it is a well known fact that the oil wealth of the Central

Asian Republics will play a key role in the 21st century because of the steep decline in the oil resources of the Gulf countries. There is also evidence to show that Kashmir too may have oil resources. Above all, Kashmir has rich resources of uranium. Thus Kashmir still occupies a very important strategic position and the developed countries, being the biggest consumers of oil, keep this factor in the forefront. Therefore, from the long-term point of view, it will be naive to underestimate the geo-economic importance of this region. That Pakistan still keeps on repeating that "Kashmir is a core question" has deeper implications than what appears on the surface. This also explains how great are Washington's stakes both in Kashmir and the Central Asian Republics.

After World War II, the USA started taking keen interest in Kashmir. Papers like *The New York Times* and *The New York Tribune* carried articles about the strategic importance of the state because of its proximity to the erstwhile Soviet Union and its new industrial centres. David Lillienthal, one-time Chairman of the US Atomic Energy Commission, wrote about it. American correspondents in India sent despatches home on "US interest" in Kashmir. *The New York Times* published a map captioned "The West's programme for containment, and the gap", and Kashmir was shown as one of the region's "gaps". Top American military experts were sent to the region for "defence" surveys. British armed forces chiefs like Montgomery and Mountabatten also visited Kashmir to discuss "the future British defence of North India". The Royal Air Force brought in bombers and war planes and carried out aerial manoeuvres in Kashmir. American interest in Kashmir began much before January 1948, when the Kashmir "case" was taken to the UN Security Council. Press reports said:

"One of the chartered civil aircrafts that flew the Sikhs to Srinagar brought back to New Delhi two American explorers, Nicol Smith, author and lecturer, of 150 Central Park South, New York, and Loren Tutell, cameraman, of Chicago. . . .

"In wide travels through Kashmir in the recent troubled period, Mr. Smith found evidence that the local rulers might take advantage of an outbreak to abrogate their allegiance to the Maharaja. In the Ladakh area Mr. Smith discovered widespread sentiment for independence."

"Nicol Smith of New York, author-lecturer, who came from Srinagar yesterday, brought reports of some pro-Russian activity in Leh, capital of the Kashmir province of Ladakh, which he recently visited. Ladakh adjoins Chinese Turkestan, which Mr. Smith also discovered was under strong Russian influence, although It was a province of China."

Major Tutell had served throughout World War II as commander of the Fifth Combat Camera Unit in the Pacific. Nicol Smith was a trained intelligence agent who had worked for the Office of Strategic Services in France, Siam (Thailand), India, Ceylon and China. In a recent book he has revealed his purpose of visiting Kashmir.

" . . . I had been nursing a pet idea. During World War II, I had often flown in a C-47 over the mountains of Eastern Tibet and had thought grimly that below us was not one level spot for a landing in all these thousands of square miles. Was the Lake Pagong area equally unfit as a landing place? That was what I wanted to know."

Smith, however could not visit Lake Pagong because of sickness and Tutell went there alone.

"Loren's observations convinced him that its northern section had a minimum width of two miles for a distance of at least 20 miles, and that its depth was considerable . . .

"Loren took from his pocket the rough notes which he had jotted down. He showed that there was ample room for a runway several miles long to be constructed at this end of the lake. In fact, he insisted, there was ample room for several runways here. The mountains to the north-west were low enough to be flown over easily by any aircraft after its take-off.

"We looked at each other in silence. . ."

The American press reported in February 1948 that an American, Haight, had served for some months in the "Azad Kashmir" forces as a "brigadier-general", and that he had boasted of killing many Hindus with his own hands. This fact was mentioned in the Security Council by Sir B.N. Rau in February 1950 (*The Hindu*, February 14, 1950).

It is clear from all these facts that the United States was for several years interested in Kashmir because of its strategic location. As Rosinger indicated, "The interests of the United States presumably arose in part from Kashmir's strategic location, close to the USSR and bordering on Afghanistan, Chinese Turkestan (Sinkiang), Tibet, India and Pakistan". (Rosinger, Lawrence K. "India and the United States").

The Indian Government was not unaware of American interest in Kashmir as a base for operations against China and the Soviet Union. Reporting the views of Indian officials, Robert Trumbull said in *The*

*New York Times* of October 28, 1947 that there was sentiment in Ladakh for independence and that "such fragmentation of Kashmir is what India wished to avoid in this strategic state next door to Russia".

These cold facts are relevant to understand that after the transfer of power to India and Pakistan, the British rulers wanted Kashmir to become an "independent" state.

For Kashmir, the status proposed by the British was "independence". Lord Mountbatten visited Kashmir in June 1947 and had long talks with the Maharaja and the then Kashmir Prime Minister R.C. Kak. Immediately after, a campaign was launched by R.C. Kak, the Kashmir Muslim Conference and the All Jammu and Kashmir Rajya Hindu Sabha demanding "independence" for Kashmir from the prospective states of India and Pakistan, and telegrams were showered on the Viceroy. Both the above-mentioned organisations, it may be noted, had opposed the "Quit Kashmir" movement and supported the princely rule, as both represented feudal reaction in Kashmir. In addition, while one represented Muslim communalism the other was a Hindu communal organisation.

The British plot for an "independent" Kashmir stood revealed in a letter addressed by the Maharaja to Lord Mountbatten when the former finally decided on accession to India. Wrote the Maharaja in his letter dated 26th October 1947, "As Your Excellency is aware, the State of Jammu and Kashmir has not acceded to either the Dominion of India or Pakistan. Geographically my state is contiguous to both . . . . Besides, it has a common boundary with the Soviet Republic and China . . . "

The only "independence" which the Maharaja could speak of was unfettered freedom for the British imperialists to treat the whole state as an occupied territory and utilise it for keeping India and Pakistan eternally at loggerheads and, of course, use it as a strategic military base.

While pressurising the Maharaja to declare "independence", the calculating British rulers were simultaneously hatching another and far more diabolical plot. They were conscious of the immense strength of the National Conference, its close ties with the Indian National Congress, which was in sympathy with the popular movement in Kashmir, as also its opposition to the Muslim League, which was supporting the Maharaja against the popular movement. In such a situation there was every likelihood that the Kashmir ruler could be finally compelled to accede to India, and his dream of an "independent" Kashmir could die a miserable death.

However, the failure of 1947 invasion of Kashmir by Pakistan, the Indo-Pak conflicts of 1965 and 1971 and, finally, the Shimla Agreement between India and Pakistan foiled the game of making Kashmir an "independent" state. Pakistan, therefore, started a proxy war against India by promoting terrorism in the state.

There is no doubt that a "Cease Fire Line" (CFL) exists between India and Pakistan in Jammu and Kashmir. It cuts the state in two, with two-fifths of the territory and one-third of the population falling under the illegal occupation of Pakistan. Quite apart from the fact that Pakistan violated this Cease Fire Line by open aggression for the third time in the 1971 Indo-Pak war, thousands of violations have occurred during the last five decades, some have been recorded, many have remained unrecorded. Nevertheless, the fact of life is that after every major violation, it has been India which has withdrawn to the old Cease Fire Line, in the hope that an amicable settlement might be arrived at through peaceful negotiations and not by armed confrontation. On the other hand, on every occasion it has been Pakistan which has violated the Cease Fire Line, notwithstanding the fact that India has taken and continues to take the position that it will not use force to regain the areas occupied illegally by Pakistan. In fact, all the Prime Ministers of India—Jawaharlal Nehru, Lal Bahadur Shastri, Indira Gandhi, Morarji Desai, Rajiv Gandhi, P.V. Narasimha Rao, H.D. Deve Gowda, I.K. Gujral and Atal Behari Vajpayee have consistently taken the position that India has no territorial ambitions in Pakistan. India has unreservedly accepted that Pakistan is an independent and sovereign state and that it will not interfere in the internal affairs of its neighbouring country.

The proxy war unleashed by Pakistan in Kashmir and its abortive attempts to promote "insurgency" among the Kashmiri Muslims cannot be equated with the rise of terrorism in Punjab, though both have certain common features, the chief among them being promotion of terrorism by the ruling elite of Pakistan to subvert and Balkanise India. For decades the ruling circles of the United States and Great Britain watched these developments passively and did not raise their voice, except on the question of what is euphemistically called "human rights". There is a linkage between terrorism in Punjab and Kashmir, which should not be ignored. Let us look at the rise and fall of terrorism in Punjab, which is the main theme of this book.

## Rise of Sikh Fundamentalism

The concept that the Sikhs in India are an ethnic or racial minority was introduced, both overtly and covertly, by the British rulers as early as in the middle of the last century. One writer emphasised :

"This is the first and most essential thing to learn about India—that there is not and never was an India, or even any country of India, possessing according to European ideas, any sort of unity, physical, political, social or religious: no Indian nation, no 'people of India', of which we hear so much."

Another British expert on India said : "The notion that India is a nationality rests upon that vulgar error which political science principally aims at eradicating. India is not a political name, but only a geographical expression like Europe or Africa. It does not mark the territory of a nation and a language, but the territory of many nations and many languages."

This is what Sir John Seeley wrote in 1883 in "The Expansion of England".

It was on this premise that British colonial policy in India, the policy of "divide and rule" was based. A British officer, writing under the name of "Carnaticus" in the *Asiatic Review* of May, 1821 declared that "*Divide et impera* should be the motto of our Indian administration, whether political, civil, or military."

*Divide et impera* implied that the British rulers should try to re-inforce the so-called separation which existed between different religions and not endeavour to bring them closer to each other.

Unlike in any other state, the British policy of "divide and rule" had its own characteristics because, apart from the fact that Punjab was quite close to the western borders of undivided India, it had three main religious communities—Hindus, Muslims and Sikhs. That explains why as early as in the middle of the 19th century, British colonial rulers had come to the conclusion that to keep India under subjugation, the tranquility of Punjab had to be maintained at any cost.

## How Was This Policy Carried Out in Punjab?

As a matter of fact, before the First War of Independence in 1857, the British had started strengthening the feudal elements among the Sikhs and thus made the interests of the Sikh landlord and the princely rulers common with those of the British rulers. After 1857 it was decided to grant *jagirs* to those who showed "active loyalty" at the time of the "Mutiny".

That the Sikh aristocracy and priests became loyalists is clearly reflected in their memorandum against the *Kukas,* the Sikhs who had taken up arms against the British Raj soon after the "Mutiny". The memorandum which was submitted to the Lieutenant-Governor in a *durbar* held at Amritsar on 22 March 1872 showed that by that time they had become supporters of the British Empire. To fight the *Kukas* they offered full support to the government and appreciated the government's "appropriate and effective measures" for controlling that "wicked and misguided sect".

In this period the British rulers adopted a new recruitment policy to win over the Sikh youth and declared the Sikhs, particularly the Jat community, to be a "martial race". It was decided that the Sikh troops should be one of the main components of the provincial armies. From 1860 onwards, the Sikhs formed a vital part of the forces sent abroad to China, Afghanistan and to many parts of the vast African continent. They constituted "the backbone of local forces as legionaries of the Empire, thus making the Punjab, what was later described as, the bulwark of defence against foreign aggression" and the "guard-room of the Eastern Empire".

In this connection it is of interest to note that the pro-British elements among the Sikhs organised themselves into the Singh Sabha of those days, which was out of bounds for those Sikhs who had proved disloyal to the government. They also decided not to discuss at their meetings anything against the British Government and thus loyalty to the British Government became an article of faith for them.

It will not be incorrect to say that all these measures were intended to cultivate and promote a sense of separate identity among the Sikhs, as distinct from the rest of the Indian nation.

This trend, which started in the seventies of the 19th century, marked a turning point in Sikh history, because it gave a new direction to the attitude and the social behaviour of the emerging upper classes among the Sikhs.

It will be relevant to mention here that the main motivation of the Singh Sabha was a search for Sikh identity and its self-assertion.

The British rulers distorted and exploited the Sikh and other religions for their own political ends to plant the idea among the people that Hindus, Muslims, and Sikhs were different entities. Various methods were used to attain this purpose.

D. Petrie corroborates this thus: "With his relapse into Hinduism and readoption of its superstitions and vicious social customs, it is notorious that the Sikh loses much of his material instincts and greatly deteriorates as a fighting machine." Again Mecauliffe, in alluding to the fact that loyalty to the British is enjoined by various prophecies in the Sikh Holy Writ, considers that "it is such prophecies as these, combined with the monotheism, the absence of superstition and restraint in the matter of food, which have made the Sikhs among the bravest, the most loyal and devoted subjects of the British Crown".

The British rulers patronised Sikhism for their own expansionist and military ends in their administrative policy.

But there is also another aspect. Some soldiers and officers, retired from service, were used to promote fundamentalist tendencies among the Sikhs in the rural areas. One of the regiments had constituted a choir of reciters to go round the villages and sing Sikh hymns at congregations. Though most retired soliders and officers were ardent devotees of the Sikh religion, some among them gave extremist and fundamentalist interpretations to Sikh principles and traditions.

On the eve of independence, the concept of a "Sikh Homeland" in Punjab was floated by certain political formations. Since the end of the 19th century and till the sixties of the present century scholars—mostly from England, Canada and America—have been working overtime to establish the separate entity of the Sikhs. There have been some Sikh scholars too who have gone abroad to make a study of the Sikh religion. All these studies tried to show that the Sikhs are an "independent" entity in every respect, notwithstanding the fact that even today many Hindus are also devotees of the Sikh religion.

Harry Izmirlian, who received his Ph.D. from the University of California at Berkley, conducted field studies in Punjab in 1961-62 and 1965-66 with a view to study the behaviour of the Sikhs in the villages in socio-political terms. After showing that the Sikhs constituted an independent entity, he underscored the fact that the Punjab and the Sikh farmer most frequently provide a surplus of agricultural products . . . it is not, therefore, surprising that Sikhs are inclined to view their contribution to the security and the prosperity of the country in terms far greater than their small number might warrant. He goes on to say that the "agitation for greater representation" in the political power structure "makes sense if viewed in this context. From the Sikh point of view, both the British and the post-1947 Indian government's responses were inadequate." To establish this thesis, he very skilfully justifies all the Akali agitations.

There are other American scholars who have been working to prove that the Hindus and Sikhs in Punjab do not have any common cultural heritage and emotionally they are poles apart. In his book " 'Arya Dharm': Hindu Consciousness in 19th Century Punjab," Jones Kenneth builds this thesis.

This intellectual exercise by the Western scholars and pro-Western Sikh scholars was directed towards creating in the Sikhs a subjective consciousness of their being an independent entity and created a sense of discrimination among the Sikh elite.

Its objective, obviously, was to declare that Sikh religious philosophy is not a continuation of Indian philosophical thought, but something entirely new. It was necessary to draw this line of demarcation in order to build the theory that the Sikhs are an independent nation. This provided the ideological basis for the demand for "Khalistan".

Quite apart from this aspect, there was only one frame of reference—Vedantic—available for the interpretation of Sikhism till this trend emerged. Western scholars offered a new understanding of Sikh philosophy and tradition and tried to isolate the principal concepts of Sikh religion from those of the main philosophical trends in India.

What were the reasons for this deliberate and conscious attempt to give a new interpretation to the teachings of the Sikh gurus?

It was directed to delink the Sikh masses from the age-old ideological traditions of the country and thus to deprive them of the national spiritual heritage. Secondly, it was aimed at emotionally disarming the Sikh masses in their fight against colonial tyranny, the exploitation of the landlords, and the princes.

What is most important to note in this connection is that as the national movement started gaining momentum and generating a new national consciousness, ideologues of imperialism started selling their own interpretations of the rich heritage of our country and some Sikh intellectuals became their special target. After independence this ideological offensive assumed a new dimension, because sowing seeds of fundamentalism and secessionism in Punjab became the prerequisite for destabilising India, on the one hand, and rendering the Sikh masses politically passive in the fight against neocolonialism, on the other.

Therefore, hostility between Sikhism and Hinduism was projected as a historical reality in the writings of such administrator-scholars. Among these scholars were Gordon, Bingley and Payne. For instance, Bingley reiterated the arguments of Lepel Griffen while explaining the adverse effects of Hinduism on the Sikhs. The chief cause of the decline of Sikhism, he wrote, was the strong alternative force of Hinduism. While repeating Griffen's argument, he further added that "the ivy-like vitality of Hinduism enfolds and strangles everything which it has once grasped." He also concluded that Hinduism has always been hostile to Sikhism and warned the Sikhs that "In course of a few generations, Sikhism is likely to be superseded by some form of Vaishnavism, which is always more popular in times of peace."

This psyche of an independent entity of Sikhs, nursed and promoted by British scholars with the active participation of Sikh landed interests and a section of Sikh intellectuals, received a new boost when the colonial rulers gave new teeth to their policy of "divide and rule" by introducing separate electorates, notwithstanding the fact that communalism and the concept of separate identity did not grip the minds of the Sikh peasantry.

The British rulers, however, did not relent in their efforts to drive a wedge between the Hindus and the Sikhs on the one hand, and Hindus and the Muslims, on the other. Under the Morley-Minto Reforms of 1909, when separate electorates were introduced and Muslims were given weightage, the upper classes among the Sikhs became active in aspiring for similar privileges.

The Chief Khalsa Dewan led by Sardar Sunder Singh Majithia articulated this hope. But till the late twenties the Sikh masses had not become receptive to the concept of a separate identity, though the British Government had offered them 33 per cent of the seats in the Punjab Council and a Sikh University.

Along with this, another alarming tendency was gathering strength. Slowly but surely, the Sikh religious shrines started becoming the hub of political activity, particularly after the Gurdwara Act of 1925. It was in the early thirties that the Akal Takht within the Golden Temple complex became a centre of Akali politics.

Nevertheless, even at that stage, there were two discernible divisions among Sikh political leaders, the anti-imperialist and the pro-imperialist. And, naturally, the anti-imperialist section of the Akalis continued to cooperate with the Congress.

However, in the forties, a fusion between religion and politics had taken place to such an extent that the trend for a separate identity of the Sikhs gained fresh momentum when Pakistan as a Muslim state began to loom large on the political horizon. The more aggressive Muslim communalism became and the more defensive the Congress chose to become, the louder became the demand of the Sikhs for recognition as a separate entity. And in this process was born what was not always noticed—the nexus between Sikh religion and Sikh politics.

In a speech at an all-party Sikh conference in Amritsar in August 1944, Master Tara Singh declared that the Sikhs were a "nation" and that, if "the country was going to be split, they should not be left at the mercy of either Pakistan or Hindustan". The Akali Dal demanded an independent Sikh state—a demand which was first made by Giani Kartar Singh. Later the Akali Dal passed a resolution on 22 March 1946, which said:

"Whereas the Sikhs being attached to the Punjab by intimate bonds of holy shrines, property, language, traditions and history, claim it as their homeland and the holy land which the British took as a 'trust' from the last Sikh ruler, and whereas the community of the Sikhs is being threatend on account of the persistent demand of Pakistan by the Muslims on the one hand and the danger of absorption by the Hindus on the other . . . . the Akali Dal demands for the preservation and protection of the religious, cultural, economic and political rights of the Sikh nation, the creation of a Sikh state which would include a substantial majority of the Sikh population and their sacred shrines and historical gurdwaras with the provision for the transfer and exchange of population and property."

Thus, long before the famous Anandpur Sahib resolution was passed and the recent secessionist forces started their violent operation, the concept of the Sikh state had been spelt out.

In this connection, another fact of history also needs to be mentioned.

Maharaja Yadvindra Singh of Patiala admitted in an article published in newspaper as late as on 19th July, 1956 that at a meeting with Jinnah at a dinner hosted by the Viceroy, Lord Mountbatten, "Liaquat Ali Khan and Begum Liaquat Ali . . . went out of their way to offer on behalf of the Muslim League everything conceivable. He was to be the head of this new Sikh state . . . the Sikhs would have their own army and so on". This admission by the late Maharaja speaks for itself and needs no comment. That the Sikhs did not fall a prey to this conspiracy speaks volumes of their sense of patriotism. Once again, the credit goes to the robust Sikh peasantry and the nationalist Sikhs.

All the same, the fact that after fifty years of independence the strident cry of "Khalistan" should have been raised by handful of people is disturbing. It shows the degree of erosion of our commitment to secularism that has taken place, notwithstanding the glaring reality that the generation of Hindus and Sikhs which migrated from the areas now in Pakistan still recall with horror how they had been thrown out of their homeland without pity and with so much violence and inhumanity.

It would be a totally subjective reckoning to conclude that the entire community of Sikhs had turned fundamentalist, though their religious sentiments were deeply hurt by "Operation Blue Star" of 1984.

An overwhelming majority of the Sikhs still believes in secularism and this does not mean that they do not adhere to the tenets of the Sikh religion.

The question arises why after Kashmir, Punjab has been selected for subversion and destabilisation? There are objective reasons for this. Punjab is among those states which form the backbone of the Indian economy. It has the highest per capita income in the country. For instance, around 81 per cent of its area under agriculture is irrigated and 98 per cent of the area under wheat and 94 per cent of area under rice produce high-yielding varieties. Punjab is thus the granary of India. Destabilisation of Punjab, therefore, will have a chain reaction on the entire course of economic development of the country. Punjab is also one of the biggest markets for industrial and consumer goods.

If one keeps in mind this factor, it will not be difficult to understand why in the operation of destabilisation of India, secessionist forces have been nursed, promoted and encouraged in their nefarious game. At one stage Harry Barnes, then US Ambassador to India, equated the "Khalistan" demand with the freedom struggle of the people of Puerto Rico in an interview he gave in June 1983, widely reported in the Indian press. This conceals more than what it reveals, because in the early eighties terrorism in Punjab had assumed a dangerous dimension. Whatever may be the stand of the United States on terrorism and religious fundamentalism in the late nineties, when it began to display an anti-American stance, these and other facts are relevant even today for any analysis of rise of terrorism in Punjab and the encouragement it received from outside.

Moreover, terrorists and extremists are trained in camps at various places in Pakistan by its intelligence agents, one of whom was designated "Station Chief" and another "Second in Command". Muslims in the guise of Sikhs are trained in Qasur by a brigadier of a Pakistani artillery regiment. Each batch consists of 300 to 400 Muslims and the term of training is three to four months.

Another centre is run in Gujranwala district specially for espionage and "black propaganda". Similar centres were run at Rahim Yar Khan near the Rajasthan border, Attock Fort and Sheikhupura city. Training is also imparted to extremists in the military college at Abbotabad in batches of 200 to 300.

The trainees in these camps are smugglers, proclaimed offenders and other bad elements operating on the border. They were recruited by Pakistani intelligence with the help of "influential persons" living in the border districts of Punjab and Rajasthan who lured them with substantial financial inducements.

After the completion of training, which included use of sophisticated weapons and ammunition and a "hate campaign against India", these terrorists were smuggled into Punjab from various points in Jammu, Bassaobarwan sector in Gurdaspur district, Khem Karan and Dull posts in Amristar district, Mamdoot sector in Ferozepore district and Ganganagar in Rajasthan.

Arms and ammunition were also smuggled into this state from Pakistan Occupied Kashmir (POK), and various points of Punjab and Rajasthan for use in Jammu and Kashmir for sabotage purposes in this period according to *The Daily* (Bombay, June 26, 1984).

It will not be out of place to mention here that the rise of religious fundamentalism and terrorism in Afghanistan started in the early 1980s because this development had a direct bearing on regional stability. In Afghanistan arms for the fundamentalists' forces came from a number of sources.

The cost of the operation as late as 1983 was no more than 50 million US dollars, with the United States financing about half and Saudi Arabia most of the rest. By the late 1980s, Washington was providing about 300 million US dollars as financial support and Saudi Arabia approximately the same; Washington's total contribution for the decade was roughly two billion US dollars. In addition to Iran's assistance to Shia resistance groups, Egyptian and Saudi arms were placed in the hands of Pakistan's military for distribution, as were those paid for by the United States. With Pakistan's approval, supplies from some Arab countries were routed to selected Sunni parties, designated by those states.

These cold facts bring into sharp focus how religious fundamentalism and terrorism were primarily promoted by external factors. These trends have now begun to surface in other parts of the world.

The smuggling of narcotics has become a prime source of financing civil wars in Southern Europe and the Eastern Mediterranean, according to a report. The report by the Paris-based *Observatoire Geopolitique des Drogues,* or Geopolitical Observatory of Drugs, identifies belligerents in the former Yugoslav Republics and Turkey as key players in the region's accelerating drugs-for-arms traffic. Albanian nationalists in ethnically tense Macedonia and the Serbian province of Kosovo have built a vast heroin network, leading from the opium fields of Pakistan to black-market arms dealers in Switzerland, which transports up to 2 billion US dollars worth of the drug annually into the heart of Europe. More than 500 Kosovo or Macedonian Albanians are in prison in Switzerland for drug or arms-trafficking offences, and more than 1,000 others are under indictment. The arms are reportedly stockpiled in Kosovo.

At the end of the 20th century, these indeed are alarming developments, having a direct bearing on international relations, peace and stability. How far these developments will influence the policy of the United States and European countries cannot be predicted at this stage, notwithstanding the balanced stand these countries have taken on the recent aggression by Pakistan in Kargil.

Nevertheless, one thing is certain: the process of building a modern nation-state in India on the basis of secularism, democracy and social justice is confronted with a more complicated situation than ever before. In this sense, the defence of secularism in India has become a basic task facing the Indian nation. Let us not minimise the importance of this national endeavour.

This book, therefore, is a valuable contribution towards evolving thought structures on this central task. Quite apart from this aspect, the concrete analysis by the author of the developments in Punjab will become a rich source of material for Indian and foreign scholars and researchers.

# CHAPTER 1
# The Punjab Crisis

## 1. Nature of the Crisis in Punjab

The recent developments in Punjab have shaken the whole country and have attracted worldwide attention. These developments, however, are not altogether isolated from what has been happening in some other parts of India. The main common factor is the imperialist conspiracy against India. There indeed are some factors peculiar to Punjab. To understand the Punjab events it is necessary to examine the common factors as they have operated in Punjab and also factors peculiar to this border state, which have aided and abetted the imperialist conspiracy.

The British imperialists who ruled India till 1947 did all they could to keep the Indian people divided and to weaken their unity in the fight for independence. When forced to quit, the British succeeded in dividing India. After India became free the aim of world imperialism, led by US imperialism, has been to weaken and even to dismember India because India chose the path of independent development, even though on capitalist lines, instead of following the neo-colonial path, and because she pursued a progressive foreign policy based on anti-imperialism, anti-colonialism and world peace.

As a part of their game of "divide and rule", the British rulers and their spokesmen not only made persistent efforts to plant in the minds of the people the patently false and dangerous concept of our nation being based on religion—of India consisting of separate Hindu, Muslim and Sikh nations, etc.—but they also encouraged our people to imbibe this belief. This was sought to be done with special vigour ever since the First War of Independence of 1857. "There is not and never was an India", proclaimed Sir John Strachey in his "India, Its Administration and Progress", 1888.[1]

In his essay on Ethno-Nationalism, K. R. Bomball has pointed out that in Cunningham's famous "History of Sikhs", written in the early years of the present century, a prominent theme is the growth of Sikhs from "a sect to a people" and from "a people to a nation".[2]

A secret CID memorandum prepared by D. Petrie, Assistant Director, Criminal Intelligence, Government of India (1911), says that "every endeavour has been made to preserve them (Sikh soldiers) from the contagion of idolatory". Thanks to these measures, the "Sikhs in the Indian Army have been studiously nationalised", M.A. Macauliffe, a highly placed British administrator, observed. According to Petrie, this meant that the "Sikhs were encouraged to regard themselves as a totally distinct and separate nation".[3]

The campaign run by some Hindu communal forces to deny the emergence of Sikhism as an independent religion led to a growing fear amongst the Sikh elite that the Sikhs might be absorbed in the Hindu social system and might thus lose their distinct communal (religious) identity. This was taken advantage of by the British to inculcate, encourage and strengthen the false and reactionary concept of an independent political identity of the Sikhs.

The Muslim League led by Mohammed Ali Jinnah had demanded Pakistan on the ground that the (Indian) Muslims constituted a separate nation and therefore should have a separate country.

In 1942, when the Cripps Mission came to India, a section of the Akali leadership demanded the creation of what they called "Azad Punjab". The "Azad Punjab Scheme" provided for the redemarcation of Punjab boundaries. The then predominantly Muslim districts were to be separated and merged with the North-West Frontier Province. The remaining districts were to be in the proposed "Azad Punjab", in which neither community would be in a dominant majority.

In case of India being partitioned, "Azad Punjab" was to be turned into a buffer state between India and Pakistan. The scheme did not get popular Sikh support. Some Akali leaders did not in the beginning rebuff the efforts of Jinnah to get their support for Pakistan (with the whole of Punjab going to it). But later on the patriotic Sikh masses forced them to do so.

Thus, notwithstanding all the machinations of the British rulers, an overwhelming majority of the Sikhs did not fall prey to the British game. They played a glorious role in India's struggle for freedom and made sacrifices of which the country can be rightly proud.

Not satisfied with the division of India into India and Pakistan, the British imperialists tried for further dismemberment of India by empowering the rulers of Indian princely states, who were notorious British stooges, to decide whether to join India or Pakistan or to become independent.

When the Nizam and his clique, in their efforts to separate the Hyderabad State from India, sought the UN Security Council's intervention, they received prompt support from the United States. The American delegate Jessup voted to take up the Nizam's complaint, and when the police action was launched, condemned India for resorting to force. The American press was almost unanimous in attacking India. After the police action, it was learnt that the Nizam's government had employed three former American Army pilots and five DC-35 aircraft.[4]

These facts[5] together with the well known anti-India role of the US in relation to Kashmir are enough to expose the real attitude of US imperialism towards India's unity and integrity from the very beginning.

The role played by US imperialism and its allies and satellites in encouraging, supporting and helping the separatist demand for "Khalistan" and the extremist-terrorists working for it is by now too well known. Even then, it may be worthwhile to mention some facts.

The "Sikhs-a-separate-nation" thesis was once again propounded in a big way by Ganga Singh Dhillon at the Sikh educational conference held at Chandigarh on March 14-15, 1981. Dhillon, a wealthy US citizen with links with US ruling circles and admittedly a close friend of Pakistan's President Zia, had been invited to preside over the conference. A resolution adopted by the conference sought for the Sikhs associate membership of the United Nations. While no resolution demanding "Khalistan" was adopted, slogans of "Khalistan Zindabad" were heard at the conference. "Khalistan" was also propagated by Dr. Sohan Singh, former Director, Health Services, Punjab, in his speech at the conference. Even the resolution moved by Dalbir Singh, an industrialist having the reputation of being a moderate, had called upon the Sikhs to "recapture their lost glory" as "the Sikhs are born to rule".

Interestingly, at this "educational" conference, a lecturer from

Khalsa College, Amritsar, was not allowed to move an official resolution on such a subject as the plight of the college lecturers.[6]

Jagjit Singh Chauhan, a self-proclaimed leader of "Khalistan" and "President of the National Council of Khalistan", was given an entry visa to the United States in 1982 despite India's strong protests and despite the fact that his passport had been cancelled by the Government of India. He received hospitality and help from some US authorities. He was even received and hailed as "President of Khalistan". It needs also to be mentioned that it was Chauhan's "National Council of Khalistan" which issued not only the maps of "Khalistan" but also "Khalistan currency", "passports" and "postal stamps"—all with the help of his friends and backers in foreign imperialist circles.

In June or so of 1983, Harry Barnes, the then US Ambassador in India, equated the "Khalistan" demand with the freedom struggle of the people of Puerto Rico, and thus in his own way justified US support for the same.

Soon after "Operation Blue Star", The BBC allowed Jagjit Singh Chauhan to make a broadcast calling for the assassination of Indira Gandhi.

A study commissioned by the US State Department had examined what would have happened in India if Indira Gandhi had died before the parliamentary elections.

"If Indira Gandhi were to die suddenly before the next parliamentary elections, Rajiv's prospects would be considerably more difficult," this study had concluded. It added :

"If she were to die in office after the elections, Rajiv's prospects for succession will be considerably more secure".

The findings of this study were received and examined by the US State Department in September 1984. Indira Gandhi was assassinated on October 31, within eight weeks.

The contract for this study was given by the American Government to Robert L. Hardgrave Jr, Professor at the University of Texas in Austin. He was guided by Edward G. Griffin of the US State Department. Griffin, formerly with the US Army, was a CIA official and is listed in "Who's Who in CIA."

To these facts[7] it needs to be added that the chosen assassins of Indira Gandhi belonged to the Sikh community. The whole thing seemed planned devilishly not only to assassinate the then Prime Minister but also to incite large-scale Hindu-Sikh riots, thus strengthening the forces of separatism.

A notorious terrorist, Talwinder Singh, had escaped to West Germany. He was wanted in India for some specific murder cases. Extradition proceedings had been initiated and were going on in the appropriate court in West Germany. When it became clear that he would have to be handed over to India, he was allowed to leave West Germany for Canada, where he was given shelter.

At one stage the existence of camps in the US and Canada to train terrorists, including those who would operate in Punjab, got exposed, thanks to some enterprising journalists. One such camp in the US was being run by one Frank Camper, who admitted having trained a number of "Khalistani terrorists". No longer in a position to deny the existence of such camps, the governments of these countries pleaded their "helplessness" to close them.

The Pakistan Government's denial of existence of camps in Pakistan to train "Khalistani" terrorists is no longer taken seriously by anyone. In fact, the revelations made by the captured terrorists, with concrete details, have made such denials look absolutely ridiculous. This writer can be proud of the fact that he was one of the first to expose the existence of such camps through an article in New Delhi's *Link* Newsmagazine. This was in the beginning of 1984. I got information about such camps from a friend who had visited Pakistan.

Significantly, an international Hindu conference in New York in July 1984 organised by the Vishwa Hindu Parishad too received the support of some US authorities. The real force behind this organisation, RSS, stands for a "Hindu Rashtra" in India and considers the Hindus a nation.

It does not have to be proved now that:

(a) the authors of the Coupland Plan and their patrons are not satisfied even today with India's partition into India and Pakistan only;

(b) US imperialism is making all possible efforts to force India to toe its line or face dismemberment. Support for the "Khalistan" slogan and terrorism is part of this endeavour. So also support to Hindu chauvinists.

These have been self-evident truths for quite some time now. Even then it would be worthwhile to make a brief reference to some recent facts which further support the above contentions.

Some leaders of the US-based World Sikh Organisation (WSO) were asked why they were campaigning in favour of continuation of military aid to Pakistan even when it had been established that Pakistan had already made or almost made a nuclear bomb. Their reply was that they were US citizens and they were seeking to serve the interests of the US. Actually, they were serving the interests of US imperialism. These WSO leaders are known to be supporters of "Khalistan" also.

On October 7, 1987, the five-member "Panthic Committee"—which claims to head most if not all the terrorist organisations in Punjab—announced the formation of the "Council of Khalistan". A majority of its members are foreign citizens and belong to the same category to which the above mentioned leaders of the WSO belong.

On November 1, 1987, the Amritsar police arrested one Balkar Singh, a Canadian citizen, who had recently come to Punjab on the pretext of visiting some ailing relative of his in Amritsar district. However, he hardly visited his native village. He was arrested from a very posh public sector hotel in Amritsar on a tip-off from a man connected with intelligence. The name and telephone number of a professor of a local college, besides others, was found on his person.

He had also brought with him a letter for this professor from Dr. Arjinder Singh, a member of the "Council of Khalistan". The letter, it is reported, asked the professor to arrange a meeting between Balkar Singh and Sukha Sipahi ("General" Labh Singh), one of the top terrorists of Amritsar district. It has also been reported that before his arrest, Balkar Singh had distributed about Rs. 38 lakhs to various terrorist organisations.

According to some newspapers, the amount had been collected by Balkar Singh from various businessmen in India, including those in Punjab. That, however, does not reveal the entire truth. The money was possibly collected in India but in non-official and illegal exchange for amounts paid in foreign currency to the relatives of these businessman in foreign countries.

According to the Superintendent of Police (Detective), Rajinder Singh, Balkar Singh had come here to "guide and finance" the "Panthic Committee", in addition to arranging arms for the terrorists.

His links with a Pakistani national, Chaudhri Liaqat Ali of Gujranwala, had been established. Rajinder Singh also said, that before his arrest Balkar Singh had met Avtar Singh Brahma, Kuldip Singh Muchhal, Gurbachan Singh Manochahal and Labh Singh (all top terrorists) and had given them Rs. 38 lakhs.

To protest against the "alleged maltreatment" of this Canadian citizen by the Punjab police, Canadian External Affairs Minister Joe Clark summoned the Indian High Commissioner. Earlier, a Canadian diplomat in Delhi had delivered a protest note to the External Affairs Ministry in Delhi over certain allegations of "torture" of Balkar Singh.

These facts are from a report from Ottawa[8]. The same report contains the following:

"Asked how Canada viewed the activities of some of its nationals who reportedly used the country as a base for launching terrorist operations in India, Georges Riou, an External Affairs Ministry spokesman, refused to comment."

On November 29, 1987, Channel I of the BBC, under the "Everyman" series, devoted to the propagation of religion, featured a 45-minute programme entitled "The Turban and the Sword."[9] The programme gave "a further boost" to the "rising militant tendencies among the Sikh youth in the UK and to the demand of separate state". Devotional singers, says the report, were projected singing songs, praising, not the ten Gurus, but the dead Bhindranwale and his nephew, Jasbir Singh, now in detention in India. The report ends by pointing out that diplomatic observers in London feel "the programme was aimed at deepening the wounds of the Sikh community. It was felt that it was more tilted in favour of separatism than in favour of those who stood for unity and integrity".

On December 12, 1987 it was reported[10] that the US House of Representatives had adopted a resolution calling upon the Government of India to open the Golden Temple for worship and to respect the "human rights" of the Sikhs in Punjab. Lying in the face of facts and presenting a totally distorted picture of reality, the resolution was obviously intended to raise the sagging morale of the terrorists.

It is unnecessary to give more examples.

India is fully reconciled to the establishment of a separate Pakistan and wishes its people well. At the same time, the vital interests of the

Indian people demand that the game of disintegrating India is defeated. The unity and integrity of India must be maintained. That is the call of patriotism today. In defending the unity and integrity of India, the people of Punjab—both Hindus and Sikhs—have a vital role to play. There is no doubt that they will play this role with credit. Our confidence is based on facts like the following:

**Majority Against "Khalistan"**

A big majority of the Sikhs in Punjab have refused to support the demand for "Khalistan". Whatever support the demand was able to gather has already started declining. The Hindu communal thesis that the entire Sikh community is responsible for the misdeeds of the terrorists and their slogans of "revenge" etc. have not evoked the response its authors had expected.

All efforts to provoke Hindu-Sikh riots in Punjab on a large- scale have failed. Thousands and thousands of Sikhs and Hindus have jointly demonstrated in Punjab and in Delhi for communal peace, for unity of India, and against "Hindu Raj" as well as "Khalistan". The Left in Punjab has played a significant role in this.

At the same time, it would be wrong to overlook the factors which have played a negative role and the negative features of the present situation. And these must be studied historically.

The British did all they could to divide Hindus and Muslims and to incite Hindu-Muslim riots. This, however, did not exhaust their "divide and rule" policy. British India's division into provinces had not been done on geographical, historical, economic or linguistic basis. This division was done with a view to following the policy of "divide and rule". The Madras Presidency, for instance, included the Tamil speaking as well as the Telugu speaking people. The Bombay Presidency included the Marathi speaking as well as the Gujarati speaking people. At the same time, many Gujarati speaking people lived in different princely states. The pre-independence Punjab province included the Punjabi speaking people as well as the Hindi or Haryanvi and Bagri speaking people. There were also a number of princely states like Patiala, Nabha etc. which were inhabited by the Punjabi speaking people.

Secondly, in the country as a whole the British rulers allowed the respective language of the people to be the medium of instruction at least at the primary stage and also to be the language of the administration below the district level. In the case of Punjab, however, even this was not done. Nowhere in Punjab was Punjabi made the medium of instruction even in (government) primary schools. Nor was it made the language of administration at any level. The British obviously wanted to exploit certain historical factors prevailing in Punjab for the furtherance of their policy of "divide and rule". And this led to the language question in Punjab getting mixed up with religion and communalism.

As a part of its efforts to defeat the British game of "divide and rule", the Indian National Congress made a firm commitment to reorganise the then provinces on the linguistic basis. However, after India won her freedom and the Congress became the ruling party, it tried to go back on this commitment. The reorganisation of Indian states on the linguistic basis came only after bitter struggles. Except in the case of Punjab, these were united struggles. These had achieved success by 1956 or so.

In Punjab the Akali Party led by Master Tara Singh came out with the demand for a "Sikh Suba". Later on it was modified to a "Punjabi speaking province in which Sikhs should be at least 60 per cent of the population." The Punjabi language—the mother tongue of all the Punjabis (Sikhs and Hindus)—was talked about as if it was a part of the Sikh religion. The Hindu communalists, on the other hand, made the false assertion that Hindi and not Punjabi was their mother tongue. They too made it a religious issue. Hindus were called upon to get Hindi recorded as their mother tongue during the census operation. Many (Hindu) Congress leaders too took this position. They would not consider the adoption of Punjabi as the official language, even with the option to use the Devanagari script besides the Gurmukhi script. Against the demand for a Sikh majority "Punjabi Suba", a demand for "Maha Punjab" (in which Sikhs would be a microscopic minority) was also advanced.

In this way, in Punjab the issue of language and of the formation of a Punjabi speaking state assumed heavy communal overtones. This enabled the ruling party to delay the reorganisation of Punjab on linguistic basis much longer than in the case of Andhra or Maharashtra, etc.

Sant Fateh Singh was encouraged to come into politics by Congress Chief Minister Sardar Partap Singh Kairon. The idea was to weaken and even split the Akali Party. Sant Fateh Singh took a progressive stand on many issues. For instance, he demanded the state takeover of the wholesale trade in food grains as well as nationalisation of banks. He was a firm supporter of India's foreign policy of non-alignment. He took the firm position that he wanted a "Punjabi Suba" comprising all Punjabi speaking areas and was not bothered which religious community constituted what percentage of the total population of this province. He also declared that he would not demand any more powers for Punjab than those enjoyed by the other Indian states. He campaigned on this basis. This brought about many healthy changes in the politics of Punjab of those days. The Communists, consistent with their own stand, lent him their full support.

The Hindi speaking people of the Haryana region of the then Punjab (overwhelmingly Hindus) now began pressing for a separate Haryana state. Active opposition from the Punjabi speaking Hindus to the formation of a "Punjabi Suba" began to go down. In the process, Sant Fateh Singh emerged as the unchallenged leader of the Akali Party in his own right and could not be called to order even by those who originally brought him into politics.

The demand for a Punjabi speaking state had to be conceded and the present states of Punjab and Haryana came into existence in November 1966. The Akalis were in power in this Punjab in 1967, in 1969-71 and in 1979-80. On the first two occasions, their government fell because of defections and internal quarrels, actively encouraged by the Congress and the Government of India. The third time, the Akali government was dismissed by the Congress (I) government at the Centre along with many other non-Congress state governments, just as many Congress state governments had earlier been dismissed in 1977 by the Janata Party government of India, of which the Akali Party too was a partner.

**Unjust Reorganisation**

The reorganisation of Punjab in November 1966 was not entirely just. Chandigarh was made a Union Territory. Many Punjabi speaking villages and even areas went to Haryana while many Hindi speaking villages and areas came to Punjab. This was the result of the tehsil and not the village being made the basis of division and also because large sections of Hindus had recorded Hindi as their mother tongue. Had Sant Fateh Singh stood for complete separation of religion from politics and had he not run his morchas from within the Golden Temple, the situation in these respects too might have been much less unsatisfactory.

In 1971, Sant Fateh Singh launched a morcha for the inclusion of Chandigarh in Punjab. He went on a fast unto death. On the basis of a behind-the-scene agreement suggested by the Akali leadership itself or its emissaries, Indira Gandhi awarded Chandigarh to Punjab while Abohar and Fazilka with a corridor through one village were awarded to Haryana. The rest of the territorial dispute was to go to a commission. The award was welcomed by the then Akali Chief Minister Gurnam Singh. However, there was very adverse and strong reaction against it in Punjab and the Akalis went back on it. It was never implemented.

When India's partition took place in 1947, all the water of the Ravi and Beas rivers was not being utilised. As these rivers flow through Pakistan's Punjab too, Pakistan rightly claimed its share. India wanted this entire water on the ground that it was needed not only for Punjab but also for Rajasthan. An agreement between the then Punjab and Rajasthan fixing their shares was arrived at in 1955. Later on, with the help of the World Bank, Pakistan was persuaded to give up its claim in return for Rs. 100 crores paid to it by the Government of India. Till 1982, no one ever raised any dispute about all this. The dispute arose about the division of the erstwhile Punjab's share between the present Punjab and Haryana when a separate Haryana state was formed. While this dispute has not yet been resolved, it was only in 1982 and thereafter that the Akali Party leaders began questioning the right of Rajasthan and sometimes even of Haryana to any water of these rivers.

The principle of riparian states was invoked in support of the assertion that neither Haryana nor Rajasthan could claim even a drop of water of these rivers—because they nowhere touched the boundaries of these states. The principle of riparian states is applicable under international law to different, separate countries. It cannot be applied to different states of one country which is developing a common economy.

As already stated, the Akalis were in power in Punjab from 1977 to 1980 (for nearly three years). In this period they also shared power at the Centre. It is true that they did nothing to settle these disputes, or the "Punjab demands" as they have come to be known. Sometimes, the Akali leaders try to refute this by pointing out that they did go to the Supreme Court regarding the water disputes. The fact is that it is Haryana that went to the Supreme Court first for the implementation of the Government of India's decision in this matter, taken during the Emergency period. The Akali Government had filed a counter case. Those cases were withdrawn after Indira Gandhi had brought about a new agreement between the Chief Ministers of Haryana, Punjab and Rajasthan—all of the Congress (I).

This agreement undid only some of the injustices done to Punjab by the earlier decision of the Government of India. For some days the Akalis did not raise any objection. The fact remained that the opposition had not been consulted. Subsequently, it became a major dispute. It was clearly wrong not to consult the opposition. Events have also proved that it would have been better to let the Supreme Court decide the matter.

**Rich Peasants, Capitalist Landlords**

As is well known the Green Revolution has been highly successful in Punjab for historical reasons. The biggest beneficiaries of this revolution have been the upper sections of land-owners. A powerful class of rich peasants and capitalist landlords has come into being in Punjab. This class has made big amounts of money and has grown quite rich. It wants avenues for investment. After a particular stage, agriculture no longer yielded as much as it did earlier. Adequate attention to development of industry in Punjab was not given at the proper time even when it had become urgently necessary from the viewpoint of agriculture itself and also from the viewpoint of the existing small-scale industry. The resulting situation gave rise to a number of demands and problems.

There has been, for instance, the demand for greater industrial development of Punjab, the demand for big industries and, above-all, the demand for agro-industries. The Akali leaders have been saying, "When we produce agricultural goods why should we not have the right to sell them at the highest available price, in the international market? Why should we be forced to sell our produce to the Government of India at the price fixed by it for Indian states who are deficit in grain?" Clearly, this is a demand for profiteering prices, as distinct from the very justified demand of the peasantry for remunerative prices.

To gain their economic aims, the landlords and the *kulaks* have been demanding greater share in state power. They are already a dominant force in the economy of the state. They want to be the dominant force in the power structure of the state. They want to rule the state and they want Punjab under their rule to have more powers than it has at present. Some have developed all-India interests including industrial interests. They have a "moderate" outlook. Others go to the extent of wanting the Centre to be very weak. And there are also such elements who dream of an independent Punjab.

Obviously, only such of their demands as are consistent with the interest of the people and the country can be supported. For instance, more industry for Punjab—Yes. More powers for the states—Yes. Only four departments for the Centre — No.

By religion, a big majority of the Punjab peasants and landlords are Sikhs. Politically, a small section of them has been with the Congress. The rest have been with the Akali Party. In fact, the Akali Party leadership is in the hands of the rural rich, the *kulaks* and the landlords. A big majority of the Punjab peasantry too is Sikh by religion. By caste they are Jats, while most of the agricultural labourers belong to the Scheduled Castes.

The caste and the religion factors help the Akali leadership to rally behind them also the middle and the poor peasants and other Sikhs. That is why they put forward even their non-religious demands as the demands of the Sikhs. They allege that the Centre discriminates against Punjab because Punjab's majority consists of Sikhs; that their demands are not being accepted because the Sikhs are treated as second class citizens, etc. They run their *morchas* from gurdwaras and to justify that, they stick to the theory that for the Sikhs religion and politics are inseparable. Those who want to go to the extreme take their stand on the thesis: the "Sikhs—a separate nation" and the "Sikhs must have separate political identity" (and not only religious identity) and demand "Khalistan". It is also argued by some that the British conquered Punjab from a Sikh ruler and therefore the Sikhs must rule Punjab again.

The conflict of interest between the established Hindu trading classes and the growing Sikh trading classes too assumes a communal colouring. This has made its own contribution to the Punjab problem.

As already stated, the demand for "Khalistan" is encouraged, supported and helped by imperialism out to destabilise and disintegrate India. The Akali Party has never demanded "Khalistan" by any resolution. It has even opposed it. However, it cannot be said that all Akali leaders have the same attitude. It is to be noted that the Akali Party as a whole has taken certain positions which provide grist to the mill of separatism, e.g. the thesis: "Sikhs-a-separate-nation."

The discontentment of the people—which is the direct result of the economic policies of the Government of India resulting in growing disparities, growing unemployment, growing atrocities on weaker sections, growing corruption, etc.—too helps the divisive forces. The educated youths coming from rich and middle peasant families of Punjab do not find avenues and opportunities desired by them.

### Anandpur Sahib Resolution

What has been said in the preceding paras should help one to understand the real meaning of the much talked about Anandpur Sahib resolution.

There are many versions of the resolution. We can leave out the one which is claimed to be the real one by the Talwandi faction of the Akali Party.

The original one was adopted in 1973 at Gurdwara Anandpur Sahib in the town of Anandpur by the working committee of the Akali Party.

It was stated in the introduction of the resolution that the English translation[11] was by Amar Singh Ambalvi, who was also a member of the 12-member sub-committee which had been constituted by the working committee to formulate comprehensive policies and programmes of the Akali Party. The introduction also stated that notwithstanding sharp differences at many meetings, the final report was adopted unanimously.

A slightly different version appeared in the press[12] on December 13, 1982. This was said to be the full text of the English version of the political goal resolution adopted by the working committee of the Dal on October 16-17, 1973 at Anandpur Sahib.

There is another version—the one which was signed by the late Sant Longowal and given to Inder Kumar Gujral. There is yet another version which appeared in the White Paper issued by the Government of India in July 1984. This was supplied to the Government by the Akali leadership.

Then there is the resolution adopted by the general house of the Akali Party in 1978 at Ludhiana. This only demanded more powers for the states. However, it makes clear that it was adopted "in the light of the Anandpur Sahib resolution."

Anyway, those who swear by the Anandpur Sahib resolution make it clear that they mean the original 1973 one.

All versions of the resolution contain certain religious as well as economic demands. Some of the latter are the real demands of the rural rich. Others are for catching votes. We need not go into all these because the essence of the Anandpur Sahib resolution lies somewhere else.

Notwithstanding some differences in the different versions of the 1973 resolution, they have the following common features:

(1) They are based on the thesis that Sikhs are not only an independent religious community (which they undoubtedly are) but are also an independent and separate political identity—which they are not.

(2) All concede only four departments to the Centre. These are: communication, currency, defence and foreign affairs. (This means good-bye to common economy. They have not conceded power even to raise finances necessary to run these departments. The Centre will have to ask for contributions from the states— presumably in proportion to their representation in Parliament. This is made explicit in one of the versions.)

(3) The political aim in every version is defined as "Khalsa Ji Ka Bol Bala". This is nothing but a demand for a theocratic Punjab. If it materialises, it will mean not the rule of the Sikhs but of the Sikh vested interests, especially of the rural rich.

Of course, extravagant claims on the territories of the neighbouring states are there in all the versions.

(4) In all the versions there is an attack on India's foreign policy of non-alignment from a pro-imperialist position.

(5) In all the versions there is the false claim that the Akali Party is the sole representative of the Sikhs.

The resolution does not spell out how "Khalsa Ji Ka Bol Bala" will be ensured, because the one-person-one-vote system may not guarantee that. Some of the Akali leaders have aired their views in this connection.

Not very long ago, G.S. Tohra came out with the theory that those not having immovable property in Punjab should not have the right to vote.

Narinder Singh Bhullar, once a dictator of the "Punjabi Suba Morcha" and later on a great admirer of Bhindranwale, has been propagating the theory of separate electorates.

There is no doubt that the demand for the acceptance of the Anandpur Sahib resolution is the demand for "Khalistan" within India but with a very weak Centre, and its acceptance can only prove a big step towards a sovereign "Khalistan".

Notwithstanding all this, it needs to be stated that during the elections to Parliament, Prime Minister Rajiv Gandhi overplayed the Anandpur Sahib resolution card—obviously for electoral gains.

**Sant Jarnail Singh Bhindranwale**

Let us now briefly deal with the phenomenon of Sant Jarnail Singh Bhindranwale.

This Sant too was brought into politics by the Congress-I. During the 1978 election to the Shiromani Gurdwara Parbandhak Committee (SGPC) his candidates were supported by the Congress. During the 1980 Lok Sabha elections, the Sant supported Congress-I candidates Gurdial Singh Dhillon and Raghunandan Bhatia. The Congress-I—at least one faction of it—continued to nurture and support Bhindranwale even after he openly called for the murder of the Nirankari Baba, Lala Jagat Narain and others. The game obviously was to split or weaken the Akali Party—as yet the only rival in its bid to rule Punjab. This game was not given up even after the Sant began organising large-scale terrorism and making serious efforts to incite Hindu-Sikh riots. The Akalis too played the game of using him against the Congress-I and the Government of India.

It is not for nothing that Bhindranwale was allowed to live first in the Guru Nanak Niwas and then in the Akal Takht. From within the Golden Temple the killing of the Hindus was preached by him. There itself the killer squads were trained and given shelter. The Golden Temple complex was converted into an arsenal with highly sophisticated weapons and a lot of ammunition. Tohra and Longowal went on denying that any such thing was happening in the Golden Temple complex. Parkash Singh Badal followed the principle: "Silence is golden".

The Akali leadership obviously wanted to use Bhindranwale as a card against the government to be able to dictate its terms. It was not for nothing that at quite an early stage the Akali leadership had demanded his release as a precondition to negotiations with the government.

Longowal went to the extent of justifying the killings of the Nirankaris. He would deplore killing of the Hindus but would blame the Congress-I for providing an *alibi* for Bhindranwale's men. Rebutting the charge that he was a Congress agent, Bhindranwale once asserted that it was, in fact, he who had used the Congress and not *vice versa.* He could have also made the same claim with regard to the Akalis.

Bhindranwale built his cells within the administration. His influence increased. The administration became more and more paralysed. Bhindranwale's became a parallel government and thereafter the only government in Punjab. Even highly confidential decisions taken by the Governor-in-Council were reported to reach him pretty fast. His men could kill anyone at his bidding and get away with it. Many began to believe that he was all powerful, almost an *avatar*.

His men fell into two categories: (a) young men indoctrinated by ideological poison, attracted also by appeal of arms and with plenty of money; and (b) smugglers and other anti-social elements. They served him in more than one way and also used the position and power he came to acquire for their own ends. Smugglers in Punjab have been wielding considerable influence over bourgeois politicians. Many of them supported the Congress as well as the Akali Party even simultaneously. They had, it seems, developed ambitions to directly share power in the state. In any case, Bhindranwale tried to use them. They in their turn tried to use him.

Towards the end of his career Bhindranwale had gone completely out of control of the Congress as well as of the Akalis. Quite a few of the Akali leaders even feared death at the hands of his men.

It is no use speculating to what extent Bhindranwale was directly linked with the US and the military rulers of Pakistan. There is, however, no doubt that he and his terrorists were playing their game of dismemberment of India and were being helped by them.

It needs to be mentioned that the Hindu communalists, who held the entire Sikh community responsible for the misdeeds of the extremists, only helped the latter. A similar role was played on more than one occasion by the then Haryana Chief Minister Bhajan Lal. Only one instance need be given. The Akali threat to disrupt the Asian Games in New Delhi deserved to be condemned and had to be met firmly and tactfully. But the way in which the ordinary Sikh passengers as also top dignitaries travelling to Delhi were humiliated by the Haryana police was a tremendous help to Bhindranwale and the Sikh communalists. At one stage Bhajan Lal had started acting on the theory of "teaching the Sikhs a lesson".

The "Blue Star" operation of the Army, when it took place, had become a painful necessity. It dealt a blow to the imperialist conspiracy to dismember India through another partition. At the same time, it created new problems. It deeply hurt Sikh religious sentiments. It made the ground more fertile for the separatists.

Could it not have been avoided? This is an important question. Our opinion is that the situation necessitating the "Blue Star" operation could and should have been avoided.

First, when DIG Atwal was shot dead from within the Golden Temple complex, Bhindranwale was in Guru Nanak Niwas, which really is not a part of the complex. He had not yet shifted to the Akal Takht. Security forces could have entered the Guru Nanak Niwas at that time and taken decisive action to smash the terrorist organisation. The failure of the government to act at that time surprised everyone, including the Sikhs, and demoralised the police force still further.

Secondly, and this is more important, had a political settlement been reached on the "Punjab demands" at the proper time, the moderate Akali leaders in all probability would have cooperated to throw Bhindranwale and his men out of the Golden Temple complex. In any case, they would have been isolated and it would have been easier to deal with them without any operation like the "Blue Star" one.

The fact that the Congress-I and its government, the Akali Party and other bourgeois parties gave the first place to their narrow electoral and other partisan interests was the main factor which hindered and prevented a political solution. Had these parties given the first place to the interests of the nation, it would not have been difficult to find a solution keeping in view the interests of national integration, doing justice to Punjab without doing injustice to Haryana and Rajasthan, and acting in a spirit of give and take. For its failure, the ruling party has, of course, to bear a greater responsibility. Much has already been written about this matter. We here need deal only with the important controversies.

The opposition parties allege that three times an agreement had almost been arrived at but each time it was prevented by the late Prime Minister. The allegation had not been refuted convincingly. The late Prime Minister alleged that settlement was prevented by the Akali refusal to give up the Anandpur Sahib resolution. This at best is a half truth. The Akalis had insisted that in the terms of reference of the commission to go into Centre-State relations, mention be made of this resolution. The government as well as the entire opposition had opposed this and the Akalis at last agreed to drop this demand. It is another matter that from Manji Saheb Sant Longowal had declared that the (original) Anandpur Saheb resolution remained their final aim. But this was not the cause of the last-minute breakdown on either of the occasions.

The late Prime Minister's charge that the Akalis kept on shifting their position is not altogether wrong. For instance, the dispute about surplus waters was really about the shares of Haryana and Punjab. Suddenly the Akalis wanted even the 1955 agreement fixing Rajasthan's share to be re-opened. But the opposition opposed them and they had to retreat. Also, they raised an altogether new demand for amending Article 25 of the Constitution. This the government almost conceded, and quite readily too, as if it had been raised by mutual arrangement. There may be some other instances too but it does not seem that they proved to be the cause of the breakdown.

Of course, it seems true that a stage had reached when the Akali leadership would not dare to arrive at any settlement that had not the support of Bhindranwale. And Bhindranwale would not agree to anything less than the Anandpur Sahib resolution.

The army action, of course, greatly injured the religious sentiments of the Sikhs and in a way helped the separatists. At the same time, note has to be taken of the fact that much before Operation Bluestar sections of the urban middle classes, intellectuals and youths had come to believe that Bhindranwale was invincible and that he would, in any case, get "Khalistan". Some such persons would gleefully ask, "What is the score today?" (i.e., "How many have been killed today?") Bungalows, houses and even mills and business premises of the Hindus had been "allotted" by Bhindranwale and his men. This writer knows of instances of even school children talking about such "allotment". Those who had thus been attuned to "Khalistan" coming into existence were more angry when they heard that Bhindranwale had been shot dead than even at the entry of the army in the Golden Temple premises. They felt frustrated.

A big majority of the Sikhs was not for "Khalistan". Operation Blue Star injured their religious sentiments too. It widened the gap between the Hindus and the Sikhs. But it is also a fact that it led to some heart-searching amongst some sections of them. The question began being asked: Why was Bhindranwale not prevented from doing what he actually did in the Golden Temple?

There is also the fact that the Sikh agricultural labourers and the class conscious organised Sikh industrial workers had been not only against Bhindranwale but also the Akalis. They even supported Operation Blue Star as a painful necessity. There are others who take more or less the same position, as for example, the Radha Swami Sikhs, the Nirankari Sikhs, etc. There were also Sikh supporters of the Left, the Congress-I etc. even amongst the peasants.

Sikh agricultural labourers belong to the Scheduled Castes. They constitute nearly 20 per cent of the Sikh population of Punjab. The landed gentry does not regard them as Sikhs but there is no reason for others to lose sight of the fact that this section of the Sikhs is firmly opposed to the demand for “Khalistan”.

Even amongst the land-owning Sikh peasantry the degree of anger and feeling of hurt was not the same in all the districts and even in its different layers in one and the same district. The fact that Bhindranwale’s call issued on June 2, 1984 to kill the Hindus everywhere was ignored, except only here and there, was also significant.

**Indira Gandhi’s Assassination**

The dastardly assassination of Prime Minister Indira Gandhi on October 31, 1984 was clearly a part of the imperialist game. Proofs of this contention were available in the US press itself. One “expectation” was that it would lead to large-scale Hindu-Sikh riots. The most shameful anti-Sikh riots that took place in the first few days of November 1984 in Delhi, Kanpur and some other places must have gladdened the hearts of India’s enemies. The fact that some Sikhs celebrated Indira Gandhi’s assassination deserved severe condemnation but that could never be a justification for anti-Sikh riots. In many cases the police connived at and even encouraged these incidents. The most unfortunate fact was that even some Congress-I leaders and workers whose duty it should have been to give correct guidance to people in those difficult days did just the opposite.

This is not to deny that some Congressmen did play a positive role too and tried to save the Sikhs sought to be attacked. It needs also to be stated that after some initial vacillation, Rajiv Gandhi did act firmly to stop the riots. Even then, in some respects, the anti-Sikh riots in Delhi, Kanpur etc. caused greater harm to the cause of Hindu-Sikh unity than anything else.

As has already been stated, during the elections to the Lok Sabha, Rajiv Gandhi used the Anandpur Sahib resolution card as his main plank and overplayed it. After the elections, however, he took many steps, one after the other, to resolve the Punjab problem and to restore normalcy. These included the release of the Akali leaders, secret negotiations with them, a firm public assurance about early construction of the Thein Dam, promise of a coach factory etc.

**Rajiv-Longowal Accord**

The late Sant Harchand Singh Longowal, who had adopted a very belligerent attitude immediately after his release, soon began speaking in a very welcome tone. And then came the Rajiv-Longowal Accord. It was widely welcomed. The entire country heaved a sigh of relief. Sant Longowal was praised for the courage he displayed by signing the accord. He could not but know that thereby he would be on the top of the hit list of the separatists and the terrorists. And he did pay with his life for his correct and courageous act. Rajiv Gandhi and the then Punjab Governor Arjun Singh too were praised rightly. At the same time it needs to be noted that it was the failure of the strategy to bring about Hindu-Sikh riots in Punjab as also in the rest of the country resulting in mass migration out of and into Punjab and the widespread desire and growing demand for normalcy on the part of the people which made possible the accord. There were of course some other factors also.

The Communists too welcomed the accord whole-heartedly. They pointed out that it could become a big weapon for completely isolating the terrorists and separatists. They also made the point that it would not mean an automatic end to and complete elimination of terrorism. They stated that imperialism would not give up its effort to destabilise India and there were factors in the internal situation to help it.

Recent events have proved all this to be entirely correct. It soon became clear that terrorists though much weakened had not been isolated. The high vote polled by Bimal Khalsa, widow of one of the assassins of Indira Gandhi, in two constituencies in the May 1985 elections to the Punjab Vidhan Sabha proves that the failure of the call to boycott the elections cannot be interpreted to mean equally strong rejection of extremism.

In his pamphlet, dated October 4, 1985, the already referred to Narinder Singh Bhuller clearly stated that the Sikh youths would either kill the traitors or get themselves killed. He openly denounced the slogan of Hindu-Sikh unity and characterised it as contrary to the teachings of the Gurus.

The Communists also stated that the implementation of the accord could not be taken for granted and that this would have to be fought for. Unfortunately, this too has proved to be correct. Some of the facts which show this are:

(1) Some important leaders of the Akali Party have been opposing openly or in actual practice the accord, for purely factional reasons. While some want to sincerely implement it, there are others who regard it as a stage for reaching the final goal—the Anandpur Sahib resolution.

(2) The initial reaction of the Congress-I Chief Ministers of Haryana and Rajasthan was to oppose the accord. They were pulled up. But then the bourgeois opposition parties in Haryana took upon themselves to do whatever they could to sabotage it, even when their counterparts in Punjab were supporting it.

(3) It is possible to argue that the territorial dispute between Punjab and Haryana for historical reasons has become so complicated that to resolve it "other relevant factors" should also be taken into account, besides "the principle of contiguity and linguistic affinity with a village as a unit". But the proper time for that was before the accord was signed. To add "other factors" in the terms of reference of the Mathew Commission (which was to decide the Hindi speaking areas to be transferred to Haryana in lieu of Chandigarh) when it was not there in the accord was certainly a very wrong act on the part of the Government of India. It is good that the Prime Minister admitted the mistake but the damage was not entirely undone.

(4) Many leaders of Haryana, including the Chief Minister, on the one hand, and the Akali leaders on the other, began saying and doing things whose obvious aim was to pressurise the Mathew Commission. Passions were being sought to be raised over Fazilka and Abohar. Each side was virtually threatening to let the accord go to hell if the Mathew Commission's decision was not to its liking.

All these and similar other facts go to show that bourgeois leaders are incapable of placing national interests above narrow partisan, factional electoral and regional interests.

No wonder then that nothing came out of the Mathew Commission. The Rajiv-Longowal Accord is almost dead now. It needs also to be noted that the accord was not free from weaknesses. For instance, it lent credibility to the false claim of the Akali Party of being the sole representative of the Sikhs, and even of Punjab. It lent a certain amount of respectability to the Anandpur Sahib resolutions. As far as Rajiv Gandhi is concerned, he signed in haste without fully understanding its implications. This alone explains subsequent attempts to manipulate the commissions.

Notwithstanding this, serious efforts and initiatives are necessary to help resolve the territorial and surplus water disputes in the spirit of the Rajiv-Longowal Accord—in the spirit of give and take and keeping in view the interests of the country as a whole. No state must be made to suffer gross injustice.

The hope that the Barnala government would be able to contain and defeat terrorism was belied. Terrorist activity was, in fact, stepped up. Terrorist killings increased. "Khalistan" was declared right inside the Golden Temple. Barnala had no option but to send police into the Golden Temple. The Akali Party got split. The Barnala government, however, survived.

Gurcharan Singh Tohra's victory in the SGPC election for presidentship was a big gain for extremists and terrorists. They acted swiftly. The five Sikh high priests were dismissed. Known supporters of the extremists and even of separatists were installed in their place. The Golden Temple and many other gurdwaras in the state were captured by the terrorists and were made full use of for their nefarious activities and poisonous propaganda.

A number of new gurdwaras began to be constructed, especially in Amritsar and Gurdaspur districts—often in uninhabited areas, but at otherwise strategic places. Many extremists would boast that these would be their centres of operation at crucial times. Kar sewa for construction work in many cases became a cover for terrorist activity.

The new high priests made a determined bid to replace the Barnala government by a government which would be completely subservient to the extremist forces. They declared that for the sake of "panthic unity" they would set up a Unified Akali Dal. They issued an edict calling upon the leaders of all the Akali factions to resign. This was a gross misuse of religion on the ground that religion and politics cannot be separated. After some vacillation, Barnala refused to resign and was, therefore, excommunicated.

The Unified Akali Dal minus the Akali Dal (Longowal) was set up with Simranjit Singh Mann, a known extremist, as President. Its constitution, based on the Anandpur Sahib resolution, was also ordained by the priests.

The priests overplayed their cards. The move boomeranged. Barnala's excommunication was condemned widely by a large number of the Sikh organisations outside Punjab and a massive Sikh convention in Punjab was held at Longowal. For the first time, a section of the Akali Dal followers began to realize the necessity of separating religion and politics.

The priests launched a counter-campaign. They held a number of "shaheedi conferences" in gurdwaras and in some of the educational institutions. Terrorist-killers who got killed in encounters were hailed as martyrs. Resolutions in support of "Khalistan" or "Khalsa Raj" were adopted.

The move to separate religion and politics was denounced as an attack on the Akal Takht.

**The So-called "Social Reforms"**

A so-called campaign for social reforms at the point of the gun was also let loose by some terrorist organisations. The 13-point charter issued in this connection and also its actual implementation made it quite clear that the real aim was not social reform but something else.

The anti-liquor and anti-cigarette campaigns by burning liquor vends and tobacco shops and by killing those running them may be said to have some connection with social reforms. Everyone, however, knows that no social reform can come through force. There were a number of reports that trade in illicit liquor increased considerably as a result of the terrorist campaign. Some of the terrorists were in league with the bootleggers. Another measure of social reform sought to be brought about by the gun related to dowry and marriage parties. In this on the one hand, exceptions were made, on the other, the move was used for extortions.

An overwhelming majority of the Sikhs is non-vegetarian. Only some small sects are vegetarians. A larger number would regard the campaign against meat as being at variance with Sikhism. This particular item seems to have had the aim of confusing some sections of the Hindus.

The campaign against barbers, the attempt to force a particular uniform in all schools and colleges (including *kesari* headgear) etc. were attempts not only to force on all the Sikhs outward rituals of Sikhism but also to force them on the Hindus. These items were not even remotely connected with any kind of social reform. One of their aims was to fuel fundamentalism of the Khomeini type and also to increase the Hindu-Sikh division.

Then there were items calling for killing those who might visit the Radha Swami *deras* or who might purchase properties of (migrating) Hindus.

The poster announcing the 13-point programme began with the slogan, "Khalistan Zindabad" and declared the Hindus as a community of the "enemy". The poster was widely distributed from within the Golden Temple.

The campaign may have helped to make the terrorists appear as the real government and to net in more youths but the sympathy it appeared to evoke in the beginning began disappearing fast. It soon became clear that their real aims remained unchanged.

It needs to be noted that Professor Darshan Singh, Acting Akal Takht Jathedar, openly and strongly supported the so-called social reform campaign through the barrel of the gun.

Moves by the Government of India to come to terms with the extremists with the help of Darshan Singh even when killings were continuing and even when no section of the extremists was willing to give up the demand for a theocratic Punjab did much harm. It meant a setback to the campaign for separating religion and politics. It gave respectability to those who had been openly backing the terrorists.

**President's Rule**

On the eve of elections to the Haryana Assembly, the Barnala government was dismissed and President's rule was promulgated with effect from May 11, 1987. Undoubtedly, the timing for this was chosen with an eye on the Haryana elections. However, the move did not help the Congress-I in Haryana.

The Barnala government had both positive and negative aspects. It did fight the terrorists to some extent. It took the correct stand that religious places like the Golden Temple could not be allowed to be used for anti-national activities. Barnala's refusal to dissolve his party when ordered by the religious priests was objectively a positive act of great significance. A number of all-party rallies held in different parts of Punjab against separatism, terrorism and for the Hindu-Sikh unity represented another positive factor of the period.

An important aspect of the other side of the picture was the considerable help which the terrorists got from within the government. Extremist leaders like Baba Joginder Singh were allowed full freedom to preach murder and spread poison against the minority community. Barnala made mockery of the Indian Constitution when he declared that his was a panthic government and tried to establish it as such by practising communal discrimination not only in the matter of jobs but also in the matter of relief for a long time. The release of many hardened killers was another negative feature.

It is generally agreed that there has been some improvement in the situation under President's rule. A big number of hard-core extremists have either been captured or killed. The fear that there may be another partition of India is disappearing. The small section which had come to believe that "Khalistan" would come into existence is getting disillusioned.

More than one factor explain this improvement. Political interference in favour of extremist killers has decreased very much. Thanks to Punjab Police Director General J. Rebeiro there has been improvement in the work of the police and para-military forces. The extremist threat to kill even Professor Darshan Singh, the Akal Takht Jathedar, only because he began to express some differences with some of the terrorist organisations, helped to disillusion many who had sympathy with the militants.

President's rule means bureaucratic rule, and the present one is no exception.

**Left Campaigns**

However, efforts made to have a dialogue at the grassroot level through *Lok Shakti Samagams* has helped to some extent. Particularly noteworthy is the statewide mass campaign launched first by the CPI and then by the CPI-M to isolate the terrorists. The CPI went even to those villages which were considered to be terrorist strongholds. These two Left parties of Punjab have been campaigning jointly too. The Communists have paid a heavy price. The CPI alone has lost 32 of its leaders and cadres including their family members. Their losses include stalwarts like Darshan Singh Canadian, Arjun Singh Mastana and *Preet Lari* editor Sumeet Singh. The CPI-M has lost 12 members including the veteran Chanan Singh Dhoot and the rising young leader Deepak Dhawan. The CPI-ML has lost at least four of its members including Baldev Singh Mann, a top leader of one of the ML groups. The mass campaigning undertaken by the Communists has forced some others to follow suit.

Improvement in the situation would have been greater if the Government of India had released the innocents out of the Jodhpur detenus and had punished such VIPs of Delhi as had helped organise the most shameful anti-Sikh riots which followed the assassination of Indira Gandhi.

The Rajiv-Longowal Accord, as already noted, is dead by now. It is no use harping on it but its spirit needs to be revived and initiatives taken to settle the territorial and water disputes. As a first step, let Rajiv Gandhi as President of the Congress (I) declare that the state units of his party would not be allowed to take conflicting stands on these issues and let him call upon all other parties to make similar declarations. Let this be followed by an all-parties meet to work out a consensus.

A negative aspect of President's rule needs to be noted. While it is quite baseless to say that innocent Sikh youths have been picked up from villages and killed, there have been excesses by the police and the paramilitary forces. Some innocent persons have lost their lives in cross firings, by mistake or due to other reasons. Along with many genuine encounters, the possibility of some dreaded terrorists being killed after being captured cannot be ruled out. This is against the rule of law. If the present law is inadequate, it can be amended, instead of the rule of law being undermined. While every excess even when it is the result of some personal enmity has been exploited by some, the Left alone has been trying to expose each and every excess and to get justice.

Here, the glorious role of the organised working class of Punjab needs to be noted. It has not allowed communalism to penetrate its ranks. It has remained fully united. Not only that; it has come out and acted in a big way against terrorism, separatism and communalism of both hues, against slogans of revenge and retaliation, for national unity and for Hindu-Sikh unity. It has done this by organising massive rallies and demonstrations consisting of thousands of people belonging to both communities at all critical times. It has resorted to work-stoppages and strikes against killings. Particularly noteworthy was the one-day strike on September 4, 1987, of more than 20,000 industrial workers and hundreds of bank employees of Amritsar against terrorist killings, for national unity and for communal peace and harmony. There was no economic or trade union demand. The call for strike was given jointly by the AITUC and the CITU. Even though the INTUC and the BMS opposed, their ranks joined the strike.

The role of the working class contrasts sharply with the role of some other classes and sections. It is a matter of deep regret that not a few intellectuals known to be progressive have been carried away by communalism and narrow class interests. While some became virtual supporters of "Khalistan", some others belonging to the other community would privately even justify the most shameful anti-Sikh riots of November 1984.

For the bourgeoisie, India is their market. The bourgeois state may still be strong enough to ensure its unity — if necessary with the help of the Army. However, it is already clear that real unity of India, based on the unity of its people — which has to be unity-in-diversity—can be fully safeguarded and made sure only if the working class becomes the leading class in Indian society and all democratic and patriotic forces rally around it. It can become so only by performing its duty to the country and by fulfilling its tasks.

Some other immediate tasks of the progressive forces, apart from those already mentioned, are us under:

1. Everything possible must be done to bridge the gulf between the Hindus and the Sikhs. An atmosphere must be created in which the Sikh minority in India and the Hindu minority in Punjab feel fully safe.

2. A powerful campaign for the separation of religion from politics and from language must be organised. No political party activity and propaganda should be allowed in religious places and no political party should have its offices in any temple, gurdwara, mosque or church. No religious place should be allowed to store arms and

ammunition and become an arsenal. No one should be a political leader and religious bigwig at the same time.

3. The Punjab Hindus must be persuaded to own Punjabi which in fact is their mother tongue.

4. Powerful public opinion must be built up against electoral opportunism which has come to dominate our political life.

5. A powerful political and ideological campaign has to be run to show why "Khalistan" is a suicidal slogan for the Sikh masses themselves. The imperialist aim to destabilise India has to be exposed day after day. False cries like the "Sikhs are second class citizens", the "Sikhs are a separate nation", have to be exposed as such. At the same time, the Hindu bias in the Centre has to be opposed and fought. An instance of this bias was seen when the Haryana Government declared Kurukshetra as a holy city and the Centre did not stop it. This was at a time when a controversy was raging about the Akali demand to declare Amritsar a holy city.

Hindu rites at state functions provide another glaring instance of the Hindu tinge in the thought processes of those who rule India at present. All really secular persons should demand that all governments—central as well as state, the Congress as well as the non-Congress ones — must function in a secular manner and keep religion and the State apart.

6. Communalism of all hues must be fought with equal vigour. Communalism of every variety is poison. Majority communalism is more dangerous in the sense that it has the possibility of rallying greater numbers under its banner. No communal party should be made respectable for the sake of electoral gains.

7. The utterly false and extremely dangerous thesis that the Hindus alone can defend India's unity must be exposed mercilessly.

It is necessary to take note of another aspect of the problem, from the viewpoint of future tasks.

With the development of the economy, self-consciousness of the linguistic groups has grown in India. This is inevitable, natural and also a healthy development. Failure on the part of the powers that be at the Centre to accord due recognition to this fact proves counter-productive and encourages separatism. The rural bourgeoisie on the other hand seeks to give it a regionalist orientation. In Punjab, even more than that, a communal orientation is sought to be given. A theory was also propounded that for the unity of India itself regional parties should come up in all states and that the Akali Party should become a non-communal regional party of Punjab.

This is a false theory and can prove dangerous. While every regional party is not necessarily regionalist, it is necessary to fight regionalist tendencies while fighting for more powers for the states. The emergence of more and more regional parties is not a welcome development, deserving encouragement.

While taking note of the growing self-consciousness of various nationalities in India, note must also be taken of the growing consciousness of Indian nationhood. The two have to be properly harmonised so that India's unity-in-diversity gets strengthened.

As regards the Akali Party, it seems to be mere wishful thinking that it can soon become a non-communal regional party. In any case, there can be no short-cut to waging a bitter and prolonged struggle against the misuse of religion and the caste factor by sections of exploiting classes for their narrow class interests. And this cannot be done successfully unless communalism and chauvinism of all hues are fought. *(1988)*

## 2. Rise of Terrorsim—Objective and Subjective Factors

Violence cannot be equated with terrorism. Even Gandhiji—the apostle of non-violence—justified the use of violence in certain contingencies by a woman to defend her honour. He had withdrawn his civil disobedience movement because of the Chauri Chaura incident in February 1922. But on the eve of the next mass civil disobedience movement in 1930-31, he had met the communist accused in the Meerut Conspiracy Case and assured them that there would be no question of withdrawing the movement in face of any similar incident.

All violence is not terrorism. It is not at all an easy job to evolve a universal definition of terrorism. I would rather leave this to more competent persons. As a political activist with a limited knowledge of history, I may make some observations. Terrorism represents an attempt to attain some political objective by creating terror through violence. This objective may be just and right as well as unjust and wrong. It may really be in the interests of the people in whose name terror is used. It can also be very much against the interests of those very people. Violence used to create terror can be targeted as well as indiscriminate, senseless and unpredictable. This often depends open the nature of the objective and the nature of the motivation of those using terrorism.

Terrorism cannot succeed even if the objective is noble and just. The justness of the objective may lead to the method of terrorism being given up. To the extent this does not happen, terrorism results in degeneration of even those who are well motivated.

There is plenty of material in our own history to support and substantiate the above propositions.

Some terrorists try to exploit the name of our great martyr Bhagat Singh. But this is what Bhagat Singh himself said on February 2, 1931 in his message to his revolutionary comrades, just a few weeks before he was hanged:

"Apparently, I have acted like a terrorist, but I am not a terrorist. Let me announce with all the strength at my command that I am not a terrorist and I never was, except perhaps in the beginning of my revolutionary career. I am convinced that we cannot gain anything through these methods."

It is not necessary to add anything to this. There were also the Babbar Akalis, who too had the purest of motives and a noble objective. Thier targets were the agents of imperialism. They would announce their targets beforehand and also the names of persons who would kill them, so that it would be almost impossible for the British rulers and their police to harass any innocent persons. Their targets never included women and children even of informers. Experience made them give up the method of terrorism.

Many of the Naxalites too have been motivated by an objective which is noble. They want a classless society in which there is no exploitation of man by man. What has been the experience of the use of terrorism by the Naxalites? Many of them have given up terrorism and have joined the mainstream of Left movement in India. Many others have left not only terrorism but have also given up politics. They have got splintered into a large number of groups. Some are moving in the direction of giving up terrorism, while those doggedly refusing to do so are degenerating into groups indulging in casteist wars.

Some may argue that terrorism has succeeded in Nagaland, Mizoram, Darjeeling, Tripura and so on. The argument has no weight whatsoever. Those using the method of terrorism in these parts of India had to give up their original secessionist objectives. They had even to give up terrorism or agree to give it up. And what they have achieved is at best equal to linguistic reorganization in the rest of the country. And let it be remembered that this was achieved much earlier as a result of mass movements, which were predominantly non-violent. It can even be argued that terrorism has in fact delayed the realisation of what was really just in the fights waged in the north-eastern parts of India.

Let us now come to terrorism in Punjab. We intend to deal with its various aspects, though not at great length, for reasons of space.

**Objective of Punjab Terrorists**

The objective of Punjab terrorists is "Khalistan", i.e. an independent, sovereign theocratic Sikh state. This is not only against the interests of India and Indian people as a whole. It is against the interests of the Sikhs themselves. Nowhere in the world has a theocratic state done any good, even to the people—the common people—professing the state religion. The Islamic State of Pakistan has not brought any happiness to the common Muslims of that country—the workers, agricultural labourers, poor peasants, middle class people etc. Almost throughout the existence of this theocratic state, people have stood deprived of even the most elementary human rights, and of course, of democracy. Unemployment among Muslim youths has not disappeared. Women have been reduced to the status of second class citizens in every field of life. Instead of Hindu-Muslim riots, Pakistan has now Shia-Sunni riots, riots between the Mujahirs and the locals. All those involved in these riots are Muslims. If India were to say that Muslims who migrated from post-1947 India to Pakistan can return to and settle in India, I am very sure a large number of them would avail of the opportunity with a great sigh of relief. Even though there is much misery, wrong and injustice in secular India, the reality of the situation in theocratic Pakistan surely has a lesson for those who feel attracted by the slogan of "Khalistan". Nepal is a Hindu state. It is even more Hindu than Pakistan is Muslim. If a Hindu of Nepal changes his religion entirely of his own free will, he can be prosecuted and is liable to be sentenced to imprisonment. It is a Hindu kingdom. Hindu landlords may be very happy, but what about the common Hindus? We in Punjab know how poor are the poor Hindus of Bihar, which is the poorest state of India. We know, because lakhs of them come to Punjab in search of work. They work in the industries of Punjab and also in the agricultural fields owned mostly by our Sikh landowners. But in poor Bihar itself you can find poor Nepali Hindus trying to find work to be able to survive. The poor of "Hindu" Nepal are poorer than the poor of our poorest state. This should provide some food for thought for those who want "Hindu Rashtra" in India and also for those who want "Khalistan" in Punjab. We had once the princely state of Patiala. It used to be described as a Sikh state by the topmost Akali leaders, because it was ruled by a Sikh maharaja. The Sikh tenants and other common Sikhs suffered most at the hands of the Sikh maharajas, their police and their minions.

There never was "Hindu rule" or "Muslim rule" or "Sikh rule" in India. These terms were coined by our British rulers. In fact, only the kings were Hindu, Muslim or Sikh. There were good kings and bad kings. But even under the rule of the good kings the common people professing the same religion as the king were far from being happy. This is true of Akbar's rule, as well as of Maharaja Ranjit Singh's. This is also true of the "Golden Age" of the Guptas.

A theocratic state in today's society can only mean greater miseries for the common people. It can at best be a state of the vested interests belonging to a particular religious community, but never a state of the common people even of the same community.

There is much material in our archives to prove that in fact the thesis that "the Sikhs are a nation" and the slogan of "Khalistan" were first inspired and encouraged by the theoreticians of British imperialism to weaken our freedom movement and our country—in the same way as was the thesis, "the Muslims are a nation" and the slogan of Pakistan.

In brief, the demand for "Khalistan" is as much anti-Sikh as it is anti-India.

**Factors behind Terrorism in Punjab**

In the earlier stages of terrorism in Punjab, the Left had to argue hard in support of its contention that behind it and the terrorists was the hand of imperialism, operating from its own soil, but mainly through the rulers of Pakistan, which has a long common border with Punjab as well as some neighbouring states of India. Today this external factor is recognised by one and all, except those who deliberately do not want to see it or are interested in denying it. The evidence which has come to light already is indeed overwhelming, and it is too well known by now.

Imperialism does not like India's anti-imperialist role in the international arena and her refusal to go neocolonial, notwithstanding the concessions which are given to the multinationals by our government. Imperialism therefore wants to weaken, destabilise and even disintegrate and Balkanise India. Towards that end it encourages, aids and abets at one and the same time such slogans as "Khalistan", "Free Kashmir" and also "Hindu Raj" in India. Not very long ago a world conference of the Vishwa Hindu Parishad, which was held in the USA and which demanded "Hindu Raj" in India, was patronised and attended by some dignitaries from the ruling classes of that country.

And towards that very end US imperialism has been helping the Khalistani terrorists from the very beginning, mainly—but not only—through the Pakistani rulers. Besides the fact that Gen. Zia was a US stooge, Pakistani rulers have their own axe to grind too. Their calculations are not difficult to see. If at a time of crisis (say, another Indo-Pak war), they can occupy parts of Amritsar and Gurdaspur districts (bordering Pakistan) Kashmir gets virtually cut off from India. This is their real "practical" objective, even when they encourage the slogan of "Khalistan", while carrying on an anti-Sikh campaign in their own country through publications in Urdu. He who pays the piper calls the tune. This is one reason, besides others, why terrorists from the very start have concentrated on these two districts, while developing the capacity to strike in any part of Punjab and even outside Punjab.

The external factor alone cannot explain the serious situation. There are internal factors too behind Khalistani terrorists.

**Internal Forces and Factors**

The capitalist-landlord class and upper sections of the rich peasants have been the biggest beneficiaries of the Green Revolution in Punjab. They are the dominant group in Punjab's economy. They want to become politically dominant too. They have their interests, ambitions as well as problems. Like the big industrialists, they too want to make bigger and bigger profits. Actually, the rate of return from agriculture has started going down. Also, their interests conflict with the industrial capitalists, who want cheap raw materials. They also want more avenues of investment. The need of developing industries in Punjab was not given adequate attention at the proper time. The scope for developing agro-industries was for long not paid the attention it deserved. To the extent the representatives or the rural bourgeoisie of Punjab were demanding the growth of industries in the state and more powers for the state, progressive forces readily supported them. Actually, they go much beyond that. While they talk of remunerative prices for agricultural produce to rally behind them the middle and poor peasants, who are denied the same, they really want profiteering prices for themselves. They want the right to sell their produce anywhere in the international market, no matter how adverse the effect of this may be on the common people of India, including of Punjab, and on Indian economy. In fact, they deny the very need of a common Indian economy. They mouth the just slogan of more powers for the states, but in fact want to make the Centre nothing more than a myth. They want to rule Punjab. It so happens that an overwhelming majority of the landlords and *kulaks* in Punjab are Sikhs, and the same is the position of the toiling peasantry. To have a strong mass base and power, the class demands they put forward are voiced in the garb of "Sikh demands". They misuse religion and thus promote religious fundamentalism.

These vested interests are represented by the Akali leadership. The Anandpur Sahib Resolution of the Akali Party mirrors their demands and their ambitions. It does contain some vote catching populist slogans, but its essence is obvious and is two-fold.

One, it demands that Punjab should be a Sikh theocratic state, i.e. a state ruled by Sikh vested interests. Two, it demands that this theocratic state should have all powers, except four departments, e.g. foreign affairs, defence, means of communication and currency. In other words, there should be no common Indian economy. The Centre will not have the power even to raise funds for the four departments. Punjab will contribute its share in proportion to its representation in the Parliament. The ruling class at the Centre has reduced the states to the status of municipalities. The Akali leaders, the moderates included, want the Centre to become a myth. They want a virtual "Khalistan" with a very weak Centre.

If conceded, it would be a stepping stone to another partition of India. Even otherwise, it would prove disastrous for the country. It would strengthen the demand for theocratic states in other parts of India, and also those who want India to become a Hindu Fascist state. The Anandpur Sahib Resolution of the Akali Party, the contention that "Sikhs are a nation", the false propaganda about Sikhs being second class citizens etc. has been a source of great help to the terrorists. In the concrete situation of Punjab, it is not surprising that sections of landlords have gone a step further and have become supporters of Khalistan as well as of terrorism. Some of the Akali leaders too have followed the same road. There are others who have developed all-India economic interests, who are moderates and who really stand for India's unity. Any positive role they can play must be welcome. Their tragedy lies in their communal outlook, in their commitment to the Anandpur Sahib resolution, and fact that they are willing to fight the separatists and terrorists only on their own ground and by appeasing them, which only proves counter-productive.

Another internal factor which has helped the terrorists in Punjab is of Hindu communalism and its line of falsely holding the entire Sikh community responsible for the crimes of the terrorists, and its slogan of "revenge" and "retaliation" against innocent Sikhs. The Hindu communal organisations have links with Hindu vested interests like the big traders, who feel threatened by the Sikh vested interests. The RSS slogan of "Hindu Rashtra" and its line that only Hindus can safeguard the unity of India brings grist to the mill of the terrorists. The Sikhs are not a homogeneous economic community. Sikh landlords and Sikh tenants and agricultural labourers have sharply conflicting interests, despite their common religion. So also the Sikh workers and Sikh capitalists. At the same time, the Sikh workers, Sikh agricultural labourers, Sikh poor and middle peasants, etc. have common economic interests with their counterparts professing other religions. In other words, the Sikhs today have no separate and single political and economic identity. But they do have a separate religious identity. Sikhism arose on Indian soil. All religions have something in common, but the Hindu and Sikh religions have much more in common than any other two religions.

All this does not mean that Sikhism is not an independent religion. It has definitely since long grown into one and is so recognised by the Indian Constitution. The RSS denies that and keeps on asserting that "Sikhs are Hindus", etc. This helps the separatists by providing them the argument that unless there is "Khalistan", Sikhism will be absorbed into the Hindu religion.

Bhajan Lal's (the then Chief Minister of Haryana) line of "teaching the Sikhs a lesson" by humiliating and harassing a large number of Sikhs travelling to Delhi by buses, cars etc., in the name of defeating the extremely ill-advised threat to disrupt the Asian Games rendered immense help to Bhindranwale.

Economically, the Sikhs are perhaps the most well-off community of India. They have a share in services (defence as well as civil) far in excess of their proportion in the total population. There are many more gurdwaras in India per one lakh Sikhs now than existed in 1947. Allegations of discrimination therefore are baseless. However, there is a Hindu bias in the leadership of the country. For instance, just when the Akali demand of declaring Amritsar a holy city was not accepted, Kurukshetra was declared one. This bias helps anti-national elements and it must go.

The internal factor which perhaps has helped the terrorists most is the opportunism of the bourgeois parties—and not only of the ruling ones—indulged in for short-term electoral or other political considerations. Many examples can be given, but the following should suffice.

As is universally known by now, Jarnail Singh Bhindranwale, a religious personality, was brought into politics by the Congress-I with the aim of weakening the Akali Party, its rival in the matter of power in the state of Punjab. The Akalis thought that they could play the Bhindranwale card better than the Congress-I. They first allowed him to stay in the Guru Nanak Niwas. Then they allowed him to stay in the holy Akal Takht, where not even a Sikh Guru had ever stayed, and to convert the Golden Temple complex proper—including the Akal Takht itself—into an armed fortress and a big training camp for terrorists.

A very prominent general secretary of the Congress-I certified that Bhindranwale was only a religious personality even when he had become already the leader of the terrorist killers and when he had already been calling for the killings. Almost at the same time not one but three respected stalwarts of the opposition visited the Golden Temple and afterwards issued certificates to the effect that they did not find any arms inside the Golden Temple complex, when anyone even from the outside could see the weapons installed in the complex and even on its outer walls.

The assassinatien of Prime Minister Indira Gandhi was the most despicable act masterminded by the terrorists and their imperialist patrons. Those who celebrated after the assassination deserved to be strongly criticised and roundly condemned. Notwithstanding all this, the anti-Sikh riots which resulted in the killing of about 3000 Sikhs in the capital alone were totally unjustifiable. They constitute one of the blackest spots on India's fair name. And they were not altogether spontaneous. Some VIPs played a big role in organising them, even though in not a few places old Congressmen too, like the Communists and others, including common Hindus, helped save many Sikhs, even at the cost of their own lives. For narrow party considerations, there has been a persistent refusal to prosecute the guilty. This grave injustice has been fully exploited by the extremists in Punjab and has done them very great service indeed.

Again and again there have been attempts on the part of the ruling party high command to strike a deal with a section of the terrorists—sometimes with the help of Sushil Muni Jain and Darshan Singh Ragi, sometimes with the help of Parkash Singh Badal (even a novice in Punjab politics knows that Badal would not even try to oblige), and sometimes through Jasbir Singh Rode. Every such effort has proved counter-productive. It has only demoralised the security forces and has strengthened the terrorists. And yet such attempts are not being given up due to electoral calculations. Not more than fifty in the Jodhpur jail are terrorist killers or organisers of killings. Yet many more are still there to be used for bargaining. The non-Left parties too do not seem averse to making unprincipled deals. Some top opposition leaders have maintained a strange silence on Punjab. Some others have been saying that the Punjab problem would get resolved only when the opposition comes to power in New Delhi. Some have even started providing *alibis* to the terrorists by saying that all the killings are being done by government agents.

The ordinance issued by the government to prevent places of worship being used to store weapons and to prevent their being used for political purposes was half-hearted. The Akalis opposed it. Other bourgeois opposition parties, instead of demanding that it be made more effective, at best only lent lukewarm support to it.

The terrorists have made full use of this opportunism of the bourgeois parties. Bhindranwale had even boasted that some thought that the Congress-I was using him, but it was actually he himself who was using the Congress-I (and also the Akalis).

The terrorists are not concerned with the territorial disputes and the dispute regarding surplus river waters. They have often said so. But they have not failed to exploit the fact that these disputes (given a communal colouring by the Akalis) remain unresolved. One of the main reasons for these disputes not getting resolved is the opportunism of the bourgeois parties. While the Communists take one and the same stand and put it forward in the concerned states, every bourgeois party takes one stand in the Parliament while giving full freedom to its state units to take different and mutually contradictory stands. It is hardly necessary to give more examples. The fact that employment avenues for the youth are not there, coupled with the lure of weapons and money, has also played a part, though this is only a secondary factor.

## Strategy, Methods, Tactics and Targets

As is the case with all terrorist movements, a key element in the strategy of the Khalistani terrorists is to create terror, in order to undermine the authority of the administration and to demonstrate their own "strength". This strategy of theirs however contains other key elements also, which are specific to them. One is to appear as defenders of the Sikhs and their religion, to widen the gulf between Hindus and Sikhs, to create situations in which large-scale Hindu-Sikh riots break out, to force the Hindus of Punjab to migrate to other states, and to create situations in which Sikhs in other states are forced to migrate from there and are also encouraged to do so. Anyone who was not with Bhindranwale during his lifetime remains an enemy.

These elements in the strategy of the terrorists have determined their methods and their targets.

They started by killing Nirankaris, including Nirankari Sikhs, because orthodox Sikhs have a strong prejudice against them. Then it was the turn of Hindus in general and such individual personalities whose killing would provoke Hindus in and outside Punjab into senseless violent acts against innocent Sikhs. Of course, those who opposed them were bound to become their targets. Thus, came also the turn of the Sikhs who dared to oppose them. They were most vindictive against Sikh families who were sympathetic to and helped them in various ways in the beginning but refused to do so later or who turned against them. They would also kill those who would refuse them shelter, food etc. Later on, they began killing even those Sikhs who did not or could not meet their demands for huge amounts of money.

Of course, policemen and persons belonging to the security forces have been killed by them in large numbers. Most men of the Punjab police are Sikhs, as is known.

A very large number of Sikhs have thus been killed—not only policemen, but also ordinary Sikhs and political activists and leaders belonging to different political parties. At the same time, Sikhs have not been killed indiscriminately, at least as yet. For mass killings such places and bazars are selected where the visitors would mostly be Hindus. True, in such incidents not only some Sikhs but also some Muslims and Christians algo get killed or injured. When buses are highjacked to kill passengers, the practice has been first to ask the Sikh passengers to get out.

In the initial stages methods such as placing severed heads of cows before Hindu temples, breaking of Hindu idols etc. were also adopted with the object of inciting Hindu-Sikh riots. (The Hindu communalists, not excluding some Hindu Congressmen, would retaliate by attacking gurdwaras, throwing cigarettes into Sikh shrines and damaging models of the Golden Temple and so on.)

An interesting but significant fact in connection with targets needs to be noted. Mass killing of migrant Hindu labourers working in

Punjab—especially in the field of agriculture—has generally been avoided. The reason is that this would hit the economic interests of the kulaks. Migrant labourers were attacked in a big way for the first time immediately after the Black Thunder operation of May 1988, which had given them a big setback. To show that they were still strong and to provoke anti-Sikh sentiments in states other than Punjab, they killed a large number of defenceles migrant labourers. Significantly, the main targets were labourers working on the Sutlej-Yamuna Link Canal, which would provide Haryana its share of surplus water. A number of agricultural labourers were killed also at least in one village of Amritsar district. This, however, was not repeated because of the negative reaction even of the supporters of the terrorists. Only in the first weeks of November 1988, the terrorists have once again attacked migrant labourers in a big way. Significantly, this attack was not on any big farm, but on a seed farm in village Longowal in Ludhiana district. The farm belongs to the Government of India.

To increase their mass support, the terrorists adopted a "social reform movement". But most of the actions were aimed not at social reform, but to encourage religious fundamentalism. For instance, barbers, those Sikhs who trim their beards, and such heads of schools and teachers who would not make their pupils wear uniforms prescribed by Sikh extremists were threatened and made targets. The only items relating to social reform concerned dowry, the numerical strength of marriage parties and consumption of liquor. Incidentally, many of those who killed liquor vendors were themselves heavy drinkers. Exemption was given in all these aspects of "social reform" quite liberally in return for large sums of money. No wonder, the movement petered out and it has not ultimately helped the cause of the terrorists.

The admission made by the "New Panthic Committee" that it was wrong to kill innocent people in the past, and the assurance given that mistakes of this type would be avoided in the future seems another attempt to overcome the growing isolation of the terrorists by deceiving the gullible.

**Degeneration of Terrorists**

A nexus between the terrorists and smugglers developed from the very beginning. One of the topmost notorious smugglers of Amritsar got killed inside the Golden Temple at the time of Operation Blue Star.

Anti-social elements were recruited into terrorist ranks from the very beginning. In course of time, many of those who were motivated initially by religiosity or some other such feeling too have degenerated. This degeneration and utter lack of humanity is reflected in the killing of even women and children, including grandmothers of over 80 years and infants not even a few months old. There have been cases of women being molested and then killed. Many have become professional killers. Most of the "normal" killings too are now being done by terrorists for money. Mutual rivalries exist amongst the terrorist groups and these lead to mutual killings.

The ugly face of terrorists was fully exposed by Operation Black Thunder in May 1988, which was carried out with the entire press watching it and was also shown on television. It became very widely known that the Golden Temple had been turned into a torture chamber. It became known that those who refused to pay up as per demand were subjected to horrible tortures and then killed; even "Amritdhari" Sikhs were not spared; that women were raped, tortured and killed.

About fifty bodies were discovered from under the debris of the Akal Takht. Only a few of those could be identified. People learnt to their great horror and shock that a number of militants had remained all the time within the Harminder Sahib proper for two days and had eased themselves therein. While this exposed their claim of being "true Sikhs", the way they surrendered, instead of living up to their boasts that if necessary they would embrace death while fighting and thus achieve martyrdom, showed them up as cowards. Their isolation became complete and this was reflected in the fact that there was no response to their call to the people to march to the Golden Temple to protest against its alleged "invasion", in spite of the fact that the same call was given by almost all the Akali leaders, the Panthic Committee as well as by the rival sets of the high priests.

It was the most opportune time for the government to continue the offensive into the Mand area (another important centre of operation of the terrorists) and simultaneously take correct political initiatives for a political solution. Opportunist considerations prevented this—thus enabling the terrorists to regroup themselves.

All that we have said above does not imply that there are no misguided youth amongst the terrorists. There certainly are, and all efforts need to be made to bring them back into the mainstream. However, such efforts are likely to bear fruit only when the backbone of the terrorist organisations has been broken.

One thing more needs to be made clear. We are not against talks with the extremists, but these should not be held when this would only help the terrorist killers and demoralise the security forces. The right time would be when they have been forced to give up the demand for Khalistan as well as for a theocratic state and after the killings have stopped. If the experience of Mizoram and the talks held with Laldenga have any lesson, it is this.

**Methods of Collecting Funds and Recruitment**

The main sources of fund collection by the Punjab terrorists have been as under:

1. Huge amounts have come from abroad from those who are sympathetic to the "cause", including from millionnaire non-Indian Sikhs. Collections in such gurdwaras as are controlled by the extremists in foreign countries have also been utilised for this purpose.

2. Large amounts have also come from large cities like Bombay, Calcutta etc., contributed and collected by supporters of the "cause".

3. Collections of gurdwaras in Punjab when controlled by terrorists or their friends have also been used.

4. Bank dacoities, robberies etc. In some cases of robberies the victims happened to be Sikhs. They pleaded to be spared. They were told they might fulfil the demand out of "sympathy" or at the point of a gun—the choice was theirs.

5. Extraction through threats. First, Hindu businessmen and professionals were the targets. Then the operation was extended to Sikh businessmen and professionals, and thereafter also to the comparatively well-off Sikh landowners.

An interesting aspect of this operation has been the bargaining indulged in to decide the exact amount to be given, with the help of mediators. In some cases terrorists, known to their targets, have also "helped" to lower the demands. Of course, at the time of the negotiations AK-47 assault rifles and other sophisticated weapons would be on display. "This one costs Rs. . . . . thousand. We need many and hence we cannot lower the demand. Pay up, or . . . ." This is the kind of "reasoning" with the mediator pleading for leniency.

Groups like teachers of a particular school have been made to pay fixed monthly contributions.

6. Ransom extracted from kidnappings. This method has been adopted in a big way only recently in sub-division Patti in Amritsar district. The main targets are owners of shellers and brick kiln owners or their children, well-off shopkeepers etc. The amounts demanded are quite substantial. In some cases the mediators would get the demand reduced somewhat. In some other cases the hostages have been shot dead. The targets are Hindus as well as Sikhs. On a smaller scale this has been happening since long and also in the districts of Gurdaspur and Ferozepur.

7. There is another method adopted from the days of Bhindranwale, which continues till today, though the exact procedure has been varying at different times. On the basis of a complaint from someone, the complainant and the opposite party are summoned. A decision is then announced and its implementation demanded under threat of liquidation for non-compliance. The beneficiary party, or both parties, are also ordered to make handsome contributions.

8. In the days of the so-called reform movement, liquor vendors and others would be spared for a consideration.

The list given above is not exhaustive.

It may be mentioned here that not all the money goes to the "cause", for buying weapons, for paying the recruits, etc. A number of the terrorists, though not all, are known to have used part of the collections for themselves, to buy items of luxury or immovable property.

Now a few words about the methods adopted for recruitment.

There is the appeal of religiosity. Also a picture of the future Khalistan, in which rivers of milk and honey will flow and where no one will be unemployed. There is also the pull of weapons and of money. Young men whose fathers do not have big land holdings easily get attracted by these. There are also many anti-social elements turned terrorists, because it makes their job easier and also "respectable".

Despite all this it is a significant fact that the number of terrorists from families of Sikh agricultural labourers, who are the poorest in the Sikh community, has been negligible. Their reactions even to events like Operation Blue Star and the killing of Bhindranwale were quite different from those of the land-owning peasantry. I wonder therefore, where is the ground for speaking of a common "Sikh psyche". In fact, some of those who speak of this themselves make it clear that what they have in view is "Jat Sikh psyche", a proposition which itself is debatable.

There is also the fact that quite a number of the terrorists have come from families of the rich, and quite a few amongst them had good decent jobs. The financiers and willing providers of shelter and stores for weapons, and members of their brains trust include some big landlords and even some IPS, IAS and other officers coming from landlord families. In general, these are retired officers, but the possibility of some serving officers being their comrades-in-arms cannot be ruled out. Some have been caught too and have had to be dismissed from service.

Whenever the terrorists are at the receiving end, recruitment goes down. When they are on top, or when the security forces get orders to stay their hand, recruitment goes up. Such has been the experience at least in Amritsar district.

I know also of more than one case of a youth getting attracted to join their ranks, and then getting disgusted and leaving them. But he had to rejoin, after being told: "If you don't rejoin us, we will liquidate you as well as your family."

**Some Other Connected Points**

1. It is rightly said by some observers that one of the causes for the trouble in Punjab lies in the fact that at one time a large majority of the Punjabi Hindus, flying in the face of truth, denied that Punjabi was their mother tongue and instead registered themselves as Hindi-speaking. This was the result of the bad advice given by the then Jan Sangh as well as many Hindu Congress leaders. This, however, is only part of the truth. The other part, equally wrong and damaging, is that the Akali Party championed the cause of Punjabi language as if it was part of Sikh religion, and as if its development was linked to their original demand for a Sikh state, and then for a Punjabi speaking state in which Sikhs would constitute at least sixty per cent of the population.

Communalists of both hues have contributed a lot to disrupting the development of common Punjabi consciousness of the Punjabi nationality within the great Indian nation. To reverse this process is a hard and long-term task. It requires a long struggle not only for the separation of religion from politics, of religion from the state, but also of religion from language, i.e. Punjabi language. Some intellectuals, including a few who claim to belong to the Left, refuse to see the need of this struggle, or are not ready for it. They are putting forward the dangerous thesis that today the Sikhs (alone) are true Punjabis, that the Sikhs are fighting the battle of the Punjabi nationality, that they are its *avant-garde* etc. I am afraid such intellectuals are only bringing grist to the mill of the extremists, and even of the terrorists, even though unconsciously.

2. There exists a viewpoint that a really big economic package by providing employment will lead to a solution of the problem. To the extent that past mistakes are rectified and proper attention given to the development of such industries in Punjab as are needed and for which there exists the necessary potential, that will be a welcome thing. It will in the long run increase the weight of the working class in the political life of Punjab, and that will be a setback for divisive forces. However, it is an illusion that any economic package can do the trick and lead to an instant solution. After all, an economic package, including a railway coach factory, was given to Punjab by the Prime Minister some years ago. And that coach factory is about to start production. Has it led to a solution of the problem of terrorism? We all know the answer.

There is also another aspect of the problem. Development possibilities within the capitalist system are much less than the needs and even the actual potential. The available resource for development must be shared equitably between all states, keeping in mind the special needs of the backward regions. All progressive forces must fight for greater development of the country as a whole and also for going forward towards the anti-capitalist path. As things stand today, no government in India can go on depriving some states of their share of development projects to give some really big economic packages to some other states. This can be done only to a limited extent. Let me recall what happened when the railway coach factory, which had originally been allotted to Kerala, was given instead to Punjab. One minister of the then Congress-I led government of Kerala threatened to create a Punjab-like situation in Kerala. Even the Left parties in that state did not find it easy to swallow the decision to take away the coach factory from Kerala. As a Punjabi, I will welcome any economic package for Punjab, but I do not entertain the illusion that this is the magic formula. Progress in Punjab can come really in a big way only as part of progress of the country as a whole, and not at the expense of other states. Any attempt to follow the latter course will only create more problems.

**Some More Negative Aspects of Government Policies**

Even apart from what has been said above, some other negative factors of the policies of the government need to be noted.

1. There are quite a few elements even today within the administration, including in the police, which are pro-extremist and which help the extremists in one way or the other. There was a time when decisions arrived at even by the Governor-in-council would reach the terrorist leadership within less than an hour, while the government's intelligence amongst the terrorist organisations was nil. The situation is not very satisfactory even today. It is necessary to adopt steps to improve this situation.

2. There is a lot of corruption in the police. There have also been excesses on the part of the police and the security forces for reasons other than corruption. For instance, there have been errors of judgement, of over-reaction, of officers or officials getting mixed up with local feuds and committing excesses against one party at the instance of the other, and so on. There have been many instances of extortion and minting of money by corrupt elements in the police. The victims of these excesses do not belong to any one community.

It is necessary to expose and fight against all excesses, not only for the sake of justice but also because some of the excesses committed by the government forces bring grist to the mill of the extremists. While the extremists have sought to exploit these excesses even by exaggerating them, the Left has been exposing and fighting against them concretely for the sake of justice. I do not, however, subscribe to the theory of state terrorism in Punjab. Excesses are one thing, and state terrorism is another. The theory of state terrorism was put forward to provide an *alibi* for those terrorists who indulge in killings. It is argued by some that individual terrorism is the result of state terrorism in Punjab. This is a case of turning facts upside down.

3. As far as the anti-terrorist fight on the administrative front is concerned the Government has been acting as if it concerns only the police and the security forces.

The terrorists have been active on many fronts.

In the field of education, they have killed a large number of teachers. School education has come to virtually an end in many parts of Amritsar and Gurdaspur districts. Some institutions of higher education, including those run by the government, have become preserves and even centres of operation of the terrorists or of anti-social elements passing themselves off as terrorists. The mass of students of these institutions feel helpless and disgusted.

A large number of the employees of the Punjab State Electricity Board, of the banks and of the Health Department too have been killed. In certain areas their branches and units have virtually closed down.

The terrorists have succeeded in paralysing the judiciary. Even those who have killed dozens get bailed out. A father is unwilling to give evidence even if his own son has been killed by terrorists before his own eyes. Very recently a government spokesman made the significant admission that it had not been possible to obtain even one conviction so far.

The terrorists walk through fields and *pagdandis*. The security forces are often unable to use even link roads effectively because these are so badly damaged that their vehicles cannot move on them at the speed at which a man normally walks. It has not occurred to the concerned departments to repair such damaged link roads in the areas which are terrorist strongholds, on a priority basis.

In short, there has been a failure to evolve a comprehensive policy to fight terrorism, covering all departments. No wonder, many secretaries of key and sensitive departments have been enjoying long foreign trips. Even proper training of the police was not started for a long time. Till very recently the security forces had weapons much inferior to those of the terrorists. For a long time they were not provided even such essential instruments as night-vision devices. There has been some improvement in this respect, but not fast enough. For long, adequate attention was also not given to the sealing of the Indo-Pak border to the maximum possible extent.

The deficiencies that still exist must be overcome at the earliest.

**The Solution**

Those who maintain that the Punjab problem is only a law and order problem are wrong. Equally wrong are those who consider it only a political problem. It is both, and must be tackled *simultaneously* on both fronts.

Immediately, the following steps must be taken:

1. The offensive against the terrorists must be a continuous affair, without any letup, until their backbone is broken. Excesses ought to be avoided.

2. All, except the killers and their organisers among the Jodhpur detenues must be released unconditionally.

3. Those responsible for organising anti-Sikh riots of November 1984 must be prosecuted.

4. All states, including Punjab, must be given more powers, but no special status of any kind should be given to Punjab, as this will lead to its becoming a theocratic state.

5. An all-parties national level meeting should be called to evolve the broadest possible consensus on the territorial and river water disputes. Prior to that, or at the meeting, all national parties must pledge that their state units will not be allowed to take contradictory stands and will be bound by the consensus. All must then go to the people of the concerned states and appeal to them to accept the agreement. Such a consensus should, of course, be arrived at, keeping in view the national interests, in a spirit of give and take and without doing gross injustice to any state. This is the only way in which the spirit of the Rajiv-Longowal Accord can be saved.

6. All secular and patriotic parties and groups must jointly as well as individually launch a new and powerful mass campaign at the grassroots level to isolate the separatists and terrorists, against killings, against excesses, against the slogan of Khalistan and of Hindu Raj, for the above demands, against the misuse of religious places, against the slogan of "revenge" and retaliation, for separation of religion from politics, religion from the state, etc.

Of course, only agreed issues should be taken up from joint platforms. There must be no attempt on the part of anyone to exploit the joint platform against the others because that will make any joint campaign impossible.

The experience so far has shown that the organized working class and the agricultural labourers have not only not fallen prey to separatism, extremism and communalism, these two forces have actively intervened in a big way at various critical junctures and have saved the situation. Narration of this in detail is being avoided here for reasons of space. The lesson is that everything possible ought to be done to augment the weight of these sections in the public and political life of the state.

**The Role of Parties**

For reasons of space we cannot go here into the role of various political parties. However, it must be mentioned that the Left has played an outstanding role on its own (the two Communist parties and some Naxalite groups acting independently and also jointly, especially the two Communist parties), by taking successful initiatives to unite all parties for joint campaigning, on more than one occasion. All parties have paid a big price but the heaviest has been paid by the Communists, and especially by the CPI. By their sacrifices the Communists have proved that they are not only internationalists but are also fine patriots.

The CPI has also run a campaign on the Punjab issue, which, in fact, is a national issue, involving the very future of the entire country, in a number of states outside Punjab. The Punjab Istri Sabha is the only mass organisation which is doing excellent work to provide relief to victims of terrorists on a non-communal basis. (The first place, of course, goes to the Shaheed Parivar Fund of the Hind Samachar group of papers.) The Istri Sabha scheme to give stipends to orphaned children to enable them to continue their education has caught the imagination of a big section of the public. Funds are coming in from all over India. An important part in these collections is being played by the National Federation of Indian Women, and many individuals from different walks of life. This is not only good humanitarian work, it helps the struggle for defending and strengthening the unity-in-diversity of our country and our people.

Last but not the least, the question is not whether India will remain one or not. No power on earth can separate Punjab from India.

The total failure of the terrorists, even though helped by the communalists of the opposite hue, to bring about Hindu-Sikh riots should convince all about the correctness of this assertion of ours. The real question is: How many more innocent lives will be lost before terrorism in Punjab is fully and finally defeated? The answer to this question depends on us all, on our response to the call of the blood of innumerable innocent persons belonging to different political parties and to no party, Hindus as well as Sikhs, Muslims and Christians, men, women and children, who have fallen victims to terrorism during the last ten years. Their call to all patriots is: Now is the time to act and prove your mettle, your real worth. Do all you can for the unity of India, of its people and for a bright future, and also act all together for this noble cause. *(November 7, 1988)*

## 3. Lessons of Punjab for Kashmir

Are there any lessons from Punjab which can help the fight against terrorism in Kashmir? For long the Union Government and its nominees in Punjab pursued a policy of battling the terrorists on the law and order front on a limited scale. This policy always proved counter-productive. An outstanding example of this was Operation Black Thunder which yielded very good results. However, these were negated when the fight on the law and order front was stopped and efforts were made instead to make a deal with a section of the terrorists. The big success that has now been achieved in Punjab came only when it was decided to continue the anti-terrorist action relentlessly till the backbone of the terrorists was broken. This has surely a lesson for Kashmir policy-makers.

**Bad Timing:** Another lesson which the Kashmir policy-makers must learn is that negotiations with the "boys" do great harm if they are undertaken at a wrong time. In fighting terrorism in Punjab, one of the things which paid dividends is that conscious efforts were made by the army not to do anything that would strengthen the mass base of the terrorists. Unfortunately, this does not seem to have been the case in Kashmir. Firing into the funeral procession of Moulvi Farooq during Mr. Jagmohan's tenure and the burning down of *mohallas* in retaliation for the killing of some jawans prove this. Special efforts were made in Punjab to train the army as well as the para-military forces in this regard. After this training the army went all out not only to fight the terrorists but also to help the people in various ways in rural areas. Such a policy does not seem to have been followed in Kashmir.

It has been proved that even those terrorists who start on the path of terrorism with noble motives soon join hands with anti-social elements. This happened in Punjab. By the time the Beant Singh government came to power and started an all-out fight, supporters of terrorists in districts like Amritsar had turned against them because by then they were not merely extortionists and killers but had also become rapists. The process of degeneration and consequent alienation of terrorists has been taking place in Kashmir too, but it does not seem to be paying the dividends it could have because of the type of mistakes referred to earlier.

It was realised in Punjab that even though the help of army and para-military forces would be indispensable, without the Punjab police going into action against the terrorists, it would not be possible to beat them back. The Punjab police is overwhelmingly Sikh. There was a time when a good section of it was helping the terrorists out of sympathy or out of fear. Another section was not willing to act because of the fear that a terrorist leader might become Chief Minister. There was a lot of conflict between the Punjab police and the para-military forces. First, Mr. Ribeiro and then Mr. K.P.S. Gill did a lot to motivate the police force. Mr. Beant Singh removed the fear that a Manochahal or a Mann would come to power in Punjab. The Punjab police then went into action bravely. A similar policy in relation to the Kashmir police is needed.

Secondly, in Punjab the political processes did not come to a halt even when terrorists ruled the state. The Left campaigned even in the terrorist infested rural areas, losing many lives.

Thirdly, when an all-out fight against terrorism was started after Mr. Beant Singh came to power, no steps were taken to ensure that at least avoidable excesses against the innocents were stopped. Such police excesses in Punjab have been many and unfortunately they continue even today. A section of the police believes that since they have brought peace to Punjab (which is only a half-truth and hence dangerous), they have the right not only to make heaps of money but also to rule

Punjab. The presumption increases its alienation from the people and in turn it can help suppressed terrorism to re-emerge.

**Avoidable Excesses:** Unfortunately Mr. K.P.S. Gill is a supercop as far as the fight against terrorism is concerned, but his policy has a negative side and this is the theory that excesses and even killings of innocents are the price which has to be paid by a people fighting terrorism. The need to prevent avoidable excesses is overlooked on the false plea that any attempt to do so will demoralise the police force. This mistake should be avoided in Kashmir.

Fourthly, there is fear of the re-emergence of terrorism in Punjab because nothing is being done to resolve political problems. By exploiting them the terrorists were able to acquire some mass base. Had this been done earlier, Punjab would not have suffered for 12 long years. In Kashmir this mistake is being made on a much bigger scale. The major opposition party in India has, in fact, been helping the terrorists of Kashmir by demanding the abrogation of Article 370, by its contribution towards the demolition of the Babri Masjid, by being a member of a *parivar* whose head is determined to convert India into a Hindu *rashtra*. The ruling party does the same when it plays the *Hindutva* card to ''fight'' the Sangh Parivar.

## References


1. Quoted by V.D. Chopra in his *Agony of Punjab*, New Delhi, p. 73.
2. *The Punjab Crisis: Challenge and Response,* Ed. Dr. Abida Samiuddin.
3. Ram Swarup, *Concept of Sikh Nation in the Punjab Crisis: Challenge and Response.*
4. *Chicago Daily Tribune,* October 15, 1945.
5. See V.D. Chopra, *Pentagon Shadow over India,* New Delhi.
6. *Indian Express,* March 16, 1981.
7. *Link* Newsmagazine, December 23, 1984.
8. *The Tribune,* December 6, 1987, datelined Ottawa, December 5, (MNS).
9. *Indian Express,* quoting a PTI Report, December, 12, 1987.
10. *Times of India,* December 12, 1987.
11. *The Tribune,* (English Translation) April 13, 1981.
12. *The Tribune,* December 13, 1982.


*(September 30, 1993)*

# CHAPTER II
# The Sikhs and Akali Politics

## 1. Is there Discrimination Against Sikhs?

For a long time now Akali leaders have been harping on the theme that the Government of India has been interfering in the religious affairs of the Sikhs. They have been alleging that Sikhs have been discriminated against and that the Centre has been discriminating against Punjab because Sikhs constitute a big portion (majority after reorganisation of Punjab in November, 1966) of its population.

Sant Jarnail Singh Bhindranwale, who has recently shot into prominence and who has taken upon himself the task of uniting all Akali factions, has been repeatedly saying that "Sikhs are slaves". According to some reports in the press, the Sant has been addressing on an average three congregations a day and the theme of his speeches has invariably been "discrimination against Sikhs", "Sikhs are slaves", etc.

Rightly or wrongly, a section of the Sikh community as well as a section of Sikh intellectuals do harbour the feeling that the Sikhs have not been getting a fair deal.

All this is sought to be taken advantage of and exploited by the separatist forces which have raised the slogan of "Khalistan" and which undoubtedly have the support and backing of US imperialism. It is therefore necessary to examine the whole matter carefully and to do everything possible to ensure that any genuine grievances are removed. To the extent the propaganda is false and motivated, it must be exposed and those indulging in it must be isolated.

Let us first examine some grievances that concern the Sikhs as a religious minority in India.

1. One of the Akali grievances has been that 15 trains have been named after religious shrines but the government declined to oblige

when the Shiromani Gurdwara Prabandhak Committee (SGPC) requested that a train be also named after Hari Mandir Sahib.

Obviously, either no train should have been named after any (Hindu) religious shrine or the SGPC request too should have been accepted. The grievance was justified. It is quite another matter that on second thoughts the demand has been given up by the Akalis. (It is reported that some Sikh religious leaders pointed out to them that many non-Sikhs would smoke in the train named after Hari Mandir Sahib and that would constitute sacrilege).

2. It has been alleged by Akali leaders that while in cities considered sacred by Hindus (like Haridwar), things which are taboo in Hindu religion have been banned by law, their demand that sale of tobacco, cigarettes, etc. near the gurdwaras and in the entire walled city of Amritsar should not be allowed was not considered sympathetically.

In this case too, every reasonable person will take the position that the government should treat all religions alike. Sentiments of followers of all religions must be respected while taboos of one religion should not be forced on followers of the others. Judged by this criterion, the demand for not allowing sale of tobacco in any form near existing gurdwaras should have been treated more sympathetically than it was in the first instance. The demand for banning smoking, etc., in the entire walled city of Amritsar was wrong and it was rightly not accepted.

3. Another religious grievance arose out of the decision of the Union Government to bypass the SGPC (which controls a large number of historical gurdwaras in the country) in the selection of Sikhs going on pilgrimage to their historical shrines in Pakistan. The decision was wrong and unjustified. Perhaps it was taken out of narrow partisan considerations (the SGPC being controlled by the Akali Party). The decision has been reversed and the matter has been settled to the satisfaction of all concerned, including the Akalis.

4. Another religious grievance about which Akalis have been most vocal is the refusal of the Government of India to grant permission for the installation of a broadcasting transmitter at Hari Mandir Sahib in Amritsar so that Sikh religious teachings can be broadcast from there to Sikhs all over the world.

The Akalis are clearly in the wrong, and the demand has rightly not been accepted. First, where is the guarantee that his facility will not be used for non-religious and partisan purposes? Secondly, such a facility cannot be given to one religious community to the exclusion of the others.

5. Another big grievance of the Akalis related to the alleged misuse of its position by the Government of India, and particularly the Home Ministry in order to get the late Jathedar Santokh Singh elected President of the Delhi Gurdwara Parbandhak Committee. The allegation, it seems, was not entirely baseless. In this case too the Government of India was motivated by narrow partisan considerations.

The above instances make it clear that as a religions minority the Sikhs do have some grievances, though not all the demands made by the Akalis (and some others) are just and correct. While some genuine grievances have been removed recently, the question remains why they were allowed to arise and why all genuine grievances were not removed promptly as and when they arose, thus giving a handle to communal and separatist forces to exploit them. There can be two reasons for this; First, some Hindu bias somewhere in the ruling circles—conscious or unconscious—notwithstanding the secular nature of our constitution and therefore of our political set-up and structure on the whole. All Left and democratic forces in the country must do all they can to ensure that this bias goes and that religious rights of all religious minorities are fully safeguarded. This will prevent disruptive forces from exploiting any genuine grievances that may be there or may arise. Secondly, there are narrow partisan considerations prevailing when certain decisions are taken by the powers that be. While far-sighted persons in the ruling circles must try to avoid this, all progressive forces must seek to ensure just and fair decisions and actions.

Before proceeding further, it is necessary to mention another grievance that has been aired. The Akalis have formulated it as "refusal to concede to the Sikhs their personal law". What exactly this demand means and what its implications are needs to be explained by those who have put it forward. In this connection, the following paragraph from a paper presented by Gopal Singh and Rajinder Kaur at the seminar on "social and political culture", held on January 26-28, 1982, in the Department of Political Science, Guru Nanak Dev University, Amritsar needs to be taken note of.

"This section (a majority of educated Sikhs) is also greatly exercised over government interference in the personal law and religious affairs of the Sikhs. Acording to it, the Hindu Marriages Act has supplanted the Anand Marriage Act which was enacted in the first decade of the current century with great difficulty for legalising the Sikh form of marriage with the exclusion of Hindu rituals. Contrary to one of the basic tenets of Sikhism, which regards marriage as an indissoluble bond, the Hindu Marriages Act provides for divorce".

One wonders if authorities on Sikh religion will agree with the proposition that indissoluble marriage at all times and under all circumstances is one of the basic beliefs of Sikhism. Any demand for enforcing this proposition by law is likely to evoke strong opposition from large sections of the Sikhs, both men and women, especially the educated ones. Anyway, this matter of personal law of the Sikhs requires debate and discussion.

Certain other propositions which hardly require any debate or discussion need to be stated.

1. Whatever one's view about the origin of Sikh religion and its relationship with Hindu religion and Hindu society in the early stages of Sikhism, it does no good to harp today on the theme that "Sikhs are a part of Hindus", as the RSS is doing. It only brings grist to the propaganda mill of the extremists who claim that there exists a serious danger of Sikhs being assimilated by Hindus.

2. Such Sikh religious leaders as are genuinely concerned about the religious rights of the Sikh religious minority in India should realise that by mixing religion and politics and by using their control of the SGPC and of a large number of gurdwaras for their own narrow partisan political ends, the Akalis do disservice to the Sikh Panth and the Sikh masses. All efforts must be made to separate religion from politics and to ensure that religious shrines are not used for partisan politican purposes.

3. Sikhs are a religious minority in India but they constitute the majority in Punjab. When the Akalis ruled Punjab from 1977 to 1980, serious efforts were made by Sikh extremists, openly supported by some top Akali leaders, to deprive the Nirankaris of their right to worship according to their beliefs and to ban their religious books on the ground that these contained insulting matter against Sikhism, without caring to give any specific instances.

The fight for justice gets weakened if those who undertake it do injustice to others. Those who claim to have a special right to speak for the Sikh religious minority in India must stand for and be vocal in defence of the rights of religious minorities in Punjab.

The Sikh-Nirankari dispute certainly can and must be resolved through discussions between the Sikh religious leaders and the Nirankari leaders.

Let us now examine some of the main examples being given to prove "discrimination against the Sikhs" in matters other than religious rights.

1. It has been argued by the Akalis that the Government of India established linguistic states in the country during the fifties but deliberately delayed till 1966 the reorganisation of Punjab on a linguistic basis because in such a Punjab Sikhs would constitute the majority.

The fact is that the Government of India resisted reorganisation of provinces on a linguistic basis all over India. It had to yield only in the face of many a bitter struggle. It was able to resist the demand in Punjab for a much longer period because Punjabi-speaking people were not united on this issue, as the question of language and linguistic State of Punjab got mixed up with communalism. For long the dominant Akali leadership demanded a Punjabi Suba which would have a Sikh majority (60 per cent), while Hindu communal leaders, including unfortunately many Congress leaders, called upon Punjabi-speaking Hindus to disown their mother tongue, Punjabi.

There is also the fact that if all Punjabi-speaking areas of post-partition Punjab including Kangra, etc., had been included in the Punjabi Suba, Sikhs might not have been in absolute majority in it.

2. The Akali charter of grievances contains the following: "Reduction of the recruitment quota (in the armed forces) for the Sikhs from 20 per cent to 2.5 per cent".

The above-mentioned paper of Gopal Singh and Rajinder Kaur has the following to say in this connection: "Their (majority of educated Sikhs) other complaint is that the Central Government has gradually and systematically reduced the proportion of the Sikhs in the armed forces from over 33 per cent on the eve of Independence to less than 12 per cent today. To reduce the Sikh share further, the Union Government in 1974 fixed Punjab's share in recruitment to the armed forces at a mere 2.5 per cent. Of this, the Sikh share works out around 1.3 per cent."

For certain historical reasons which need not be gone into here, Sikhs got a very big share in the armed forces under the British. It was natural that after Independence different sections of the Indian people wanted a just share in the armed forces for themselves, which had been denied them under the British. Justice and fair play demanded that this aspiration of theirs should be met to the extent possible without impairing the efficiency of our defence forces. Keeping this in view, no injustice in this respect should be done to any section and any injustice done should be undone. However, it is not fair to cry discrimination if justice is sought to be done to other sections.

The issue of Sikh share in the armed forces has perhaps acquired importance recently because of growing unemployment in the country and the bleak prospects in the country for all. In view of this, it is understandable that the Akali cry should find response among sections of the Sikh youth. However, the real solution of the probem will be possible only through a united fight against the policies and the capitalist path itself which give rise to unemployment.

3. The Akali charter of grievances also contains the following example of discrimination against the Sikhs: "Nationalisation of the Sikh bank, that is, the Punjab and Sind Bank".

If the Akali position were to be accepted as correct, some Hindu leaders might as well say that nationalisation of Birla's bank was an attack on Hindus. Some Parsi leaders would claim that nationalisation of Tata's banks was an act of discrimination against the Parsi minority.

One may also mention that the Sikh employees of the Punjab and Sind Bank (and they constituted a big majority) did not consider its nationalisation as discrimination against Sikhs. In Amritsar at least they danced with joy when they got the news of the nationalisation.

Examples of alleged discrimination against Sikhs being given by Sant Bhindranwale are even more hollow. Here are some of them:

1. The two Congress-I workers who had hijacked a plane during the Janata regime were later rewarded by the Congress-I with legislative positions. A different attitude was taken towards the hijackers of an Indian plane to Pakistan a few months ago. This is said to be an example of discrimination against Sikhs.

Those who hijacked the plane during the Janata regime deserved to be condemned and were condemned by all except the Congress-I.

Also, the Congress-I was criticised sharply by many for making these hijackers legislators. How can this wrong attitude of the Congress-I, adopted for narrow partisan considerations, justify refusal to condemn the hijacking of an Indian plane to Pakistan by supporters of Khalistan? Only those who in their heart of hearts have sympathies with this separatist slogan, can do that and call criticism of this action an act of discrimination against Sikhs.

2. Sant Bhindranwale considers the transfer of former Delhi Police Commissioner, P.S. Bhinder, as another case of discrimination against the Sikhs. Of course, the Sant does not have anything to say about all that this officer did during the Emergency and the way he was promoted and made Delhi Police Commissioner superseding dozens of senior officers including many Sikhs.

3. According to the Sant, whenever Sikhs were killed, no judicial enquiries were ordered. But whenever Hindus became victims, enquiries were immediately instituted. This is just not true. The fact is that the rulers of India have generally sought to avoid judicial enquiries into police excesses. Only very powerful and united outcries or struggles made them institute such enquiries.

The conclusion is clear. There is hardly any weight in the argument that a deliberate policy of discrimination against Sikhs has been followed.

Let us now deal with the allegation that Punjab has been discriminated against and that this has been done because of anti-Sikh communal considerations.

It cannot be denied that on occasions injustice has been done to Punjab. For instance, the recent agreement on division of Ravi-Beas waters is itself proof that the earlier award given by Prime Minister Indira Gandhi during the Emergency did considerable injustice to Punjab. But then many other States inhabited mostly by Hindus may point out similar injustices done to them.

There is also the fact that for a number of years Punjab was very much neglected in the matter of industry. But perhaps some other States too were neglected. Factors responsible for this have nothing to do with communalism. As against the neglect of industry, it can be pointed out that agriculture and irrigation in Punjab did receive much help from the Centre.

Such instances of "injustice" therefore do not prove discri-mination against Punjab because of communal considerations.

A brief examination of some of the examples being given by those who allege discrimination against Punjab will help us understand the real nature of the problem.

1. It is alleged that delay in clearing the Thein Dam project is discrimination against Punjab because of communal considerations. This is belied by the fact that many other states have similar grievances about projects vital for them being delayed and even given up. The truth is that the capitalist path to which the ruling class is wedded makes development at the needed rate very difficult and even impossible.

The matter is also connected with the fact that states do not have adequate resources and powers. United struggles are necessary for speedier development. To allege communalism in such common issues as the Thein Dam is to hinder the growth of such united struggles.

2. It has been alleged by the Akalis that non-payment of remunerative prices to Punjab peasants for their produce is another act of discrimination because of communal considerations. If the Sikh peasants of Punjab have not been getting remunerative prices, can anyone assert that non-Sikh peasants in the rest of India have been getting remunerative prices? If not, where is the question of discrimination against Punjab or against the Sikhs? Really, it is a question of the pro-monopoly character of the economic policies of the Government of India, harming the interests of peasants all over the country.

3. Akalis have been loudly making the allegation that refusal to give greater autonomy to Punjab is an act of discrimination against Sikhs and against Punjab. The allegation is obviously without any basis. Demand for more powers for the states is just and in the interest of the country as a whole. It is being denied not only in the case of Punjab but in the case of all states. The Akalis, by giving the matter a communal colour and by demanding a Punjab in which Sikhs will dominate (Anadpur Sahib Resolution), are only harming the struggle for greater autonomy for the states.

From what has been stated above, it should be clear that the allegation of discrimination against Punjab because of communal considerations is not at all justified. It only hinders the unity of the

Punjabi people on common issues, including issues involving injustice to Punjab. It also hinders the process of raising class consciousness and class solidarity and of strengthening the unity of the people.

In today's situation, it also brings grist to the mill of the separatists, just as is done by the failure to promptly remove the genuine grievances of the Sikh minority in India. *(1982)*

## 2. How Akalis Misinterpret Article 25 of the Constitution

From time to time some of the Akali leaders have been alleging a conspiracy to end the separate and independent Sikh religious identity. Recently some of the most vociferous leaders of this category have made the point that Article 25 of the Indian Constitution defines Sikhs as a part of Hindu religion. And this has been cited as a proof of the fact that the conspiracy was hatched almost immediately after India won her independence.

It would be necessary therefore not only to have a close look at Article 25 but also to make a study of what happened in the Constitutent Assembly in connection with this Article—what position its Akali members took, to what extent the allegation and even the misapprehension behind this is well or ill founded, etc.

Article 25 of the Constitution of India reads as under:

1. Subject to public order, morality and health and to the other provisions of this part, all persons are equally entitled to freedom of conscience and the right freely to profess, practise and propagate religion.

2. Nothing in this article shall affect the operation of any existing law or prevent the state from making any law;

(a) regulating or restricting any economic, financial, political or other secular activity which may be associated with religious practice.

(b) providing for social welfare and reform or the throwing open of Hindu religious institutions of a public character to all classes and sections of Hindus.

**Explanation I:** The wearing and carrying of kirpans shall be deemed to be included in the profession of the Sikh religion.

**Explanation II:** In sub-clause (b) of clause (2) the reference to Hindus shall be construed as including a reference to persons professing the Sikh, Jain or Buddhist religion, and the reference to Hindu religious institutions shall be construed accordingly.

Quite clearly, the Article recognises Sikh religion as a separate religion and the wearing and carrying of kirpans as a part of the profession of the Sikh religion. By no stretch of imagination the article can be said to even imply that Sikhs are a part of Hindu religion.

What is stated in Explanation II is only a drafting device to say that the State can make laws to ensure that religious institutions of public character of not only Hindus but also of Sikhs, Jains and Buddhists are not barred to any section of Hindus, Sikhs, Jains and Buddhists.

Obviously, this was to make sure that in the name of religious freedom the believers in untouchability etc. were not able to continue banning the entry of scheduled castes to Hindu temples etc.

Guru Nanak, the founder of the Sikh religion, was a crusader against the caste system. It is, however, a fact that the evils of caste system have penetrated even amongst followers of this religion. Even in many small villages, there are separate gurdwaras of Mazhbi Sikhs on the one hand and Jats on the other. Entry in these is not formally banned to anyone but in actual practice the reality is not very happy. Under these circumstances, any true follower of Guru Nanak should welcome the provision contained in Explanation II instead of misinterpreting it as a conspiracy to assimilate the Sikhs into the fold of Hindu religion.

Had the authors of Explanation II forseen that their drafting device would be misinterpreted, they would have added the words "Sikh(s), Jain(s) or Buddhist(s)" after the word "Hindu/Hindus" in sub-clause(b) of clause (2), instead of having Explanation II.

Some Akali supporters have argued that whatever be the obvious meaning of Article 25, its hidden intention is shown by the fact that the provision in question has not been made applicable to Muslim religious places. The argument has no weight. The problem arising out of caste system does not exist as far as Muslim religious places are concerned.

It is true that Muslim women do not go to mosques. But given the consciousness of the common Muslims, it would be counter-productive to try to get the mosques thrown open to Muslim women by legislation.

An example will help to understand the point: Ultimately, we must have a common personal law which should provide besides other things that no male can have more than one wife at a time. But till such time as such a law can be enacted, should we refuse to have such a law for Hindus, Sikhs, Buddhists, Jains etc. just because we are not yet in a position to make such a law applicable to Muslims too?

The answer to this question is obvious. We hope that those who are putting a wrong interpretation on Article 25 will not succeed in misleading the Sikh masses.

As is well known, almost every article of the Constitution passed through many stages before it was passed and became a part of the Constitution in its final form. So did the article in question.

According to B. Shiva Rao's "The Framing of Indian Constitution", the Fundamental Rights Sub-Committee first discussed freedom of religion on March 26, 1947 and at the instance of a Sikh member, Harnam Singh, "the right to wear and carry kirpans" was recognised as a part of the practice of the Sikh religion.

The article in question was numbered 20 in the Draft Constitution as prepared by the Constitutional Advisor in October 1947. It read as under:

1. Subject to the public order, morality and health and to other provisions of this part, all persons are equally entitled to freedom of conscience and the right freely to profess, practice and propagate religion.

**Explanation I:** The wearing and carrying of kirpans shall be deemed to be included in the profession of the Sikh religion.

**Explanation II:** The rights conferred by this sub-section shall not include any economic, financial, political or other secular activity which may be associated with religious practice.

2. Nothing in this section shall preclude the State from making laws for social welfare and reform and for throwing open Hindu institutions of a public character to any class or section of Hindus.

The Draft Constitution prepared by the Drafting Committee improved upon this article and numbered it 19. The Drafting Committee elected by the Constituent Assembly consisted of experts and did not have any member from Punjab.

Article 19 read as under:

Subject to public order, morality and health and to the other provisions of this part, all persons are equally entitled to freedom of conscience and the right freely to profess, practise and propagate religion.

**Explanation:** The wearing and carrying of kirpans shall be deemed to be included in the profession of the Sikh religion.

2. Nothing in this article shall affect the operation of any existing law or preclude the State from making any law—

(a) regulating or restricting any economic, financial, political or other secular activity which may be associated with religious practice;

(b) for social welfare and reform or for throwing open Hindu religious institutions of a public character to any class or section of Hindus.

As has been pointed out by B. Shiva Rao in his book, the clause by clause consideration of the Draft Constitution was taken up by the Constituent Assembly on October 15, 1948 and concluded on November 17, 1948.

A number of amendments were moved to the article in question. Dr. Ambedkar accepted only two. By one of these, the word "preclude" was substituted by the word "prevent". The second amendment replaced the words "any class or section" by the words "all classes and sections" in sub-clause (b) of clause (2).

All other amendments were either not pressed or were negatived. No Sikh member had moved any amendment.

Incidentially, one of the amendments which were pressed and which Dr. Ambedkar refused to accept, wanted to provide for the right of the Muslims to have their personal law in a way as would have prevented any reform in it. Dr. Ambedkar in refusing to accept this amendment was not abrogating the Muslim personal law. He was only refusing to undermine or contradict the objective of having ultimately one personal law for all Indians as provided in the Directive Principles.

The Draft Constitution with the amendments adopted by the Assembly was referred again to the Drafting Committee.

It was at the revision stage that the Drafting Committee added a new Explanation II in the draft Article 19 providing that the reference to Hindus (in the context of throwing open of religious institutions of a public order to all classes and sections of Hindus) would be construed as including a reference to persons professing the Sikh, Jain or Buddhist religion etc. and this draft article was re-numbered as Article 25.

Members of the Constituent Assembly had the right to give notice of amendments to any of 395 articles of the Revised Draft Constitution. Many amendments were in fact given notice of and were considered by the Assembly. However, no notice of any amendment to this article was given by anyone. If the Akali members had thought that Explanation II was a conspiracy against Sikh religion, they would have surely moved for its deletion.

During the third reading of the Constitution, the very alert and intelligent Akali member, S. Hukam Singh, made a strong speech on November 12, 1949. He criticised every aspect of the Constitution which he could from the "Sikh" angle. He criticised the denial of the demand for a Punjabi-speaking province. He criticised the majority community for disowning the mother tongue. He asserted that provincial units had been reduced to municipal boards. He also made the point that the proportion of the Sikhs in the army was being reduced every day.

In his long speech, he did not make any criticism of Article 25. Obviously he did not consider it as an attack of any kind on Sikh religion.

The foregoing should make it clear that some of the Akali spokesmen are these days deliberately misinterpreting Article 25 to suit their narrow, partisan and communal interests.

Interestingly it is this very Article on which the Akali leadership relies whey they assert the "exclusive religious" right of the Sikhs to wear and carry kirpans even during flights—internal or over-seas.

*(September 25, 1983)*

## 3. The Akali Who's Who

Almost all political parties as well as the Government of India recognise that there are moderates as well as extremists amongst the leaders of the Akali Party. It is also accepted that it will not be in national interest to ignore this fact. Since the Punjab problem has become a national issue, many from outside Punjab have been wanting to have a fuller pictures of the top Akali leaders. This article is an attempt to help such friends at least to some extent.

**Parkash Singh Badal:** Soft-spoken, twice Chief Minister of Punjab, a big landlord owning land not only in Punjab but also in some of the neighbouring states; also a transporter whose vehicles run not only in Punjab but also to some places in Haryana. According to some, he also owns *benami* a good deal of landed property in New Delhi.

Undoubtedly a moderate; least communal of all Akali leaders at the top-most level. Not long ago had the biggest mass base of all the Akali leaders; commanded respect of considerable sections of Hindus in the State.

When during his chief ministership (1977-80) the extremists from outside as well as inside the Akali Party demanded a ban on the scriptures of the Nirankaris, he did not yield. At the same time he did not oppose the demand frontally.

Two Akali leaders opposed to him submitted to the head priests a memorandum against him alleging corruption etc. He was summoned to apper before the Akal Takht. In a statement to the press, he said that he could appear only as a Sikh but not as the Chief Minister because as Chief Minister he was bound by the secular Constitution of India. Within a couple of days, he gave up this position. On a subsequent occasion, he himself became a party in the matter of seeking arbitration of the head priests to resolve the differences within the Akali Party regarding distribution of seats for elections to legislatures.

He has never supported the demand for Khalistan. Quite often he opposed it openly though on some occasions he might have chosen to remain silent. He was a party to the resolution declaring that the Sikhs constituted a separate nation.

Of the top Akali leaders he did not go to Chowk Mehta when Bhindranwale was to court arrest. Again, he did not go to Ferozepore to welcome him on being released from the Central Jail there. In fact, he and Bhindranwale were not on talking terms and Bhindranwale had indulged in a lot of character assassination of Badal, making an issue even of the marriage of Badal's daughter to the son of a Congress leader. Badal was known to be on Bhindranwale's "hit list."

Badal never made the false statement (which many other Akali leaders did) that no arms were being collected inside the Golden Temple, that no terrorists were being trained there, etc. He was reported to have advised Sant Longowal not to make such patently wrong statements but to maintain silence on the issue.

Why did Badal himself choose to be silent instead of speaking out the reality and opposing it? Some say: out of fear of isolation as well as of physical liquidation. Others say: Badal too wanted the activities of the terrorists to act as pressure on the Government of India. Still others believe that all these factors operated together.

Immediately after Operation Blue Star, Badal issued a highly inflammatory statement to the press. Not a few considered it to be unlike Badal. Some believed that he did so because he wanted to be arrested. (Actually, after the statement he was immediately arrested.)

Badal has always been at loggerheads with Tohra. He has always been keen to oust him from the presidentship of the Shiromani Gurdwara Prabandhak Committee (SGPC). At the last moment, however, he would invariably give up the battle. Only at the time of the latest SGPC election held only a few weeks ago he gave the green signal to his supporters outside the jail to fight it out. Atma Singh contested against Tohra but lost by a narrow margin, reflecting the weakened position of Badal—weakened by his refusal or failure to fight extremism frontally.

**Gurcharan Singh Tohra:** Besides being one of the three topmost Akali leaders, has been the President of SGPC for many years.

Undoubtedly an extremist, he managed for long to have an image of a "progressive". For long he was said to be close to CPI-M leader Harkishan Singh Surjeet, who was widely reported to have written Tohra's speech at the Ludhiana convention of the Akali Dal held in 1978 which adopted the Second (Ludhiana) version of the Anandpur Sahib resolution. (This version was an attempt to make the resolution presentable to others.) Tohra's opponents inside the Akali Party sought to hit him by falsely alleging that he was a card-holder of CPI-M.

Some years ago when abroad, he (and another Akali leader, Sukhjinder Sikh) happened to meet the late Navtej Singh, the then editor of *Preet Lari* and a son of Gurbux Singh, doyen of Punjabi literature. They frankly told Navtej: "Khalistan is bound to come. We will work for it when Indira Gandhi is no more, because then nobody can hold the country together."

As SGPC President, it is Tohra who permitted Bhindranwale first to live in Guru Nanak Niwas and then in the Akal Takht. At an early stage, Singh Sahib Giani Kirpal Singh banned anybody going to Akah

Takht with arms. This affected Bhindranwale and his guards. Giani Kirpal Singh was made to retreat by Tohra.

Notwithstanding all this, it was widely believed that Tohra was willing to settle with the Centre in his bid to become the Chief Minister. It is even said that a settlement was reached but it did not come off because Bhindranwale did not agree.

**Sant Harchand Singh Longowal:** He became President of the Akali Dal with Badal's help. Many believed that he was Badal's man. Others had their doubts. At a later stage, some supporters of Bhindranwale openly alleged that he had been all along a Tohra man but had manoeuvred to get Badal's support to become president. In any case, it soon become clear that he was not dittoing the Badal line. In private, Badal bitterly complained to some of his friends that Santji first would agree with him but would then act differently. Longowal did not accept Badal's advice not to issue certificates about there being no arms etc. inside the Golden Temple. Longowal issued such false certificates repeatedly. Once he explained his refusal to condemn Bhindranwale by saying: "Why should I condemn him? He is our *dang* (a stick) for the government." And later he complained that his name too was likely to be included in the "hit-list".

In the latest election for the presidentship of SGPC, Longowal from within the jail fully supported Tohra against Atma Singh. The head priests too did all they could for Tohra's victory.

Sometime back, Jagjit Singh Chauhan released to the press a letter written to him by Longowal long long ago. In this, Longowal had forecast the establishment of Khalistan towards the end of the century. This has not been contradicted. However, on more than one occasion Longowal has opposed Khalistan and supported national unity and integrity.

Many believe that he is not a extremist but is a vacillator and also has been trying to utilise Badal-Tohra differences to become the sole leader of the Akali Dal. This is also the view of the writer of this article.

This much about the top trio. Now some others.

**Balwant Singh:** An ex-government officer, an ex-Congressman, a former Finance Minister (Akali). Besides being a landowner, he has big industrial interests in and out of Punjab as well as outside India.

Has links with some foreign big business too. He has often complained in private that though he deserves most, he cannot be an (Akali) Chief Minister because he is not a Jat by caste.

A moderate, he was for long reported to be a loyal member of the Badal group. His house was attacked by extremists. He had a narrow escape. It may be accidental, but thereafter a change in his attitude was noted by some observes. After the second killing of Hindu passengers of a bus towards the end of 1983, Badal was for a resolution by the Akali Legislature Party recommending the withdrawal of the Dharam Yudh Akali Morcha. This wholesome move was sabotaged by Balwant Singh.

In a seminar held after Operation Blue Star, he asserted that till a settlement was arrived at, killings etc. in Punjab would go on. In the recent election for the SGPC President, Balwant had supported Tohra—maybe because of acute rivalry with Atma Singh. In any case, another change in his attitude—a change for the better—can now be noted. In a press conference held on January 24, 1985, Balwant Singh contradicted Akali Dal *ad hoc* convener Surjan Singh Thekadar and SGPC acting President Lalpura when they said that the Anandpur Sahib resolution adopted in 1973 was the real document the party would like to stand by. Balwant Singh interjected to say that the latest version of the Anandpur Sahib resolution amended and adopted at the party's All-India Conference at Ludhiana in 1978 was now the final document.

**Surjeet Singh Barnala:** An advocate by profession, soft-spoken, with the reputation of a gentleman. A former Education Minister and the Akali nominee in the Janata Government (1977-78), he is considered a moderate, has been taking a moderate position though maintaining silence on some crucial questions; said to be close to Longowal.

**Sukhjinder Singh:** A former police officer. In the faction-ridden Police Department of the Punjab Government, he prepared and submitted a report against a senior officer "proving his corruption". A report was prepared against him. This was shown to him and he was asked to resign or face a charge-sheet. It is said that it was because of this that he resigned. Some also allege that before becoming an Akali, he had tried for a Congress ticket for the Punjab Assembly. Was Education Minister in the second ministry headed by Badal. Visited Yogi Harbhajan Singh (an American Sikh leader) in USA when he was still a minister. Later on, had to resign because of acute differences with Chief Minister Badal. Some allege that he had close contacts with the Congress Chief Minister Darbara Singh. An open protagonist of Khalistan.

Like Balwant Singh and Barnala he too was at one time a member of Akali Dal's negotiating team.

***Moral:*** There are moderates in the Akali leadership but they will act as consistent moderates only under mass pressure. *(March 2, 1983)*

## 4. The Anandpur Sahib Resolution

Akali leaders again assert that the Anandpur Sahib Resolution does not demand Khalistan. It is not necessary for them to do so because no one has alleged that it puts forward such a demand. What is alleged is that this resolution contains seeds of secessionism (besides being otherwise objectionable also). The Akali leaders refute this too. They would like us to believe that the resolution demands nothing more than a real federal structure for India. And at least one prominent Opposition leader, Inder Kumar Gujral, has been more or less supporting this contention of the Akali leaders for more than two years. His latest pronouncement in this respect perhaps is contained in *Mainstream,* Republic Day Number 1985. Here is what he writes.

"The main difficulty centres round the Anandpur Sahib resolution. Much has been said and written about it. It will be useful to discuss only its official version. Sant Longowal had given me, in October 1982, its authenticated version under his own signature. To treat it as *secessionist* is a serious folly. Its main thrust has to be interpreted in terms of modifications in Centre-state relations. Although the resolution has asked for addition of more territories from the adjoining states, the Akalis' discussions had confined their demands to retention of Abohar and Fazilka and transfer of Chandigarh. Similarly, they had expressed satisfaction with setting up the Sarkaria Commission. In very unambiguous language, the Akali leadership and many others had repeated their dissociation with any concept of Khalistan." (*Emphasis in the original.*)

The main purpose of this article is to examine whether or not the Anandpur Sahib resolution has any seeds of secessionism. Since Gujral had not discussed the matter but had only made an assertion, I requested him to send me a copy of the authenticated version with him. He was good enough to promptly accede to my request and I received a photostat copy last week. Clearly and obviously, it is not the resolution adopted at the All-India Akali Conference held at Ludhiana on October 28 and 29, 1978. (According to the Dal, the Ludhiana resolution was adopted "in the light of the Anandpur Sahib resolution".)

The official version with Gujral would thus appear to be the one adopted by the Working Committee of the Akali Dal on October 17, 1973. Interestingly, there are other "authentic" versions of the 1973 resolution, though not signed by Longowal.

One appeared in *The Tribune* of April 13, 1981. It was stated in the introduction that the English translation was by Amar Singh Ambalvi who was a member of the 12-member sub-committee which had been constituted by the Working Committee to formulate comprehensive policies and programmes. The introduction also stated that there were sharp differences at many of the meetings of the sub-committee but the final report was adopted unanimously. (Version Tr-1).

*The Tribune* of November 13, 1982, carried the "full text of the English version of the political goal resolution adopted by the Working Committee of the Dal on October 16-17, 1983, at Anandpur Sahib". (Version Tr-2).

We shall refer to the version with Gujral as the "official" version.

There is also the version contained in the White Paper issued by the Government of India in July 1984. It will be helpful to compare the relevant clauses in the different versions.

1. The very first sentence of the "official" version reads as follows: "The Shiromani Akali Dal is the supreme body of the Sikh Panth and as such is fully authorised to represent and lead them."

The first sentence of the Tr-1 version reads: "The Akali Dal is the only body which represents and is duly authorised to represent the collective will of the Sikh Panth".

Tr-2 version does not have the whole of the first section of the resolution, being confined to the section headed "political".

The White Paper version's (Hindi) first sentence is on the same lines but speaks of Sikh "Rashtar"—perhaps a case of wrong translation.

2. The second para in the section entitled "Aims" in the "official" version reads as follows: "Maintaining the realisation of Panth's independent entity and creation of such an environment where Sikh sentiment can find its full expression . . . ."

Corresponding para in the Tr-1 version reads: "Maintaining the feeling of a separate independent entity of the Sikh Panth and creation of an environment in which the "national expression" of the Sikhs can be full and satisfactory . . . ."

Tr-2 version omitted this whole section. The White Paper version is on the lines of Tr-1 and speaks of fulfilment of "national aspirations" of Sikhs.

3. The section headed "Political" in the "official" version has the following as the first para: "The Panthic *political aim* is definitely based in the directives of the Tenth Guru, which is engraved on the pages of Sikh history and is in the mind of Khalsa Panth. Its aims is, *Khalsa ji ka bol bala"*. (*Emphasis added.*)

The corresponding para in the Tr-1 version reads as follows: "The political aims of the Panth are definitely ingrained in the orders of the Tenth Guru in the pages of Sikh history and in the perspective of the Khalsa Panth the purpose of which is the pre-eminence of the Khalsa. To give the 'birthright' of the Khalsa a practical shape, creation of the necessary environment and achievement of a political constitution are the basic ideological planks of the Akali Dal".

This para in the Tr-2 version reads: "The political goal of the Panth, without doubt, is enshrined in the commandments of the Tenth Lord in the pages of Sikh history and in the very heart of the Khalsa Panth, the ultimate objective of which is the pre-eminence of the Khalsa. The fundamental policy of the Shiromani Akali Dal is to seek the realisation of this birth right of the Khalsa through the creation of a congenial environment and political set-up."

The White Paper version is exactly on same lines.

4. The (b) part of the section headed "political" in the "official" version reads as follows: "In this new Punjab and other States, the Central intervention should be restricted to defence, foreign affairs, post and telegraph, currency and railways. The rest of the departments should be under the direct control of Punjab."

The corresponding para in the Tr-1 version is as below: "In new

Punjab the authority of the Centre should be confined only to the defence of the country, foreign relations, communications, railways and currency. All the residuary subjects (departments) should be under the jurisdiction of 'New Punjab', which should have the right to frame its own constitution for these subjects. In the Central subjects New Punjab should contribute its share of necessary finances in ratio of its members in the Lok Sabha."

Tr-2 version in this respect is as follows: "In this New Punjab and in other States, the Centre's interference should be restricted to defence, foreign relations, currency and general communications. All other departments should be in the jurisdiction of Punjab and other States, which would be fully entitled to frame their own laws on these subjects for administration. For the above departments of the Centre, Punjab and other States contribute in proportion to their representation in Parliament."

The White Paper version is the same as Tr-2 version.

5. In the same Political section of the official version, the following too occurs. "Shiromani Akali Dal will also try that the Indian Constitution becomes federal in the real sense and all States are equally represented at the Centre."

The corresponding para in Tr-1 version is on the same lines except that it also speaks of equal "authority" of all the states at the Centre.

Tr-2 version and the White Paper version in this respect are similar to the official version. They speak of only "equal representation".

The above exercise makes the following clear:

1. The official version like the other versions is based on the thesis that Sikhs are not only an independent separate religious community (which they undoubtedly are) but are also an independent and separate political community, which they are not—an extremely dangerous thesis.

2. Other versions contain formulations which make it explicit that the resolution is based on the theory that "Sikhs are a separate nation". These have been omitted from the official version.

3. The political aim in every version including the official one is defined as *Khalsa ji ka bol bala*. This is nothing but a demand for a theocratic Punjab.

No version poses the question how this will be achieved, because it cannot be achieved on the existing basis of one person-one vote type of democracy. Tr-1 version, however, provides a clear answer to this unposed question. The answer is by framing (such) a separate Constitution for Punjab (as will ensure it). Tr-2 and the White Paper versions speak of laws and not separate Constitution. The official version is altogether silent. However, if the Centre is to have only four departments mentioned in the resolution and in all other respects states are to be virtually sovereign, what is explicit in the Tr-1 version would seem implicit in the official version.

4. According to every version including the official version, India will not have any common economy. Nor is that all. The Centre will not have any powers to raise finances to run its four departments. Where will the money for these come from?

The answer is given in some versions. It is that states will contribute money in proportion to their representation in Parliament. (Since equal representation is demanded for all states, it is not clear why it is not said that all states will equally contribute). The official version maintains silence regarding this question.

Gujral may be of the view that omissions effected in the version given to him are substantial and this makes the resolution harmless. Others may be of the view the omissions are only an attempt to hoodwink the gullible but do not change the essence of the resolution which is for a Sikh Raj in Punjab within India with a very weak Centre. And this is quite a different proposition from the genuine demand for more powers for states, for strong states with a strong Centre.

Secondly, many may not feel as sure as Gujral that the version given to him really holds the field or will continue to do so.

In the circumstances, will it not be only correct and reasonable that all should tell the Akalis: "Decide once and for all what is the final and official version of the Anandpur Sahib resolution. It should not be vague on crucial questions. Place the same before the Sarkaria Commission for its consideration".

After all, according to the Akali leaders, the resolution only demands greater autonomy for the States. And to consider this very question the Sarkaria Commission has been set up. According to Gujral himself the Akali leaders did express satisfaction over it.

The Prime Minister has done the right thing by saying that he does not demand scrapping of the resolution as a precondition for talks. Let others advise the Akalis not to insist upon the resolution being made the basis for talks. Let them take the resolution to the Sarkaria Commission and argue its merits before it. Perhaps at one stage the Akali negotiators themselves had agreed to it.

*(March 30, 1985)*

## 5. BBC Looks at Punjab

The book* has attracted wide attention and also much appreciation from varied quarters for good reasons. Already its translation in some Indian languages has also appeared.

A number of books were published about the Emergency immediately after it was lifted. The same thing happened immediately after Operation Blue Star. A number of books made their appearance about the tragic events of Punjab. In either case, most of these books neither gave any new facts nor made any deep analysis of the events and facts already generally known. However, these books were sold in quite large numbers because of very wide interest that existed about these subjects. And that must have brought much money to the publishers and authors. Possibly, some of these books were written only with this objective and with no other purpose. Certainly this cannot be said of Mark Tully and Satish Jacob's book. The book has a purpose. This is made clear in Mark Tully's "Note to Readers". According to him:

"We started work on this book before Mrs. Gandhi's assassination because we were convinced that Operation Blue Star would have the gravest consequences for the unity of India if it was not recognised that the Sikh leadership was as much responsible as the government for the disaster . . . . The danger of the alienation of a large section of the Sikh community was magnified by the government's failure to control the violence unleashed against Sikhs after Mrs. Gandhi's assassination. We therefore felt there was all the more need to tell the story of Bhindranwale and the mistakes which led up to the disaster in the Golden Temple."

---

* **Amritsar: Mrs. Gandhi's Last Battle** by Mark Tully and Satish Jacob. Published by Rupa & Co., by arrangement with Pan Books Ltd. London; 1985; Pp 238. Price paper-back Rs. 30.

It needs to be stated that to a very considerable extent the book achieves this purpose by marshalling and analysing facts in a very readable manner. In analysing the facts, the authors have been quite impartial on the whole. They have spared neither the Congress leadership nor the leadership of the Akali Party. They have also exposed the role played by factional fight in the Congress between Darbara Singh and Zail Singh as well as by the factional fight inside the Akali Party. Their efforts to present and analyse facts objectively and impartially has made the book convincing to a great extent and that is the chief merit of the book.

The authors cannot be faulted in the matter of exposing the responsibility of the government and the Congress leaders for the Bhindranwale phenomenon. The book contains powerful exposure of how for "petty political gains the government itself created the ogre who was to dominate the last years of Mrs. Gandhi and to shadow her until her death."

If at all, there is some underestimation in the book of the role and responsibility of the Akali leadership. The authors expose the role of Tohra "who was hoping the Akali Morcha and Bhindranwale to discredit Badal" and take over himself as head of the political wing of the Akali Dal, becoming the party's candidate for the chief ministership." The authors in the last chapter conclude. "No Shah, No Khomeini, no Indira and no Bhindranwale . . . . she was responsible for the political atmosphere which made the fundamentalism of Bhindranwale relevant. The Akali Dal Trinity must also bear their share of the responsibility. Badal and Longowal lacked the courage to stand out against a force they knew was evil. Tohra tried to use it for his own ends."

The fact is that it was not merely a question of lack of courage on the part of Longowal and Badal. They had come to believe that Bhindranwale was a good stick to beat the government with and to get better terms. While Badal did maintain silence, Longowal not unoften praised and defended Bhindranwale. This aspect and the facts relevant to it have been overlooked by the authors.

Another merit of the book is that it has revealed some little known but important facts. This author, like many others, believed that Bhindranwale could not be arrested by Darbara Singh's police at Chando

Kalan because he was tipped off by Haryana Chief Minister Bhajan Lal at the instance of the then Home Minister Giani Zail Singh. The Punjab police had set on fire Bhindranwale's vans. Bhindranwale had been accusing those responsible for burning copies of Gutka Sahib and even of Guru Granth Sahib which were said to be there in these vans. According to the authors, the fact was as below:

"Bhindranwale used to have a secretary with him wherever he preached, whose job was to copy down every word he said so that it could be recorded for posterity. It was the immortal words of Bhindranwale which went up in flames at Chando Kalan and the preacher never forgave the government for that. In fact it was the burning of his sermons, not his arrest, which turned Bhindranwale against his godfather, Zail Singh, and against Mrs. Gandhi."

The book has quite a few weaknesses too. The authors concede that Pakistan had a role to play in the Punjab crisis but only in a minor way. The extent of its hand is very much underplayed and there is no reference at all to the role of US imperialism and its allies out to disintegrate India even though more than enough evidence was available when the book was written.

Another weakness of the book is the complete absence of any reference to the role of the Left and more so of the common people—both Hindus and Sikhs—in foiling attempts to provoke large-scale Hindu-Sikh riots in Punjab. The two Communist Parties are not very strong in Punjab but they do matter and their role, particularly of CPI, was noted and appreciated even by sections of the press usually quite hostile to the Communists.

The book also contains some factual errors and weakness of analysis. Here are some instances:

1. The authors write:

"But Mrs. Gandhi stepped in before the Sant (Fateh Singh) was put to the final test and announced that Chandigarh would go to Punjab. She also insisted that Punjab would have to surrender two tehsils, Abohar and Fazilka, to Haryana. This was a messy award too. The justification for giving the two tehsils—the smallest Indian revenue unit—to Haryana was that they were Hindu majority areas. They were Punjabi not Hindi speaking."

Some vital facts have not been brought out in connection with the award of 1971. Firstly, about 50 villages in Abohar and Fazilka are Hindi speaking, though the Hindi spoken there is more akin to that spoken in Rajasthan. They have no contiguity with Haryana. The contiguity is broken by village Kundu Khera which has always been Punjabi speaking.

Secondly, the award was made on the basis of a prior agreement. In fact, the transfer of Abohar and Fazilka to Haryana had been suggested by the Akalis. It is not without significance that the then Chief Minister Gurnam Singh (Akali) hailed the award as their victory and called for deepmala to celebrate it. It is a different matter that under various pressures and for various reasons, the Akali Party went back on the award.

2. The seeds of secessionism in the Anandpur Sahib resolutions are underplayed in the book. The fact that its goal is a theocratic Punjab is not brought out.

3. Tohra's friendship and connection with CPI(M) leader Harkishen Singh Surjeet (wrongly referred to in the book as a Sikh leader) at one stage is overplayed and Tohra is described as a "politician with Communist connections."

4. The authors wrongly say that Bhindranwale along with Fauja Singh had marched at the head of a procession shouting anti-Nirankari slogans in 1978, the procession which ended in a clash. Bhindranwale had backed out at the last moment after instigating his audience to take out this procession. The explanation given by his admirers is that it would have been wrong to send the main leader himself in this procession. The contention of the authors that the Akali Dal leaders did little to encourage the agitation against the Nirankaris so long as they remained in power too is incorrect. Tohra and some others did a lot to encourage this agitation even when Akali leader Badal was the Chief Minister.

5. Some correct decisions and bold pronouncements of Darbara Singh are mentioned and even praised. The negative role he played is completely overlooked—for instance, his role in relation to the dispute in Jalandhar in connection with the Sodal Mandir. His role there for the sake of narrow political reasons accentuated Hindu-Sikh tension.

6. The reference in the book to "the Left wing of the Akali Dal" is unwarranted and not supported by any facts. Reference to moderate section and extremist section would be in order.

7. According to the authors, Bhinder was sent to Punjab by Indira Gandhi as Director General of Police to crush the terrorists. Actually, he was sent to try to pave the way for an agreement with Bhindranwale. A real uncle of Bhinder was quite close to Bhindranwale.

8. The authors describe what happened in the Golden Temple during Operation Blue Star. Some statements in this connection are disputable, and no facts or sources are given in support of them.

Mistakes and omissions of this type do not take away from the merit of the book, even though some of them may be indicative of some prejudice. Such mistakes, however, have been taken advantage of by some to denounce the book and the authors. For instance, a publication of the All India Sikh Students Federation notes some wrong facts and asserts that these "white lies" have been written in the book at the instance of the Government of India. The factual mistakes mentioned are:

1. One trader's arm was cut off at the hands of the anti-Nirankari procession of 1978. No such thing had happened.

2. Fauja Singh, leader of this procession, drew this sword and swiped at the neck of the Nirankari Guru. This too is incorrect.

3. The DIG Atwal died in the Parikrama of the Golden Temple. Actually, he was shot dead just at the main gate of the Golden Temple from inside. And his body had fallen at a site where one could not go bare-headed and with shoes on. It is, however, not correct that he died in the Parikrama, which is very much inside the four gates of the Golden Temple.

Mistakes of this type do not affect the main line of the argument of the book but can be and have been used, as seen above, to denounce the authors as virtual government agents and thus to damage their credibility and to undermine the positive features of the book.

To sum up, the book, notwithstanding some more or less serious weaknesses, is a good contribution towards the understanding of a tragic and turbulent phase of Punjab's contemporary history.

*(May 10, 1986)*

## 6. Mischief of Priests

Widespread negative Sikh reaction to the hukumnama ex-communicating Surjeet Singh Barnala should have made the five Sikh priests do some rethinking. In actual practice, after some efforts to regain lost ground, they have further moved in the wrong direction.

On February 27, three of them including Ragi Darshan Singh, Acting Jathedar of Akal Takht, addressed a gathering within the premises of Khalsa College, Amritsar, called by some organisations of the militants. The declared aim was to pay homage to the "Sikh youths killed in encounters." Incidentally, these would include such dreaded terrorists as Billa of Taran Taran subdivision at whose death all the people of the area, including Sikhs had heaved a sigh of relief. No one disputed the official claim that he had been killed in a genuine encounter with the CRPF. Amongst his many victims were the 8-year old Babla of Fatehabad, who was shot dead at 11 p.m. in the night while asleep.

Beside the three priests, other speakers or participants included Baba Thaknar Singh (successor of Sant Bhindranwale as head of the Damdami Taksal) and Bimal Khalsa (widow of Beant Singh, an assassin of Indira Gandhi).

The real purpose of the convention, however, was to justify the recent controversial action of the priests and to call for social boycott of Surjit Singh Barnala.

Slogans in favour of Khalistan were frequently raised during the speeches.

An interesting sidelight of the convention needs to be mentioned. Those who claim to have "united" the Panth by setting up a new United Akali Dal and by excommunicating Barnala could not keep the militants united at the convention. According to the report of the Convention in *The Indian Express*, "Earlier, members of the All India Sikh Students Federation (Gurjit faction) objected to the presence of the leaders and activists of the AISSF (Presidium). After an exchange of hot words, members of the Manjit Singh group staged a walk-out from the convention." *The Tribune* reports: "According to Miss Rupinder Kaur, member of the women's wing of the Presidium, trouble arose when Mr. Ram Singh, an uncle of AISSF leader Manjit Singh now in Jodhpur jail, was not allowed to speak on behalf of the mother of Manjit Singh on the plea that he was not recognised by the Damdami Taksal. At this, the Presidium leader and a section of the audience staged a walk-out".

The incident, no doubt, provides some indication of the real esteem in which the priests are held by the militants, whom they are trying to help.

By misusing their religious positions to help the pro-extremist factions of the Akali Dal, the priests are only undermining their own authority and are also being forced to use unpriestly methods to defend their indefeasible positions.

On February 28, 1987, a number of newspapers carried a half-page advertisement under the signatures of Ragi Darshan Singh and the four other priests. It denounces Barnala and those who have stood by him as anti-Sikh and anti-Guru. It appeals to the Sikhs to boycott them, not to attend their public meetings and gatherings etc. The advertisement tries to ridicule the allegation that they are not for the unity and integrity of the country. There is however no refutation of the fact that three of the signatories made speeches in favour of Khalistan at Bhawanigarh in Sangrur district, nor of the fact that on January 26, the "Sarbat Khalsa" of the extremists adopted a resolution in favour of Khalistan with the explicit or implicit agreement of all the five priests. Ragi Darshan Singh, in fact, had approvingly quoted Bhindranwale to the effect that the foundation of the Khalistan was laid when the Army entered the Golden Temple. The irony lies in the fact that the papers which carried this advertisement also carried the report about pro-Khalistan slogans at the convention held in the Khalsa College one day earlier and addressed by the three priests, including Darshan Singh.

One can always expect such acrobatics from unscrupulous politicians but when they are indulged in by priests and that too in the name of Akal Takht, one can only feel sad.

The advertisement seems to justify the right of the priests to interfere in the affairs of the Akali Dal; it asserts that the Akal Takht has and alone has the right to issue hukumnamas, and it seems to justify the ex-communication of Barnala from the Sikh religion as ordered by the priests.

All the five priests including Darshan Singh are undoubtedly admirers and perhaps followers of Jarnail Singh Bhindranwale. Let us remind them what at one time Bhindranwale had said about their predecessors, occupying the same religious positions as they occupy now. Sant Bhindranwale had bluntly stated that the priests could not be regarded as anything more than the paid employees of the SGPC, that he regarded Sarbat Khalsa (of militants) and not the priests, as supreme.

Another known follower of Sant Bhindranwale has reiterated once again this position and has explained it as the basis of the history and traditions of Sikh religion, as he understands them. He is Narinder Singh Bhular who was once Dictator of the Punjabi Suba Morcha of the Akalis and who later on took upon himself the task of expounding and justifying the views of Bhindranwale to the extent of justifying killings and denouncing the slogan of Hindu-Sikh unity. He now holds the view that the Akali Party is a party of self-seekers and is not a Panthic organisation. He is angry with the priests because they have not declared openly and in writing that Khalistan is the objective of the Akali Dal set up by them. He is of the view that they should work for the unity of the militants instead of wasting their time on working for the unity of the Akali Dal.

Bhular expressed these views in the 15th February 1987 issue of his journal *Dehati Janata*. In the same issue he has explained his views on the right to issue hukumnamas to excommunicate, etc. Here are the main points made by him:

1. Shri Akal Takht Sahib was founded by the Sixth Guru, Shri Guru Hargobindji. He himself stayed there. From Akal Takht itself he issued all his hukams (orders), religious as well as political. The Guru himself would appoint the Akal Takht Jathedar. It was the Guru who was supreme. The Akal Takht Jathedar only looked after the Takht and carried out the orders of the Guru.

2. The Seventh and the Eighth Gurus did not make much use of the Akal Takht. The Ninth and the Tenth Gurus could not come to Amritsar and hence did not issue any hukumnamas from Akal Takht.

3. Shri Guru Gobind Singh, who had founded the Khalsa, died in 1708. After him, the Khalsa Panth began holding its gathering at the Akal Takht. These Sarbat Khalsas took all decisions concerning the Khalsa dharma. These decisions had to be unanimous. These decisions were called "Gurumatas". Thus, after the Gurus, Sarbat Khalsa became supreme. However, a Gurumata cannot be called a hukumnama because hukumnamas were issued only by the Gurus under their own signatures.

Gurumatas were released under the seal of the Akal Takht. It is the Sarbat Khalsa which appointed the Akal Takht Jathedar.

Gradually, it became a tradition that only the Akal Takht Jathedar would call the Sarbat Khalsa and he would release as Gurumatas the decisions, which had to be unanimous. It is these Gurumatas which were binding on all Sikhs. Akal Takht itself is only a building and idol-worship is against the Sikh tenets.

4. The Akal Takht Jathedar has full rights to declare a Sikh as Tankhaya for violating or not observing his religious duties and to ask him to do some particular "seva" as punishment. Akali Phoolan Singh in his capacity as Jathedar Akal Takht had declared Maharaja Ranjit Singh as Tankhaya because he had illicit relations with a prostitute. This was purely a religious misconduct. Akali Phoolan Singh himself had thereby established that the Akal Takht Jathedar was not supreme in political matters. In fact, he does not have the right to declare anyone even a Tankhaya on political grounds.

5. With regard to matters which are political the position of the Akal Takht Jathedar is that of the speaker of the Parliament with one difference: He has the right to call Sarbat Khalsa which is supreme in political matters. But its decisions have to be unanimous. Only such decisions are to be released by the Jathedar as Gurumatas. The Akal Takht Jathedar himself has no right to interfere in or give decisions about political matters.

6. According to Sikh religion, others can be converted to Sikhism but no one has the right to throw any Sikh out of Sikhism or out of the Panth.

It is a fact of history that 40 Singhs of Amritsar district had differences, given in writing to the Guru, that neither was he their Guru nor were they his Sikhs. Even in such a case there was no hukumnama excommunicating them.

Then there is the example of Jassa Singh Ramgarhia. He had gone over to the side of the Lahore rulers and had fought the Khalsa Panth. The institution of Sarbat Khalsa was at its peak in those days. But no Sarbat Khalsa ex-communicated him.

On the basis of these and other examples, Narinder Singh Bhular asserts that there is no provision in the Sikh religion to ex-communicate anyone and neither the Akal Takht nor anyone else has this right.

Even the Sarbat Khalsa does not have this right. This wrong practice has been started as a part of the factional game.

In short, Bhular on the basis of Sikh history, asserts that: 1. The Akal Takht Jathedar can declare a Sikh a Tankhaya on religious grounds alone and can award punishment. He has no right to excommunicate anyone or to interfere in matters political. 2. Hukumnamas could be issued only by Gurus. Neither the Akal Takht Jathedar nor anyone else has this right. 3. With regard to political matters only Sarbat Khalsa can adopt binding decisions which have to be unanimous and are called Gurumatas.

It is as clear as daylight that proposition No. 3 is no longer a practical proposition because of vast changes which have taken place in Sikh society. Since long, it has ceased to be a unified group fighting the feudal rulers, who happened to be Muslim by religion. The Sikhs are not a unified class. They belong to different classes having even opposing and contradictory interests—tenants and landlords, workers and capitalists, peasants and big traders, etc. All Sikhs do not and cannot have common political interests.

Nor is this all. Sikh workers have common political interests with Hindu and Muslim workers but have no common political interests with Sikh capitalists, etc. Can anyone imagine a genuine Sarbat Khalsa in today's situation being able to adopt unanimous decisions on matters political. And with Sikhs spread all over India and even outside India, is a real and genuine Sarbat Khalsa at all possible? And can patriotic Sikhs of Punjab and American millionaire Sikhs like Ganga Singh Dhillon, stooges of US imperialism and in league with Zia of Pakistan, agree on vital political issues concerning our country and the world as a whole?

To ask these questions is to answer them. The institution of Sarbat Khalsa has outlived its utility; only unscrupulous politicians have been exploiting it for their own narrow, selfish, and factional interests. One Sarbat Khalsa has been cancelling the decisions of another Sarbat Khalsa. Is this a happy situation? Sant Bhindranwale and Narinder Singh Bhular would recognise as genuine only such a Sarbat Khalsa as is fully controlled by the extremists. Communists too can hold a gathering of some lakhs of Sikhs which would unanimously denounce Khalistan. Suppose they were to call it a Sarbat Khalsa, how would the priests relish that? After all, Sarbat Khalsas have been called by persons other than the Akal Takht Jathedar and at places other than the Akal Takht.

Will it not be better for Sikh religion, for Punjab and for India to recognise the changed realities and to admit that the interests of all today demand that religion and politics should be separated fully and completely and that this holds good for all including the common toiling Sikhs and the noble and humanistic traditions of Sikh religion?

Will more and more Sikh leaders have the courage to state boldly that some anti-national forces in the process of exploiting Sikh religion are trying to completely distort its real traditions and are trying to change it altogether? Those who have already moved in this direction should move forward and not stop half-way. Others should follow them. *(March 14, 1987)*

## 7. Sanctity of Golden Temple Ensured

The nation understandably heaved a sigh of relief over the Golden Temple having been cleared of the terrorist killers. The manner in which the security forces carried out their Operation Black Thunder has won praise all around, including from UAD leader Amarinder Singh and leading Sikhs in all walks of life.

All this, however, does not mean that the fight against the terrorists and terrorism is over. The killings which have been going on on a big scale, day in and day out, should leave no room for complacency. The fight has to continue and, as we have always emphasised, must be waged simultaneously on the law and order front as well as the political front.

The latest round of killings by the terrorists has a new feature. There is much greater and, in a way, new concentration on migrant labourers in Punjab. The main aim of this is to provoke attacks on Sikhs in states outside Punjab, that is, states from which these labourers come. Such attacks, the terrorists hope, will help them to regain the sympathy which they have lost to a considerable extent even in areas in Punjab considered their strongholds.

This game must be foiled by the governments and the secular forces of the states concerned. Effective and immediate action must be taken within Punjab to deal with terrorist killers outside the Golden Temple, together with the correct type of political initiatives.

An immediate and important question being debated is: how to ensure that the Golden Temple is not recaptured by the terrorists? Vital interests of the nation as well as of devout Sikhs and of the Sikh religion demand that this must be ensured.

The fact that Sikhs in Punjab, including Amritsar district, did not respond to appeals to march to the Golden Temple shows considerable realisation on their part of the truth, namely, that it is the terrorists who had deprived them of their right to worship in the holiest of holy shrines and who had desecrated it. This should give confidence to all concerned that steps to prevent recapture of the Golden Temple can win the support of the Sikh masses, provided the sensitive nature of the issues involved is kept in mind.

There is not likely to be any opposition worth the name to the construction of a security road around the Golden Temple. Besides aiding the task of ensuring security, it will also help in beautifying the Golden Temple and attracting more people. A proposal to this effect was mooted after Operation Blue Star. It was dropped for reasons best known to the government. But past mistakes must not be repeated. Of course, those uprooted must be given compensation at market rates and all, including tenants, must be rehabilitated suitably and in consultation with them and their representatives.

There is talk of amending the Gurudwara Act to ban taking of all types of arms, except the kirpan, into the Golden Temple. That is necessary but why only in the Golden Temple? For that matter, why only in the gurdwaras? Let us recall that at one time weapons were stored in, and were distributed from the Seetla Mandir, Amritsar, as a retaliatory measure against Sikhs. And one should take into account all contingencies.

There should be a new Act for this purpose. That should cover places of worship of *all religions.* And it should override any provision in any existing law, which may be to the contrary. At best, a limited number of licensed weapons may be allowed for the managing committees for protection of the treasures and objects of sanctity and historical value. And, of course, traditional weapons known to be symbols of some religions.

Such a legislation can also make illegal for any political party or for any organisation, except the lawful managing body of the place of worship, to have its office in places of religious worship. This too should prevent organisations like the AISSF to function from within the Golden Temple. It is also necessary to prevent organisations like the Hindu Shiv Sena and the Rashtriya Suraksha Samiti to function from within the Seetla Mandir. And this is only an example to illustrate the point.

The proposed legislation should similarly make illegal all political activity within the places of worship. That will also help to prevent their misuse for anti-national purposes. Of course, it will not be easy to enforce this provision. That will require building up of a powerful public opinion—a task which the secular forces can ignore only at great risk, as the experience hitherto has shown. The task will be made easier if the Government of India gives up the Hindu tinge in its functioning. The ruling party must resist the temptation to use the Hindu card in the electoral game on the one hand and of having alliances with communal parties on the other.

Even the provision banning weapons in a place of worship will not get implemented automatically. After all, almost all the weapons with the terrorists within the Golden Temple were illegal. Why was their entry not prevented? True, these were taken hidden in vehicles supposed to be meant for Kar Seva and Dharam Prachar. The government says that their search would have injured the sentiments of the Sikhs. On the contrary, a sizeable section of the Sikh opinion in Punjab has been very critical of the government for not preventing arms build-up in the Golden Temple that it should have. Some even accuse it of allowing the same with a view to take "strong action" later on (and at an appropriate time) to impress the Hindu voters. There must not be a repetition of this mistake.

There are also some aspects which relate only to the Golden Temple. The Shiromani Gurdwara Prabandhak Committee (SGPC) wants the entire huge complex to be treated as sacred. There are others, including Sikhs, who are of the opinion that only the area within the four gates should be treated as such. The SGPC itself twice resolved to demolish all rooms around the Parikrama. However, this was never implemented. There is also the fact that the SGPC goes on claiming a road of the Municipal Corporation as belonging to it.

The road divides the Golden Temple complex proper, Manji Sahib and the Langer buildings on the one hand and Sarais etc. on the other.

These aspects must be settled and can be settled keeping in view the option of the really devout Sikhs and the common Sikhs and also the need to defeat the designs of the separatist terrorists. It would be ideal if they could be resolved in cooperation with the SGPC. However, there is no prospect at all of the SGPC being cooperative.

In fact if the SGPC were to be trusted, the Golden Temple may once again become the hide-out of the terrorists. That is why some would like the SGPC to be disbanded and a board for managing its affairs to be set up. This, however, is a rather very sensitive matter. It should be resolved through a national consensus. That is why an all-parties meeting at the national level needs to be called urgently. Such a meeting can and should try to evolve national consensus on other aspects of the matter too. *(May 25, 1988)*

## 8. Analysing S.S. Mann and His Activities

Our Deputy Prime Minister is as powerful as the Prime Minister, if not more. Reliable reports say that he is determined to make Simranjit Singh Mann the Chief Minister of Punjab. Some may object that this right belongs to the people of Punjab and not to him. That objection must be dismissed as frivolous. Did not Mann's Akali Dal prove its "popularity" by defeating the great Tau himself by a convincing margin in the Ferozepur parliamentary constituency? Never mind if his own son, who was in charge of his election campaign and who is now the Chief Minister of Haryana, is on record that Mann's candidate won with the help of terror and rigging. What matters is that he "won". The Deputy Prime Minister is reported to have even persuaded his old friend Badal not to object but to line up behind Mann.

And Mann has been talking and acting as if he is already the ruler of Punjab. In any case, he has no doubt that he is the future ruler.

Bhindranwale and Longowal were both alive at that time. Mann was the SSP in Faridkot. There were reports that more than once Mann had invited Bhindranwale to address his men in the Lines. Some colleagues of his assert that these reports were not correct. Let us accept them at their word, even though Mann has been admittedly a disciple of Bhindranwale since long and remains so even today.

Bhindranwale's outfit became the only government at least in the Amritsar and Gurdaspur districts. So much so that he could get anyone killed within the time specified by him. And many innocents were being killed day after day. Once Longowal said about these killings: "Killers come out of police stations and go back there after doing their job." The Akali leadership following the Congress-I leadership had been trying to use the Bhindranwale card in its game of power-politics. It was, therefore, generally thought that Longowal was providing an alibi for the terrorists and their leader as a part of this game. There are some who believe that what Longowal said was not altogether baseless.

They allege that a killers' squad had been organised by Mann, the SSP, out of some serving policemen. Mann has admirers even amongst the Punjab Police officers still in service. They include officers who have honestly and fearlessly fought terrorism risking their own lives. They believe that Mann is an extremely emotional man gone astray partly because he was handled wrongly. I asked one such officer if Mann did organise a killers' squad out of serving policemen. He said that there was such a squad and its members used to visit Mann. However, he did not think that Mann had organised it. Let us take him at his word and let the matter rest here.

A CPI member of the Rajya Sabha and the leader of the CPI group in the Punjab assembly alleged on the floors of the respective houses that as an SSP Mann had helped a number of "boys" to get licences for weapons, pretending to be Nirankaris in need for weapons for self-defence. Even their names were given. Even though the AISSF leader, Amrik Singh, had listed the Communists as one of their four enemies, it was not their policy yet to kill the Communists. However, these two CPI leaders were on the hit-list of one squad of killers and each of them had a very narrow escape at least once. Members of these squads had been recruited out of the police force.

Mann was transferred and sent to Bombay. Operation Blue Star pained most of our people and rightly so. It was not unavoidable and it should have been avoided. Responsibility for it has to be shared by Bhindranwale on the one hand and the Congress-I and the Akalis on the other. Mann held only the government responsible and resigned. One wonders why he chose to write to the then President, Giani Zail Singh.

Mann was nabbed while trying to escape to Nepal. He was in jail till recently when he was released after this election as an MP.

Mann was still in jail and quite sometime before the controversy over the Thakkar Commission Report erupted that the police succeeded in nabbing Atinder Pal Singh, a leading light of one of the four main "militant" organisations. It was as a result of the statements made by him during interrogation that the name of Simranjit Singh Mann figures as having been (possibly) involved in a conspiracy to assassinate Indira Gandhi. No case, however, was registered either against him or against Atinder Pal Singh on this account.

When much later a case was registered against both of them and some others, the controversy over the needle of suspicion pointing to Dhawan was at its peak. The registration of the case was wrong. Also it was bound to and did prove counter-productive. An impression was created that the case was false and had been registered to take the limelight away from Dhawan.

The sympathy factor no doubt helped Mann and other candidates of his group. But one major factor responsible for their victory was terror and rigging. Governor Ray's instruction to the security forces was not to interfere during the election campaign and on the polling day itself. His game was to help Mann and Bimal Khalsa to win so that the Mann group could help the Congress-I to win about eight seats by dividing the Akali votes. Known terrorists and killers had, therefore, full freedom and they used it to their advantage. But Ray's strategy boomeranged. The Mann group "won" nine seats including the Independents supported by it, the AISSF and the Damdami Taksal. They helped the Bahujan Samaj Party to win one seat.

More than the Mann group, it is the "boys" who emerged stronger out of the elections.

Many hoped that after his release Mann would act to help in restoring peace in Punjab. There is no sign of these hopes being fulfilled.

Let us examine the experience so far.

No doubt, Mann has said more than once that he wants a solution of the Punjab problem within the framework of the Indian Constitution. He has not demanded or supported the demand for Khalistan.

At the same time, he has not opposed this demand either. He is neither for nor against it. He has been emphasising his total loyalty to Bhindranwale's philosophy. He has firmly stuck to the demand for a state/region which would be ruled by Sikhs, that is, for a Khalistan within India, which would in fact be ruled not by the common Sikh masses but by the Sikh landlords and other vested interests. In any case, the demand for acceptance of the Anandpur Sahib resolution or for a "self-determined political status for Sikhs" is not a demand within the basic framework of the Indian Constitution.

Mann has not even once condemned the terrorists in Punjab. On the other hand, he has been providing alibis for them.

At first he alleged that all the killings, kidnappings, etc. were being done by the RAW and such other agencies of the Government of India. When this theory became patently untenable, the killings were then ascribed to Black Cats. This theory was also not convincing because the victims have been mostly men of the security forces, families of special police officers, etc. Others killed include hawkers who are declared as the targets of the "militants". It then began to be said that the killings were being done by groups of the Congress-I. This did not explain the killings of Congressmen. There was also the fact that in many cases known and established terrorist groups were taking responsibility for the killings.

Whenever an innocent person is killed, the killers are anyone but the terrorists. When a killer gets killed by police, he becomes a "martyr".

In the name of punishing those who committed excesses, dismissal/prosecution/removal of even such officers has been demanded who have been fighting honestly and against whom there are no complaints of harassing innocent persons.

Mann has not only been threatening "Nuremberg type" trials of police officers but has also started warning the Chiefs of the Army, Navy and Air Force.

He has been demanding wholesale releases which would also set free hardened killers.

His authorised spokesman has demanded that changes in the administration must be effected in consultation with them. Obviously they want their men in key positions. Mann has not taken the trouble of trying to know the views of the common man and even of the other political parties.

All in all, speaking objectively, Mann has only brought grist to the mill of the terrorists—whatever the subjective considerations and whatever the pressures.

Some still hope that Mann will take a turn. Even such persons have begun to say: "The day he decides to confront the terrorists, he may be no more."

According to a very recent statement made by Mann, the Prime Minister has agreed with him that the Punjab problem is the result of Indira Gandhi's policy of genocide of Sikhs and destruction of their gurdwaras. He said that this was a big "ideological break-through".

The governments headed by Indira Gandhi and Rajiv Gandhi have to bear a good deal of responsibility for the tragedy of Punjab. The above charge of genocide, however, will not have many takers. Moreover, anyone who fails to see the hand of imperialism and Pakistan behind terrorism in Punjab, the responsibility of Bhindranwale, the Akali Party and even some others who, like the Congress-I and the Akali leaders wanted to play the Bhindranwale card for short-term political gains, cannot find a correct way to peace in Punjab. Nor can those who think that terrorism in Punjab began only after Operation Blue Star. It began as early as 1978. Bhindranwale had become the only government by 1983.

Operation Bluestar and the anti-Sikh riots of November 1984 broadened the social base of the terrorists and made the Punjab problem more complicated. But those who do not see all the factors that resulted in the rise of terrorism in Punjab cannot help restore peace.

The solution of the Punjab problem cannot be found unless all the factors are taken into consideration.

Mann's ideology and analysis do not give much hope that he can play a positive role. We will be happy if we are proved wrong, if he changes and does help to restore peace in Punjab. It is necessary, however, to warn that it will indeed be very tragic not only for Punjab but for the entire country if the Prime Minister accepts the present ideology, philosophy and analysis play a positive role. We will be happy if we are proved wrong, if he changes and does help to restore peace in Punjab. It is necessary, however, to warn that it will indeed be very tragic not only for Punjab but for the entire country if the Prime Minister accepts the present ideology, philosophy and analysis of Mann and if his government frames its Punjab policy on this basis. The only correct policy today is a combination of correct political initiative, a no-holds-barred fight against the terrorists while avoiding excesses and mass mobilisation plus the groundwork for giving greater autonomy to all states including Punjab and for resolving the territorial and river water disputes.

These are not preconditions for the holding of elections to the Punjab assembly. Elections to the Punjab assembly should be held only when free and fair elections are really possible. Those who are keen on early elections should advise the "boys" to hand over all their arms. *(February 17, 1990)*

## 9. Tohra's Bid to Emerge as Akali Supremo

There have been interesting but important developments in Akali politics in Punjab. Efforts to unite Akali factions under one or the other leader having failed, Jathedar Gurcharan Singh Tohra hit upon a "new" strategy to get himself accepted as the leader.

He and the SGPC appointed Akal Takht Jathedar Manjit Singh gave a call for a three-day long "Khalsa March" starting from Wadali Guru on October 15 and terminating at Anandpur Sahib on October 17. The erstwhile village Wadali Guru (now a part of Amritsar Municipal Corporation) is the birth place of the Sixth Sikh Guru. The Khalsa Panth was founded at Anandpur Sahib by the Tenth Guru. It was stated that the Khalsa March was in honour of the 400th birth anniversary of the Sixth Guru and 300th anniversary of the Khalsa Panth, though neither of these anniversaries fell during the days of the march. Many were of the opinion that the march was to help establish Tohra's supremacy. The Chief Minister, Mr. Beant Singh, smelt politics and there were reports that the march might not be allowed. Assurances were forthcoming very promptly that the march was a purely religious affair. The government decided not to ban it. Before the march began, the Akali leaders declared that there would be no political slogans. Subsequently, however, leaders made political speeches though the themes of their speeches were dissimilar.

Nor is that all. At the concluding gathering, a resolution was adopted regarding the serious situation which had developed in Srinagar in connection with the Hazaratbal Dargah which enshrines a holy relic of the Prophet. The resolution did not decry the "militants" for misusing the mosque for their political ends. It did not decry the sacrilege which was committed by them by taking weapons into a place of worship. It did not ask them to vacate the mosque and surrender. All this was in line with the Akali thesis that religion and politics cannot be separated . By urging the Government to lift the siege, the resolution was meant to extend backing to the terrorists of Kashmir, just as Akali leaders had helped the Khalistani terrorists. It is to be regretted that the moderate Akali leaders too became a party to the resolution.

That apart, Tohra had once again misused religion and had dragged the Akal Takht Jathedar into his politics. Jasbir Singh Rode, backed by the Damdami Taksal which was once headed by Bhindranwale, and by Simranjit Singh Mann who continues to openly demand Sikh homeland or Khalistan, has re-emerged on the scene and has claimed that he is the real Akal Takht Jathedar.

For quite sometime now, Tohra has been having a running battle with the Damdami Taksal. Outwardly, the fight is about the Rahat Maryada to be followed in the Golden Temple. In fact, it is for control over the SGPC.

On October 14, speaking to press persons at Amritsar, Tohra made a frontal attack on the Damdami Taksal, holding it responsible for Operation Blue Star. He enumerated a number of facts to substantiate his charge, but all of them represented only a partial truth. Tohra conveniently "forgot" to mention his own responsibility. After all, he had been calling upon Sikh youth to get motorcycles and automatic weapons. It was Tohra who had forced the then Akal Takht Jathedar to let Bhindranwale and his armed men occupy the Akal Takht and to convert the Golden Temple into an armed fortress and a training camp for terrorists. Nor is that all. Tohra even "forgot" the role of the Congress, whose government had allowed Bhindranwale to smuggle weapons into the Golden Temple. Tohra invited sharp criticism from certain quarters and ridicule from some others. He made a half-hearted denial of what he had said but none were deceived. Incidentally, all this has vindicated the CPI position regarding Operation Blue Star. The CPI had regretted this most unfortunate event. It had held Bhindranwale, the Congress-I government and the Akalis responsible for the tragedy. The Congress-I was more responsible than the Akalis only in the sense that it was in power and had therefore greater responsibility to act in time which it did not, deliberately. Except for this, the Akalis were no less responsible.

The next step in Tohra's strategy is the march to Delhi starting on November 1, to protest against the sacrilege committed by the police, which entered the gurdwara in Gujarawal in Ludhiana district on September 15, and disrupted the Akhand Path of Guru Granth Sahib. It is said that the police had entered to nab some terrorists. There was, however, no justification for disrupting the Akhand Path. The CPI and some others too condemned the incident and demanded action against the guilty officials. Beant Singh was criticised by the CPI leader, Jagjit Singh Anand for not visiting the gurdwara and apologising. Later the Chief Minister did that and also expressed regrets. He promised that the guilty police officials would be punished.

The Director General of Police only transferred them. However, Tohra and the other Akali leaders are not satisfied. They want an "apology" from Beant Singh and dismissal of the police officials alleged to be responsible for the sacrilege. The planned march is in support of these demands. Not a few Akali critics have pointed out that Akalis did nothing when some bigger sacrileges took place just because no political capital could be made out of them, because those responsible were not policemen but connected with granthis themselves. In other words, behind the proposed march, politics is a bigger factor than a genuine religious grievance.

The All India Sikh Students Federation (Manjeet), which has declared itself a political party, has dissociated itself from the Tohra-led proposed march to Delhi as a protest against his attack on Damdami Taksal.

Beant Singh perhaps could have been more forthright in condemning the sacrilege in question and the guilty policemen could have been given greater punishment than mere transfers, which in the eyes of law are no punishment. Beant Singh, however, appears to have decided to take advantage of the weakness in the Akali game plan to foil the march. A large number of Akali activists including many leaders have been arrested. Beant Singh has openly declared that the march would not be allowed. This is bound to evoke criticism from various quarters, though the likelihood is that Beant Singh will get away with it.

It is interesting, though not surprising, that most of the Akali factions have decided to support the BJP during the coming mini-general elections. After all, the BJP goal of establishing a Hindu Rashtra in India helps the demand for a Sikh theocratic state in Punjab, just as it helps the terrorists of Kashmir. *(October 2, 1993)*

## 10. Buta Singh's Penance Sets the Clock Back

Much has been written about Mr. Buta Singh's appearance before the Akal Takht, the apology tendered by him for his role in what happened in the Golden Temple during the days when it was occupied by the terrorists and his acceptance of the punishment awarded to him. It has been rightly noted that this action of Mr. Buta Singh—nine years after the event—has only helped fundamentalism. It can strengthen only those who are against the separation of religion and politics.

Operation Blue Star in 1984 was a deplorable incident. The responsibility for it lay on three parties: Jarnail Singh Bhindranwale who converted this sacred place into the main training and operating centre of terrorists, the Congress rulers in New Delhi who allowed this to happen and the Akalis who neither took steps to stop the Golden Temple from being converted into an armed fortress nor asked the government to do so.

A survey done by some impartial organisations revealed that about 34 per cent of the Sikhs were of the view that at the time it took place Operation Blue Star could not have been avoided. The majority felt, however, that whatever the factors, Operation Blue Star should not have taken place. As far as the government is concerned, the responsibility fell on the then Prime Minister, Indira Gandhi, and not on Mr. Buta Singh. But if he felt that Operation Blue Star hurt his religious sentiment or went against his religious convictions, he could have resigned from the cabinet. He did not.

The Akali leaders wanted the Akal Takht to remain damaged for as long as possible and wanted it to be reconstructed in a manner and at a time that would give them maximum political mileage. Mr. Buta Singh took upon himself to get it reconstructed and got Nihang leader Baba Santa Singh to undertake the kar seva for this. With the active help of the government, the Akal Takht was reconstructed and even approved by the five jathedars. Later on, however, Mr. Gurcharan Singh Tohra, who was the President of the SGPC, had it pulled down on the grounds that it was not the real structure. The real reason was, of course, political. Mr. Buta Singh could not possibly be regretting his role in the reconstruction. Baba Santa Singh has not tendered an apology yet.

Before the reconstruction of the Akal Takht began, a Sarbat Khalsa (gathering of the entire Sikh community) was held in gurdwara Shaheedan to sanctify the plan. A historical Sikh tradition which had become outdated was revived. Mr. Buta Singh's idea of calling a Sarbat Khalsa was subsequently used by the terrorists. Such meetings were called in the Golden Temple by pro-terrorist organisations to appoint Akal Takht jathedars of their choice who could legally be appointed only by the SGPC. The establishment of Khalistan was adopted as its goal by a Sarbat Khalsa. It was thus made to appear as an objective to be achieved by the entire Sikh community, when, in reality, a majority of Sikhs did not support it.

The concept of hukumnama (edict) was also distorted when at some stage such authority was misappropriated by the priests in charge of the Akal Takht. The SGPC's jathedars were not averse to being used in factional squabbles between the Akalis. At one stage, the Akal Takht jathedar issued a hukumnama that all Akali factions must unite on the basis of a constitution decided by it. At least one Akali faction defied it.

It is time for religious leaders to review the utility of the Sarbat Khalsa and the concept of hukumnama. Priests in charge of the Akal Takht have had the authority to punish Sikhs violating the Sikh religious code. Maharaja Ranjit Singh was awarded such punishment. In due course, this power began to be misused for political and factional ends. For instance, at one stage Mr. Parkash Singh Badal was summoned to appear before the Akal Takht to answer charges of corruption at the instance of this rivals, Mr. Tohra and Mr. Talwandi. Punishments have been awarded for political acts and also to Sikh scholars for their research work at the instance of fundamentalists and even academic rivals.

But Buta Singh's appearance before the Akal Takht was clearly motivated by political considerations. His action suited the Akali leaders controlling the SGPC. It is time, therefore, to confine the functions and powers of Akal Takht jathedars to strictly religious matters. If this is to be achieved, the first step should be to depoliticalise the SGPC, and to ensure that it functions as a body to manage gurdwaras as places of worship. No political party must be allowed to have its office in a place of worship. *(April 18, 1994)*

## 11. Akal Takht and Akali Politics

Not many outside Punjab know fully the intricacies and oddities of Akali politics. They will find the present developments in Akali politics quite amusing or intriguing, or both. Nevertheless, the widespread debate which has started on some basic issues has the potential of giving a very healthy turn to Punjab politics, provided the vested interests do not succeed in aborting it midway, and provided it is taken to its logical conclusion.

Prof. Manjit Singh, acting Jathedar of Akal Takht (not recognised as such by Akali leader Simranjit Singh Mann) had given a call for a Khalsa march to culminate at Talwandi Sabo in Bhatinda district on April 13, i.e. on the birthday of the Khalsa. Repeatedly the Jathedar had declared that the project was entirely religious and no political speeches or slogan would be allowed at any stage. At Talwandi Sabo, however, one after the other almost all Akali leaders, barring Badal, got up on the stage and requested the acting Jathedar to use the authority of the Takht to bring about unity amongst Akali factions, which included open votaries of sovereign Khalistan on the one hand and also those who had always claimed that they stood for the unity and integrity of India. In between were others who wanted a theocratic Sikh state within India with a very weak Centre.

Prof. Manjit Singh allowed the political issue of Akali unity to be raised in violation of all that he himself had said about the function being entirely religious and notwithstanding what he had himself said only some days before the Khalsa march started.

He had made a categorical declaration that Panthic unity and Akali unity were two different things. He was quite right in that. Panth means the Sikh religious community. Akal Takht is sacred for all Sikhs and is held in high esteem even by non-Sikhs. All Akali factions put together are a communal-political party of only a section of the Sikhs. It represents the interests of Sikh landlords and rich peasants though, for selfish political ends and to have a bigger mass base, it has always sought to equate itself with the Panth and has exploited religion for its own ends by taking the position that for Sikhs politics and religion cannot be separated. The fact of their control of the SGPC, which has the duty of maintaining and managing various historical Sikh gurdwaras, including the Golden Temple, has helped Akali factions to do that quite successfully notwithstanding quite a sizeable opinion amongst Sikhs themselves against this.

The professor had also declared that he would not want to be involved in the factional squabbles of the Akalis.

Parkash Singh Badal, before submitting a signed blank paper to acting Jathedar, denounced the calls for unity as a conspiracy to isolate and downgrade him. He was not wrong in this.

During the heyday of terrorism, Akali leader Gurcharan Singh Tohra (who has also been for long years President of the SGPC of which the Akal Takht Jathedar is an employee), made speeches echoing Bhindranwale calling upon Sikh youths to buy motor cycles and AK-47 guns. With terrorism overcome even though not yet buried deep, Tohra is reported to have revived his old ambition of becoming Chief Minister of Punjab after the next elections. That can become possible only if he is the head of a united Akali Dal. Frustrated Akali leaders like Simranjit Singh Mann, Jagdev Singh Talwandi, Surjeet Singh Barnala and Amrinder Singh, notwithstanding their mutual sharp differences regarding the desirable goal of the Akali party and other vital matters, and also their differences with Tohra, have lined up behind Tohra's strategy and game of downgrading Badal as the first essential precondition for realising their own ambitions.

The hurdles in the way of Tohra and his strange bed-fellows realising their objective are many.

Firstly, when Prof. Manjit Singh summoned the chiefs of all Akali factions to appear before him, Parkash Singh Badal resigned the presidentship of his Akali Dal, appointed a Presidium to run the party and himself went underground. The Presidium in its turn suspended all political activities. Only Tohra and his known supporters have deserted the Badal Akali Dal. Realising that Akali unity without Badal would be meaningless, immense pressure is being put on him and the Presidium members. They are not sure that this pressure will succeed.

Secondly, every previous attempt to achieve Akali unity by orders issued by the Akal Takht Jathedar had failed miserably. One such attempt was made by Prof. Darshan Singh who even framed a constitution of the United Akali Dal he ordered into existence. This was in 1987. Prof. Darshan Singh has asked Prof. Manjit Singh to get that implemented instead of starting *de novo*! This is perhaps a way of telling the professor that he should not burn his fingers as Prof. Darshan Singh did.

Thirdly, there is the recent Supreme Court judgement holding that a party cannot be religious and political at the same time. Any "united" Akali Dal that may come into existence (even though temporarily) will run the risk of being deregistered as a political party by the Chief Election Commissioner of India. Prof. Manjeet Singh is therefore doing a good deal of tight-rope walking. The Akali leaders who have responded to his summons have been asked to do Sewa (cleaning utensils and shoes of the Sangat, etc.) and to come to agreement between themselves. It is now being said that the clergy will not issue any directive.

Fourthly, and above all, a lively debate has started on certain basic issues. Some of these are: (a) whether it is at all worthwhile to try for unity when political goals are very different; (b) whether Akalis and the Panth are synonymous; (c) whether the Akal Takht Jathedar can be equated with the institution of Akal Takht; (d) whether the Akal Takht Jathedar should intervene in the factional squabbles of Akalis, etc.

According to press reports, preparations are on to let loose a mass campaign denouncing Badal as a traitor to Sikh religion, if he does not fall in line. It is also being said that "no Sikh can survive in Akali politics by defying the Akal Takht". The protagonists of this view underestimate the lessons which even sections of the Akali following have learnt from the bitter experience of the recent past, e.g. Akal Takht Jathedars being used not only by the Akalis as a whole for their political ends, but even by one faction against another, by terrorists against Akalis, and by one terrorist group against another, and the fact of there having been rival Akal Takht Jathedars recognised as such by opposing Akali factions and terrorist groups.

Support on the other side is, however, swelling. For instance, a large number of lawyers have supported some of the correct positions taken by Badal. The editor of the Punjabi daily with largest circulation has also supported Badal, though he is also reported to be acting as a go-between. As already noted, there have been no defections from the Badal group. On the other hand, some papers reported on April 23 that many leaders and activists of the Mann Akali Dal of Bhatinda district had joined the Badal Akali Dal. Some renowned Sikh intellectuals have come out with the pithy formulation that "it is Shri Akal Takht and not an Akali Takht", which can be manipulated at will by the entrenched religious establishment in the SGPC (Jasbir Singh Ahluwalia).

There are, however, serious weaknesses in the situation.

First, Badal is not likely to come out for separation of religion and politics and that will help his opponents. Ahluwalia considers that the Akal Takht is "the symbol of the temporal authority vesting in the collectivity of the Khalsa Panth" and that "its proper domain is that of *universal* temporal concerns—social, cultural, political, economic—of the Sikh community as a whole . . . . ." The fact is overlooked that with the developments which have taken place even while continuing to have common (universal) religious interests and a common religious identity, Sikhs do not have today common economic or political interests, nor do they have a common political identity. For instance, what is common between the economic and political interests of Sikh landlords and landless Sikh agricultural labourers? Only by divorcing religion and politics and by barring the Sikh clergy from dabbling in politics of Akali or any other variety, can the sanctity of religious institutions be maintained. Nor is this all. Certain other issues need to be debated. For instance:

(a) Should the Sikh clergy have the right to excommunicate any Sikh from Sikh religion? It is this "right" which has been used in the past in the political and even factional struggles. My many Sikh friends who are well versed in Sikh history are of the view that this right was never conferred on the Sikh clergy either by the tenets of Sikhism or by any Sikh Guru.

(b) Should the Sikh clergy have the right to issue hukumnamas? Historically heads of Sikh Misals used to gather at Akal Takht to iron out their differences and then the common agreement was issued with the seal of the Akal Takht Jathedar as a hukumnama. Gradually the Sikh clergy began to be used to issue hukumnamas to suit some political force or the other. Even in its original form, the institution of hukumnama is very much out of date today, just as the institution of Sarbat Khalsa which originally was the gathering of the heads of Sikh Misals.

(c) Should the Sikh clergy have the right to impose "tankhah" (i.e. religious punishment) on Sikhs at least for religious misconduct? Views on this differ, and this writer is not competent to take a definite view in the matter. One thing is certain—the Sikh clergy should not have the right even to impose "sewa" (religious service) for any political reason or with any political objective. Real sewa can only be voluntary.

There is no real debate on these issues as yet.

The other weakness in the situation is Badal's own make-up. Once regarded as most liberal and least communal of all Akali leaders—had he played the role expected of him the history of Punjab from 1978 to 1992 would have been very different. Punjab might not have seen the bad days it has.

Even though not on speaking terms with Bhindranwale, Badal would not fight him. There were two reasons for this. One, Badal's lack of courage. Two, Badal too, like the Congress on the one hand and the Akalis on the other, wanted to use the Bhindranwale card.

Long ago, Tohra and Talwandi had submitted to the Akal Takht a chargesheet against Chief Minister Parkash Singh Badal who was summoned to give his explanation. Badal first said that he could be summoned as a Sikh but not as Chief Minister. He even quoted the Indian Constitution. He retreated pretty soon.

Once, Parkash Singh Majitha, a very firm supporter of Badal at that time, had taken the position that SGPC members should not contest assembly and parliamentary elections and MLAs and MPs should not be on the SGPC. Badal did not support even this position. Maybe Badal will show greater courage this time. If he does, all Punjabis will hail him, forgetting even the tons of grist he brought to the mill of the terrorists over a long period. The million dollar question is: Will he? *(April 30, 1994)*

## 12. S.S. Mann—From Terrorist Recruiter to Writ Petitioner

Simranjit Singh Mann, an Akali Dal (A) leader is a very colourful person. He is also a man of strong convictions and believer in the theory of "the ends justify the means".

I have never met him but I have had the opportunity to discuss him with one of his former colleagues when Mann was an officer of Punjab Police. This former colleague has been a staunch anti-terrorist and has made a good contribution in the fight against terrorism. His view about Mann was that he is an emotional man and could be brought round through discussions. Rightly or wrongly I could never share this view.

Once Shri Mann's name cropped up during some discussion between a very upright and anti-terrorist Deputy Commissioner and myself. He had on an earlier occasion worked in the same district in which Mann was SSP. We too could not agree.

When Mann was an SSP he had no hesitation in shooting some Nihangs with his own hand because they were suspected to have murdered some police constable. At a later stage Mann was to quote chapter and verse from the UNO Charter to denounce the Punjab police for "false encounters" even when the victims of these "false encounters" were killers of many innocent persons—men, women and children, each having to his "credit" a good number.

### SSP Mann

Mann the SSP recommended weapons for many "militants" and their friends posing as Nirankaris. There were widespread reports that he invited Bhindranwale more than once to lecture his force.

Once the late Sant Harchand Singh Longowal, replying to the charge of the government that the Akalis were helping terrorists, thundered: "The killers come out of police stations and go back there". I was one of those who ridiculed this contention. At a later stage I realised that perhaps what Sant Longowal had said had some basis. This was when it came to be known that some police officers had organised terrorist groups consisting of serving policemen. The needle of suspicion pointed to Mann, the SSP.

Prime Minister Indira Gandhi and Rajiv Gandhi had objectively helped the terrorist groups in Punjab by their policy of playing the Bhindranwale card against Akalis and Akalis had done the same.

Prime Minister V.P. Singh had the simplistic idea of solving the Punjab problem by managing to make Mann the Chief Minister of Punjab. Chief Minister-designate Mann fully exploited this position with the result that recruitment to the ranks of terrorists reached unprecedented heights.

Governor Ray had worked out a strategy to win elections to Lok Sabha for the Congress by making a deal with Mann. Just as Bhindranwale had outmanoeuvred the two Prime Ministers, Mann outmanoeuvred Ray. He not only won hands down himself but many of his candidates too became MPs. He emerged as a powerful Akali leader. However, he never entered the Lok Sabha because of his insistence to take along with him a very long kirpan, in violation of the rules.

Ever ready to quote the Indian Constitution whenever it suited him, Mann openly called upon the Sikhs to support Pakistan in case of an Indo-Pak war only because he wished to see India's dismemberment and the emergence of a sovereign Khalistan.

**Decline**

Thanks to the patriotism of the Sikhs, Mann's decline as a mass leader has been as rapid as was his rise.

Mann remains a Khalistani—at least he says so. It is an enigma how he and Barnala can get on well and comfortably in one party, even though ordained by the Akal Takht Jathedar.

Perhaps Mann fully realises his present position as well as his inability to get on with some other Akali leaders. Maybe it is because of this that he has now taken to filing Public Interest Litigation cases in Punjab and Haryana High Courts and even the Supreme Court. His Katia case in Punjab High Court got a good deal of publicity. His latest one is about the distribution of confiscated weapons by the Chief Minister of Punjab at throw-away prices.

In his Writ Petition Mann has named the beneficiaries and the throw-away prices at which they have been given the weapons. Names mentioned by him in his Writ Petition are on the basis of newspapers reports—mostly police officers and bureaucrats.

**New Profession**

Mann will be doing very useful service to the people if he makes filing of such petitions his main preoccupation not for getting political mileage out of it but for ensuring justice and just policies. Sh. K.P.S. Gill once suggested that Mann should rejoin the police. My suggestion is that he should bid good-bye to politics and take to such useful work as public interest litigation. Let me help him with his latest writ petition about confiscated weapons.

In reply to Starred Question 1312 which had been jointly given notice of by CPI MLAs Hardev Arshi and Vimla Dang, Sardar Beant Singh, Chief Minister Punjab, gave the following information during the Budget 1994 Session on 16 March, 1994:

"The Government of India redelegated powers to the State Government for allotment of confiscated weapons of non-prohibited bore with effect from 15th September, 1993. Since then, persons alloted such weapons were:

"(1) Sh. Kishore Patil—allotted .32 bore pistol for Rs. 900, (2) Smt. Gargi Devi .32 bore revolver for Rs. 1,000 and (3) Shri Ram Lal Rahi .32 bore revolver for Rs. 900".

(Late) Gargi Devi was the wife of (late) the then Governor Shri Surindar Nath.

Daily *Ajit* (Punjabi daily published from Jalandhar) reported the Chief Minister's reply on 17 March but also gave some additional information. It stated that Shri Kishore Y. Patil was the son-in-law of the Home Minister of India while Shri Ram Lal Rahi was Minister of State for Home Affairs in the Government of India.

The Chief Minister had said in the Assembly that the market price of the three weapons could not be stated as they were old. According to *Ajit,* each of these three weapons was worth more than Rs. 1 lakh.

It is hoped that this information will be found relevant to the Writ Petition pending in the High Court. *(December 18, 1994)*

# CHAPTER III

# The Ugly Face of Terrorism

## 1. The Grim Scenario

The last few weeks have seen a further worsening of the situation in Punjab.

Firstly, Sikh separatists and extremists have greatly stepped up their activities. Killings of Nirankaris and others have increased. Two new methods have been introduced. First, sending of parcel bombs. Second, killing of Hindu priests. The obvious aim of the first is to strike terror and a feeling of insecurity amongst the minorities in Punjab and those opposing the imperialist backed slogan of "Khalistan". The aim of the second is also clear. When cow heads, etc. were placed before Hindu temples, some Hindu communalists had retaliated by throwing cigarettes into some gurdwaras and by attacking some of them. Contrary to the expectations of the separatists, communal riots did not break out, despite the help rendered to them by Hindu communalists. Behind the murder of a Hindu priest the calculation seems to have been that at least this would provoke riots, especially if some Sikh priest was murdered in retaliation.

Along with these new methods, other efforts to widen the gulf between Hindus and Sikhs continue. For instance, huge printed posters issued by Sant Jarnail Singh Bhindranwale have appeared in many villages of the State. These reproduce the original Anandpur Sahib resolution which demands a virtual Khalistan within India with a very weak Centre and call upon Sikhs not to tolerate any compromise. These posters call upon Sikhs to arm themselves with such weapons as will not fail them when they are needed to be used.

Other exponents of the original Anandpur Sahib resolution etc. are circulating pamphlets and leaflets which raise new disruptive slogans. For instance, one such pamphlet says that "all the minority communities should demand separate electorate, which they were enjoying under British rule". It argues that "joint electorate alone is sufficient to finish the minorities politically . . . ." This pamphlet even says that the "British though foreigners were very good and just administrators." It declares that "Khalsa Raj" is the only target of the Khalsa Panth.

Cassettes of highly provocative speeches of Bhindranwale are being played to Sikh youth in many villages of the state.

The failure on the part of the Akali leadership and the Government of India to reach agreement and the continuation of the Akali Morcha provide a favourable atmosphere for Sikh extremists and separatists to carry on their nefarious activities.

The total failure of the government to get at the killer gangs, the murders of Nirankaris and others in broad daylight with the police looking on—all this has created fertile ground for Hindu communalists. In the past calls for Sikh hartals as well as for Hindu hartals evoked no response whatever. This time the call for hartal on June 27 given by some Hindu communal organisations did get substantial response in some towns. The BJP has called upon Hindus to be ready to defend themselves with arms, knowing full well that such a slogan can only help those working for Khalistan.

Secondly, what has happened in Jalandhar recently is more dangerous than what took place in Patiala. In Jalandhar there have been clashes, however small, between sections of Hindus and Sikhs. And that is the biggest danger signal so far. A brief review of what happened in Patiala and what has happened in Jalandhar recently will be worthwhile.

**First about Patiala**

On April 21, 1983, Ramnavami day, the Hindu Surakhsha Samiti took out a procession armed with trishuls and raising provocative slogans. The authorities allowed it. On April 30, an armed Sikh procession was taken out. The occasion was the birthday of Guru Tegh Bahadur, though it is not customary to take out processions on this day. The Akali leaders freely distributed swords to the processionists, many of whom had been brought from outside. Organised by the

Naujawan Khalsa Dal, this procession too raised provocative slogans. The authorities permitted this too.

It was in this background that the trouble in Patiala started over an objection raised by a Hindu leader to the use of a loudspeaker. Shops were set on fire. Curfew had to be imposed for many days.

Significantly, the same district authorities who had allowed the processions have been refusing permission for peace marches. On May 4, the Deputy Commissioner refused even to meet a deputation of Communist, trade union and other representative people of the city, who have been most active in Patiala in maintaining communal peace.

Events in Patiala drew national attention. And yet ordinary people in villages were saying: "The fight is not between Sikhs and Hindus, but between *Banias* and *Bhapas*."

Sikh traders in Patiala are mostly immigrants from Rawalpindi and other places in Pakistan and are called *Bhapas*. They have become prosperous in acute rivalry with traditional Hindu traders of the city, called *Banias*. They have no mutual interrelationships. It is not an accident that Patiala has thrown up the worst type of communal leaders like Shambhu Prashad (RSS-BJP) Sardara Singh Kohli (Akali) and Pawan Kumar (Congress-I, and president of Hindu Raksha Samiti).

The nature of relationship between Hindu and Sikh traders of Patiala is not typical of such towns of Punjab as Amritsar and Jalandhar. In these towns many Hindu and Sikh traders are interrelated. And yet in Jalandhar Hindu-Sikh clashes have taken place. There was a clash even between some Hindu and Sikh passengers at the railway station. Here is the sequence of events.

There is a 70-year or so old temple in Jalandhar called Sodhal Temple. In an adjoining room there has been a Granth Sahib since the very beginning. Mahant Gurmukh Dass managed these, and after his death Mahant Chanan Dass. At some stage a board of trustees was set up. Perhaps in the beginning it represented only the Chadha *biradari* (Hindu) and later on some other (Hindu) trustees were also added.

From 1953-54 or so, the price of land began to shoot up. It is said that the Mahant allowed people to construct shops provided they agreed to pay rent to him. It is reported that a dispute arose between the Mahant and the trustees. The Mahant called in some Nihangs to help him and this consequently took the shape of a dispute between the temple on the one hand and the gurdwara on the other.

There was prolonged litigation and a Letters Patent Appeal is said to be pending in the High Court even now.

Police has been posted in and around the area for the last three to four years.

Recently the Mahant died, reportedly in mysterious circumstances, but his body was allowed to be cremated without a post mortem.

By the morning of June 25, 1983, a Nishan Sahib 125 feet in height, had gone up near the mandir. It is said that it was put up with a rig brought by the Nihangs from Ludhiana and the job could not have been done in less than four hours. It is also contended that the police, who had been forewarned, had said that no such thing would be allowed. Police complicity is alleged by Hindu leaders and the trustees of the mandir. Communal tension began to build up.

In this background came the explosion of a parcel bomb in the office of the Urdu daily *Pratap*, resulting in the death of two persons. A Hindu priest was murdered and another seriously injured in Sultanpur Lodhi not far from Jalandhar.

Groups of Hindu youths marched in the city. It is said that they attacked a gurdwara and that a Nihang was beaten up.

The Punjab Hindu Sangathan called for a statewide bandh on June 27. The Akalis called for a procession in Jalandhar on the same day for protection of the gurdwaras. In the District Communal Peace and Harmony Committee, the Akalis agreed to drop the procession and have only a protest meeting in a gurdwara. The proposal was made by a CPI member.

On June 27 a truck of Sikhs was coming from outside. It was allowed to come via a particular route, though this route was known to be communally dangerous and other routes were available. A clash took place outside the Balmiki Gate. A large Hindu crowd gathered and was on the offensive. Lathi charge and teargas failed. The police force was small. Some responsible persons told me that the reinforcements reached after about $1^1/_2$ hours. Before that the police had opened fire, which led to the death of three Hindus.

On the same day, due to an accidental explosion in a bomb "factory", two Sikhs died on the spot and another was injured. This too happened in Jalandhar. According to latest police reports, the "factory" was being run by the extremists.

Much of Jalandhar has since been under curfew. As always, the common people are the worst sufferers. Non-VIP pass-holders are harassed by the police. When there is relaxation of curfew to enable people to make essential purchases, people have to pay fancy prices. Contradictory and confusing announcements are made by the authorities, adding to the difficulties of the people.

What do the Patiala and Jalandhar examples show? They show that disputes which normally should not result in clashes and riots can lead to them in the situation which prevails in Punjab today. Ordinary criminals too have stepped up their activities, adding to the insecurity. Some of these too are the handiwork of separatists and extremists.

Punjab can be saved if all healthy and patriotic forces do what the situation demands of them. There are many positive factors operating. Punjabis do not want a repetition of 1947. They do not want Hindu-Sikh unity to be disrupted. In many places, the bandh call for June 27 got no response from the Hindus. In some places like Rajpura, Sikh shopkeepers too observed hartal. Nor is this all.

When the situation was at its worst in Patiala, all the Hindus and Sikhs of Mohalla Angatpura held a joint meeting. They decided that (a) they would jointly defend themselves against mischief-makers of all hues; (b) not a paisa would be contributed either to Hindu Raksha Samiti or Naujawan Khalsa Dal; and (c) no volunteer of either of these organisations would be allowed to come into the mohalla.

This example was followed by many other mohallas and can be spread to the whole of Punjab.

This is what all the healthy forces must aim at. "Communal peace, come what may" must be the slogan. At the same time, people must be mobilised to tell all the bourgeois parties to place national interest above their narrow partisan, electoral and factional interests. All bourgeois national parties must be told to ask their state units to stop taking opposing stands on the territorial and water issues. They must ask their state bosses not to think of the interests of their states alone but of the interests of the country as a whole. The Akali leadership must be told that the interests of the Sikhs and even of Punjab cannot be isolated from the interests of the country as a whole.

They need also to be told that India is and has to remain secular, fully safeguarding the interests of all religious minorities—be they Sikhs in India or Hindus and Nirankaris in Punjab. Misuse of places of worship is wrong and in the present times launching of morchas for economic and political demands from religious places of one community does more harm than good.

The Government of India must be told to give up the policy of delay and do everything possible to reach a joint settlement with the Akalis so that extremists can be isolated and fought effectively. The government must ensure the safety of all and that will be the biggest blow to Hindu communalism.

The moderates among the Akali leaders like Parkash Singh Badal must be asked to realise that their policy of using extremists to put pressure on the government and their argument that they will fight extremism after they have got something worthwhile from the government is proving counter-productive. They must fight the extremists here and now, without any conditons.

Last but not least, politicians who do not mind promoting riots in their own selfish interests must be exposed and isolated. Behind the present Hindu-Muslim tension leading to riots in Malerkotla are said to be one Akali politician and one Congress-I politician. Both happen to be Muslims, and a divorced husband and wife. The hands of a Hindu and a Muslim, old rivals, are also reported to be behind the recent riots in Malerkotla, which remained completely free from riots even in 1947. Two officers—since transferred—made their own "contribution" towards these riots. *(July, 1983)*

## 2. Healing Punjab's Wounds

How have the people in Amritsar reacted to the recent developments of June 1984—developments which have had repercussions not only in India but in many parts of the world too? What is the situation now? And what tasks face the Left, democratic and patriotic forces?

Comprehensive answers to these questions will be possible only some time after communications, etc., have been restored. Even then, it is necessary to try to answer these questions to whatever extent is possible just now.

After the premises in which the Golden Temple is situated had been surrounded by the Army units deputed for the purpose, Jarnail Singh Bhindranwale, called upon his killer gangs to implement his standing instructions which were known to have been to indulge in mass massacre of Hindus. Some newspapers reported this directive of his.

It is already known that attempts to implement this directive were made at a number of places. In Chheharta (Amritsar) some members of the killer gangs entered the area about 5.30 p.m. This became known to many including the police. And yet they were able to shoot down and murder as many as seven persons some hours after their entry.

On June 4 morning, two banks, a number of factories and about 32 shops were burnt down by a crowd of 50 to 150. It had started from a gurdwara. What was intended to be done was proclaimed from a loudspeaker. Here too the police did hardly anything to prevent the mischief.

Two young girls belonging to the same family in village Muradpur near Tarn Taran were murdered during June 3-4 night. Their mother and brothers were injured.

A few other reports of this type are already there. But it is already clear that by and large Bhindranwale's followers did not succeed in putting into practice the instructions given to them. Nor is this all.

As many as nine persons have been killed by extremists in the Chheharta area of Amritsar in three operations. In no part of Chheharta has there been any act or any attempt at any act that may smell of "retaliation" or "revenge".

In Kittias all the shops that were burnt down belonged to Hindus. If the building belonged to a Sikh, things were taken out and burnt. In other cases the buildings themselves were set on fire. In quite a few cases neighbouring Sikhs saved as many things of their Hindu brothers as they could. One of the shops burnt down completely belonged to Boota Ram. (He had been a special target of the extremists. On an earlier occasion an attempt was made to set fire to his shop. An attempt on his life had also been made. On June 3, 1984, evening his son was fired upon but had a lucky escape.) Two shops of a nephew of Boota Ram were also burnt. The shop of his two brothers was also set on fire. Some of those who had done this, had looted some of the goods from this shop and were taking them to their houses. Some elderly Sikhs met them on the way. They asked them how they got the goods they had. When they learnt the truth, they took them to task and made them deposit all the goods in a gurdwara. They were later returned to the owner.

As already stated, the police were not to be seen. Curfew had already been imposed. To scare away those who were indulging in arson, some persons having licensed arms fired shots from their houses. They were Sikhs.

There is no doubt that as days pass we will know not only about what extremists may have done but also and much more about the good sense of the common people—Hindus as well as Sikhs.

Left with no other choice, the Army men entered the premises of the Golden Temple on June 5. They had no idea about the type of the situation they were going to face, and the first to enter suffered heavy casualties. It does much credit to the Army that no damage at all has been done to the Golden Temple proper. A part of the Akal Takht no doubt has been damaged, but responsibility for that must be borne by Bhindranwale. Considerable damage has been done in some of the adjoining shopping and residential centres.

While Punjab was cut off from the rest of India, Amritsar was cut off completely for a number of days. Telephone services have been restored only two days ago. For about a week, there was no relaxation at all in the curfew. Thanks to false and exaggerated reports given by Pakistan Radio and TV, many false rumours were afloat. One such report repeated by Pakistan Radio and TV more than once was that a Communist leader (no name was given) of Amritsar had been shot dead. Pakistan mass media did all it could to widen the gulf between Hindus and Sikhs, though this was not done in a very crude manner. The extremists were invariably referred to as "Sikhs".

The unscrupulous amongst the traders minted a lot of money. Sugar was sold in many areas at Rs 8 per kilo. So also milk. And these are not the only examples.

Attempts were made to collect crowds of Sikhs to send them to the Golden Temple to fight/protest against the Army which was alleged to have attacked the Sikh religion itself by entering the Golden Temple. Efforts were also made to spread the false rumour that the Golden Temple had been badly damaged

These attempts did succeed in a number of places, but generally the crowds that marched were small. In several other places, the attempts failed altogether. There have been instances in which the crowds went back after they were satisfied by the Army authorities that no damage whatsoever had been done to the Golden Temple. At least in one case, two representatives of those assembled were flown over the Golden Temple in a helicopter. They then went back to the crowd and reported the truth. The crowd dispersed.

Reports already coming in show that invariably Mazhabi Sikhs (agricultural labourers) as a whole refused to join these crowds or to listen to the extremists and their supporters. There are already confirmed reports from some villages of the extremists or their hot-headed supporters saying "Not only Hindus but Mazhabi Sikhs too must be killed." The latter as a section/class were ready for the confrontation, if it came to that. Fortunately, there is no report (so far at least) of any such confrontation having actually taken place.

The writer of this article happened to be staying with a friend in the interior of Amritsar city, when for more than a week curfew was imposed with no relaxation.

This friend had in his house a teenager boy to help in household chores. After the TV had announed the death of Bhindranwale, the helper was asked by the master of the house: "Do you still insist on returning to your family in UP?" He replied: "No, now Bhindranwale is dead." I learnt that he had been terribly afraid that he might be killed and therefore had wanted to go back to his family?

We were watching on Doordarshan Gurbani being recited in the Golden Temple (after the Operation). My friend's son, 14-15 years old, asked: "Why have these people not been killed?" His father said: "They are not extremists. They are Sikh priests." The boy replied: "I know all Sikhs are not extremists. But these have *peela datkas* (yellow cloth over the head)." He, of course, did not consider every Sikh to be an extremist, but he had come to regard every Sikh with yellow headgear as an extremist.

In Chheharta, two or three days after the Operation was over, one Sikh said to another: "Thank God, Bhindranwale is no more." The other Sikh angrily shot back: "You are saying this even though you are a Sikh!" The first said: "In my opinion Bhindranwale was not a genuine Sikh, much less a sant".

These instances to a considerable extent reflect the reality.

A large majority of the Sikhs are bitter and angry. In the villages not a few go to the extent of arguing that the propaganda being done by television about the Golden Temple having been turned into an arsenal is all false. Some seek to justify the storing of arms in this holiest of the holy shrines. At the same time, there is the other opinion too. In a village, one elderly Sikh was heard telling a group of about 50 Sikhs: "We are sorry and pained at the entry of the Army in Darbar Sahib. But why did the Akali leaders allow Bhindranwale to convert Darbar Sahib into a cantonment? And if Bhindranwale had been really sincere about the sacredness of the Golden Temple, why did he not go out with his armed men to fight the Army outside its premises?"

Activists of the All-India Sikh Students Federation have been heard saying: "We will show them when the curfew is not there and when the Army has been called back". They are propagating the myth that Bhindranwale is not dead and will reappear at some appropriate time.

Some hot-headed Hindu young men bitten by the bug of communalism have been heard taunting Sikhs: "What has happened so far is nothing. A real good lesson will be taught in the days to come". Of course, such elements are not many, and they are often made to shut up by other Hindus.

Clearly, Punjab is not yet out of the woods. For all patriotic forces there are immediate jobs to be done and there are long-term tasks:

(a) All-out efforts must be made to maintain Hindu-Sikh unity. Communalism of either hue must be given no quarter. The gulf created between Hindus and Sikhs must be bridged.

(b) Such innocent persons as have suffered heavily must be rehabilitated.

(c) As soon as possible, new initiatives must be taken to settle what is known as the Punjab problem, that is the dispute about river waters, Chandigarh etc.

For a long time to come, an extensive as well as intensive political and ideological struggle will have to be waged not only against imperialist-backed separatism but also against Sikh as well as Hindu communalism.

As far as the Sikhs are concerned, a massive campaign will have to be run to expose and repudiate many wrong theses that have been widely progagated from various gurdwaras, including the Golden Temple. For instance that: (a) Sikhs in India are slaves/second-class citizens and are discriminated against. (b) Sikh religion and Sikhs can prosper only if Sikhs have a homeland of their own. (c) Sikhs are a separate nation. (d) The Akali Party is the sole representative of the Sikhs. (e) For Sikhs, religion and politics must go together. (f) Sikhs must have a separate and independent political identity of their own. (g) The Constitution of India lays down that Sikhs are a part of Hindu religion and thus denies the fact that Sikhism is a separate religion.

While wrong and false propaganda must be exposed, this must be done in a convincing manner. Steps must also be taken to remove genuine apprehensions, doubts and complaints.

Strong public opinion in general and Sikh public opinion in particular has to be created that no arms must be allowed inside places of religious worship. Steps have to be discussed to ensure that what happened in and from the Golden Temple during the recent past does not happen again, either there or at any other place of worship.

In the field of administration, appropriate lessons must be drawn from the now freely admitted facts, for example, colossal failure of intelligence and almost complete paralysis of the administration in Punjab. There is need for a thorough overhaul of the administration in the border state, especially of the police administration.

If the above tasks are to be performed successfully, many lessons from the past are to be drawn.

First and foremost, the Congress-I leadership as well as the moderates among the Akali leaders must learn never to encourage, shelter or support separatist extremists for narrow party or factional considerations.

Second, the Congress-I leadership must understand that most of the Congress-I activists and even leaders of today have no deep commitment to secularism. At least in Punjab, at the time of any crisis they become only Hindus or only Sikhs. It would be no exaggeration to say that in some places at least Hindu Congressmen played a worse role than the BJP, while many Sikh Congressmen were no better than the Akalis.

It needs also to be pointed out that many Congress leaders just disappeared from the scene to avoid risk to their own lives. They have not yet re-emerged from their places of safety in Delhi or elsewhere.

Third, all bourgeois national parties must learn to place national integration above their electoral interests and calculations.

As far as the Left is concerned, it did whatever it could according to its capacity. At the same time, certain weakness need to be noted. Perhaps the Left could and should have launched ideological and political propaganda on a bigger scale than it did. It should have done much more than it did to mobilise Sikh public opinion in particular. in and outside Punjab.

It needs also to be examined if all segments of the Left were completely free from electoral considerations.

It needs to be examined if the Left was fully ready to physically face the type of the situation that developed in Punjab.

Whatever the weaknesses, the Left can be proud of the role it has played so far. In Amritsar, for instance, even the class enemies of the working class concede that Communists alone stood up to the extremists and refused to quit the field. The CPI is the main Left force in Amritsar. The CPI (M) acted jointly with it.

Last but not least, Doordarshan and AIR Jalandhar, have been doing a good job for communal peace and harmony and they deserve to be praised on that account. But they have as yet hardly run an ideological and political campaign of the type indicated above. And that is needed not only in Punjab. *(June 14, 1984)*

## 3. Why Amritsar and Gurdaspur Only

Often the question is asked as to why the extremist-terrorists have been able to develop a mass base in Amritsar and Gurdaspur districts and not in the rest of Punjab, even though they have the capacity to strike anywhere in the state. Some imagine that these two districts must be economically the most backward. This is not at all correct. Economically these are not the most backward districts. Amritsar, in fact, is one of the advanced districts of the state. What then is the real reason?

It is now common knowledge that extremist-terrorists are aided and abetted by foreign imperialism and the aid is given mainly through the puppet rulers of Pakistan. The aid, including training and sophisticated weapons, can be given easily and effectively only if those sought to be helped are strong near the Indo-Pak border. For obvious reasons, therefore, extremist-terrorists would concentrate on border districts.

The extremist-terrorists of Punjab have been acting under the banner of "Khalistan", i.e., a theocratic Sikh state. To justify this, they falsely characterise India as a Hindu state in which Sikhs are second class citizens. They characterise Hindus as enemies and grossly misuse and exploit Sikh religion to develop a mass base. Therefore, out of the three border districts of Punjab, they would select Amritsar and Gurdaspur because their border areas have an overwhelmingly Sikh majority, unlike Ferozepur district whose border areas have a Hindu majority.

The Pakistani rulers have their own objectives too. A serious study of recent writings in Pakistan regarding this matter makes one thing clear. They know that "Khalistan" is not a realisable slogan. Some sections in the ruling circles are even opposed to it for reasons of their own. A campaign is on to inculcate among the people of Pakistan hatred not only against India and Hindus but more so against the Sikhs. Why then do they pretend to support the slogan of "Khalistan"? And why have they been encouraging the belief that at the decisive moment Pakistan will intervene in a big and even military way to help those fighting for the establishment of "Khalistan"? The reasons are not far to seek. At the crucial time they would want to occupy at least parts of Amritsar and Gurdaspur districts, so as to cut off Kashmir from India and grab it. And if they can also capture Amritsar and Gurdaspur districts, nothing like it. After all, in 1947 the Muslim League leadership was confident that these two districts would go to Pakistan. The fact that they remained in India was considered a victory for anti-Pakistani forces. That these are the Pakistani calculations is amply proved by a Pakistani book in Urdu "Amritsar Was Burning—1947", which this writer recently reviewed. This is also proved by the articles written by Rajinder Sareen in *The Tribune* about his reading of the Pakistani scene after a recent tour of that country. It is, therefore, in the Pakistani rulers' interest that extremists-terrorists should concentrate in these two districts and especially in areas bordering Pakistan. And those who pay the piper call the tune.

The existence of large-scale smuggling across the border, the large number of people involved in it in various capacities, the close terrorist-smuggler nexus, thc political clout which the smugglers enjoy with the Akali as well as the Congress (I) leaders—all this too has helped the terrorists to become strong in the border areas of these two districts.

There is another important factor too. The hold of religion on the land-owning Sikh peasantry of Amritsar district has always been great. For instance, smoking by Sikhs has been a common phenomenon in some districts of Punjab, especially the Malwa region, since long, even though smoking is strictly prohibited by Sikh religion. In Amritsar, generally speaking, this taboo has always been strictly observed. One reason for the greater hold of religion in Amritsar district is perhaps the fact that the most sacred shrine of the Sikhs, the Golden Temple, is located in Amritsar. Many of the historic gurdwaras are also in this district. Amritsar is considered a holy city by the Sikhs. The institution of kar sewa has developed most in Amritsar. Originally it developed in relation to the Golden Temple—mainly in the form of cleaning the Sarovar (holy tank) by voluntary labour. Baba Jeewan Singh and Baba Kharak Singh developed it and used it for constructing gurdwaras, roads, colleges, deras etc. There are others who have used this institution for constructing deras-cum-gurdwaras and educational institutions.

All these Sants are not necessarily non-political, religious-minded and interested in selfless service. They have their political sympathies. And many of them have had a soft corner and sympathy for the late Bhindranwale and his extremist followers.

All the five Sants who took over kar sewa work for reconstructing the demolished Akal Takht from the SGPC, courtesy Jathedar Tohra, belong to Amritsar district.

It is perhaps not an accident that a very large number of deras, gurdwaras, dera-cum-gurdwaras have come up in parts of Amritsar district through and even without kar sewa. Many of these are without any doubt being used as hideouts by the terrorists. In some cases, kar sewa vehicles have been used to remove injured terrorists and weapons from one place to another. It is not easy for the paramilitary forces and the police to search these because that would be exploited as an attack on religion. Actually, the extremist-terrorists are exploiting the religious sentiments of the peasantry to the maximum for their own nefarious ends and some of the so-called Sants, dera heads and gurdwara heads are helping them.

The kar sewa phenomenon has developed a lot and has a widespread network in Amritsar district. Sooner or later the issue has to be faced and tackled with a correct approach, difficult though it may be.

Another interesting fact needs to be taken note of. The Tarn Taran sub-division of Amritsar district is the strongest base of the terrorists. They have been calling it their "liberated area". This sub-division has only one government college while it has three colleges controlled by kar sewa Sants. These are situated at Sarhali (Guru Gobind Singh Khalsa College), Khadoor Sahib (Guru Anand Dev Khalsa College) and Baba Budha College Bir Sahib—a part of a big gurdwara complex near Jhabhal. A very reliable source told this writer in these areas very recently some facts about one of these three colleges. According to this source, the college had only two Hindu lecturers. Their services have now been dispensed with. In almost every period in every class in the college the first five minutes are devoted to talks aimed at motivating the young Sikh students to become supporters of extremists. They are told that Sikhs are slaves in India, the Sikh "nation" is in danger and Sikhs should be ready to make every possible sacrifice to win their goal. The position in other colleges may not be much different. Incidentally, all these colleges are recognised and aided by the government to the extent of 95 per cent of the deficit. The Akali government cannot be unaware of the goings-on in these colleges.

All that has been said above is not to deny the existence of such other factors as unemployment etc. which too have been fully utilised by the extremists. But these prevail throughout the state. It also needs to be noted that even in these border areas the extremists have not been able to develop a mass base amongst landless Sikh agricultural labourers, who are much poorer. Most of them are Mazhabis—one of the Scheduled Castes amongst the Sikhs. Sometimes they openly oppose the extremists, and sometimes they maintain a discreet silence—depending upon the concrete situation. But they are not with the extremists and the separatists.

The above observations are not the result of deep and thoroughgoing research. They are the result of observation and discussions held with various cross-sections of the people in the course of practical work. It is, however, hoped that these observations will be of some use to research scholars and social scientists interested in the subject.

*(October 4, 1986)*

## 4. Terrorists Down But Not Out

A statement issued by the five-member "Panthic Committee" on December 17 this year is surprising. Through this statement, "militants" have been called upon not to kill women, children and innocent men. According to press reports, "they were also asked not to involve themselves in private feuds". Not only that, the statement wanted all Sikhs—including Congressmen, Communists and Naxalites—to be treated as Sikhs. "Whatever their political ideologies, they are all Sikhs and we as Sikhs are up in arms against the government which we believe is bent upon eliminating the community", the statement of the Panthic Committee said.

This statement is significant because it is clearly the result of realisation that the terrorists have begun to lose mass support which they had succeeded in building up in some areas. This became clear the very next day when Gurbachan Singh Manochahal, a leading member of the "Panthic Committee", issued another statement, in which he put forward the proposition that 90 per cent of the informers were Sikhs—the usual pretext to kill such Sikhs who openly oppose separatism or have become wiser and have stopped supporting the terrorists. Even otherwise, the statement of December 17 cannot be taken seriously.

A good section of the terrorists have become degenerate to the extent of being ready to be hired to kill anyone at anyone's bidding for a price. And they are not going to stop this on their own. Notwithstanding the perceptible improvement in the situation, Punjab is not yet out of the woods. After a comparative lull for a few weeks, terrorists have again gone on a killing spree. Three senior and brave police officials—an SSP, an SP and a DSP—have been among the victims.

Some other facts too need to be noted. Both the above mentioned statements were issued from the Akal Takht. That shows the complete control which the terrorists exercise over the Golden Temple. The number of threatening letters coming out of the Golden Temple complex demanding huge amounts of money is perhaps not as big as it used to be. It is however significant that for the first time such letters have started using the official letterheads of Sri Darbar Sahib. This writer has before him one such letter dated December 3, 1987, asking a Sikh landowner to report and hand over Rs. 50,000 on December 12, 1987, failing which the whole family would be liquidated.

Forcible collections are also being made from teachers of a number of schools in parts of Amritsar and Gurdaspur districts. For obvious reasons, this is not being reported in the press. It is not necessary to give more instances to make the point that notwithstanding the improvement that has taken place in the Punjab situation, the fight at all levels has to continue. Some had entertained the hope that Mr. Parkash Singh Badal after his release would turn a new leaf, would take a stand against the terrorists and would help bring back normalcy to Punjab. Mr. Badal has belied these hopes. At his first press conference held on December 12, 1987 Mr. Badal made five demands. All people of reason would fully support the demand for the punishment of those guilty of the November 1984 riots. There has been a widespread demand for the release of the innocent among the Jodhpur detenus. But the demand made by Mr. Badal for general amnesty cannot even be considered when the killings as well as the demand for Khalistan continue.

Mr. Badal demanded the "stoppage of fake encounters" and "unprecedented repression" and the repeal of "black laws". However, he would not say a word against the killing of innocent people by the terrorists nor against the gross misuse of the Golden Temple by the "Panthic Committee" and other terrorist organisations. He replied to such questions by saying that he was for the "unity of Sikhs". When asked about the prospect of unity between the UAD and the Barnala faction of the Akali Dal, he said he always stood for unity but hastened to refer to "basic differences" such as the "attack" on the Golden Temple during the Barnala government's tenure. He did not speak of any differences, much less basic ones with the "Panthic Committee" or the militants.

While Mr. Badal must have disappointed many, Mr. Barnala has also disillusioned many. His hope of being called upon to form a government after the first six months of President's rule not having been fulfilled, he has been speaking the language of the "hawks".

No Akali leader has condemned the murder of the SSP and the SP of Patiala. Belatedly, Mr. Barnala characterised these as "unfortunate" but held the repressive policies of the government responsible for these killings. This provides an alibi for the killers.

The tragedy of Akali politics lies in the fact that even the moderate leaders are not prepared to take a forthright stand against separatism and terrorism as a matter of principle. Nor have they learnt the lesson that appeasing the extremists does not help them. There is little hope just now of any Akali faction really trying to isolate the extremists.

The mass contact campaign of the Congress has done some good but it has suffered from serious limitations. Excessive security arrangements have prevented real contact in many cases. While during the 1985 election campaign not a word critical of the Akali Party was uttered by Rajiv Gandhi, in the present mass contact campaign criticism of the Akali Party has been one of the main themes. The impression has gone round that the campaign is in fact intended to serve as preparation for elections.

The Left in Punjab has to continue to shoulder the main responsibility for political campaigning at the grass-roots level. Apart from its own independent campaign, it must continue its efforts to unite all patriotic forces.

There are reports that the Government of India will try for a package deal with some Akali faction, and failing that, it is likely to go in for elections. It is necessary to warn against any compromise of principles which will prove counter-productive in the long run. All emphasis for the time being must be on carrying on the fight against the terrorists. At the same time all excesses and harassment of innocent people by the police and the security forces must stop.

Certain political initiatives must also be taken immediately. For instance, the innocent amongst the Jodhpur detenus must be released forthwith. Those who helped organise the November riots must be prosecuted.

*(December 12, 1987)*

## 5. Terrorism Thriving on Wrong Policies

Some new features of the situation in Punjab following stepped-up killings by the terrorists from the start of the new year need to be noted.

Some Sikh families from terrorist-ridden areas of Amritsar district have shifted to Amritsar city and some are thinking of even migrating to UP. The number of instances of this type may not be very large as yet, but they are an indication of large-scale extortion of money by extremists from people, irrespective of their religious community, under threat of liquidation. Even those officials or non-officials who had helped the terrorists in the past are not being spared.

Kot Khalsa, an erstwhile village and a part of Amritsar Municipal Corporation for more than 12 years, saw its first killing by terrorists on February 16, 1988. A young man of 22, belonging to a Congress-I family and to the minority community was shot dead at 6.30 p.m. at his shop. The two terrorists who had come on a scooter went away leisurely.

With the exception of Amrinder Singh, more and more leaders of the "Unified Akali Dal" (UAD), following the example of Parkash Singh Badal, are making speeches which only help and strengthen the terrorists. Some are even outdoing Badal.

According to reports in the press, "pro-Bhindranwale and pro-AISSF slogans were frequently raised" at the UAD rally in Sangrur on February 1, 1988. And "some of the speakers asked party leaders to join hands with the militants."

On the same day (February 1), General Secretary of the Unified Akali Dal Ranjit Singh Brahmpura, "appealed to his party workers to appreciate the services and sacrifices being rendered by the militants." Brahmpura drew parallels between the militants and his party workers. "Only the approach is different," he pointed out. He was speaking at Amritsar.

While talking to pressmen at Jalandhar on February 17, Kuldip Singh Wadala, a Senior UAD leader, warned the government that if it failed to solve the Punjab problem peacefully, UAD "would be forced to side with the militant organisations", and it might even "be forced to support the demand of Khalistan."

Besides the UAD, others too have once again begun speaking this kind of language.

The Punjab Sikh Lawyers' Council has in a resolution declared "full autonomy with right of self-determination" as the goal of the Sikh Panth. It has appealed to Sikhs living abroad "to concentrate on protection and promotion of human rights of Sikhs and other oppressed nations in India." Of course, there is not a word of condemnation of killings of innocent persons including Sikhs by the terrorists.

About two or three weeks ago, three Congress leaders took tea at Bhikhiwind in Amritsar district at the house of a person at whose instance terrorists had shot a CPI member, Jatinder Kumar—a fact known almost to everyone in Bhikhiwind. The Secretary and Assistant Secretary of the Gurdaspur District Council of the CPI have named a Congress leader whose gunman is linked with the terrorists and whom this Congress leader got released after he was taken into custody. The CPI leaders have also alleged that this Congress-I leader had hatched a plot to get a local CPI leader liquidated because the latter is his potential rival in elections to the Punjab Assembly. All this with more details is given in a signed article by the two CPI leaders of the district.

On January 26, 1988, at about 9 p.m. three armed persons alighted from a Maruti car in front of the house of an advocate belonging to the minority community in Amritsar city. They wanted to enter the house. Due to the vigilance of the people and the chance arrival of some CRPF men, they could not. Two escaped but one with a revolver was nabbed. This revolver was a licensed one but the weapon as well as the Maruti car belonged to someone else. The police, to whom the nabbed person was handed over, through persuasion and also indirect threats brought about a "compromise". The story was trotted out that the intruders had no bad intentions and were only under the influence of liquor. Some gazetted police officers were instrumental in bringing about this "compromise."

People throughout India are perturbed about the sudden worsening of the situation in Punjab after the security forces had gained the upper hand, during the months of October to December 1987. The conclusions this writer has reached are as under:

While the security forces had gained the upper hand, the terrorists' backbone had not yet been broken. What was needed was: (1) to let the security forces continue their offensive and not let the terrorists reorganise themselves; (2) to take right type of political initiatives—for example, release of innocent ones among Jodhpur detenus, prosecution of the VIPs who took part in organising anti-Sikh riots, and an all-parties meeting to evolve a broad consensus regarding territorial and surplus river water disputes; and (3) to intensify the mass campaign against terrorism, separatism and communalism at the grassroots level.

What the Government of India did was just the reverse. It decided to try for a package deal with a section of the Akali Party as well as a section of the terrorists, and failing that, to go in for elections and take strong action on the eve of the poll to help the Congress-I come to power. This resulted in wrong type of political steps—for example, the release of Badal. And only this explains the welcome accorded by the Prime Minister to the move of Jain Muni Sushil Kumar to become a mediator even when he was demanding the release of some firm supporters of the Khalistani terrorists. It is strange that even while preaching separation of religion and politics, the Prime Minister should want a religious personality to become a mediator.

This writer can assert with a full sense of responsibility that, side by side with the wrong type of political moves, sensible proposals which would have enabled the loyal-to-uniform officers to go ahead to break the backbone of the terrorists were either turned down or put in cold storage. This enabled the terrorists to reorganise themselves. This policy led to demoralisation in the security forces and an upswing in the morale of the extremists.

This policy must go. The battle has to be and must be fought simultaneously at three levels—at the administrative level, at the level of mass campaigning and on the political front by taking initiatives that would help isolate terrorists and find a political solution.

*(February 21, 1988)*

## 6. The Extent of Terror

The unending agony of Punjab is continuing. Hundreds of innocent people are being killed in selected attacks, indiscriminate firings, bomb blasts and so on. These killings result in hundreds of women becoming widows and thousands of children becoming orphans.

The death toll in the first four months of this year according to the Home Minister of India is 585.

It seems that the daily killings at the hands of terrorists have deadened the sensibilities of most of the people and political leaders living outside Punjab and they take it as routine news. Nobody seems to think of the misery each family has to face when its breadwinner is killed.

The situation has worsened a great deal in the past five months—firstly, due to the parting kick of the Rajiv Gandhi government, who allowed the terrorists to browbeat other political parties by open threats of violence, which was responsible for the victory of so many terrorist-backed candidates in the parliamentary elections, and secondly, by the wrong signals sent out by the National Front government, particularly by the new Governor, who seems to think that by a few conciliatory gestures and by entering into an agreement with a section of the terrorists (incidentally, the previous government also followed this policy) a solution of this long-standing malady can be found. They failed to understand the deep-rooted conspiracy of imperialist powers who were working through Pakistani rulers and the committed Khalistanis to destabilise and destroy the unity and integrity of the country.

Before the parliamentary elections, Amritsar district, Batala police district of Gurdaspur district and the Mand areas of Ferozepur and Kapurthala districts were the worst terrorist-ridden areas, but now many areas in other districts, i.e., Ferozepur, Faridkot, Patiala, Bhatinda and even certain areas in Jalandhar, Ropar and Hoshiarpur have become terrorist-ridden.

It is most unfortunate that apart from treating the daily killings as routine news, the perception of the all-pervasive and silent terror in Punjab is either totally underestimated or is ignored, especially by many Punjab experts and by some newspaper writers and even by many parliament members as well as ministers, who have no time to come to Punjab and study the situation first-hand, by going to the villages and meeting ordinary people. The people in the villages and towns in the terrorist-ridden areas are leading a miserable life. They are harassed and exploited, on the one hand, by the terrorists, and on the other, by a section of the police. There is self-imposed curfew in the villages and towns after 7 p.m. Nobody feels safe. Each night that passes is a blessing for them and they heave a sigh of relief that they are alive. Nobody stirs out during night time, even for watering the fields or for other urgent work or in case of an emergency in the family.

In the villages and small towns in terrorist-ridden areas in Punjab, the terrorists rule. They issue edicts, firmans and orders which are scrupulously obeyed, not because the people like them or love them but because of the fear of AK-47 rifles which are very much evident in the villages as the terrorists openly move about in groups with these rifles slung on their shoulders. Some of these orders are:

(a) Each kisan must cultivate half an acre of sugarcane per every five acres and this sugarcane must not be cut unless the wheat crop grows up, although the sugarcane may go waste in the meanwhile, and tall grass (*sarkanda*) in the Mand areas or near canals must not be cut or destroyed. All this to provide hiding places for the terrorists in the fields.

(b) All dogs should either be destroyed or kept chained.

(c) There should be no lights in the streets and in the houses at night.

(d) Each kisan must pay Rs. 50 to Rs. 100 per acre, each employee Rs. 100 per month, each combine owner Rs. 100 per acre and each commission agent must pay Rs. 1.50 per bag, in the village gurdwaras for buying arms or for building gurdwaras as memorials for the terrorists who get killed in inter-group clashes or in encounters with the security forces.

(e) Teaching of Hindi in the government schools is banned. Anybody violating the ban is killed, as happened in the case of a woman teacher in the Majitha police district. Bonfires of Hindi books have been lit in some schools. .

(f) The singing of the National Anthem stands banned in many schools.

(g) The students, both boys and girls, must wear a particular type of dress, especially yellow turban or dupatta.

(h) After the killing of every terrorist by the police or as a result of mutual infighting, handwritten orders are pasted and all shops in the area are ordered to be closed for 4 days, a week or even a fortnight. In some areas of Tarn Taran, Majitha and Batala police districts, shops hardly open for a few days in the month.

(i) A ban on having more than eleven people in a marriage party. In some cases those violating have been killed or forced to take a dip in the village ponds of dirty water.

(j) A ban on inviting Hindus on the occasions of marriages in Sikh families has been imposed in certain towns and cities.

(k) In many villages, Khalsa panchayats have been set up. But apart from that, roaming groups of terrorists force the people to settle to their liking civil and criminal cases pending in the courts. Those who resist are threatened or even shot dead. Because of this one out of three civil courts in Tarn Taran has ceased to function due to a sharp reduction in cases.

(l) Reports of massive gatherings on the occasion of bhog ceremonies of slain terrorists appear in the newspapers. These gatherings are by order. From each gurdwara in every village an announcement is made that each kisan with a trolley tractor must carry people to the bhog ceremony. These orders are obeyed out of fear. Highly inflammatory anti-national and secessionist speeches are made and young people are invited to join the terrorist gangs.

(m) There is a report that a Sikh doctor has been warned not to treat Hindu patients.

Recently there has been a big increase in bomb blasts and bomb plants. Bombs are planted in busy thoroughfares, buses, at railway stations and even in running trains. The casualties in case of bomb blasts are heavy. This has created a sense of fear amongst the people and they are afraid to travel.

Fortunately, many of the bombs which had been planted were discovered before they exploded. If all these bombs had exploded, the death toll would have run into hundreds in a few weeks.

Certain newspapers which print anti-terrorist materials are special targets of the terrorists. So far twelve journalists have been killed. A ban has been imposed on the sale of certain newspapers. Twenty-nine newspaper hawkers have been killed by the terrorists for violating this ban. This has resulted in a decrease in the sale of those newspapers.

On the other hand some Punjabi newspapers are printing all the anti-national, secessionist and provocative material given out by the terrorists. Even calls for killings are printed, apart from appeals to participate in the bhog ceremonies of killed terrorists. Because of this atmosphere in many terrorist-ridden areas, only one Punjabi newspaper, which is the mouthpiece of the terrorists, is allowed to be sold.

A large number of people are being kidnapped. These include industrialists, businessmen, brick kiln and sheller owners, doctors, rich peasants, etc. or their children, not only in villages but in big cities.

After kidnapping them, huge ransoms are demanded. These are invariably paid and the release secured. Most of these cases are not reported to the police or to the newspapers.

Some terrorist groups have started kidnapping or abducting young girls and women for a few days. They are molested and returned after some days. Forced marriages too have been taking place. The victims do not even tell their neighbours or relatives out of fear.

The extent of extortions cannot be imagined. More than 95 per cent of the victims never report to the police. The fact is that there is hardly a farmer living in a farm-house or a businessman in the village or a brick kiln owner, or a sheller owner, or a commission agent, or a teacher or a doctor, or even big industrialists and businessmen in the cities, from whom the terrorists have not extorted from moderate to huge amounts. Most of them are forced to pay on a regular basis, i.e. every month.

Extortions are being carried out not only by terrorists but also by many gangs of ordinary looters or criminal elements who have links with the terrorists, on the one hand, and with certain sections of the security forces, on the other.

State apparatus in the villages is totally paralysed. Most of the government employees, especially Hindus, do not report for duty or have got themselves transferred—whether they are doctors, teachers, bank employees, revenue officials or others.

Moreover, the government employees have to obey the orders of terrorists on pain of being liquidated. Even if there is ban on new recruitment, persons sent by terrorists are appointed to various government or semi-government jobs. Even the Central Govern-ment officers obey these orders. Telephones are installed in the houses of terrorists or their friends out of turn, and even without depositing the security.

In most of the schools there is no teaching, as most of the teachers have got themselves transferred, or they do not attend, because dozens of teachers have been killed. Many bank branches in the interior villages have been shifted to *addas* or towns because many bank employees have been killed and many banks have been looted. Some petrol pumps have been closed down.

The revenue recovery is decreasing because revenue officials are afraid to go to interior villages; many revenue officials have been killed.

Recently a meeting of the All-India Sikh Students Federation and Punjab Government employees was held in the Golden Temple complex. It was decided to carry forward the struggle launched by Sant Bhindranwale by government employees. It was further decided that in each government office a small organisational committee consisting of AISSF activists and government employees will be set up "in order to safeguard the rights of the government and semi-government employees."

The Punjab Electricity Board Employees Union office bearers and members have been threatened because they dared to go on strike or have held rallies and processions when some employees were killed by the terrorists. Dozens of these employees have been killed. Now the office bearers of the union have been ordered to resign and paste their resignations on the notice board, on pain of death. Many lower-level office bearers have obeyed these orders.

Many electricity, FCI *palledars* and transport unions are ordered to induct the terrorists' nominees as their office bearers. Some unions have obeyed these orders.

A large number of gurdwaras and "martyrs' gates" are being constructed in the villages to honour the killed terrorists. Terrorists who kill innocent people are called martyrs—the higher the number of innocent people killed by a terrorist, the greater a martyr he becomes when he is killed.

Previously the authorities stopped allowing the construction of such gurdwaras or gates but the new Governor of Punjab has openly announced that the government has not banned this activity. After his announcement there has been a big spurt in the building of such gurdwaras and martyrs' gates.

So now the terrorist killers are martyrs and the innocents who are killed are . . . . .?

In the recent months attacks on security forces, even on officers, have multiplied. Rockets are fired at their camps, mines are laid, ambushes are laid and individual policemen or home guards are killed when they visit their villages.

In the first five months of this year hundreds of security personnel have been killed by the terrorists. Entire families of some security personnel have been killed. Many cases have been reported in which the parents and relatives of policemen or home guards have been forced to make the security personnel resign their jobs.

In some cases children and relatives of police officers are kidnapped and release of terrorists is demanded in exchange. This swapping has taken place in many cases. Severe attacks by the terrorists have resulted in the demoralisation in the security forces.

This demoralisation has increased due to the open threats held out by Mr. Simranjit Singh Mann and his followers to liquidate certain police and CRPF officers or to launch prosecutions against them. Lists of such officers have been printed in some newspapers.

The new National Front government sent signals that a settlement with Mr. Mann was in the offing and that he would be the new Chief Minister of Punjab.

All this has further demoralised the security forces and hundreds of special police officers and home guards and some policemen have resigned or have deserted.

What has been stated in the above paragraphs has resulted in a spurt in migration. Thousands of families have migrated—these include not only Hindus but also affluent Sikh kisans and even some poor people.

This migration is of many types, i.e. from a village to a small town, from a village or a town to a city, from one district to another district, and from Punjab to other states. Exact figures have not been compiled by the government but there has been large-scale migration.

In the end, we wish to emphasise that life in villages in the terrorist-ridden areas is beyond description. It can only be believed if it is seen and studied from close quarters. After 7 p.m. there is self-imposed curfew in most of these villages. Every night there is sound of firing. The terrorists move about openly in group of 5, 25, 60 and even 90 with AK-47 guns slung on their shoulders. The villagers are at their mercy. They must perforce feed them, give them shelter etc., and if they refuse, whole families are shot dead, and when some of them are arrested and they immediately blurt out as to where they slept or where they had food, then these villagers are at the mercy of the police, who harass them and extort big amounts from them. Thus life in the terrorist-ridden areas is indeed miserable.

Some friends are insisting that elections must be held even in the present atmosphere of all-pervasive terror. They think that the democratic process must be gone through. They think only a "democratically-elected" government can solve the Punjab problem. These friends are honest and sincere and are well wishers of Punjab but, alas, they are sitting far away from the terrorist-ridden towns and villages of Punjab. If they could spare their valuable time and study the situation from close quarters, we are sure they will change their opinion.

In a recent article in *The Tribune* this writer quoted the following observation of the U.S. Supreme Court:

"An election to be free must be without coercion. If the voter casts his valid vote as a result of intimidation, if he is deterred from the exercise of his free will by means of any influence whatsoever, although there is neither violence nor physical coercion, it is not a free and equal election within the spirit of the Constitution (Needly *vs* Fari, 61 Colo 485, 158, Page 458)."

If elections can be held in the spirit of the above-mentioned observation of the U.S. Supreme Court, these are welcome, but the extent of all-pervasive terror in Punjab forbids any free and fair election, as was evident in the recently held parliamentary elections. It is agreed by everybody that the situation in Punjab has worsened a great deal after the parliamentary elections.

Hence the agony of Punjab cannot be ended by the magic wand of elections—in fact, elections in the present atmosphere may worsen the situation and the situation may go out of control.

The need of the hour is, on the one hand, suppression of terrorism with a firm hand, and, on the other, that all political parties which are opposed to terrorism and secessionism and are for the unity and integrity of the country should unitedly go to each village and explain to the people the whole situation and boost their morale, to stand up to the terrorists and secessionists. Also some political steps need to be undertaken by the Central Government, e.g. granting more powers to the states, transfer of Chandigarh to Punjab, a solution of the canal waters problems, etc. *(April 1988)*

## 7. Operation Black Thunder Gains Being Squandered

Dead bodies cannot speak—they cannot say how they died. Nor can they cry for justice against foul play which may have led to their death.

The dead bodies being discovered from below the debris of the holy Akal Takht, collected near the Langar building in the Golden Temple complex, can hardly be called "bodies". They are more like skeletons but many still emit foul smell. Of the 20 such bodies dug out so far, only three have been identified. One of the three was of a woman. It is now known that she was awarded capital punishment for this "crime" by those who claim that all they are doing is to establish the "land of the pure" (that is the literal meaning of "Khalistan"). The dead body of this Sewadarni, however, cannot tell what all was done to her before she ceased to breathe and was buried under the debris.

The "devout Sikhs"—these terrorists—did not even cremate her as she would have liked to as per her religious beliefs. Those who are getting new gurdwaras constructed to perpetuate the memory of terrorist killers like themselves, did not hold even "Antim Ardas" and "bhog" ceremony for this woman, a true Sikh and a decent human being.

Dead bodies cannot tell their tales. But surely there are ways to find out how they became dead and then to do justice. The SSP, Amritsar, had called upon families to report their missing members. This he believes may help to identify the bodies. He rightly says that earlier out of fear such reports might not have been lodged. But then the big majority of the terrorists are still at large. In many rural areas of Amritsar district their writ continues to run as before.

Terrorists belonging to the group of Avtar Singh Brahma don't look demoralised at all. Maybe because Brahma had supported Mr. Jasbir Singh Rode with whom the government has worked out some secret understanding. The "purist" Babbar Khalsa, hopes about whose being won over are still high, continues in its killing spree of men, women and children through explosives of different types. Other terrorists continue to indulge in killings, though ways and means are being adopted to win back some of the sympathy they have lost. So, many may not come out even now to report, again out of fear. Other methods must therefore be found to get at the truth.

The nabbed terrorists have told the police that in all about 50 bodies were thus buried. They must also give the names of the killed, reasons for killing them, the methods adopted to kill them and what all was done to them before they were killed. All this can and must be verified. Verified and fully established facts, including the names, etc. of the torturers, must be made known to the public.

And then steps must be taken to ensure justice. This the state owes not only to the dead but also to the sanctity of the holiest of the holy shrines of the Sikh religion. People too have a duty to perform in this respect.

Considering the type of politics the Government of India as well as the Akali Dal have been playing, there is serious danger of the entire issue being pigeon-holed after some time. The Tohra-led SGPC at first adopted a defiant resolution refusing cooperation even in the matter of removing fortifications and of constructing a road around the Golden Temple. Then there was a *volte face*. It gave all the undertakings demanded from it, but also removed the five high priests whose release it had demanded only two days earlier. Now it blamed them for all that had happened in the Golden Temple. It installed new priests—political personalities belonging to the Badal-Tohra factions of the Akali Dal.

The government did a lot of arm-twisting to make the authors deny having passed such a resolution. This was done so openly and so crudely that all the denials being made now by the Governor cannot fully undo the harm done to the credibility of the government. People just cannot forget that the removed priests had been made high priests originally by the terrorists. What the government did was also against the recent ordinance issued by it to keep politics out of all places of worship. It was also seen as interference in religious matters.

The moves of the Tohra-led SGPC on the one hand and the government on the other were rightly seen by the people as moves on the chess-board of power politics—even though some of these were welcome.

The parallel SGPC headed by the men of Mr. Barnala's Akali Dal this time chose to keep silent. It has now lodged a mild protest against the government's action in not consulting it and against the recognition which the government has accorded to the rival body.

Chess players are known to be addicts. People will not get convinced by mere declarations of the Governor that the government is not concerned as to who are the head priests and that it only wants to depoliticise the Golden Temple and other places of worship. People will watch the actual practice of the government in the days to come—whether it continues the offensive against the terrorists, what political initiatives it takes, etc. People therefore have to remain vigilant.

Vigilance is also needed to ensure justice for those whose bodies are being discovered. Also, justice in connection with other crimes committed in the Golden Temple. For instance, it has been estimated that Rs. 35 lakh were being extorted every month. Crimes of all the criminals may not be of same order.

Then there are those whose job it was to maintain the sanctity of the Golden Temple but who allowed it to become an operation theatre of murderers, extortionists and rapists.

The government has also to explain why it did not prevent weapons from being taken into the Golden Temple, when it could have done so.

Have any cases been registered in connection with the bodies discovered? The million-dollar question is: who will investigate these cases and unmask all aspects of the sordid affair? *(June 9, 1988)*

## 8. Amritsar—A Case Study

Two views are being expressed about the situation in Punjab. One view is that the situation has improved a lot. The other is that the gains of Operation Black Thunder have not been consolidated; that they have been allowed to go waste and that in Amritsar district at least the situation has been worsening once again.

Which view is correct? Here are some facts relating only to some parts of Amritsar district. These should help readers to decide for themselves, for they will also give some idea of the type of activities which the terrorists are carrying on—besides killings.

It was on August 31, 1988 or September 1, 1988. Three extremists, each having one AK Chinese assault rifle, were moving on foot about 4.30 p.m. on the main Harike-Amritsar Road. They signalled a passing car to stop. It did not. They fired at it. It is not known whether or not anyone got injured. The terrorists went away. Obviously the police were informed. The police came to the spot only about 7 p.m., fired some shots in the air and went away.

One day before this incident, a group of terrorists brought someone from his house to a place only about 125 yards from the police station of Harike and shot him dead.

The victim was a Sikh Jat. This is what is said in the area about this incident. The terrorists had told a particular patwari to pay Rs. 1 lakh or face death. This Sikh Jat had stood guarantee that the patwari would pay up. The patwari disappeared from the area. The terrorists shot dead the guarantor. No attempt was made by the police to pursue the killers.

On September 1, 1988, a group of terrorists attacked the house of ex-sarpanch of village and P.O. Booh, Karnail Singh. A Sikh Jat, Karnail Singh is also a transporter. He and his men fired back. Exchange of fire took place for more than two hours. The Harike police station is only three kilometres away. The time was after 10 p.m. The police could not but have heard the shots. They did not move out of the police station. There was no casualty on either side.

The same night, perhaps the same terrorist group, killed two persons in village Sabrawan. The first to be shot dead was 65-year old Chanan Singh—a Harijan, a good Congressman and a member of the village panchayat. One of his sons argued with the terrorists. He was told that they wanted to kill only his father. He was asked to go away. The son left but went straight to the police post in the village, which also houses a big group of CRPF men. The information was given at the police post within five minutes, at least this is what many in the village say. Chanan Singh was forcibly led away and shot dead. He was falsely accused of being a police informer. The security forces reached the site much later.

After killing Chanan Singh, the terrorists group of five went to the house of Simranjit Kaur, a widow and a private nurse in the village. She had no parents. It is said that she had distributed sweets when she got the news of the assassination of Indira Gandhi. Later on she got the sad news that her father in Delhi had been killed in the anti-Sikh riots. Now she was shot dead by the terrorists at 3.30 or 4 a.m. The allegation against the victim was that she was not of good character. She has left behind her only son—a student of eighth class. He lay in his room weeping. The police visited the site at 8 a.m. and registered a case.

Terror prevails in the whole area. There is no patrolling by the security forces during night. No one feels safe after evening.

On September 7, about 7 p.m. a passenger train was attacked by a big group of terrorists at railway station Rure Asal, only three kilometres from Tarn Taran. The aim was to kill passengers belonging to the minority community. Eight including one clean-shaven Sikh were shot dead. Some more including Sikhs were injured. Quite a few Hindu passengers were saved by their Sikh brethren. The police guards in the train did not act. They fired in the air after they felt sure that the terrorists had left.

Mr. Parshotam Lal Jain of the sub-divisional town of Patti has a shop in village Kairon. He used to commute to Kairon and back to Patti every day. One day towards the end of August, as he got out of Kairon railway station about 8.30 a.m. he was forced to sit on the carrier of a bicycle by two armed terrorists. He was driven away. He had shouted for help. No one went to his help. The police station is about 20 yards from the railway station. The terrorists left behind a chit demanding Rs. 3 lakhs. Mr Parshotam Lal was released after six days. No one can be sure about the amount of ransom paid by the family. They are all tight-lipped. The rumour in the area is that more than Rs 1 lakh was paid.

On September 6, one Ashok Kumar was kidnapped by two terrorists from the same village Kairon about 9 a.m. He had tried to grapple with them but in vain. He was whisked away on a scooter leaving behind a chit demanding Rs. 3 lakh. The police post about 500 yards away from the site of the incident was informed within 5 to 10 minutes. No policeman visited the spot.

Ashok Kumar and his family used to live in village Kairon but had shifted to Patti. He continued to carry on his business in Kairon, however. He has been released in exchange for a big sum.

It is feared that all the Hindus may leave Kairon. Incidentally, the late Pratap Singh Kairon hailed from this village.

*The Tribune* of September 8 reported that at least 12 such cases, including the two mentioned abovc had been reported from Patti town and surrounding areas during the preceding one month. Those kidnapped included Sikhs—for example, Ram Singh and Swaran Singh (an SDO of the PSEB).

The report further adds: "Several Sikh landlords have shifted from isolated farm houses to the town, while several others have fled the villages. Due to large scale extortions, over 12 bricks-kilns in the area have closed down—several shopkeepers of the main Ghati Bazar in the town (Patti) told this correspondent in hushed tones that small groups of terrorists were extorting money at gun point from each shop even during the presence of security forces".

On September 12, *The Tribune* carried the following news item: "The bullet-ridden body of a businessman, Manohar Lal, who was kidnapped by terrorists for a ransom of Rs. 1 lakh from his village Thatian Mahanta under Sadar Tarn Taran police station on September 8, was found this morning . . . . His elder son, Janak Ram, was shot dead by the terrorists who had also seriously wounded his relative, Mr Suresh Kumar, at the Tarn Taran bus stand last night".

More than one paper has reported (September 12) that 12 to 15 strong groups of terrorists move about freely in the Tarn Taran sub-division. They hold courts and mete out punishment. Bullet-ridden bodies are being discovered at many places. The terrorists enter wayside farm houses and at gun-point demand and take food, rape girls and women and take away cash and ornaments. And they have the cheek to give verdicts about the character of others!

Papers have also reported that terrorists entered village Tur one evening and made all the agricultural labourers come out of their houses. Women were forced to beat their men and then *vice versa*—all at gun-point. Faces of all were blackened. They were also made to shout certain slogans. The terrorists, 15 in number, remained in the village the whole night.

Some may think that everything is now all right at least in Amritsar city. That is not true. At least half a dozen cases of robbery wherein armed persons in trucks raided factories and took away goods worth lakhs of rupees have been reported in the past one month. Following such incidents, some factories have been closed down and the owners are planning to shift to other states.

There is no room for complacency. A no-holds-barred offensive against terrorists must be launched. Terrorists from within the entire Mand areas including that of Amritsar district must be nabbed. Political initiatives which will help to further isolate terrorists must be taken. *(September 26, 1988)*

## 9. No Soft Options

The Deputy Prime Minister has claimed that ever since the formation of the National Front government, the situation in Punjab has been improving. This does not tally with ground realities. In some respects, there has been a downslide.

Killings, including those of political leaders and workers, continue, as do bomb explosions and the blowing up of railway lines. Kidnappings for ransom have increased considerably and are now taking place, once again, even in Amritsar city. Amounts demanded and obtained now are no longer in the thousands but in lakhs. Victims have sometimes had to sell all their merchandise and to borrow from relatives and friends to pay the ransom.

A meeting of the association of rice-sheller owners of Rayya in Amritsar district was called in the first week of January on the orders of a terrorist organisation to decide how much every owner would pay to it. A representative of the terrorist group attended the meeting.

One owner, Mr. Ram Rattan (a Congressman), said at the meeting: "There is not going to be any end to such demands. One day we will have to say 'no' and face the consequences. Why not today itself? However, if you have a different opinion, then I too will pay but I can pay only a few thousand."

Within a few days, on January 12, Mr. Ram Rattan was shot dead by terrorists in broad daylight in a crowded place. His sons were told on the phone: "You will have to pay up or be prepared to meet the same fate as your father." This when the body had not yet been cremated. The *rasam pagri* was seheduled for January 23. The daily *Ajeet* of January 22 carried an advertisement placed by sons and brothers of the deceased. It did not even say that Mr. Ram Rattan had been a victim of terrorists. It was so worded as to give the impression that it was a natural death. Such was the haunting fear.

Regular forcible collections from teachers of a large number of schools have started again. Big groups of terrorists move about openly in the rural areas even during the day with their AK-47s decorated with flowers and bells. They fire at random. Their calls for bandhs evoke a prompt response not only in rural areas but also in towns. In small towns, they continue even beyond the specified time as in the sub-divisional town of Patti where a bandh was observed for more than four days in the third and fourth week of January. Many gurdwaras and their public address systems are also being used by terrorists.

During the days of Bhindranwale, parallel courts operated only from within the Golden Temple. "Khalsa courts" are now being set up in villages not only in Amritsar district but also in a district like Bhatinda which had been completely free from terrorism before the elections. In some rural areas of Amritsar district, big amounts are collected from landowners. Orders not to cut sugarcane are issued on gurdwara public address systems.

The number of security men of various forces killed by the terrorists during November-December 1989 and January 1990 would be higher than the number killed during any previous full year. Police SPO and CRPF posts are attacked almost every day.

First, it was Hindus who migrated from rural areas. Then many Sikhs began to migrate followed by employees of the Punjab State Electricity Board, most of whom are Sikhs. Now policemen have started shifting their families from villages to towns. Previously, schools heads were ordered to ensure use of the uniform prescribed by the terrorists instead of the one prescribed by the department. Now teachers are being told to be ready to face the consequences if they do not stop teaching English and Hindi. (In government schools in Punjab, Punjabi is the medium of instruction and is taught as the first language. Hindi is compulsory as the second language from the 6th standard).

With the NF government came a system of flying squads of officers to hold darbars and listen to public grievances, especially regarding police excesses. It is proving a total failure. People just don't speak up.

The NF government has taken some correct political initiatives. At the same time the simultaneous suspension of the fight to enforce law and order led to a rapid worsening of the situation. Even the correct political steps have been seen as a sign of weakness by the terrorists. Terrorism in Punjab cannot be contained without a no-holds-barred fight against the terrorists combined with mass mobilisation based on appropriate political and economic steps. Continuous talk of early elections, instead of emphasis on restoration of peace and the giving up of arms to ensure free and fair elections, only helps the terrorists.

Extremist outfits are keen to get changes made in the administration and the police set up. They want men of their choice in key places. Succumbing to pressure in this matter even partially will send wrong signals to the security forces.

The political decisions announced should be implemented rapidly. The Home Minister and even the Prime Minister should have a meeting with top police, CRPF and BSF officers with knowledge of the ground realities in Punjab and with no complaints of harassing innocent persons against them. They should be asked: (a) why they are feeling they are being asked to fight terrorism with their hands tied behind their backs; (b) how police excesses can be avoided; (c) how deliberate mischief must be dealt with and how *bona fide* mistakes should be treated.

What is just and right must be done unconditionally. The groundwork to give more powers to all states, including Punjab, and to evolve a national consensus on territorial and river water disputes must be intensified. There must be no attempt to appease the terrorists and even Mr. Simranjit Singh Mann. That will only boomerang. Bilateral talks have an important role, but so have all-party meetings. In any case, no agreement must be attempted only with one group and even one party. The sad fate of the Rajiv-Longowal accord must not be forgotten. *(February 8, 1990)*

## 10. Targetting Hindus and Sikhs Alike

Ever since Operation Black Thunder the Golden Temple has ceased to be the main centre of the terrorists for planning and carrying out their operations. Terrorist boys, however, are there in the Temple quite often. They often rub shoulders with security men in plain clothes.

About fifteen days ago the terrorists whisked away two Sikh youths from right in front of the Akal Takht. They were asked to join their ranks. The two youths did not want to. They were sought to be persuaded and also threatened and even tortured to make them agree. After a few days one was let off. The other joined up.

There is a cluster of villages under P.S. Jhabal in Tarn Taran police district. A large number of terrorists roam about in these with their weapons even during the day. It is no secret that many hostages are also kept in these villages till amounts to be paid as ransom money are agreed upon and actually paid up.

These villages are not on any main road. The link roads to these villages are in an extremely bad condition. They have not been repaired for years. A *pucca* road from Tarn Taran to Jamastpur to Bhojian to Panjwad was to be constructed. That would not have suited the terrorists. The contractor who had been allotted the work was made to flee and told that neither he nor any other contractor must dare enter the area to repair a road or to build a new one.

According to a news item in *Vir Pratap* of 18th February, 1990, the terrorists have now started threatening Sikh families of dire consequences if they invite any Hindus on the occasion of a marriage or any other similar function. Some specific instances are given in which armed terrorists forced the hosts to send away their Hindu guests.

Another news in the same paper of 16th February says that a doctor was warned not to treat any Hindu patients, failing which he would have to face dire consequences.

Recently a granthi was killed by the terrorists in Tarn Taran police district. Another granthi suspected to have links with the terrorists and involved in the killing was taken into custody. No respectable person made any representation on his behalf. Some All-India Sikh Students Federation (AISSF) boys asked for his release and he was let off immediately.

The worst effected areas from the viewpoint of terrorism are the police districts of Tarn Taran and Batala. In both these districts, the majority of gazetted posts of police officers have been lying vacant since long.

The Punjab police has received instructions to get tough with the terrorists. The CRPF does not seem to have received similar instructions or, because of infighting at the top, it is not fully cooperating.

Shri Kishan Kishore, a Hindu Brahmin, continues to live in Goindwal Sahib. His ancestral property consists of one haveli, six shops and a room for residential purposes behind the shops. The shops have been rented out since long. Some "boys" now have been threatening Kishan Kishore's tenants to execute rent deeds in their favour on the ground that they have purchased the property from the Waqf Board. (The property does not belong to this board. Moreover, the board cannot sell even property which is in its charge. It only rents out such property.) The "boys" have not yet succeeded in their game thanks to the intervention by an S.P. known for his uprightness as well as fearlessness.

Not long ago, the terrorists put up notices outside various offices of the Punjab State Electricity Board in Amritsar district, ordering the office bearers of the local units of what were described as Communist trade unions to quit or be ready to face dire consequences.

On 8th April 1990, Jugraj Singh alias Toofan Singh, a "Lt. General" of the "Khalsa Liberation Force", was killed in an encounter with the police. No one has alleged that the encounter was not genuine. According to *Punjab Tribune*, Toofan Singh was second in command of the KLF He had managed to escape from the Hoshiarpur jail in 1987. He was wanted by the police in 150 murder cases. According to the Director General of Police the death of Toofan Singh in an encounter is the biggest achievement of the police this year.

The daily *Ajeet* carried an article based on interviews with various persons eulogising Toofan Singh. The article was printed in two instalments on 27th and 28th April 1990.

The bhog ceremony of Toofan Singh on 18th April was addressed amongst others by Darshan Lal Chopra, the BJP leader of Hargobindpura in Gurdaspur district. He praised Toofan Singh who had, he said, "died fighting against an oppressive government."

According to the Union Home Minister, 50,000 persons attended the bhog ceremony of Toofan Singh. *(May 4, 1990)*

## 11. Disturbing Signs

Recently the Governor of Punjab characterised the situation in the State in these words: “More innocent people are being killed, even when more terrorists are being nabbed and killed." Even though some terrorists are being killed as a result of mutual infighting, it is also a fact that security forces including Punjab Police too have been trying to fight the terrorists for the last two or three months in some areas.

It is also true that they have had some good successes. Why then have killings of innocent persons been rising, instead of going down? The Governor has not tried to answer this important question. The reasons are not far to seek.

To put things in perspective, for about two months before the elections to the Lok Sabha and during the elections, the then Governor Mr. S.S. Ray virtually called off the fight against terrorism and let the terrorists have a free field. The National Front government in the main followed the same policy for about six months sending signals that it would bring peace to Punjab by settling with the terrorists via Mr. Simranjit Singh Mann, who would be made the Chief Minister. In other words, the N.F. government too gave a free hand to the terrorists, notwithstanding some correct steps to begin with.

As a result of all this terrorism gained immense strength from October 1989 onwards. The fight has been resumed on the law and order front, but it is not accompanied by necessary political initiatives, which are essential for isolating the terrorists. Moreover, terrorists have their friends in the police as well as in the civil administration. Corruption and excesses on the part of the police continue to bring grist to the mill of the terrorists. Wrong signals about friends of terrorists being put in power have not stopped, and these provide encouragement to the terrorists. Even otherwise, the harm done during eight to nine months will take considerable time to be undone.

Recently, this writer had the opportunity of attending a meeting in which many keen observers of the situation in Punjab were present. Living as they do in various parts of Punjab, what they said about the situation in their respective areas gives a really vivid picture of the Punjab situation which people all over India should know.

Here is what some of them said. First, the scene in Gurdaspur. Not only have killings increased, but the terrorists' mass base has also expanded. The policy of releases on the assurance of Sarpanches has boosted the morale of the terrorists. In the border areas, not a few of the Sarpanches are linked with smugglers and, as is well known, there is a nexus between smugglers and terrorists. Recruitment into the ranks of the terrorists increased in a big way because of the feeling amongst sections of youths that at worst they would have to spend a few months in jail. In the meantime, they would be able to amass a good deal of wealth and build good houses for their families and for themselves.

Police has developed vested interests in terrorism. Not only many Akali leaders but even quite a few Congress leaders have their sympathies with the extremists. Sons of some are in the ranks of the extremists. Fathers do nothing to dissuade them. People are coming to the conclusion that even Communists are not in a position to fight the terrorists. In a particular area of Gurdaspur district, a majority of the Sikh Jat youths are in one terrorist organisation or the other. This is the area from which the Panthic Committee member Wassan Singh Zafarwal comes. Many others are related to Wassan Singh. They came from poor peasant families but now these families have grown quite rich. This is true of Wassan Singh's own family too. Quite a number of such families have built very good new houses in their fields and have purchased new motor cycles; arms and ammunition continue to come from across the border through the river Ravi and also with the connivance of the corrupt elements in the border security forces.

Next, Amritsar. Terrorist boys hold their meetings in broad day-light even in a well known garden of Amritsar city. Also in some posh hotels. In the terrorist-ridden rural areas of Amritsar district, there are queues for being recruited into the ranks of the terrorists. Often, some are told to come after a month and even later. Arms and ammunition going round are unlimited.

Many are of the view that the possibility of there being some tunnels between some of our border areas and some areas across the border for bringing in weapons etc. cannot be ruled out. Sometime ago, various organisations of shopkeepers of Tarn Taran (sub-divisional town in Amritsar district) decided that they would carry out bandh orders of the terrorists, only if they are given through their letter-heads. In July 1990, an order to observe a bandh for one day appeared in the town. It was not on any letter-head. Even then about half the town observed the bandh. The very next day, a new notice–now on a letter-head—appeared in the town. It said, "Our earlier order was not carried out properly. Now there must be a complete bandh for 3 days." The order was carried out *in toto*.

In Faridkot district, it was observed, instead of improving, the situation has been worsening. Motivations for recruitment to the terrorist ranks are varied. At the same time, degeneration has been quite rapid. There are terrorist boys who will take away any girl and rape her. Not long ago, a group of terrorist boys kidnapped and gang-raped a girl of village Rode. Amongst the gang members was a son of a brother of Jarnail Singh Bhindranwale. The girl was a courageous one. She lodged an FIR in the police station of Bagha Purana. So far as is known, no one has been arrested.

Bhatinda was another sensitive area. Here, immediately after the elections to the Lok Sabha, terrorists were on top. They began virtually running a parallel government. Within a few months, they collected crores from various Mandis of the district. A good S.S.P. was then posted in the district and he succeeded in containing terrorism to a considerable extent. He would nab all the new recruits, would deal with them tactfully but also firmly, and would succeed in bringing them back to the right path before they became hardened and criminalised. The hardened ones were dealt with differently. This S.S.P. incurred the wrath of Mr. Simranjit Singh Mann because he dared to raid the house of a local leader of the Akali Dal (Mann) and recovered an illegal weapon from his house. He himself used to mediate and settle the amounts to be paid as ransom. Mr. Mann personally led a morcha against this S.S.P., who was ultimately transferred, even though on some other ground.

The situation has again been worsening since then. Mr. Mann's prestige had gone down very much but he is again gaining ground. New recruitment is on into the ranks of the terrorists. Some of these "militants" say, "We will collect 5 to 6 lakhs in a very short time. If we go to jail, we are sure to come out after a few months. If we get killed we will become martyrs."

Another queer thing that happened was the recruitment in Bhatinda district of 400 SPOs not very long ago. They were asked to get their uniforms made at their own cost. They were given training for 21 days. After less than two months, they were all thrown out. They were not paid any salary or allowance for the period of their training and service. The reason given for dismissing them was that instructions now were to recruit only those who were fit to be recruited as policemen. One need not wonder if some of these young men, out of sheer disgust and anger, join the ranks of the terrorists.

One has also to take note of two serious developments which, unless dealt with immediately and firmly, could lead to a serious relapse. First, the terrorists have succeeded in stopping the construction of the SYL canal. Why was the Chief Engineer, recently killed by terrorists (together with his S.E.) in his office in broad day-light, not provided security even though he had asked for it in view of the many threats received by him? This essential point does not seem to have been probed thoroughly. And now the engineers are refusing to work even if they are given adequate security. Their argument is "Who will protect us after the canal has been completed or when we are no longer in service?"

The second critical development is that the terrorists' attack on the freedom of the press has been stepped up.

Here are a few examples. About three months ago, Mr. Jagan Nath Sharma of Bhatinda was shot dead because he dared continue selling a particular daily despite terrorist orders to the contrary. The sale of the paper stopped. But then one Romesh Kumar began selling the "banned" paper. Last month he and his wife were shot dead late in the night. The result: one leading journalist, known for his anti-terrorist views and his objective reporting, has very recently made a right about turn for reasons which can easily be guessed.

Till recently only some Punjabi papers were printing whatever the terrorists desired to be printed, including their calls for killings and their advertisements eulogizing the killers and the struggle launched by Sant Jarnail Singh Bhindranwale. These papers have perhaps been acting more because of threats than out of sympathy. The terrorist dragnet has now been extended. Recently, the two English dailies published from Chandigarh too carried the full text of the "Open Letter" of assassins of General Vaidya, released to the press by the Panthic Committee headed by Sohan Singh. This was as per orders of the terrorists. Incidentally, in the first instance, one of these two papers had already printed a large summary of the letter. But the very next day they had to print the full text—and that took a full page of the daily. If this goes on, very soon the terrorists may be in a position to dictate even editorials.

But that need not be. The hearts of a big majority of the people of Punjab, including the big majority of the Sikhs, are sound. Those who had gone somewhat astray can be won over. It is not for nothing that the terrorists are killing not only Hindus but also Sikhs—perhaps more Sikhs than Hindus. There is also the fact that even the worst efforts of the terrorists have not resulted in any big Hindu-Sikh riot during the last 12 years of terrorism in Punjab. The need of the hour is a correct policy on the part of the government, correct political initiatives, and strengthening vigil on the border, which is a MUST.

*(May 4, 1990)*

## 12. Story of an Undauntable Village

Kotli Naseer Khan is a village about six kilometres from Chheharta in Amritsar district. There are only three or four houses of Jat Sikhs in this village. Most of the landowners are Kamboh Sikhs. Out of the total population of about 3,000, almost 50 per cent are Scheduled Caste Sikhs, mostly agricultural labourers.

Traditionally this village has been a stronghold of the Congress on the one hand, and Communists on the other. Akalis have hardly any influence here. During the last 12 years of the rampage of terrorism in Punjab, not a single terrorist has been given shelter in this village either out of sympathy or out of fear.

For the brave fight put up by the people of this village, the Deputy Commissioner of Amritsar announced not long ago a special development grant of Rs. one lakh for the village.

However, the worsening of the situation in the state, and particularly in Amritsar district, has not left even this village unaffected. Here is the story of this village and its people. On August 20, 1988, a farmer belonging to a landowning family of the village was working on their agricultural land. With him was the family's agricultural labourer—a Mazhbi Sikh. Suddenly, five armed "militants" appeared on the scene. The agricultural labourer was ordered to go home and bring with him the head of the family, who was told: "Our orders are to get from you Rs. 25,000 at least (for the 'cause')".

The family-head went home and came back with Rs. 1,600 only. He told the "boys": "This is all that I have". The head of the family was ordered to appear at a specified site the next day and to pay up the irreducible minimum of Rs. 20,000 or face the consequences.

The wise men of the village took counsel. They were able to identify the ''boys'' and the village from which they hailed. Security forces were informed. Four of the culprits were nabbed. One of them, an ex-serviceman, was let off for reasons best known to the police.

The same serviceman got nabbed about eight or nine months later for indulging in the pastime of extorting big sums from various persons on the point of the gun. The other three culprits were prosecuted and convicted.

Inside jail, they graduated in terrorism. (It is the terrorists who control certain jails in Punjab and run them as colleges for terrorism, a dangerous feature to which no attention whatsoever has been paid by the authorities.) On release the three convicted ''boys'' became killers. Two of them were nabbed by the police and the CRPF in Chheharta about three months ago. They committed suicide by taking cyanide.

The scene a year later, on December 12, 1989: Life in the village was disturbed again. A youth was kidnapped for ransom by the terrorist gang of Kashmir Singh of village Thathgarh. But the people of the village managed his release without paying anything.

They did so by securing the help of a Baba of a nearby village to whom the terrorists were obliged in one way or another. About a week later, the terrorists took away a scooter from the village. The scooter was not recovered by the police, despite a case of theft having been registered.

Came February, 1990. In one Kamboh family, one of the sisters was to get married on February 16, while the second sister was to get married on February 17. Tea was being served to the marriage party. Two ''militants'' made their appearance. They demanded a scooter. They were told that the family did not have any. They were offered tea.

They angrily refused the offer and went away. They returned at 8 at night but now there were seven of them. They fired about 12 shots and broke many glass panes of the house. Some members of the family were beaten up. Later, early on the morning of February 17, some CRPF men reached the village and took positions. Thanks to this, the marriage of the other sister too could be performed, though without the normal festivity.

The village people now demanded the setting up of a police post.

An SPO's post was given. All the SPOs were outsiders—two of them were ex-servicemen. They have been doing their duty very well and have proved their mettle.

On their request some young men of the village were given guns for self-defence and for defence of the village. But soon on April 15, the SPO's post was attacked by the terrorists. About 900 rounds were fired in the exchange of fire between the two sides. There was no casualty on either side.

Then, on April 28, two agricultural labourers were kidnapped by the same Kashmira gang and were taken away to another village. They were sent back with a letter on the letter-head of the ''Khalistani Commando Force''. It was addressed to the sarpanch of the village.

Serious consequences were threatened if demands listed in the letter were not met. These were: (a) Rs. three lakh; (b) guns obtained from the government to be handed over to the terrorists or returned to the authorities; and (c) SPO's post to be removed from the village.

It was after that the district authorities announced a special grant of Rs. one lakh for the village, gave Rs. 10,000 for building some morchas and added one police post in the village.

Thereafter came a turn in the scenario of this brave village. On June 19, two terrorists visited five houses in the village in search of a scooter. It seems someone informed the SPO's post, and they were arrested. One was identified by the people, as also his village.

One of them, a younger brother of the terrorist who had taken cyanide in Chheharta, was let off for reasons not known. The other, a deserter from the police, is in jail. Soon thereafter, on June 27, two Kamboh Sikhs were kidnapped from the fields. However, their release was managed without paying any ransom money.

Then, the terrorists came with a vengeance. On July 30, the terrorists launched a big attack on the police post as well as the SPO's post in the village. They occupied some houses and opened fire. There was very heavy exchange of firing.

The terrorists then fired a rocket and also threw a grenade. Harcho, wife of Beera Singh, a very poor, pregnant woman, was seriously injured. Her one leg is still in plaster. The injuries which her other leg and one arm received too have not healed as yet. She is still in hospital. In the meanwhile, she gave birth to a child who was either stillborn or who died immediately after birth.

On August 16 the terrorists attacked village Kotli Naseer Khan again. This time they indulged in firing at random. Five transformers were hit and went out of action. This means no electricity and irrigation water for paddy. The Punjab State Electricity Board has not yet replaced the transformers. Some officials have been heard to say: "If we replace them, the new ones too will be put out of order".

Now migration has started from the village. It began on July 30, the speed of migration picked up after August. By now about 50 per cent of the population has already migrated—all Sikhs. (The only Hindu family of this village migrated long long ago.)

*(September 3, 1990)*

## 13. Shahkot: Venue of Anti-terrorist Upsurge

During the night of August 8, a young Sikh girl of village Budhanwal of police station Shakot in Jalandhar district was kidnapped. There was a great outcry throughout the block.

An all-parties action committee was set up, with representatives of the Congress, both the Communist Parties, Akali Dal, BJP, Bahujan Samaj Party, Janata Dal and all the Naxalite groups. The attitude of the police was however as is usual—taking the matter as a routine case.

The action committee gave an ultimatum to the police to arrest the culprits by August 16, 1990.

During the night of August 16, two more girls of two villages in the area, both students of +2 class of Nikodar College were kidnapped. One of the two girls resisted strongly and was therefore killed. The other was taken away.

This incident added fuel to the fire. Spontaneously people came out of their homes. By noon, more than 2,000 were sitting on dharna before the Shahkot police station. Blocking the gate of the police station, the gathering was boiling with rage at these misdeeds of the terrorists and was demanding immediate arrest of the culprits.

In the evening, the action committee gave a call for "Rasta Roko" on August 21. The gathering on August 21 was much bigger. In the meanwhile, the SHO was transferred and a new SHO took charge of the police station. In view of this, the "Rasta Roko" programme was changed to a programme of massive dharna.

The new SHO was given time till August 28. The police now came into action. On August 23, there was an encounter in village Gill. In the encounter, two terrorists and the Budhanwal village girl got shot dead. The second kidnapped girl was rescued.

This spontaneous wave of anger and the united front of all the parties not only made the police act more promptly and move effectively. The happening also generated a lot of self-confidence among the people. This can still be seen in high visibility. Those who previously considered keeping of weapons as inviting death are now demanding weapons from the government for self-defence and are receiving them.

On the other hand, this incident has spread panic in the ranks of the terrorists. Of course, some terrorists group are characterising the group responsible for the kidnappings as a group of anti-socials (whose leader has not been nabbed) with whom they have nothing to do.

However, sophisticated weapons, including two AK-47 rifles and documents of the Khalsa Commando Force recovered by the police from some of the group's members do not show them up as just ordinary anti-socials. People are also asking whether the killing of a retired sub-inspector during August 6 night by this group too was an ordinary anti-social act.

The wave of anger which has arisen in the Shahkot area of Jalandhar district has a lesson. Such a wave must spread to the whole of the state and through mass mobilisation people must be reactivated to fight terrorism.

*(September 13, 1990)*

## 14. Visiting Families of Victims of Terror

Long ago, two journalists came to me. They wanted me to provide a volunteer who would take them to some families who had lost more than one member at the hands of the terrorists. They were from a national paper published from New Delhi. They wanted instances not of families in which more than one member had been killed in one single operation but of families which had lost quite a few members, but one by one. I told them: "Come when you are ready to visit such families. A volunteer will take you in some streets of Chheharta. Visit the families house to house. You will come across a large number of such families."

They said they would fix some time and come with a camera etc. They could not manage the time. I wish they had come as such a survey even in the streets of Chheharta published by some national papers would have helped the rest of India to understand better the agony of Punjab. I was reminded of it when a family living in Chheharta lost yet another relation very recently. This was not an exceptional case. There are a large number of families of this type. Witness the story of the family of Surindar Nath and his wife Kamal. Here is the list of relations which Kamal and her husband have lost.

1. Dharam Parkash of village Dera Sahib tehsil Tarn Taran. He was shot dead by terrorists on 29th April, 1986 in his village. He was Kamal's real brother. He was a Congress-I activist and an R.M.P. by profession. He also owned some land in his village. His son Parveen Kumar was seriously injured and was in hospital for more than a month.

The widow of Shri Dharam Parkash, his three unmarried daughters and two sons migrated to U.P. The old mother migrated to Chheharta to live with her daughter and son-in-law. After about a year she said she would go back to her village because she wanted to die there. Nothing could persuade her against her resolve. She returned to Dera Sahib and ten days after her arrival in the village she passed away.

2. Karam Chand, son of Durga Dass. He was shot dead on 6th August, 1987 when he was returning to his residence in Patti, in Amritsar district from his duty in a nearby village. He was a para-medical employee of the Government of Punjab and a member of the CPI. He was married to the real sister of Surindar Nath. His widow with her children migrated to Amritsar.

3 & 4. Sheila Devi, widow of Swaran Dass and her son Babbu were shot dead on January 23, 1988 in their village Khalchian in Amritsar district. Another son of Sheila Devi was at home. He fought back with a *datar* and managed to escape, but could not save his brother and mother. Swaran Dass, who had passed away earlier, was a brother of the wife of Dharam Parkash, mentioned above at No. 1.

5. Sixty-five year old Durga Dass was shot dead in his village

Gaggarbhans tehsil Baba Bakala in Amritsar district on 16th February, 1988. A petty shopkeeper in the village, he was the father-in-law of one of the daughters of Dharam Parkash, brother of Kamal. His widow and two married sons migrated to Jalandhar.

6. Twenty-four year old Tilak Raj was shot dead in his village near Tarn Taran in October 1989. A petty shopkeeper in his village, he was a son-in-law of Kamal's aunt. His young widow with her two children migrated to Tarn Taran.

7. Narender Mohan, son of Gurdial Chand was shot dead on 26th June, 1991 by terrorists in district Shahjahanpur in U.P. He was about 30 years of age. His mother is a real sister of Kamal. Originally, the family was living in village Mattewal tehsil Kathunangal in Amritsar district. After some killings in the village, the family had migrated to U.P.

8. Twenty year old Ashvini Kumar, son of Narinder Mohan (he is a different Narinder Mohan than the one mentioned at No. 7) was shot dead by terrorists in July, 1991 on Fatehpur Road near Amritsar. He with his younger brother was going to Amritsar to his elder brother's house from village Fatehpur, a village just outside the city. He belonged to a family of shopkeepers in this village. Their father had sent the two brothers to go to the city and spend the night with their elder brother because "It would not be safe in the village". The younger brother managed to escape somehow while Ashvini was shot dead. His dead body remained lying on the road until next morning. Only when Surindar Nath went to the police station concerned a police party went to the site and removed the dead body for post mortem etc. The family has now shifted to Amritsar city. Ashvini Kumar was one of the sons of a niece of Kamal.

One has to see Kamal to understand what these deaths have meant to her. Her health is completely shattered. And there are many such Kamals in Punjab today. *(August 15, 1991)*

## 15. Kidnapping and Hostage Taking

Terrorism has become a serious menace which people of entire India must face and overcome. Already, in three states it is playing havoc. It is spreading to some more. It has encouraged and strengthened violence all over the country.

Everywhere terrorism has some common features. At the same time in every country and even in different parts of one and the same country it may have some specific features. One universal feature is that terrorism can be successfully dealt with only if it is not treated as merely a law and order problem, but also as a political one. It is not my intention to deal in detail with either of the two aspects. At present I intend only to express some thoughts of mine about the aspect of taking hostages by the terrorists—a problem which has assumed serious proportions in Kashmir, Assam and Punjab.

In Punjab, kidnappings for ransom began quite sometime ago and this is taking place even today. Most of these cases are not formally reported to the police, and the kidnapped persons are got released after paying the ransom. The amounts paid are generally less than originally demanded. These are negotiated and settled with the help of some middlemen. More often than not such middlemen become active immediately after kidnappings take place. Sometime they are Sarpanches or other respectable people. There have been some cases in which kidnapped persons for ransom have been freed by police action. There have also been cases in which kidnapped persons have been shot dead. Sometimes this has been done because ransom has not been paid. In some cases kidnapped persons were shot dead when they tried to escape. In some other cases, they got killed during encounters between the police and the kidnappers.

Kidnapping for ransom has been followed by kidnapping to keep hostages to get some terrorists released. Persons kidnapped for this purpose generally belong to two categories. They are relatives either of VIPs or of top security officers. The policy followed in these cases has not always been the same. In fact, different policies have been followed at different times and even at one and the same time by different officers.

Let me illustrate by some concrete instances without giving names.

The grandson of one VIP was kidnapped and made a hostage. The release of a top terrorist was demanded. The demand was conceded. This top terrorist went straight to his village on release from the jail. There he was given a welcome salute by his group by firing their AK-47s etc. Within a few days of his arrival in the village, quite a few innocent persons were killed in the area.

Sometime after this, the grandson of another VIP of another district was kidnapped. This VIP too at first wanted the demand for the release of a top terrorist to be accepted. Once persuaded by some top officers not to press for that, he is reported to have stood firm. The police was able to identify the gang responsible for the kidnappings. The VIP was also told. Through some middlemen a large amount of money was offered. The offer was not accepted. They wanted their man to be released. The police then took into custody some relatives of the members of the gang. The message was sent: "Treatment would be reciprocal". It was not long before the grandson of the VIP was released. The police too let off the persons it had taken as hostages.

From time to time, relatives of top officers of the security forces too have been got released by this very method—clearly an illegal one. At the same time there have been cases in which top terrorists nabbed by some police officers at very great risk to their own lives were ordered to be released by higher officers to buy their own security. This produces demoralisation in the security forces without ensuring security for long of even those ordering releases of terrorists nabbed but as yet with the police.

The illegal method mentioned above may have the approval of some and strong disapproval of some others. It must be said to the credit of the terrorists as well as of the police that generally they have not been harassing their respective hostages.

In Punjab there also have been cases in which the condition for release of hostages was to return the weapons and ammunition seized by the police. Of course, persons kidnapped and made hostages were relatives of policemen or policemen themselves.

The phenomenon of taking hostages for getting terrorists released assumed bigger proportions in Punjab after the episode of the daughter of Mufti Mohd. Saeed, then Home Minister of India. The manner in which it was handled invited many adverse comments. There was a widespread belief that in view of the worldwide reaction against the kidnapping of the lady doctor, the kidnappers could have been forced to release her without the government having to release some top terrorists.

Kidnappings of relatives of top officers of security forces for keeping them hostages to get terrorists released has got a big fillip in

Punjab after the kidnappings in Assam on the day the new Saikia government assumed office and after the Doraiswamy episode in Kashmir.

It is time for the powers that be to take steps to pool the experience of our own forces, and also take into account international experience, to evolve a sound strategy to tackle the problem. Maybe this will have to be a flexible strategy, but it is necessary to evolve it, as has already been proposed by some writers in our press. It may be worthwhile to make an effort to come to a national consensus on this matter. *(August 10, 1991)*

## 16. Open Letter to Militants of Punjab

Dear Militants,

Let me through this open letter appeal to you to ponder over seriously the 13 years long course of your struggle during which thousands have lost their lives or suffered otherwise.

You believe that by fighting for Khalistan you are fighting for the interests of the Sikh community. Can you give one instance from history or the present day world of a religion-based state having brought happiness to the common people of even that religion? (I am not talking of vested interests.) On the other hand Zia's Nizam-e-Mustafa in Pakistan, the pre-democracy Hindu Kingdom of Nepal and the erstwhile Sikh states like Patiala prove to the hilt that theocratic states serve only the vested interests professing the official religion but not the common people professing even the same faith.

Perhaps the main argument in favour of Khalistan is that it is the Hindus who rule in Delhi. Surely, you are aware of the pitiable condition of lakhs of Hindu labourers of Bihar who are forced to leave their kith and kin behind and come to work in the fields of our landowners, mostly Sikhs. Would that be so if common Hindus were in power? The vested interests who dominate in New Delhi may be having some Hindu bias but common Hindus are as much the ruled as common people belonging to other religions. And they can come into their own only through their unity notwithstanding their different faiths. The slogan of Khalistan or of Hindu Raj can only divide them, thereby strengthening the vested interests of all hues.

Let us leave this point. You have adopted the path of terrorism to achieve your objective. Should not all learn from history? What successes has terrorism achieved anywhere? Whether the objective is just or wrong, terrorism leads nowhere. Our great martyr Bhagat Singh began his revolutionary life with terrorism but gave it up very soon, realising its futility. The same thing happened in case of Babbar Akalis of Punjab. Palestinians too gave it up. Many more examples could be given, but that is not necessary.

Terrorism has brought nothing but much suffering for Punjab. Inevitably, it has strengthened the coercive apparatus of the state and that too has resulted in much suffering. And yet you are nowhere near achieving your objective. In fact, your mass base is shrinking and not increasing. If you have the courage of conviction, you should argue your case in the court of the people in a peaceful atmosphere. One thing is certain. The way to redressal of any genuine grievances is through the unity of the common people on a just basis. Grievances may be political, economic, cultural and even religious. Even the rights of religious minorities can be guaranteed best by the unity of the people—both in case of minorities in the country as a whole and minorities in individual states.

It is time you gave up the path of terrorism. The interests of India as well as of Punjab, of all the people, of Sikhs and of yourselves demand that. It will also be in line with the great humanistic traditions and heritage of the Sikh religion.

*18 August 1991* Yours sincerely,
Satya Pal Dang

## 17. What is Happening in Chheharta?

The following will give the reader some idea about the grim situation in Punjab. Chheharta constitutes a small outer suburb of Amritsar city. Its total population may be about 30,000 or so. It has been a CPI stronghold, with the Congress as the second biggest party. Akalis have been far behind and so also the BJP.

The population of Chheharta has been undergoing a substantial change. Many industries have closed down resulting in many workers going to their original villages in other districts. A very large number of families of victims of terrorism as well as other families, Hindu as well as Sikh, have migrated to and settled in Chheharta. Many have been settling in Chheharta and not in the city proper because of higher land prices in the latter.

For long, Chheharta was considered one of the safest areas in Amritsar district. The situation now can be judged from the incidents which have taken place here during the last 8 to 10 days. These will also help readers to know some aspects of terrorism in Punjab, which are not very well known so far.

The Bhallas are a big inter-related family of Chheharta, mostly brick kiln owners. More than half have already migrated to other states as they found it impossible to carry on their business by paying huge sums to the terrorists every month, and even more frequently, and in some cases having also to pay salaries of special police officers provided at their brick kilns for security. (One of them was kidnapped despite all this and was released only after a fat amount was paid as ransom. This happened about a year ago.)

On October 25, 1991, Rohit, a young student, son of Shri Onkar Nath Bhalla, was kidnapped in broad daylight. A Hindu young man of Chheharta requested Rohit to give him a lift on his motorcycle. Rohit did that. At the place in Chheharta where the Hindu youth got down and "went his own way", two armed terrorists got hold of Rohit and whisked him away. He was released after five or six days in exchange for a big amount as ransom.

The incident was not reported in any paper. It is generally believed in Chheharta that the Hindu youth who got a lift on the motorcycle was in fact an agent of the kidnappers. The police knows his name etc. He is not now traceable in Chheharta. There are other agents of this type. It is reported that they are paid 10 per cent of the ransom money as commission. The failure of the government to curb terrorism is having many side effects. Attraction of easy and big money is corrupting and criminalising many youths.

On October 10, 1991, at noon, some CRPF men happened to go to the premises of the Himalaya Woollen Mills in Chheharta. They learnt that there were some terrorists already there. Four of them had come there and wanted to kidnap two brothers belonging to the proprietor's family. One had been traced. They were locating the other. The terrorists were surprised at seeing the CRPF men. One managed to escape in their Maruti van. Three took positions.

More force was requisitioned. Three commandos broke open a wall and tried to take one terrorist from behind. The terrorist and one commando (19-year old Naresh Kumar) opened fire at each other almost simultaneously. Both died. Another terrorist was also killed while the third managed to escape. A sister of Naresh Kumar lost her mental balance with the shock and had to be hospitalised.

On the same day (October 10), at 7.45 p.m. Dr. Balwinder Singh RMP, a CPI-M activist, was attacked at his clinic in Naraingarh, Chheharta. His guard had a sten-gun. He too had a weapon. So he was first fired at. When there was firing back from the locality, the terrorists escaped. Comrade Balwinder Singh's hand was injured but his life was saved. Balwinder Singh is still in hospital. During the elections to the Amritsar Municipal Corporation held not very long ago, Balwinder Singh was a CPI-M candidate.

People of the locality allege that a police vehicle was there nearby at the time of the incident but it disappeared and came back after the terrorists had gone. This allegation is being verified.

On November 2, Iqbal Singh, about 40 years old, son of Pritam Singh, proprietor of a small factory H.K. Textiles was kidnapped between 7 p.m. and 7.30 p.m. from his home in Abadi Hargobindpura of Chheharta. He was released on November 4, after ransom money was paid. No paper reported the incident.

On the same day and at almost the same time, one Santokh Singh (a porter at the Attari railway station) was kidnapped from the same abadi and by the same gang. He was released on November 4 perhaps for Rs. 12,000 only. (Usually the ransom amounts are above Rs. one lakh. He being a mere coolie was perhaps let off for this small amount.) Porters at the Attari railway station earn comparatively more because it is at this station that Pakistani passengers coming to India change trains. This incident too went unreported.

On the same day, two armed terrorists appeared at the shop of Gurdial Singh of Naraingarh, Chheharta at 12.50 p.m. or so. They wanted to kidnap his recently married son, Surinder Singh. Gurdial Singh resisted and was shot dead. The son escaped because some citizens of the locality fired back. The police reached after 20 minutes or so but could not nab the killers.

Some papers did not report this incident while some others wrongly described Naraingarh as a village and only said that one Gurdial Singh was shot dead.

On November 2, one young man, son of Shri Dev Raj Puri of Wadali, was kidnapped from a neighbouring village of Mahal from a brick kiln there. He was let off for a ransom. The incident was not reported by any paper. Wadali adjoins Chheharta and is part of Amritsar city. Mahal also is very close to Chheharta.

Last but not the least. On November 6, a working day, this writer wanted to draw some money from his account in the bank on GT Road, Chheharta out of his pension as an ex-legislator. The bank was closed as there was a bandh in Chheharta as per orders of the terrorists. The bandh had been ordered because Baldev Singh Hoathian, a "militant" belonging to a particular group, had been shot dead on October 25, by terrorists belonging to another gang and his bhog ceremony was on that day. "There is a bandh in Chheharta. Obeying the orders of the terrorists may alone ensure some security." Such is the feeling of the people and for good reasons. Baldev Singh had been living in Chheharta for some years.

If such is the situation in an area like Chheharta, the situation in the rural areas can be imagined. One can be certain that the seriousness of the situation is not fully understood in the rest of the country. A political solution is nowhere in sight. More people want army help to be taken by the civil administration. Of course, people do realise and also demand political initiatives to isolate the terrorists completely. Some have begun fearing that it may not be very long before they may start kidnapping girls. *(November 20, 1991)*

## 18. Some Observations and Conclusions

It stands out clearly that the largest number of terrorist-killers hail from Amritsar district, followed by Gurdaspur district. The reason for the terrorists deciding to concentrate on these two border districts is their ability to get arms and ammunition from across the border without much difficulty, utilising also the services of smugglers. The ethno-religious composition of the population of these border districts suits best the Khalistani terrorists for building a mass base with the help of religiosity and religious fundamentalism. Concentration on these two districts also suits the strategy of the rulers of Pakistan. Even while encouraging and helping those who want Khalistan, they know that no Indian government would allow another partition of India, come what may. The Pakistani rulers, however, do hope that at a critical time they will be able to occupy such parts of Amritsar and Gurdaspur districts as would virtually cut off Kashmir from the rest of India.

There is enough material in the bio-data of terrorists contained in this book* to prove that a good part of training in sophisticated weapons to the brain-washed youths has been and is still being given in Pakistan. No one in India now has any doubt about it. It is also now well established that US imperialism, and some of its Western allies too, have been actively encouraging and helping the Khalistani terrorists. A number of facts which bear this out have been mentioned in the chapter entitled "Punjab Crisis". Another significant fact was reported only a few days ago. According to these reports a Canadian citizen Balkar Singh, who recently came to India to give money and guidance to the terrorist organisations in Punjab and who figures in the above-mentioned chapter, belonged to an official secret service agency of the Government of Canada.

The members of the Sikh religious community in India are economically much better off than the members of any other religious community except perhaps the Parsees. The poorest amongst the Sikhs are the Sikh agricultural labourers of Punjab and Sikh industrial workers, particularly the unskilled ones not yet organised in trade unions. It is significant that out of a fairly large number of terrorists about whom information is contained in the book, only one belongs to a family of agricultural labourers. He too became a terrorist-killer under the influence of a Jat Sikh youth and the sarpanch of his village. There may be some more terrorists belonging to Mazhabi Sikh agricultural labourers' families.

No one, however, can dispute the fact that they would constitute an insignificant minority of terrorists in Punjab. It is also significant that in some cases at least, Sikh agricultural labourers had come out openly against the activities of the terrorists There is the instance of the village Sakheera, in Amritsar district. It needs to be added that when Sant Bhindranwale called for the killing of the Hindus at the time

---

*The reference here and in other parts of this extract is from the author's book **Genesis of Terrorism,** Patriot Publishers, New Delhi, 1988.

of Operation Blue Star, in many villages the Hindus were saved by Sikh agricultural labourers.

During the so-called social reform movement launched by the extremists, it was the agricultural labourers of Faridkot district who resisted their violence and accepted their challenge.

It should also be noted that the number of terrorists coming from industrial workers is also almost nil.

**The Role of the Working Class**

The glorious role played by the organised working class of Punjab in fighting separatism, terrorism and communalism of both the hues finds mention, even though a brief one, in another part of the book.

As will be noted by the readers, some of the terrorists belong to Backward Castes and also to the urban middle class. Their number however is not large.

The largest number of terrorists come from landowning Sikh Jat peasants. Some of these belong to large families with holdings which are not large. They are from poor and middle peasant families. However, the data collected does not bear out the view put forward by some that a large majority of terrorists belong to poor peasant large families with little land. Quite a sizeable number comes from well-off rich peasant and even prosperous landlord families. Similarly, the view expressed by some that most of the terrorists are illiterate or very little educated is not borne out by the data collected in this book. Many are well educated—matriculates, undergraduates and graduates and even post-graduates. Some of them are also technically qualified.

Some of the terrorists have close links with influential and well-off politicians, including ex-ministers and ex-MLAs as well as with class I officers—retired or serving.

Another significant fact came out of the data: Gurtej Singh Brar, an IAS officer-turned one of the principal advisors of Bhindranwale, comes from a very affluent Sikh Jat landlord family. Then there is Simranjit Singh Mann. He comes from a big landlord family—who misused his official position as a Senior Superintendent of Police to help the extremists and is even reported to have organised some terrorist groups out of policemen. The data mentions some ex-Army officers whose big bungalows and houses provided shelter to terrorists and/or were used as store houses for weapons. It is a well known fact that most of the Sikh Army officers came from landlord families—some of them were pro-British, when the British ruled the country. There is also the fact that amongst the military advisors of Sant Bhindranwale were such top Army officers as Shabeg Singh (dismissed) who got killed during Operation Blue Star and Jaswant Singh who escaped from India and now heads the World Sikh Organisation (WSO) in the USA.

To find out which classes or groups a movement in fact seeks to serve, it is not enough to examine which classes or groups its active cadres come from. It is also necessary to see which classes or groups are financing the movement, which classes or groups its advisors come from, which classes or groups constituting its brain trust belong to, etc.

The data does help us to understand that it is the vested interests amongst the Sikhs, especially the landlords and the rural elite, who stand for a theocratic state within India with a very weak Centre (Anandpur Saheb resolution) or even a "sovereign Khalistan"—which demand fits in with the imperialist conspiracy to dismember India because India refuses to become a satellite state. Clearly, a theocratic Sikh state will serve their interests and not the interests of the common Sikhs.

The data in the book should help any impartial reader to understand various factors which help them to mobilise some mass support and to get "militants" even from other groups and classes to fight their battle. One of these is the religious and caste appeal which the landlord class is able to make because of the ethnic composition of Punjab. A big majority of the landowning peasantry in this state belongs to the Sikh religion and the Jat caste. These two factors are fully misused and exploited to the maximum.

Some educated youths who do not see much prospect of the types of jobs or avenues in life they seek in the present set-up become victims of false propaganda that in "Khalistan" alone all the hopes and expectations of all the Sikhs will get fulfilled. Even well-established middle classes get affected by the propaganda that they will have still better prospects in a theocratic Sikh state—especially when such propaganda is combined with the prospect of the "Sikh rule", with the appeal of religious fundamentalism, with continuous and false propaganda that the Sikhs are a separate nation having an independent political (as distinct from religious) identity, with the equally false propaganda that the Sikhs are discriminated against, which is helped by the Hindu bias which willy-nilly does exist in the Government of India.

Operation Blue Star, the anti-Sikh riots of 1984, the unpardonable failure of the Government of India to prosecute such VIPs as helped in organising these riots, also egged on the terrorist organisations backed by imperialism and pro-imperialist millionaire Sikh US citizens and the like, to get more recruits. Besides, the spirit of adventurism, lure of weapons, easy money, etc. too have played a big part. In some cases, more than one member of a family have become terrorists. Quite a few are, otherwise, inter-related.

**The Terrorist-Smuggler Nexus**

As invariably happens, the terrorist movement of the type which has come up in Punjab cannot but provide shelter to all types of anti-social elements. There have been a large number of such elements amongst the Punjab terrorists too. Some who became terrorists were really lumpen elements, and some because it provided an opportunity to take revenge, etc. The data in the book also brings out the fact that there has been a nexus between the terrorists and smugglers from the very beginning and this nexus has been to their mutual benefit. Some of the most notorious smugglers had made the Golden Temple their headquarters and were operating from there until Operation Blue Star. One of them, Satinder P.T., got killed inside the complex. There might have been differences between him and Bhindranwale, but obviously they were not of the type which would make Sant Bhindranwale throw him out. Some terrorists were originally smugglers.

Mutual suspicion, rivalries, mutual killings and utter degeneration amongst terrorists would seem inevitable under the circumstances. According to Amritsar SSP Azhar Alam, only one group, namely, the Babbar Khalsa, has remained clean. That is quite possible because a number of good youths believing in good values and traditions of the Sikh religion got swayed into the wrong path under the influence of false propaganda and religiosity. All efforts should be made to persuade such youths to give up the futile path of terrorism, to surrender their arms and return to the path of genuine struggle for a just society, which struggle can be waged only on the basis of the unity of toilers irrespective of their religion, and not on the basis of communalism or with the help of terrorism. Those who surrender and pledge to give up the path of terrorism should be treated leniently.

There is, however, no doubt, and this is fully brought out by the data, that many if not most of the terrorist killers have become absolute degenerates in their personal lives. Some have become even professional killers ready to be hired by anyone. How many of them can be brought to the path of sanity is to be seen.

**The Truth About Naxalites**

A question is often asked about the relationship between Naxalism and Khalistani terrorism. On more than one occasion Home Minister Buta Singh, on the one hand, and Gurcharan Singh Tohra, on the other, have alleged that in the ranks of terrorists a large number of Naxalites have penetrated. This is far from the truth. The real situation is somewhat different.

Some ex-Naxalites did become followers of Bhindranwale and terrorists. According to a pro-Naxalite journalist, out of about 12 groups of Naxalites in Punjab, nine are opposed to the killing of innocent people and to attempts to divide the Hindus and the Sikhs. They are also against the misuse of gurdwaras by the terrorists and are opposed to the demand for Khalistan.

At least one group is fully with the Khalistani terrorists and it has characterised their ''struggle', as the ''struggle for the liberation of the Punjabi nation''.

Out of the nine groups opposed to them, only three or so have some pockets of influence in Punjab. Some of them have done some good work against separatism, terrorism and communalism, both before and after Operation Blue Star. In my view their work on the whole suffers from serious weakness because of some of their wrong theoretical positions. One group believes that terrorists can be fought only by revolutionaries with arms in hand and it is futile to try to make the present state take any effective action. This group has been carrying on a virulent campaign against the CPI, because it does not agree with it. It also came out against Baldev Singh Mann, who was shot dead by terrorists and whose group has been sincerely working for cooperation between the Left parties to the maximum possible extent.

Even groups firmly anti-communal and strongly opposed to theocracy share the belief that the path to Indian revolution lies through creating liberated zones. One of the Naxalite ideologues wrote in his journal that unity of India is something about which only the bourgeoisie need worry and not the Left. Unlike the CPI and the CPI(M), Naxalites do not think that disruption of the unity of India will cause a great damage to the forces of Indian revolution and the world revolutionary process. This fact is one of the factors which have made some ex-Naxalites and at least one Naxalite group line up with the terrorists. Others have not let this wrong belief overwhelm their convictions and above all their firm belief in the need for the unity of toilers.

Another weakness from which some of the Naxalite groups suffer is their inability to work out a correct attitude towards the police and other security forces of the bourgeois state in the concrete situation prevailing in Punjab today. The need of the hour is to support and demand strong action against terrorists while also demanding and taking political initiatives and exposing and opposing all excesses by the police and the para-military forces. Any acts which violate the rule of law should also be opposed while amendments to law to make it adequate to effectively deal with the phenomenon of terrorism should be demanded. Some, though not all of the Naxalite groups, seem unable to adopt or appreciate such a flexible stand.

While the ruling Congress-I refuses to see any excesses on the part of the police and the para-military forces, some Naxalite groups believe that their attitude must be of total opposition (irrespective of the concrete situation and balance of forces) to all limbs of the coercive apparatus of the bourgeois state. This leads them to characterise excesses as state terrorism and this helps those who falsify facts to propagate the false theory that individual terrorism in Punjab is the result of state terrorism.

Their own wrong positions have led some pro-Naxalite intellectuals to completely overlook the really good work done by the CPI and also the CPI-M and declare that they have been sacrificing their cadres and leaders without any purpose. Some of them have wrongly accused the CPI and the CPI-M of having reached an agreement with the bourgeois parties not to criticise each other. This is nothing but a travesty of truth. Both the CPI and the CPI-M have run independent mass campaigns during which they have exposed and explained to the people the responsibility of the bourgeois parties—especially of the Congress-I and the Akali Dal—for the Punjab crisis. They also believe that on specific points of agreement there should also be a joint campaign going beyond the Left parties. And they have worked for it and stand for it even today. There is no contradiction between the need of an independent campaign and the struggle by the Left and the need for uniting all patriotic forces which stand for India's unity in diversity and for communal peace and harmony.

Some bourgeois politicians have often tried to blame the Naxalites for terrorism in Punjab. We have therefore dealt with the question at some length—as we see it. *(1988)*

## 19. A Truthful and Objective Assessment: Gen. K.S. Brar on Operation Blue Star

Authored by Lt. General K.S. Brar, who led it, the book* should help to know the truth behind the episode which shook the country, particularly the border state of Punjab. The book has come out at a time when Punjab has been freed of the grip of terror making possible an objective assessment of this highly controversial and most unfortunate event. This is clearly illustrated by the fact that on the 9th anniversary of Operation Blue Star in June 1993 there was no shrill demand asking Government of India (alone) to apologise to atone for its alleged sins. Instead, even many pro-Akali intellectuals argued that both the Congress government and the Akali leadership owed an apology for it.

The author very aptly describes the situation in which the Operation Blue Star had to be undertaken when he says: "The militants had desecrated a sacred place of worship by converting it into an arsenal, and a base from where heinous crimes were planned and mounted, sentences proclaimed, and executions carried out. Their secessionist activities had posed a very serious threat to the security of the country as a result of which we had been assigned the task of flushing out the militants from within the Golden Temple, to thus restore its religious sanctity at the earliest".

Himself a Sikh, the author was asked by a foreign news reporter soon after the action in the temple : "General, how could you have

***Operation Blue Star—The True Story** by Lt. Gen. K.S. Brar, UBS Publishers & Distributors, pp 173, Rs. 150.

ever agreed to carry out a military operation inside the temple?'' The reporter had nothing to say when the General replied, ''What would you do if St. Paul's Cathedral was desecrated and converted into an arsenal? If it was made into a military fortress by militants, from where secessionist forces were working towards the disintegration of your country?'' The author adds: ''At times like this, if clear thinking is to prevail, our emotions need to take a back seat''.

Facts narrated in the book establish clearly that the Akal Takht was the lynchpin of the defence system of the terrorists. For instance: ''of the fifty or so light machine guns, as many as thirty were around the Akal Takht itself. Normally, an army unit would deploy this quantum of fire power to cover an area of about eight kilometres''.

The book convincingly refutes the allegation that Operation Blue Star was directed against Sikhs and the Sikh religion. It also strongly refutes the propaganda that in the course of the operation, Sikh religious sentiments were disregarded. It also explodes such myths as the alleged use of chemical gas, the Sikh Library being deliberately set on fire by the Army, etc. etc. It clearly brings out the fact that it was not the Army but the terrorists who did not hesitate to kill the innocent devotees trapped inside the complex. The author's narration of facts would convince any impartial reader that the Army suffered extremely high casualties for two reasons: One, total absence of operational intelligence. Second, its determination to use minimum force, and its concern for Sikh religious sentiment and protection of the innocents. The security personnel had also been ordered to prevent damage to the *sanctum sanctorum* at all costs. The author justifiably lauds the jawans and the officers who carried out the operation, not a few of whom were Sikhs. He also pays a tribute to the bravery which some terrorists displayed.

The book convincingly explains why a Black Thunder style operation would have been sheer madness when Operation Blue Star was undertaken.

Some reviewers have made extremely biased and prejudiced criticism of the book. For instance, one critic has described it as only a ''differently written version'' of Government of India's white paper. How totally wrong this criticism is would be clear from the fact that the author himself admits that Operation Blue Star could have been avoided, but for the follies of both the Akali leadership and no less of the Congress-I government at the Centre. He refers to Bhindranwale as ''Frankenstein'' and a ''monster of Governments' own creation''. While he charges the Akalis of ''playing'' Bhindranwale against the Centre, he also makes pointed reference to ''the manoeuvres for power by various competing interests, which the politicians at the helm of affairs, both at the Centre and in the state'', resorted to in their selfish pursuit of power.

Elsewhere in the book, he refers to the widespread belief that Bhindranwale was propped up by Giani Zail Singh to ''break up the 'big three' of the Akali party and spearhead himself as the new messiah of the Sikhs''. The book also indicts the government as well as the Akali leadership for letting Bhindranwale and Shabeg Singh convert the ''Temple of God into a full-fledged battlefield of those very people who profess to be protectors of religion''.

How unsparing the author is in his criticism of the role of the government can be judged from the following observation made on page 28 of the book: ''The Temple and hostel complexes were at the same time being fortified at a feverish pitch.... It would be foolish for anyone to believe that those in power did not realise what was going on and that they failed to gauge the gravity of the situation . . . . Yet no one in authority took any action. To charge those in authority for dereliction of duty would be putting it very mildly, and to forgive them for it, naivety.''

The book makes some positive references to the Anandpur Sahib resolution (with which this writer is not in agreement) but makes very justified criticism of the Government of India for not implementing even the recommendations of the Sarkaria Commission.

All this and much more constitute a telling refutation of the uninformed criticism of the book by those who read it with their own coloured glasses on. This does not mean that it does not contain any drawbacks and mistakes.

For instance, the book sharply criticises the policy of the Congress as well as the Akalis towards Bhindranwale, policies that contributed a lot towards the Punjab tragedy. However, it ascribes that more to the government's alleged fear of inflaming Sikh passions and the Akali leaders' fear of terrorists. However, the truth is that both were playing a dangerous game for the sake of their power politics and vote banks.

The author of the book, however, tends to overestimate the mass influence commanded by Bhindranwale even when his popularity was at its peak. Although it is true that many had begun to believe in his invincibility and had even begun to regard him as the 11th Guru, the fact remains that Bhindranwale was not invincible. The author overlooks the silent majority of the Sikhs who were never either for Khalistan or for terrorism. These included Sikh agricultural labourers and many others. He also fails to take note of the active anti-terrorist role of the working class, including Sikh workers as well as of the Left-leaning Sikh peasantry. He ignores the fact that terror paralysed the people's psyche. The book does not throw light on the external factors responsible for stoking the sentiments of separatism and terrorism in Punjab. Even Pakistan's role is not properly brought out.

The book poses the question why Operation Blue Star was undertaken two days after the martyrdom day of Guru Arjan Dev even when it had become unavoidable—why it could not have been undertaken a week before or a week after. Real explanation, if any, for this can be given only by the government. Lt. General Brar has given more than one possible explanations but they don't carry conviction.

In the chapter entitled "A Backdrop to the Punjab Imbroglio", the author fails to bring out adequately the reasons which accounted for the failure of negotiations between the Akalis and the government. While he does not blame the Akalis alone for the failure, he does not make a convincing case, when he refers to the responsibility of the Congress government and Mrs. Indira Gandhi in aborting these negotiations.

The author concedes the possibility of the Sikh Library having caught fire as a result of some action of terrorists or by a grenade thrown by the Army while acting in self-defence. The author rightly puts the main blame on the terrorists who had made the library a launching-pad for attack.

The author, however, does not concede the possibility that some jawans, under very grave provocation, might have fired in the direction of Harmindar Sahib from within which the terrorists were firing on the Army resulting in the outer wall of the *sanctum sanctorum* being hit.

He is certain that these bullet marks were the result of cross firing by the militants.

The book contains some smali factual errors, such as about the period of the Emergency, about the exact developments regarding Chandigarh, his statement that Bhindranwale accompanied the Akhand Kirtani Jatha to the Nirankari Samagam in Amritsar in April 1978, and his assertion that Fauja Singh attacked the Nirankari Guru, etc. These however, don't in anyway undermine the importance of the book. Similarly, the author does less than justice to the Nirankaris by not bringing out the fact that their requests for protection against repeated attacks on them were not being heeded by the Punjab Government even though these attacks were totally uncalled for and unjustified.

For reasons not known, the author has not thrown any light on the material besides the weapons, captured from the Golden Temple. Such an account would have thrown much light on the degenerate and anti-Sikh life-style of terrorists, though degeneration of militants became a widespread phenomenon much later.

There are, no doubt, some shortcomings in the book, but these surely are not such as to impart a one-sided bias to the author's account. The book is written truthfully in accordance with the author's knowledge and convictions. It is a book which must be read widely. And for this very reason, one wishes that a cheaper paper-back edition is brought out early. One also wishes its publication in Punjabi.

# CHAPTER IV

# Role of Media

## 1. Terrorism in Punjab and Role of Media

The case registered by the Government of Punjab against the leading Punjabi daily *Ajit,* the refusal of the Prime Minister to advise the State Government to withdraw it, his charge against the Opposition that it was seeking leniency for those who were helping the terrorists by making this demand, and the consequent uproar in the Parliament—all these have brought to the fore the question: What role is the mass media playing in Punjab vis-a-vis terrorism?

Let us begin by paying our homage to the 11 journalists of repute and two sons of two journalists, who have been shot dead by the terrorists. These sacrifices are a telling testimony to the fearlessness with which the journalist community as a whole has discharged its professional and patriotic duty notwithstanding the threats held out by the terrorists.

Some other journalists sought to be killed by terrorists escaped death narrowly, though some got seriously injured. Two employees of a paper also fell victim to the bullets of the terrorists. Of considerable significance is the fact that of the 11 journalists who got killed, seven were either Sikhs or hailed from Sikh families.

For obvious reasons, these facts alone are not adequate to judge the role of the mass media in Punjab. Some may as well point out that at least two journalists had to be hauled up by the government. The charge against them was that they were helping the terrorists. It is not necessary here to go into the correctness or otherwise of this charge.

TV has become perhaps the most powerful mass media these days. On the whole, its role in the fight against terrorism has been positive. However, we have no hesitation in saying that it could have played a far bigger role. For instance, it could have come up with many more features to rouse anger against the doings of the terrorists. Some good features were dropped at the last moment and then shown at very inconvenient hours, and that too without adequate publicity. Repeated requests were made by leaders of some political parties that Door Darshan should educate people as to how they should behave and what they should do at the time of actual, and as a precaution against possible, attacks by the terrorists. The demand fell on deaf ears.

Of late, Doordarshan has been showing the sites of the murders committed by the terrorists. There is some controversy about it. There is an opinion that this gives publicity to the terrorists that the latter are eager to win and thus helps them. In the opinion of this writer, this view is not correct. Visual exposure of the atrocities committed by the terrorists can be done in a manner as will rouse people's anger and hatred. In fact, Door Darshan should do this job much more effectively than hitherto. Often, Door Darshan reaches the sites much later—after cremation etc. One obstacle in its way perhaps is fear. The government should make adequate security arrangements for its teams.

It also needs to be mentioned that the coverage of anti-terrorist mass campaign by the Left could and should have been much more. (This criticism is equally valid in relation to the non-Left newspapers.) It is strange that Jalandhar DD should not have found it possible to accept the request of the Government of Punjab for time for a feature on its relief measures for the innocent victims and about the state of their actual implementation. For obvious reasons, DD has been more or less silent about the excesses by the security forces, which have been taking place even though it is wrong to characterise them as state terrorism. TV has not been utilised to fully answer the terrorist propaganda.

What has been said above about DD is generally true of the AIR as well.

Let us now come to the non-official mass media, that is, the newspapers. First the English press. On the whole, the English papers have played a positive role. While various viewpoints have been given publicity, the approach on the whole has been more or less correct. One of the two English papers of Punjab has, however, evoked criticism from certain circles for being soft towards Badal and the Akalis in general. This paper has Punjabi and Hindi editions too. One and the same news would get displayed quite differently in them. Some difference is natural, but often the differences would be the result of efforts to cater to different types of readers with communal bias of different types. This may as well be true of the other English paper also that has a Hindi edition. Be that as it may, the two English papers of Punjab cannot be faulted very much.

The case of the Indian language newspapers is more complicated. The Hind Samachar group of papers is the most powerful. Its three daily papers are—Hindi *Punjab Kesari,* Punjabi *Jagbani* and Urdu *Hind Samachar.* Together they have a very big circulation. They have been active opponents of terrorism. In the matter of killings by the terrorists, this group of papers has suffered the most and has paid the heaviest price. The Shaheed Parivar Fund started by it to help the families of the victims of terrorists has turned out to be the biggest ever non-official relief project in India. Help has been given on a strictly non-communal basis. Victims of anti-Sikh riots in Delhi too have been helped on an equal footing. Its editorial policy has been quite sober and with the passage of time it has been improving, judging from the viewpoint of secularism. However, one wishes it were more critical of the ideology and line of Hindu communal organisations like the Hindu Shiv Sena. Yet in the matter of news and their display its Hindu bias has been much too obvious.

*Ajit* is the leading Punjabi daily of the state. Undoubtedly, its editorial policy has been to oppose terrorism and killings. Its editorials have been generally quite sober. In the matter of news and their display etc., however, the Sikh bias has been much too obvious.

It is a pity that neither the Hind Samachar group of papers nor *Ajit* have been able to live down their reputation of being Hindu and Sikh papers respectively. Perhaps for commercial reasons they do not want to.

There are some other papers which have been playing the communal card all round. The worst has been the role of one paper which writes sober editorials only when the extremists are at the receiving end.

An interesting summing up of the role of the non-English press of Punjab (barring the Left press) was done by the well-known Punjabi poet and writer Santokh Singh Dheer of the CPI. He said that he had written two open letters, one addressed to the Sikhs and the other to the Hindus. The first one was carried by all the papers regarded as "Hindu" but was blacked out by papers regarded as "Sikh". Just the opposite happened in case of the second letter.

There are only two Left dailies in Punjab—*Nawan Zamana* of the CPI and *Lok Lehr* of the CPI(M). Notwithstanding their limited circulation, they, and especially *Nawan Zamana,* have made a significant contribution to the fight against terrorism. The editor of *Nawan Zamana* has been on the hit list of the terrorists since long before even Operation Blue Star.

Last but not the least is the question of the ongoing controversy about Ajit. Advertisements about the bhog ceremonies of the terrorists killed in police encounters, eulogising them as martyrs, have been appearing in more than one paper—but most of all perhaps in Ajit. The Punjab Government has registered a case on the publication of an advertisement related to the bhog ceremony of Labh Singh alias Sukha Sepahi, the leader of one of the four main organisations of the terrorists in Punjab, which was carried on the front page. One does not know whether such advertisements are paid for or are carried free—out of fear. In the opinion of this writer, the registration of the case against *Ajit* was not a wise and correct move, taking into account its overall role. The government could have moved the Press Council against the advertisement in question. It should have specifically put a ban on advertisements of this type for the future and taken action against anyone violating the ban. The Prime Minister's virulent attack on the Opposition for suggesting withdrawal of the case against *Ajit* was not at all justified. It was an attempt to make political capital out of the issue. The Prime Minister should note that the demand has been made by all the parties, including those whose anti-terrorists *bona fides* are recognised by one and all. The Opposition should also understand that publication of the type of advertisements which appeared on the front page of *Ajit* has to stop.

*(August 13, 1988)*

## 2. The Media Under Attack

On June 1, 1989, a new dimension was added to terrorism in Punjab. Two hawkers in Mohali in district Ropar and one in Amritsar city were shot dead by the terrorists for daring to distribute dailies belonging to the Hind Samachar group of papers published from Jalandhar. Earlier, more than one terrorists groups had issued warnings that anyone distributing, selling and even reading these papers would be liable to be shot dead. This was obviously the beginning of a serious attempt to force this group of papers to close down and to force others to carry out the orders of the terrorists and to toe the line. Shri Rajan Kumar, who was shot dead in Amritsar, was an unmarried young man, a college student who had taken to selling newspapers to earn some money as he came from a poor family. On June 2, there was a protest strike by newspaper agents and hawkers in Amritsar. All went without their newspapers in the political capital of Punjab.

On June 8, another unmarried young man, Kuldip Kumar of Phagwara, was shot dead and two others of the same town got bullet injuries for the same reasons. Incidentally, the late Muni Lal, father of Kuldip, was an industrial worker, a trade union activist and a member of the CPI. He was seriously injured in a parcel bomb explosion during a strike in his mills, of which he was one of the prominent leaders. The bomb had been posted by some henchmen of the management. Muni Lal got disabled for life. It was after this that he had taken up the work of sale of newspapers.

For various reasons, I have not been very fond of television and even of radio. Faced with the prospect of having to go without newspapers, I sent for repairs a very old transister of mine. I was told by a journalist who had come to see me on June 10 that another newspapers hawker had been shot dead in Amritsar. Ashwani (that was his name) was a student of ITI. His father used to be an industrial worker in a local mill and was now retired. He is from Himachal Pradesh.

I got back my transister the same evening and listened to the news. Poor Ashwani did not feature in the AIR news bulletin. Somewhere in India the Prime Minister had said that the situation in Punjab was fast returning to normal. This was the lead news.

No newspapers came on 11th morning. We learnt that the protest this time would be for five days. At 8.30 a.m. or so I left for village Chabal to attend a function. One Punjabi daily was being sold there. The Prime Minister's observations about the situation in Punjab were reported in it and quite prominently.

At the function I happened to meet many people from different villages of the Tarn Taran and Patti sub-divisions. Here are some of the recent facts which I learnt from them and which have not been reported in the press.

In a village under P.S. Tarn Taran Sadar, a terrorist climbed on the roof of the house of a Sikh Jat at about 1 o'clock on the night of May 30.

After feeling sure that everyone inside was fast asleep, he shouted to the members of his gang outside the house to follow suit. The head of the family was not quite asleep and had a weapon. He fired at the intruder. This was followed by exchange of fire for 40 minutes. The Special Police Officers (SPOs) manning the local SPO post fired two shots only after the terrorists had left. However, they sent out wireless messages to the police. One SHO after getting the message went to the CRPF post. He was told by the CRPF guards there that no CRPF men could be sent with him as except for those whose duty it was to guard the post all the men had gone for an operation in Mand area. The SHO did go to the village but that was after the terrorists had left.

Two or three days before the above incident, some terrorists in a jeep entered the Tarn Taran mandi (grain-market) sometime after 8 p.m. and started firing. The SPOs and the Home Guards hid themselves quite successfully, instead of firing back. They must be "praised" for saving their arms. In the mandi, there is a building of the Market Committee. A part of it is somehow in the possession of the police department. Some guards of police officers live there. They fired back. The terrorists were quick to escape thereafter.

An activist belonging to a village very near Tarn Taran narrated an experience of his in a meeting in this subdivisional town. He was warned by the SPOs of his village to be careful because some armed persons were seen moving about in the village. When asked what the SPOs had done or intended to do about that, the reply was: "Why should we make enemies?"

I was told more facts of this type. It is not necessary to enumerate them all. More than one person whose judgement can be relied upon told me: "Terrorists have managed to have many new hideouts . . . . They are likely to launch attacks in Tarn Taran and Verowal areas in the near future. There are quite a few indications to that effect." People in Amritsar city too fear more attacks in the city itself. Even the city is not free from kidnapping of persons for ransom. Families of those kidnapped do not report to the police but pay up, sometimes after some bargaining with the help of some middlemen.

No one would grudge it if the Prime Minister were to emphasise the positive aspects—a number of killers have been nabbed or killed in encounters and isolation of the terrorists has been increasing, as demonstrated by two recent incidents. (In one case a top terrorist was done to death by people of his own village. In the second two young Sikh passengers of a bus grappled with the terrorists, laid down their own lives but saved many Hindus.)

Perhaps more effective patrolling of the border from both sides is now taking place. But should the Prime Minister overlook the negative factors and give an assessment of the Punjab situation which does not accord with reality and which is not truthful?

What is the game behind this? Or is the Prime Minister being fed with wrong reports?

*Tailpiece*. The Speaker Shri Balram Jakhar has asked why some very loud champions of freedom of the press have chosen to keep quiet when press freedom in Punjab is under a very serious attack by the terrorists. The question is pertinent and very valid. However, it does not seem to have occurred to the Speaker that a correct reply to his question will embarrass the leader of his party. *(August 13, 1988)*

## 3. Advertising the "Martyrdom" of Terrorists*

For a successful fight against terrorism, it is necessary to study carefully the terrorists' strategy and changes in it on various fronts, including the propaganda front. Only then counter-strategies can be devised and implemented. As far as the propaganda front is concerned, adequate attention has not been paid to this, to say the least. We shall give here only one example.

Various terrorist outfits have since long adopted the method of eulogising the terrorists killed in police encounters as "martyrs". People are mobilised through persuasion as well as threats to attend their bhog ceremonies. At these gatherings, not only are these "martyrs" praised, but highly provocative speeches based on half-truths and untruths are made to preach terrorism.

The insertion of advertisements, with photographs, of the "martyrs" in some Punjabi papers inviting people to attend these bhog ceremonies also began long ago. A paper, which claims the largest circulation of all

*This article, written sometime towards the end of 1991, had to be signed "By a Research Scholar" by the author, as he was on the top of the "hit-list" of Punjab terrorists in those days.—*Editor*.

Punjabi dailies, has been printing the largest number of such advertisements.

In the beginning every one of such advertisements used to mention and elogise the "(Sikh) struggle launched by Sant Jarnail Singh Bhindranwale" and every slain terrorist was described as a "martyr".

It was after quite a long time that the Punjab Government took notice of these advertisements. It seems that a new format for them was agreed upon. Bhindranwale's name disappeared. Instead of the words "Sikh struggle", the words "ongoing struggle" began to be used. This loss in the propaganda value of these advertisements was sought to be made up by press notes containing reports of functions, including many held at "some secret place", to pay homage to the "martyrs". These press notes began to be carried in a big way in the Punjabi press.

This matter was also debated before the Press Council of India. Here is a small extract from the report of the Council.

"More than all this, *Ajit* says that over the past year it has itself stopped publishing *spashtikarans*, reduced the size of bhog advertisements to two columns by 2 cms. and limited their text to a standard format. Now bhog advertisements are being issued solely in the names of relatives, excluding all 'militants'. All the assertions contained in this except one are wrong.

"*Spashtikarans* continue to appear, but just now we are concerned only with the bhog advertisements.

"The only correct statement made is about the 'standard format'. We have already dealt with it."

There are 21 bhog advertisements in *Ajit* of 14.9.91 which relate to persons killed in "the current struggle". All are of 2 columns, no doubt, but only 6 would be less than 5 cms. Even these six are of more than 2 cms. The remaining 15 are much bigger—some even as big as 10 cms. and even more.

Of the 21, only one is in the names of two individuals. The relationship of the two with the deceased is however not given. Of the remaining, one is in the name of "Sikh Students Federation, (Daljit Singh Group)" and another "All India Sikh Students, Federation, District Faridkot" Some are by "All the people of the region and colleagues." Others are by "Comrades and colleagues". Except one, all others give the names of those who have issued these advertisements but no relationship is indicated. Some, perhaps many, of these names are well known terrorists, including those who are wanted by the police such as Bhai Wassan Singh Zafarwal. He is the leader of one of the Panthic committes, though this fact is not mentioned. His name is well known in Punjab as also the fact that all the three or four Panthic committees are terrorist outfits. Of course, there are some other advertisements besides these 21 which are issued by relatives but these do not mention "the current struggle". Relationships are also indicated. Obviously, in these cases the deceased were ordinary citizens. Occasionally, in some issue of the paper a bhog ceremony advertisement in the names of relatives of some terrorist may also be there. But one invariably finds in the same issue one or more advertisements relating to the same terrorist issued by one terrorist or pro-terrorist organisation or the other.

Some new significant features have been introduced in connection with these advertisements.

First: Not infrequently more than one advertisement appears relating to the bhog ceremony of one and the same "martyr" in the same issue.

Second: Advertisements relating to one and the same "martyr" may appear for a number of days prior to the day of the *bhog* ceremony. This generally takes place in the case of terrorist leaders and of those who have a very large number of murders to their "credit".

Third: Every advertisement has been carrying the photograph of the killed terrorist from the very beginning. Now photos of some others who may have been killed much earlier are there in the same advertisements.

Fourth: Advertisements have started appearing in which the place of the bhog ceremony is not given. Instead it is said that it will be held "at some secret place". Such advertisements too appear for more than one day and also more than once in the same issue of the paper. For instance, in *Ajit* of 6.9.91, there were two advertisements in connection with the bhog ceremony of Bhai Major Singh Butala on 8.9.91 "at some secret place". Both were issued by one and the same organisation i.e. Sikh Students Federation (Bhai Daljit Singh Khalsa). Both carried not only the photograph of Major Singh but also of a top terrorist Dr. Baljinder, who had been killed earlier and whose bhog ceremony had already been held. Two similar advertisements appeared in *Ajit* of 7.9.91 while two had appeared on 5.9.91. In all the 6 advertisements the venue of the bhog ceremony is given as "some secret place". The issue of *Ajit* dated 8.9.91 carries as many as 5 such advertisements—two on page 8, one on page 9 and two on page 11. Two are in the name of "Comrades and colleagues" while three are in thc name of one and the same organisation i.e. "Sikh Students Federation (Bhai Daljit Singh Khalsa)". In all the five, the venue is said to be "some secret place". The names of those who are said to have issued these are the same in some, and different in some other advertisements. In *Ajit* of 9.9.91, there are two advertisements on the same page 7 regarding the bhog ceremony of "Bhai Avtar Singh Tari Banjara (close to Bhai Gurjant Singh Budh Singh Wala)". Both of them have the same wording, both are issued by "Comrades and colleagues". Both have a photo of Bhai Manohar Singh Dhura, besides that of Bhai Avtar Singh Tari. The only difference, apart from the size, is that one says that it has been issued by "Bhai Gurjant Singh Budh Singh Wala, Bhai Gurvinder Singh B.A." and the other gives no name at all. Gurjant Singh Budh Singh Wala is a very well known terrorist wanted by the police and with a big prize on his head.

Not infrequently the total space occupied by such bhog and death anniversary advertisements is as much as nearly one page out of the total of 8 pages.

Some important questions arise:

1. To what extent do these advertisements bring grist to the mill of the terrorists?

2. Do repeat advertisements in the same issue and even on the same page add to their propaganda effect?

3. Are these advertisements issued by different persons for one and the same "martyr", as a form of homage, *or* is there some planning in the whole exercise?

4. Should these advertisements be allowed when they are in the name of "Comrades and colleagues" or "People of the area" or by some pro-terrorist organisations, and not in the name of relatives? And even when they are issued by such known terrorists as Wassan Singh Zafarwal, Gurjant Singh Budh Singh Wala and so on?

5. Who maintains contacts with the papers which print these advertisements on behalf of Wassan Singh, Budh Singh Wala, and others for giving the drafts and making payments etc.?

6. Are repeat advertisements even on the same page issued not only

for more propaganda but also to give financial aid to papers which help them by printing their press notes etc., which often call even for killings—sometime directly and sometimes indirectly, which print the reports of their "functions" held at "unknown places", reports which are claimed to have been received by post?

Finally, should the press carry such advertisements or not?

These are important questions which organisations of editors and journalists and the government should discuss. All possible efforts should be made to evolve a mutually agreed code. Once evolved, it should be adhered to by all.

The following points may help in evolving the code:

1. There should be no controversy about the dead.

2. Bhog ceremonies should be purely religious and should not be converted into occasions to promote terrorist and secessionist propaganda.

3. Advertisements announcing these bhog ceremonies should be the same as in the case of other citizens.

## CHAPTER V

# The Law, The Police and Human Rights

## 1. Police, CRP and BSF and Terrorists

In a letter written in the second week of June 1984 to the Inspector General of Police, P.S. Bhinder, the Prime Minister appreciated the role of the Punjab Police. She conveyed through him to the officers and men of his force her appreciation of the sense of duty and courage displayed by them in very difficult circumstances in Punjab. She also sent her heartfelt sympathies to the families of those who lost their lives or were injured in terrorist violence.

This is as it should be. For, nearly 40 officers and men of the Punjab Police were killed and 50 seriously injured during the two years of terrorist violence in the state. And yet there is another side of the picture. To shut one's eyes to that would be extremely dangerous. Here are some facts which will help to see this side of the picture.

On February 22, 1984, a killer gang of the terrorists shot down a number of persons at Lopoke near the Indo-Pak border. Those killed included Sumit Singh, editor *Preet Lari.* The in-charge of the police station was very much there. He left the place instead of nabbing the terrorists.

On February 23, 1984, a responsible local leader of Chheharta (Amritsar) informed the local police station that an attack by terrorists was expected. Two likely places were also indicated. Adequate security arrangements were also requested. On February 24, 1984, the writer of this article took up this matter with the SHO of the local Police Station as well as with the SSP. Within 15 minutes of this, the attack took place. One person was killed. Two were injured. The two police officials posted hardly 25 yards from the site of the shooting ran away.

It was about the beginning of March 1984 that the All India Sikh Students Federation (AISSF) organised bhog of Akhand Path just adjacent to the OCM Mills at Chheharta. Police force present was ordered to move away by about 100 yards. It complied. Most provocative speeches calling for killing Hindus were made. The speakers included a proclaimed offender. The police force just heaved a sigh of relief that the function ended "peacefully".

In February 1984, some innocent persons were murdered in a gruesome manner at Amarkot in Amritsar district by some extremists. It was known in the area who the murderers were. The police too knew. On one occasion, these very persons had threatened some Communists with the same fate right in the police station. The police, of course, did not so much as raise a little finger against them.

The banned AISSF announced a convention of theirs in Gurdwara Chheharta Sahib for May 6, 1984. This was done through an illegal printed poster which was widely pasted again and again at Chheharta and the surrounding villages during the preceding week. The convention was also announced through *munadi* done from a loud speaker for three days or more. There were rumours that the control of this historic gurdwara would be forcibly taken over by AISSF from the elected managing committee dominated by Congressmen. Had this plan succeeded, this gurdwara would have become another operation centre of the terrorists.

The Adviser to the Governor issued strict orders that the organisers be arrested and the convention not allowed. The orders were not carried out. Instead, a compromise was arrived at with AISSF. The convention was allowed. After the convention about 40 extremists took out a procession through the main bazar. One of the slogans shouted was: *Bank loote ga Khalsa* (Khalsa will loot banks). There were also slogans in support of Khalistan and AISSF. In the convention, highly provocative speeches calling for killing Hindus were also made.

No action was taken against anyone. A false claim was made that five activists of AISSF had been arrested. Of course, AISSF did not try to capture the gurdwara. And perhaps this was their part of the bargain.

CPI had announced a public meeting in Kot Khalsa at Amritsar for May 25, 1984. It was known that AISSF activists would make a serious effort to disrupt it. CPI volunteers had made arrangements to defend it. Some volunteers had with them their licensed weapons. The police officials led by the SHO himself did all they could to harass the CPI volunteers. The house of one of them was searched. The police just looked on when an attempt was made by AISSF activists to snatch the rifle of one of the CPI volunteers. When the attempt was foiled, this CPI volunteer was harassed by the police but the AISSF activists were not touched.

The public meeting lasted for two-and-a half-hours. If it could not be disrupted, it was because of the arrangements made by the CPI itself.

Earlier, in connection with a public meeting at Chheharta on May 16, 1984, the threat to disrupt it was sent through the police. The meeting started at 5.30 p.m. and ended at 8.30 p.m. A group of 25 extremists had come to attack it. They dared not when they realised that any attack would be paid back in the same coin. A few policemen of course were present. But the main force came from the city to provide protection for the public meeting at 8.45 p.m., that is, 15 minutes after the public meeting had ended!

The local unions of AITUC and CITU had called for a one day strike of industrial workers on May 31, 1984 for the revision of minimum wages. The AISSF had openly come out in opposition to it. The strike was a huge success and the rally and the demonstration were bigger than even Communist election rallies.

In connection with the rally we had information that the AISSF activists would try to attack it. The District police authorities confirmed it. We were assured that adequate police force would be there for protection. Actually, this "force" consisted of one ASI, two constables and two Home Guards—not one of them with any weapon except small sticks. The extremists did collect in a nearby street to march to the rally to attack it. They gave up their plans when they learnt about the arrangements the trade unions had made to defend the rally and the procession.

On June 3, 1984 at about 5.30 p.m. some extremists entered Chheharta. It was noted that at least one of them had a sten-gun. The police too learnt about it. Nothing was done by the police to apprehend them. At about 8.30 p.m., the extremists shot dead five persons and injured some.

This took place on the GT Road exactly where the banned AISSF had held a bhog of Akhand Path on that very day. The "Path" had been going on for the earlier 48 hours. The AISSF banner put up there remained there even for some subsequent days. Of course, no killer was nabbed.

A few hours after this incident at Chheharta, some extremists murdered a chowkidar of the Food Department of the Punjab Government in another part of Chheharta. This chowkidar died on the spot. A Sikh colleague of his, it seems, tried to protect him. He too was attacked. He died in the hospital later on. Some persons saw the killers enter the gurdwara. They went to the SHO, Police Station and informed him. They were told that an SP or DSP was on duty in the area and that he should be informed. These persons found out the officer and informed him. They were rebuked and spoken to rudely. According to these persons, this police officer did intervene but only to let the murderers escape.

Deputations from Abadi Killais outside Sultanwind Gate, Amritsar had met various police officers and informed them about the actual position and activities of the extremists in this area. Nothing was done. On June 3, 1984, besides others the SSP too was met. He was told that some of the local police officers appeared to be virtually in league with the extremists. The SSP was also informed that an attack was apprehended.

Next morning on June 4, about 30 shops, 10-12 factories and two banks were set on fire. The police was nowhere to be seen.

Many more examples of this kind can be given but that is not necessary. A part of the Punjab police was definitely in league with the extremists. Another part was not prepared to discharge their duties for fear of being included in the extremists' hit-list.

There is now much talk of screening and reorganisation of Punjab Police. What is needed is screening and reorganisation of the entire Punjab administration. And screening should start not from below but from the top. In fact, it is needed most at top levels.

Amritsar was the headquarters of the terrorists as well as of the Akali Morcha. One would think that the best available officers would be appointed as police chiefs in Amritsar. It would be worthwhile for the powers that be to examine the records and the conduct of three or four SSPs in Amritsar (prior to the present incumbent who took charge only last week), who appointed them and why they had to be transferred out of Amritsar after short and even very short periods. Startling facts are likely to come to light.

And the position in some other districts may be as bad and even worse. The conduct of top district officers of Jalandhar, for instance, in connection with the murder of Romesh Chander, *Hind Samachar* Edior, became a big scandal.

In any case, the need for an overhaul of Punjab police in particular and Punjab administration in general is all too obvious.

For quite some time, para-military forces too have been posted in some parts of Amritsar and in other parts of Punjab. They are likely to remain for some time to come. They too have not been free from blame altogether. On April 3, 1984, the day of the funeral of BJP leader Harbans Lal Khanna, the Punjab police had been withdrawn from the sensitive areas on the insistence of the BJP; only the CRP was incharge. Six Sikhs were killed by the CRP bullets. That might or might not have been the result of *bona fide* mistakes, but there is no doubt that these Sikhs had no connection whatsoever with the extremists.

We got any number of complaints against the Punjab police for treating leniently Sikh violators of curfew while Hindu violators were dealt with severely and even brutally. We got an equal number of complaints against the CRP for acting exactly in the same manner with the opposite communal bias—that is, the Sikhs were treated roughly or even brutally, while Hindus were shown leniency.

Once some of us had an opportunity to discuss such complaints with a top CRP officer. He frankly conceded that the complaint might not be baseless. Interestingly, besides other things, he expressed the view that CRP personnel should not have been put up in temples. He conceded the need for taking steps to prevent Hindu communalism making inroads into CRP, howsoever difficult the circumstances might be.

As regards the BSF nothing needs to be added to what the BSF Director-General Birbal Nath has himself said. The corruption within the BSF helped in the smuggling of arms and ammunition.

It is to be hoped that urgent and adequate attention would be given to these aspects too.

*(June 28, 1984)*

## 2. Why is Punjab Police Ineffective?

The name of the Punjab police is in mud. Even today not a few police officers in the Tarn Taran Subdivision of Amritsar—and not only there—are either in league with the terrorists or are more anxious to be in their good books than to discharge their duties.

It is commonly believed that the reason for this state of affairs is the sympathy which sections of the Punjab police have developed for the Sikh extremists out of communal considerations. This is not incorrect. There is also the fact that a few police officers of high rank, having developed such sympathies, helped the extremists to establish links with the Punjab police. All this, however, is only part of the truth.

The disease that has overtaken the Punjab police cannot be fought effectively unless some other main reasons are also gone into.

It needs to be recalled that when killings had just started, no effective steps—political and practical—were taken to ensure that the Punjab police would prove equal to the new tasks. On the contrary, the then Union Home Minister was known to have nurtured a soft corner for the extremists and some of their doings to embarrass his arch rival, the then Chief Minister, Darbara Singh. This discouraged the upright officers and encouraged the black sheep and the weaklings. The Akali leaders too did not want an end to the activities of the extremists. Some were in league with them while others calculated that killings would help them to strike a better bargain with the government. Police officers having links with Akali leaders were therefore not anxious to deal firmly with the extremists.

Both the Government of India and the Akali leadership had for narrow considerations tried to use Sant Bhindranwale against each other, while Bhindranwale, guided by his Indian and foreign advisers, was trying to use both. This played havoc with the morale of the Punjab police.

It is in this background that the terrorists adopted the strategy of killing such police officers as dared fight or interrogate them. Financial and other assistance admissible in such cases was extremely inadequate for a long time. This too was a negative factor.

When Deputy Inspector General (DIG) of Punjab Police, Atwal—a Sikh—was shot dead from within the Golden Temple, almost everyone in Punjab felt sure that the police would enter Guru Nanak Niwas and nab Bhindranwale and his men. (As yet the Sant had not shifted to the Akal Takht.) Darbara Singh's advice to this effect was not accepted by Delhi. This further demoralised the police.

In the period preceding Operation Blue Star, three SSPs were posted at Amritsar who had either links with Bhindranwale or had no will to fight him. All of them were posted according to Delhi's wishes. A Director General to head the police was sent from Delhi because he could help in arriving at an agreement with Bhindranwale. No wonder he gave a certificate that there were no arms inside the Golden Temple.

The effect of all this on the Punjab police can be imagined. The soft attitude adopted by the Akali Chief Minister, Barnala, for some months after he assumed power, encouraged the extremists and discouraged any strong action against them. When Barnala subsequently began acting tough and strong, some of his ministers would not desist from helping smugglers and extremists. Revolt by Badal and company and their link with the extremists was a big morale-booster for the terrorists and a big demoralising factor for the police and the administration.

Communalism is only one of the factors. The havoc played by the "political" factor must not be underestimated. Let it be remembered that not a few Sikh police officers and ranks have remained loyal to their uniform.

The havoc wrought by the political factor can be judged from one instance. In Police Station "A" in District Amritsar, a person had been taken into custody. A Sikh resident of the village told the thana in-charge that this person was the main link of the extremists in the village/area. This was not within the hearing of the person concerned. The "in-charge" immediately communicated this to the person. Soon after, the Sikh resident received threats that his two sons would be killed. The "in-charge" was not a Sikh but a Hindu.

We had an SSP in Amritsar who was dead set against the extremists. He, however, in the case of every incident (big or small) would want the culprits within hours. So not unoften his subordinates, to save their own skin, would nab innocent persons and declare them culprits.

Only recently, on June 23, a police Inspector took into custody two autorikshaw drivers and fitted them into a case registered on June 21 against a crowd which was said to have shouted slogans calling for murder of Sikhs and for burning of Sikh shops. This happened when we had an SSP for whom many unbiased citizens had a lot of praise. Interestingly, one of the autorikshaw drivers is a Sikh. Both are in jail. Even their bail applications have not yet been heard. They are victims perhaps of the "quota" system. (Only recently, this writer came across a case in a town other than Amritsar in which a police officer posted at one place had challaned all the scooterwallas—two-wheelers—passing that point. Even then he was taken to task because he had not fulfilled the "quota". Bitterly he said: "Now onwards we will have to go to houses and challan so that we fulfil our quotas".)

As recently as July 1986, three leading Communists of Tarn Taran Subdivision, known to all as firm fighters against extremists and also known to have received serious threats from them, were tortured and beaten up inside a police station by or at the instance of one police inspector. The inspector also flouted a court order to get one of them medically examined. We have a new SSP who had earlier saved one small town from an orgy of killings, and who was sought to be victimised. Nobody doubts his will to fight the extremists. However, in the case in question he would not agree to at least transfer the Inspector from Tarn Taran pending enquiry. "Prestige" of police above all—even above justice and public interests—has been the code of the Punjab police for long.

It is well known that the Sikhs are as allergic to the CRPF as Hindus in Punjab are to the Punjab police. As in the case of the Punjab police, some allegations against the CRP including some serious ones, are not wrong, but these too are exaggerated. That apart, here is another incident that throws some light on another aspect of the Punjab police.

In village Vallaha (Amritsar) a woman belonging to a poor Sikh Jat family was stripped and paraded by a Sikh rich landlord Jat family. There was an uproar. The Akali Istri Dal and the Punjab Istri Sabha led a joint deputation to the officers. The ASI was merely transferred. Some culprits were arrested. A protest public meeting had been announced in the village. One culprit had already been bailed out. Apprehending mischief at the time of the public meeting, the leader of the Akali Istri Dal wanted the CRP to be requested to be present. Why the CRP? The reason was that while Punjab police officials at the spot had sided with the rich, two of the accused had been caught by the CRP.

The long and short of all that we have said above is that the problem is many-sided. Reorganisation is needed. Those linked with terrorists must be sent to jail. Re-education is also required to strengthen secularism in the police force. Some outdated codes also need to be revised. Political interference to help extremists must stop. Good officers and ranks must be encouraged. Links with vested interests must be broken. Representation of the minority community in the Punjab police needs to be increased as representation of minorities in India needs to be increased in the para-military forces which too have often behaved communally in various parts of India. *(August 2, 1986)*

## 3. Significance of Chaman Lal Episode

The decision of Mr. Chaman Lal, Inspector General of Police (Border) with headquarters at Amritsar, to proceed on leave and his press conference announcing this attracted a great deal of attention. Recently, a leading English daily has said that with the exit of Mr. Jasbir Singh Rode from the Golden Temple, the entire episode has become a non-issue. This is not entirely correct.

The decision to let Mr. Rode and his group enter the Golden Temple was clearly taken at the highest level. The widespread criticism of the move was fully justified. It is not generally known that there was much vacillation and dithering before it was finally decided to let him in without weapons. Quite a few contradictory orders were issued during the preceding four or five days, and many police officers were equally (if not more) exasperated and disgusted. The reference is to police officers known to be genuinely anti-terrorist due to patriotism or loyalty to their uniform or both. It is not necessary to analyse the reasons for the government's vacillations: serious students of the Punjab situation already know them.

Mr. Chaman Lal had given another reason for the step he took. It was about the line to be followed for a successful fight against terrorism. The differences he hinted at existed in the top layer of officers responsible for conducting anti-terrorist operations. These differences may be summed up as between a "hard" line and a "soft" line. And this aspect of the matter has certainly not become a non-issue. These differences got reflected in the press too, though not very directly. Before we deal with the differences which existed in the top layer of the police and the para-military forces, it is necessary to state some facts so that the differences are seen in proper perspective.

Mr. Chaman Lal has been known as an upright officer. His integrity could not be doubted. His dealings with the public are good. And he was absolutely genuine in fighting terrorism. All this has been correctly highlighted in the media. What needs to be pointed out is that those differing with the line Mr. Chaman Lal represented included at least some who also possessed all these qualities. Some of them would even concede that Mr. Chaman Lal would be one of the best police officers for normal times.

What then were the differences? Those differing with Mr. Chaman Lal seemed to hold the opinion that the present law is not adequate to deal with terrorism and therefore it is necessary to take some liberties with the law—even while agreeing that excesses prove counter-productive and must be avoided to the maximum extent possible. It seemed that Mr. Chaman Lal's emphasis was to stick to the law in letter and in spirit. If a known extremist died during interrogation because he had some disease like enlarged liver, spleen, etc., one view would be to register a case against the police officials involved while the other would take a "lenient view" if the killing was not deliberate and if the victim was really a terrorist or an extremist actively helping the terrorists.

Possibly, there also existed differences on the emphasis about the objective during encounters with the terrorists. One view would be to do everything possible to capture them alive to interrogate them and to register cases against them in accordance with the law. The other view would readily concede the need to capture the terrorists alive and to get information from them. But it would not risk their escaping even if it meant their being killed in encounters.

Those holding this view seemed to argue that the judicial system had been paralysed, that many of the killings were being done by those released by the Barnala government or by those who had been released on bail, etc.

Possibly, there also existed differences about what have been described as false encounters between the security forces and the terrorists. Differences could also be noted with regard to how exactly to handle the situation if some relation of a victim of terrorists took the law into his own hands and managed to kill a member of the gang responsible for the killing of his relation. There were differences also about non-official anti-terrorist squads, created by some officers at one stage and these being armed.

Strange though it may seem, even votaries of the "soft" line took some liberty with the law. No case was registered by them against some known targets of the terrorists, who fired first to kill the terrorists before the latter could fire and kill them. According to the law, it is not for the police but for the courts to decide on the plea of self-defence even in such cases. In other words, the difference in the top brass was about the extent to which liberty could be taken with the law.

In the opinion of this writer the present law is inadequate. Instead of making it adequate by necessary and correct amendments, the government has been passing draconian measures which have not really helped in the fight against terrorism.

There were differences also about the need and desirability of combing operations in some areas of Amritsar district—areas in which terrorists admittedly rule the roost even today. One view is that these must be avoided as they were bound to result in many excesses. The other view seemed to be that they were absolutely necessary and they should be undertaken while taking every possible precaution to avoid excesses and harassment of innocent people.

There was general agreement that there was a lot of corruption in the police ranks and that corrupt officials and police officers would often so act as to bring grist to the mill of the terrorists. In the opinion of this writer too the actions of such officials and police officers have been a contributory, secondary factor for the growth of terrorism.

The difference even among the few upright officers was about the extent to which corruption should be made an issue. One would give priority to the fight against terrorism and would fight corruption to the extent it helped the terrorists on a priority basis and would give lower priority to the fight against corruption in general. The other view was that the fight against terrorism and corruption could not be separated to any extent and must be fought simultaneously on an equal footing.

As stated above, the differences appeared in the press. This writer referred to them in a press statement three or four weeks before the Chaman Lal episode. It was pointed out that the differences would harm the fight against terrorism. It is a pity that the government did not take any steps to resolve them on a just and principled basis. Perhaps it was not correct to expect the government to do so because the government itself has been playing politics with Punjab.

There is however no doubt that had the differences been resolved on a just and principled basis, that would have been in the interest of the fight against terrorism. This would be clear from another fact. Officers having differences included some on both sides who shared the correct belief that the problem was simultaneously an administrative problem and a political problem. To say this, one does not have to agree fully with either of the two sides. Life itself will prove to what extent each side was right and to what extent wrong. *(October 29, 1988)*

## 4. K.P.S. Gill Exaggerates Improvement

Mr. K.P.S. Gill, Director General of Police, Punjab, had claimed "big improvement" in the situation in Punjab. To substantiate his claim he has given figures of persons killed by the terrorists and the terrorists killed by the security forces during the first quarter of 1989. He has compared these with the corresponding figures for the first quarter of 1988. This by itself presents a comforting picture. Such a picture, however, is not true. Mr. Gill errs in not taking other relevant factors into consideration.

To mention only one: By October 1987, the security forces had achieved considerable successes. Many hardcore terrorists had been killed or captured. The number of killings by the terrorists had come down considerably. The backbone of the terrorists, however, had not yet been broken. What was needed was correct political initiatives and continuation of the offensive, but what was done was just the opposite.

The offensive against the terrorists was called off. Mr. Parkash Singh Badal was released as part of a policy to make a deal with sections of terrorists and the Akali leadership. Consequently, the security forces were demoralised, and the terrorists were able to reorganise themselves. Terrorists launched a big offensive on January 1, 1988. Despite that the policy of trying to make a deal with a section of the terrorists was not given up.

Comparison of the figures of the first quarter of 1989 with those of 1988 gives one picture. Comparison of the same with those of the quarter ending September 1987, or October 1987, will not give the same picture. That apart, there are other factors to be noted. Some of these help understand the real situation prevailing today, while some others throw light on the long-term plans of the terrorists and of their think-tanks.

First, about the immediate situation. Here are some instances from facts reported at a recent meeting of the Punjab State Council of the Communist Party of India. In the Batala sub-division of Gurdaspur district, firing by terrorists goes on during night time in village after village. People do not move out of their houses after sunset, whatever the compulsion. Forcible collections are made in the name of kar sewa. Villagers—100 to 300—are rounded up by police and taken to police stations for "questioning". Their relations manage to get them released. They get let off in the evening but only after the corrupt amongst the police officials have netted tidy sums. If isolation of the terrorists has been increasing, it is mainly because of their own misdeeds.

In the small district of Kapurthala in March, 1989 terrorists killed Youth Congress-I leader Bikramjit Singh, an ex-MLA and an ex-Congress-I leader who had joined the Janata Party Mr. Sadhoo Ram; and Sarpanch Shangara Singh of Togawala village of the Sadar Kapurthala police station. All three were killed only because of their anti-terrorist and anti-Khalistan views. Serious efforts were made to kill Mr. Niranjan Singh (of Ucha village, P.S. Kotwali Kapurthala), Secretary of the Kapurthala District Council of the CPI.

Finding his house very well guarded and well defended, efforts were made to get someone to bring him out on some plea from his house one night. A person was even offered Rs. 50,000 for this. It is a different matter that the terrorists did not succeed. (It was also in March that Gajjan Singh, a member of the Amritsar District Council of the CPI was shot dead.) Piara Singh, Sarpanch of Bhungrani village of Hoshiarpur district, bordering Kapurthala district, was shot dead also for purely political reasons.

These facts should be enough to blow up the theory put forward by no less a person than the Prime Minister that the link between fundamentalism and terrorism has been broken. Kidnappings for ransom continue also in this district, and by no means on a small scale.

Mr. Gill has claimed that the Nishan Singh gang is not able to indulge in more killings in the Mand area of Ferozepore district because some of its members have been liquidated by the police. People in the area tell a different story. They claim that they have brought about a truce. The BSF post has been removed from the house of Nishan Singh. His relations have been allowed to return and live in their house. In the bargain, Nishan Singh has promised not to do any killings in the particular area.

In Amritsar district, even well-off Sikhs continue to shift from rural areas to towns or from their farm houses to the interior of the village proper. At a recent function at Jalandhar, Dr. Baldev Prakash of the BJP cited an instance from Amritsar city itself. Someone's son was kidnapped, Rs. 1 lakh was demanded for his release. The amount was sent. The father was informed that the amount had somehow gone into the hands of some other group and another Rs. 1 lakh must be kept ready. Soon thereafter, in broad daylight a group of terrorists visited the father. He was told: "If you want you can inform the police but then you will get the dead body of your son within one hour". We have serious and irreconcilable differences with the BJP. But it needs to be stated that Dr. Baldev Prakash is not known for exaggerating facts.

In most of the government schools in the rural areas of the affected districts, the national anthem is not sung.

Improvement to the extent it has come about must be publicised but it would be dangerous to exaggerate it. There should be no complacency, and long-term plans of the terrorists should be taken serious note of.

Long ago the attention of the government was drawn to the construction of many new fort-like gurdwaras in the unpopulated border areas of Amritsar and Gurdaspur districts and also at strategic points. This is now being done in Ferozepur district also. New gurdwaras even at unpopulated places, very near the Indo-Pak border, are being constructed by the extremists. Forcible collections in cash and in kind are made in their name in broad daylight. Some of the new gurdwaras can easily have underground tunnels going up to territory on the other side of the border.

And let it not be forgotten that Benazir Bhutto has not been able to end even the training of terrorists in Pakistan. Sophisticated arms and ammunition continue to flow. Terrorists from Punjab go to Pakistan and are put in touch with their leaders there by the Pakistan Rangers. They return after consultations and with a lot of arms and ammunition. During friendly chats, some Pakistani Rangers even tell our terrorists: "What you did to your woman, we will do to ours if she tries to interfere and stop the help you are getting from our country." Benazir has as yet only partial power. She is as yet not in a position to determine Pakistan's policy either in relation to our Punjab or in relation to Afghanistan.

Not complacency but correct political moves are the need of the hour—as also continued offensive against the terrorists without excesses against innocent people and mass campaign at grassroots level. The Punjab problem is a national problem. It must be treated as such, instead of being sacrificed at the altar of electoral opportunism—a god which not only the ruling party but also the non-Left opposition parties seem to worship.

*(April 27, 1989)*

## 5. False Encounters : Claims and Counter-Claims

The Governor of Punjab on several occasions claimed that there has not been a single false police encounter after he took charge. Of course, some terrorists have been killed either in genuine encounters with the police or as a result of infighting among terrorists. The number of men of the security forces killed by the terrorists in this period is indeed very high. Mr Simranjit Singh Mann and some others, however, continue to assert that false encounters continue to be organised by the police. Though this assertion is being made without citing any instance, it may be worthwhile to go into this business of "false encounters".

If the police get information about some terrorists being in a particular place, it is their duty to conduct a raid. If instructions are that the police should go there to arrest them, they are certain to suffer heavy casualties as the terrorists would open fire first. The correct thing would be to allow the police to open fire first when it is certain that armed terrorists are there. If some terrorists get killed in such an operation, it cannot be called a false encounter except in the vocabulary of men like Mr. Mann.

Some innocent persons have undoubtedly been killed in Punjab. One got killed near Jandiala in Amritsar district when he was running away from a genuine encounter which was on. A bullet hit him. In another village in the same district, some off-guard CRPF men were shot dead by terrorists who escaped. A big CRPF force arrived soon and opened fire indiscriminately. Two innocent persons were killed. Out of enmity someone told some CRPF men that a particular person was a terrorist and pointed to him. He was asked to stop. Out of fear he ran. The CRPF men ran after him and opened fire. The man was killed. This incident took place in Tarn Taran sub-division. These and some other incidents of this type took place during the earlier regime. In connection with such incidents there were agitations and enquiries also. In the majority of cases at least partial justice was obtained.

Two innocent persons were killed recently in Tarn Taran town when some CRPF men opened fire on a crowd two days after the terrorists had killed four CRPF men. The incident took place after the present governor had settled down in office. The battalion at fault was transferred and an enquiry was ordered. Obviously, incidents of this type cannot be called "false encounters", though some men of the security forces might be guilty. Incidents of this type must be agitated against.

But one thing should be made clear. There is absolutely no truth in the propaganda of terrorists and their supporters that security forces have been picking up innocent youths in villages, taking them to the border and shooting them dead.

If a terrorist were to be nabbed, disarmed and then shot dead (before or after some interrogation) that would surely be a "false encounter". There is no doubt such "encounters" were staged from time to time. Some officers admit the fact off the record. One police officer was reported by a daily to have said at a public meeting something to this effect: "Yes, I have killed some terrorists like that, but not one of them had to his 'credit' less than five murders of innocent persons . . . . Name any innocent person I have killed or even a terrorist who had committed less than five murders and whom I have got killed after nabbing him, I will take any punishment you may decide to give me."

Killing of even hardened terrorist killers in this manner is not only illegal but also wrong. There are, however, people who justify such false encounters. Their argument runs as under: "You cannot deal with terrorism as you can deal with ordinary crime . . . . Terrorists in Punjab have completely paralysed the judiciary. More often than not, even a hardened terrorist killer gets bailed out immediately or pretty soon. Out again, he gets back to killing more persons. If some are not bailed out and reach the trial stage, no one is ready to give evidence, not even the father or brother of a victim. In some cases the accused are acquitted out of fear, even when evidence is adequate to convict . . . . It is many years since terrorism began in Punjab. Convictions obtained may be less than even half a dozen."

There is much weight in these arguments. Recently, one terrorist was nabbed by the police in Amritsar. He had three bombs which were to be exploded in three crowded places of the city on the same day. This terrorist admitted before pressmen that two bombs expolded earlier in Amritsar city, resulting in heavy casualties, had been planted by him. He also admitted having got the training and know-how from Pakistan. When asked by a pressman what he would do if he were to be released, he said: "The same thing."

I have been asked by many how the situation in Punjab can ever be controlled if even such persons are not to be liquidated. Some others have asked: "Should killings be allowed to continue day after day till some political solution is reached? Is there no way to prevent or at least to reduce killings by the terrorists till a political solution is arrived at?"

Men like Mr. Mann, who are against false encounters but who are supporters of the terrorists or are not ready to speak against them, and even go to the extent of supporting them out of fear for their own lives, do not feel called upon to answer such questions. But those who are genuinely concerned about human rights must try to answer such questions.

One proposal which can be considered is to amend the law so that hardened terrorist killers can be sent to high security jails in other states, to be kept there till peace is restored. Of course, the amended law should have some procedure to ensure that only hardened terrorist killers are sent to such jails. Simultaneously, steps must be taken to build up the morale of the judiciary and to ensure that jails in Punjab cease to be universities in terrorism which at present they seem to have become.

If such steps are taken simultaneously with correct political and economic steps (e.g., giving more powers to all states including Punjab, providing employment to the unemployed, mass mobilisation, etc.) and also a no-holds-barred fight against the terrorists, the problem will become much less acute before long. Also the need for false encounters will not be felt by anyone.

Let us get back to people like Mr. Mann who are most vocal about false encounters and police excesses. Since Mr. Badal too has been talking in the same vein, some facts need to be stated. During the chief ministership of the late Gurnam Singh, some Naxalites were killed in false encounters. The CPI and the CPI-M agitated against this, inside and outside the Assembly. Mr. Badal was then aspiring to be Chief Minister. He promised that on becoming Chief Minister he would order enquiries into those false encounters. He became Chief Minister very soon thereafter. He not only went back on his promise but allowed the police to continue with false encounters to kill Naxalite cadres. Someone has calculated that about 45 persons, mostly Sikhs, were so killed during Mr. Badal's regime—after being nabbed and disarmed. Some of them had no arms and were just picked up from their places.

As regards Mr. Mann, I would like to mention only one thing. One policeman of his district was murdered when Mr. Mann was the SSP. Three Nihangs were suspected. Mr. Mann got them nabbed and produced before him. All three, it is widely believed, were shot dead by Mr. Mann himself.

Of course, two wrongs don't make a right. However, those like Mr. Mann who have been giving open calls for killing Congressmen, have been justifying the killings of Indira Gandhi and General Vaidya and have been offering alibis for killings of innocent men, women and children by terrorists, carry no conviction with those who believe that some false encounters are necessary in the type of situation that prevails in Punjab and which has been worsening after the National Front government took over, despite some correct political steps taken by it.

Police excesses of various types continue. These can be reduced to the minimum only if every excess committed for money or any other motive is also agitated against specifically and concretely. Even a wrong resulting from a *bona fide* mistake cannot and must not be overlooked. The CPI and the CPI-M have been doing this; perhaps both should have done more. There is however serious doubt about the genuine concern of Mr. Mann in this matter. *(March 20, 1990)*

## 6. Police Force Needs Cleaning Up

Mr. Simranjit Singh Mann and leaders of some terrorist organisations claim to have prepared a list of some corrupt police officers who have been minting money by branding innocent persons as terrorists, nabbing them, and then letting them off in return for big sums of money. On the basis of this claim, they want a thorough restructuring of the police department in Punjab.

No doubt there are corrupt police officers who make money by harassing persons who they know are innocent. Such officers deserve no mercy. It is the duty of every citizen to cite concrete cases, demand an enquiry, and see that it is completed. Mr. Mann and his friends are not known to have adopted such a course. Corrupt police officers make money not only by harassing innocent persons but also by letting off terrorist killers in return for huge amounts.

Recently, Bakhshish Singh Sona, a notorious terrorist, was killed in an encounter. He had to his "credit" more than a hundred murders and numerous kidnappings for ransom. He used to move about with his gang during the day, all carrying sophisticated weapons. Policemen would avoid a confrontation with the gang: they were afraid. More than a year ago, he was nabbed by a police party. It was given out that he had managed to escape from police custody. Actually, he had purchased his "escape" by paying two lakh rupees to some corrupt officers. Will Mr. Mann and his friends demand action against these and other such police officers or will they praise them for helping the "cause" for which Sona in the end gave his life and was made a "martyr"?

Are Mr. Mann and his friends not aware that in many other departments of the Punjab Government, corruption is as rampant as in the police department, and that as a result, a large number of persons suffer much harassment? Why do they not speak up against corruption in the other departments? Sometimes, they characterise the entire police department as corrupt. But they demand that police officers of their choice be posted in key positions.

The real aim of Mr. Mann and leaders of terrorist organisations is not to end harassment of innocent people but to demoralise police officers who have been loyal to their oath and uniform and have been fighting terrorism to the best of their ability. Their aim is to get pliable officers placed in key positions so that their job becomes easier. To let Mr. Mann have his way in this matter would be to play with the lives of the people of bleeding Punjab.

There are others who take the opposite position, quite wrong and harmful to the state—those who do not want to see anything wrong in the police force and who, in case of *mala fide* steps, would not like any action to be taken. The argument is that this would demoralise the police force and help the terrorists. Little do they realise that by making no distinction between *bona fide* mistakes, errors of judgment and *mala fide* action to make money or for any other reason, they actually help the terrorists and increase the alienation of the people from the government.

It is necessary to realise that some wrong and unintelligent ways of police functioning do harm to the fight against terrorism. Even senior police officers concede privately that some have joined the ranks of the terrorists only because they were beaten up or tortured and their parents had to pay big amounts to get them released—in some cases more than once.

Saroop Singh alias "Super" of Ramoowalia village in Amritsar district was an anti-social element. He was recruited as an informer. He did help the police to nab some terrorists. At the same time, he misused his weapon and position. He formed a gang of his own and indulged in extortions on a large scale. One family was able to nab him and another member of his gang on January 26, 1990. Both, along with a pistol and a motorcycle, were handed over to the police. "Super" was let off for services rendered. It is learnt that for some time now he has been operating in Uttar Pradesh.

Labh Singh (this is not the real name), an employee of a local body, was recruited as an informer and given a weapon. He misused it to browbeat his colleagues. When he was shot dead by terrorists, his own colleagues were not enthusiastic about helping his widow.

On June 7, 1990, a young man of village Ghanupur (Amritsar) was whisked away by the police. Someone—an anti-social element, possibly having links with terrorists—had told the police that this young man was involved in a killing. The allegation was because of personal enmity. The innocent young man was hung upside down and beaten. Later, he was let off as he was found innocent. The only relieving feature in this case was that an apology was tendered to the parents and the public. Actually, some questioning and cross-checking would have established his innocence.

Parminder Kumar of Amritsar was whisked away by the police on September 6, 1989, at about 5 p.m. He was taken to Majitha police station. His only fault was that he had, as a part of his profession, written the registration deed of sale of a house in which, later, a terrorist was found living. No one would object to the questioning of Parminder, for that would have revealed that he had no connection with any extremist. But he was hung upside down from the ceiling. The deputation which went to the SHO to demand his release was treated rudely. Someone was told the amount that would have to be paid for his release. A complaint was made. Parminder was released on the orders of the SSP or the SP. An enquiry was demanded and ordered. Perhaps some punishment was given, but certainly not commensurate with the offence.

Baldev Raj, an anti-social element, who had cheated and was estranged from his own mother, brothers and sister, managed to get recruited as an SPO. Soon, he established links with terrorists and ran away with three weapons. The police nabbed his brothers and another relative. The absconding SPO's real link with terrorists was soon discovered and the girl was taken into custody. The three innocents were let off after six or seven days. One brother had been subjected to some minor indignity. It seems that someone, not of the police force, offered to get one of three released for a consideration. However, no bribe was actually given. The facts are so glaring that the innocence of the three should have become evident on the very first day.

**Two Versions:** On June 17, young Jaswant Singh, the son of Mohinder Singh, a mason by profession, was coming from his place of work in Wadali Guru in Amritsar district. Near the railway crossing at Chheharta, he sat at a tea-shop for a cup of tea. He had his tools with him. A passing police party ordered him to put his hands up. There are two versions of what followed. One is that he did not know English and did not comply. The other is that he did raise his hands, though not fully, and his tools fell to the ground.

There is, however, no dispute that the DSP heading the police party pumped four or so bullets into him and did not let anyone give him even the water he was asking for. It was the SHO, Chheharta, who reached the site after the police party had left, who let him have water and rushed him to hospital. Jaswant Singh is struggling for his life in hospital. As for the DSP, it was clearly not a case of *bona fide* wrong judgement, but of being trigger-happy. The main bazaar of Chheharta observed a bandh in protest. Action against the offending officer has been promised, but is still awaited.

These examples should suffice to emphasise that much improvement in the police force is necessary even to fight terrorism. Those in charge must analyse such examples and draw appropriate lessons and educate the security forces accordingly. These examples also have a lesson for Mr. Mann and others of his way of thinking. *(July 14, 1990)*

## 7. Informers and Extortionists

An avoidable confrontation took place between the new Governor of Punjab, Mr. Virendra Verma, and some top police officers at the meeting of top bureaucrats and police officers called by the Governor. The Director General of Police is reported to have walked out in protest against some remarks said to have been made by Mr. Verma. In his speech on return to the meeting, Mr. K.P.S. Gill defended the police force.

Such a confrontation is unfortunate when Punjab is faced with a very serious situation. If press reports are correct, the Governor tarred the entire police force with black paint by saying that it was engaged in making money through extortions. This was neither correct nor conducive to raising the morale of the security forces in the fight against terrorism.

This also overlooked the fact that a number of police officers have been loyal to the uniform and oath and have been fighting the terrorists honestly though from time to time the powers that be did a lot to demoralise them by indicating their intention to put in power certain figures supported by the terrorists, despite their open threat to all police officers who have fought relentlessly against terrorism.

It seems the Governor also forgot the fact that a large number of men and officers of the security forces, including those belonging to the Punjab police, have died fighting or have been killed by the terrorists. If the Director General of Police reminded the Governor of these facts, he did no wrong.

At the same time, the Governor would have been right if he had emphasised the necessity of putting an end, to the maximum possible extent, to excesses against innocent people. He would have also been right if he had said that a section of the police was in league with gangs indulging in extortion, etc. He should have called for prompt and deterrent action against such elements while assuring that *bona fide* mistakes and errors of judgement would be treated differently. Top brass of the police must concede the fact of large-scale corruption in the police force and also the tendency to cover up even blatantly wrong actions of a section of police officers. Realities must be faced.

No amount of general declarations will help. What is needed is to get public cooperation and to ensure fair and impartial examination of every complaint, and action in accordance with the facts of each case. It is also necessary to draw appropriate lessons from every complaint and from every wrong done or mistake made. This is necessary not only for the security forces in Punjab but all over the country because terrorism is not only a Punjab phenomenon. Soon it may spread to states other than Punjab, Kashmir and Assam.

Let me give one instance to illustrate my point. A gang had been indulging in extortions on a large-scale in the area under Lopoke police station in Amritsar district (police district Majitha). Complaints to the police did not result in any effective action.

At night on 26 January, 1990, three members of the gang visited the house of Balwinder Singh (s/o Gurdial Singh) of village Bhangwan P.S. Lopoke and demanded money, etc. They were somehow put off. On January 27 two of them came again at noon. They were confronted. They ran away. The police who had been informed beforehand had laid a *naka* and nabbed them and seized from them a motor-cycle without number and a revolver. One was "Super" and the other was "Bindra". On information given by them, other members of the gang were also brought to the police station.

After some time, "Super" and others except "Bindra" were let off. It was in March that the case was brought to my notice. I took up the case with the concerned SSP and also did some investigation on my own.

I found out that "Super" of village Ramuwala near Chheharta, an anti-social element, had been recruited for intelligence by a top police officer. "Super" had helped this police officer in nabbing some terrorist-killers. At the same time he had formed a gang and was indulging in extortions on a large scale.

The police officer who had recruited him was no longer in Amritsar. Obviously "Super" was let off because of his (past) connection with this police officer.

The SSP assured me that he would nab "Super" and others and get them prosecuted. Perhaps he issued orders also. But nothing happened. On the contrary, I learnt that "Super" had managed to get recruited in the police force. Soon thereafter I contacted the SSP and asked him about it. He confirmed the information but added: ''He has been thrown out already''.

I checked up and found this to be correct. However, till today I do not know whether "Super" and his gang were arrested and prosecuted or not. The SSP who had promised arrest and prosecution got transferred.

Some police officers argue that to fight terrorism, informers are necessary. ''Not very good people agree to become informers and help the police. And some of them misuse their position like 'Super'. What to do?"

Fighting terrorism is a patriotic job. It should not be impossible for really good officers to motivate good persons to help in the fight. In any case, there should be no question of informers or ex-informers being allowed to indulge in extortions, kidnappings, etc. This can only further lower the credibility of the police. *(September 5, 1990)*

## 8. Police Prowess and Prize Money

Twenty-two-year old Kabal Singh, s/o Narinjan Singh, belongs to the erstwhile village, Kale, now part of the municipal corporation of Amritsar. He and his uncle Daya Singh decided to go to UP to meet some relations who had left Punjab and settled in the Terai area of UP, about 20 years ago. Close relations of Daya Singh live in village Fazalpur near Jaspur, where near relations of Kabal Singh live. Kabal Singh decided to take with him some new blankets to sell there and to earn some money.

They first went to Jaspur and from there took a rickshaw for village Fazalpur. This was in January. On the way they were checked and questioned by the police. Out of panic, they said that they had come from Amritsar to attend a marriage in the family. When the police checked up with the family, it was found that there was no marriage. However, Daya Singh was set free as he was identified by his near relations even though he was meeting them after a very long period. Kabal Singh could not be identified and was taken away by the police and would not be let off.

Relatives from Amritsar went there armed with certificates from some responsible persons. The police there still did not agree to let Kabal Singh off. The relatives were told that the SSP, Amritsar, should inform the SSP, Nainital, on telephone that Kabal Singh was OK.

After satisfying myself fully, I requested the SSP, Amritsar, to help in the matter. He asked for a report from the SHO concerned. On the basis of this report, he gave a letter for the SSP, Nainital. Along with a relative, Comrade Charan Singh of the CPI went to Jaspur and then to Kashipur where the letter was delivered to the ASP. It was on December 24, 1991 or so. The ASP said that there should now be no hitch in letting off Kabal Singh.

The SHO, Jaspur, however, went on putting off the matter. He had even said that Kabal Singh would not be allowed visitors. The ASP was approached again.

He said that Kabal Singh was now in the police station, Kashipur, and that they should go there. The relatives and Comrade Charan Singh were allowed to meet Kabal Singh at PS Kashipur. He told them that he had been treated well and not given any beating, etc. However, his release was put off again and again. And this despite the fact that some UP papers had been highlighting the long illegal detention of "a Sikh from Punjab". He was let off only late in the evening on December 31 on the assurance that he would stay there for 3-4 days before returning to Amritsar. Comrade Charan Singh has this to tell as to why Kabal Singh was not being let off for a long time.

Some days after Kabal Singh was taken into custody, one night shots were heard near the village. The police went there. Nothing could be found. Next morning Shri Mukhtiar Singh, Sarpanch, came across a dead body. He informed the police. The dead body turned out to be of a dreaded terrorist, Balwinder Singh alias "Binda" who had a prize of Rs. 5 lakh on his head.

The Jaspur police wanted to claim that Binda had been killed in a police encounter by the police. Actually he, it seems, had been killed by some terrorists because he had developed some intimacy with a sister of one. In any case, he had not been killed by the police. Kabal Singh was being kept and not let off because the police wanted the relations there to give in writing that there was an encounter. This they refused. The Sarpanch too refused. Pressure on the police also increased. Local parties also demanded his release. There was also the continuous pressure from the press.

Kabal Singh was, at last let off before the New Year, after full one month in police custody. He was required to stay on there for a few days for reasons which were not clearly spelled out. Possibly, the police wanted to make sure that no rumour went round that he had been liquidated. That apart, after the letter of the Amritsar SSP, the police had not the least justification to keep him, either legal or moral. He was kept in the hope of using his detention as a pressure to help the police to grab the Rs. 5 lakh prize.

It is hoped that appropriate lessons will be drawn by all those who are against police excesses even while standing for strong action by the security forces against the terrorists. *(January 12, 1992)*

## 9. A Case Study of Police Functioning

We give below some of the cases of persons nabbed by the police which this writer had to handle during the last one month or so—a sort of case study of police functioning in Punjab. Of course, all the cases belong to Amritsar district. Useful lessons can be drawn from this and such other studies, if there is a desire and will for that.

1. The erstwhile village of Ghanupur, now a part of Amritsar Municipal Corporation, is adjacent to Chheharta. At about 6 a.m. on 25 January 1992, a police party raided the house of 45-year-old Charan Singh, son of Doolah Singh—a Jat Sikh, and took him into custody. Some prominent as well as ordinary residents wanted to know why Charan Singh was being taken away. The reply was: "Come to the police station Raja Sansi to find that out". (Ghanupur is under the jurisdiction of the police station Chheharta and not of Raja Sansi.) Some relatives with an ex-sarpanch of the village went to Raja Sansi. All that they were told was that Charan Singh had been picked up on orders from above and that they could approach the higher police authorities.

It was at 8 in the evening that some comrades of Ghanupur met me and told me that Charan Singh had nothing to do with terrorists and in fact was strongly opposed to them. The SSP concerned could not be contacted. In any case I wanted to know the possible reason for Charan Singh having been picked up. The comrades came again early next morning with some family members. It came out that there was a land dispute in the village between two families. One party had been getting members of the other party "arrested" by the Chheharta police by making false reports. Charan Singh had been intervening to get them released. This could be the reason of a false report against Charan Singh. Those who had gone to Raja Sansi police station on 25th January had managed to find out that someone had sent a complaint that Charan Singh had illegal weapons. I got ascertained that this was not true and that in fact he had only a licensed gun for his own self-defence.

Due to their preoccupation with the Republic Day, I could not contact any senior officer. The Raja Sansi police station, recently upgraded from a police chowki, had no telephone as yet. I gave a letter for the SHO introducing a responsible comrade, requesting that he be heard and no injustice should be done.

I was able to contact the SSP only at 8.30 p.m. and gave him the facts of the case and demanded Charan Singh's release. The SSP told me that he would check up and that I could find out from him the next morning. However, he had to go out of Amritsar unexpectedly and I therefore drew a blank. (There is no really high-powered police control room to deal with such cases.) I was able to contact the DSP. He told me that there was a complaint against Charan Singh having illegal weapons of some slain terrorist. That would warrant a thorough search of the house, which had not taken place. After some discussion, the DSP accepted our version and assured that he would order his release. Charan Singh was let off on the 27th afternoon.

He met me on the 28th. On being asked, he told me that he was given some usual police "treatment" on the first night but not afterwards. He pleaded not to be asked the details of this "treatment". He had not been asked for any bribe but feared that he might be asked as he had been called again on the 28th. I was able to contact the DSP who agreed that there was no need for Charan Singh to report at Raja Sansi police station.

2. Surjan Singh, son of Lachhman Singh is about 60 years old. He is an ex-armyman, a pensioner. On retirement from the army, he settled down in Chheharta. After sometime he joined the Home Guards and was posted at Jandiala. He received threats from the terrorists and quit. He then took to business of selling vegetables in streets. He is a Mazhabi Sikh. He has four sons—all unmarried so far. Three are powerloom weavers and the fourth is a driver.

One of the sons with a young comrade of the area came to me on 23rd January 1992. A police party had entered the house of Surjan Singh at 10.45 p.m. on 21st January by scaling the walls and had taken him away. They checked up from the Chheharta police station. They had not done this. A cousin of Surjan Singh's wife was a fishy character. He had recently purchased a truck worth more than Rs. 1.5 lakhs. The police was after him to know from where he got the money. A police party from Jandiala police station had raided his house. He was not there. The police took away his elder brother, a vegetable seller. It was suspected that Surjan Singh too had been taken in the same connection. Before being taken away, he was asked by the police about the whereabouts of Bagga Singh, his wife's cousin. Bagga Singh had visited the house of Surjan Singh once after he bought the truck and had asked him to accompany the family to visit the gurdwara for thanks-giving. Charan Singh had refused to go and knew nothing about his where-abouts thereafter. The police could have ascertained the truth of this assertion from respectable persons of the area but it chose to take him away.

I was able to take up the case with the S.P. (Operations) and later with the SSP of police district. Majitha on 23rd January itself. On 24th I was informed by the office of the SSP that our version was correct and Surjan Singh could be brought from police station Mehta. This was done. He met me the next day. He told me that he was not tortured in any way but was asked again and again the whereabouts of Bagga Singh, which he did not know. However, he had been whisked away and kept in police custody unjustifiably.

3. Narinder Kumar (25), son of late Chaudhry Ram is a small shopkeeper in village Kalair under Raja Sansi police station. He is married and has one child. He was taken into custody by a police party of Amritsar Civil Lines police station on 2nd January and was being kept there. A relation of his in Chheharta met me with a Lambardar from the village. It turned out that Balwinder Kumar (22), an unmarried younger brother of Narinder Kumar, was originally a powerloom weaver but for some reason had joined a terrorist group. The possibility of his being a killer and kidnapper could not be ruled out. He had been absconding for the last six months. Because of him his uncle had left the village. Narinder Kumar had nothing to do with the terrorists and did not know the whereabouts of his younger brother. The Lambardar of the village told me that Balwinder Kumar had not been seen in the village for the last six months. Narinder Kumar had been whisked away and detained in the police station with the calculation that this would make Balwinder Kumar surrender. This was confirmed by the SHO of the Civil Lines police station. To me the police calculation seemed to be totally wrong. I was able to contact the SSP and take up this case with him on 5th January. It was on the 9th that he was ordered to be let off, our reading of the situation having been accepted as correct.

Narinder Kumar had not been subjected to any torture but the humiliation at the hands of the police because of his brother having gone astray has made him migrate from his village.

Incidentally, the Lambardar of the village who vouched for this innocent Hindu young man is a Sikh. Hindu youths going astray and joining the terrorist gangs for one reason or the other is no longer a rare phenomenon any more.

4. Rajinder alias Kali, son of Dharam Pal of Chheharta, was reportedly nabbed by some police agency on 4th January. He enjoyed by no means a good reputation in the town. He was believed by some to have been a member of the gang of the notorious Hindu terrorist

"Whiskey" who had been shot dead in an inter-gang fight. Kali's father, however, insisted that he was with Whiskey but had left him when Whiskey turned a terrorist. His father insisted that this was a false rumour spread by someone out of enmity. The matter was taken up by us only to demand that the matter should be decided without undue delay. He was let off on 29th January. According to one report, he is said to have surrendered to the police and repented. Of course, he had been subjected to a lot of torture.

5. About 50-year old Satpal, son of Lajpat Rai, was a tonga driver in his village Makhanwindi under police station Jandiala. Besides his wife, he has three sons and one unmarried daughter. He was picked up by men of police station Sadar in Amritsar on 24th December 1991 along with another Sikh youth. Both were let off on the 25th on the surety of perhaps the Sarpanch who said that they would appear when wanted. The police went to the village again on the 26th. Satpal was nabbed, but the other person Sukha, had disappeared.

I was approached on 29th December 1991 for help to get Satpal released. After satisfying myself that he was innocent, I took up the matter with the police authorities. It was said that Satpal had been found praising a top terrorist of his village and was also suspected to have transported weapons in his tonga for the terrorists. My argument was that no Hindu could possibly live in the area without praising the terrorists of his village and carrying out their commands. I also argued that his being kept in police custody would not act as any pressure on Sukha. He was let off on 5th January 1992. Satpal met me on his release. He had been hung upside down and beaten off and on till I took up the case with the SSP. After that he was only asked questions. He admitted having praised the topmost terrorist of the village, but did not admit having transported weapons. However, he said: "You cannot remain alive in the village if you don't carry out the orders of the terrorists". He told me that he would migrate from the village. He expressed the hope that he would not be picked up by the police again.

6. Jagtar Singh (35), son of Mohinder Singh, originally of village Baserke had purchased land in village Bhindian Aulakhandi under police station Lopoke. Having a wife and three minor sons, he was whisked away by the police on 6th January 1992. I was approached for help on the 11th. His relations admitted that till the posting of the Army in the

area some terrorists used to visit his house and take food, etc. He had to comply with this not out of sympathy but fear. Baserke comrades vouched for this. The SSP concerned told me that according to a report against him from the village, he was involved in smuggling of arms. However, Jagtar Singh was ordered to be released on 13th January, this complaint having been found to be false. Jagtar Singh met me on the 14th January. He was not in good shape and could not walk straight. He had been kept in the Lopoke police station for two days and then shifted elsewhere. He used to be hung upside down and given lathi blows. He was also given "vatna" treatment—a notorious method of physical torture. No information about arms smuggling could be extracted from him because he had none. Torture was stopped after the SSP rang up and discussed with the police officer who was interrogating him. Jagtar Singh told me about the person who had made the false report against him because of a village feud. This man, also a Sikh, was known in the village as helping the police as well as the terrorists—a sort of double agent. No persuasion on our part could make Jagtar Singh agree to demand action against this man and the police officials who tortured him. Neither he nor his relations would agree. Nor did they want any agitation on the issue. Of course, the police authorities should have taken action at least against the man who deliberately made the false report. This, however, was not done. Forums to discuss such cases have been promised and even formed more than once but they never function.

7. On 25th December 1991, I was approached for help to get one Angre Singh, son of Balwant Singh of village Mandiala near Bhauru in Amritsar district, released. I was told that he had been whisked away by the police on 16th December, had been tortured a lot and was now in hospital. Before intervening, I, as usual, wanted to check up. The relations who had sought my help admitted that he was an extortionist and kidnapper but was not a killer and was not a member of any terrorist outfit. Some others told me that he had killed ten or so innocent persons. The police denied that he had been nabbed and was with them. Some thought that he had been liquidated by the police in an encounter—genuine or false. His relations, however, believed that he was with the police and was still alive. The police, however, have struck to their version. There was, of course, no question of my intervening on his behalf. It is only very rarely that such cases come to me.

**Tailpiece**. The state level Republic Day function was held in Amritsar. The Governor hoisted the flag. As a precautionary measure a large number of Sikh youths allegedly suspicious-looking were picked up by the police and were released only two or three days after the 26th. In the bargain the corrupt amongst the police officials made a lot of money.

*(January 31, 1992)*

## 10. Terrorism and Human Rights

Any genuine concern for human rights should be welcome for all democrats and all those who cherish human dignity. However, when the banner of human rights is sought to be used to bring grist to the mill of terrorism and to undermine the sovereignty of independent states—including India—all democrats and decent people must refuse to fall prey and should expose and oppose these false champions of human rights.

Let us take the example of Punjab. Terrorists have been depriving innocent persons including six-month-old children and 8-year-old grandmothers of their most basic human right—the right to life. For ransom, innocent persons have been kept hostages, families are forced to give them food and shelter while unmarried daughters are molested, raped and forced to marry at the point of guns. A case has recently come to light in which a six-year-old boy was shot dead by a terrorist because he was witness to the rape of a 10-year-old girl. Of course the girl too was liquidated. This happened in a village of Amritsar district. Except a few, human rights organisations in Punjab as well as in countries of the West refuse to condemn these most horrible violations of human rights. When forced to deplore some mass killings by the terrorists, they in fact provide alibis for the killings by falsely ascribing the killings to the government. These champions of human rights have been keeping quiet at the killings of journalists who dared defy the orders of terrorists and also of hawkers who dared to sell papers, the sale and reading of which is banned by "militants".

Some will argue that these organisations are concerned only with violations of human rights by the state. This would mean that they have partisan political ends to serve and have no genuine concern for human rights. Even apart from this, the argument is false. When a killer guilty of a dozen or more murders gets killed by the security forces in a genuine or false encounter they kick up a big row. When an innocent person gets killed by the security forces by over-reaction, by mistake or as a result of false information or for some ulterior motive, they generally do not speak up. In any case they do nothing to get justice for the families.

It is good that the Prime Minister has done some plain speaking on the issue. However, it is necessary to go beyond what he has said. The Western governments should be told that a lot of money which comes for the terrorists from their countries is directly responsible for violation of human rights. Their first concern should be to stop this flow of money, if they are really concerned about human rights.

Of course, there have been some violations of human rights by security forces too. The corrupt among the police have made money not only by helping and letting off terrorists but also by harassing innocents. Third degree methods have been used during investigation of terrorists and those suspected to be so. All this needs to be exposed, deplored and stopped. But then such things happen in all countries even in normal times while investigating normal crime. It seems true that some terrorist killers have been shot dead after having been captured.

The police have an argument. It is impossible to get them convicted. The judiciary is almost totally paralysed. If a son is murdered by terrorists in the presence of his father, the latter will not give evidence—such is the fear of terrorists. All this is true but we do not agree that it is correct to kill even a killer except in accordance with the law. But then it must be recognised that laws which may be adequate to deal with ordinary crimes may be inadequate to deal with terrorism and insurgency.

Some of our laws need to be changed, especially in relation to trials, etc. It also needs to be recognised that, as in case of war, in case of insurgency or terrorism too some violation of human rights is unavoidable due to human errors and various other factors. The need is to devise ways and means to minimise these. It must be admitted that adequate attention has not been paid to this aspect. Secondly, victims of police excesses must be helped exactly on the same scale as victims of terrorist crimes. This has been achieved in Punjab. When killing or an excess is not the result of a *bona fide* error the culprit must be punished. The false thesis that it will demoralise the force must be rejected.

Today the matter concerns not only Punjab or Kashmir but the country as a whole. The banner of human rights is sought to be used by some

Western powers to have the right to interfere in the internal affairs of various countries as a part of their strategy to establish their own hegemony over the world. They are trying shamelessly to convert the UNO into a tool for this purpose, forgetting their own black record in the matter for support to regimes which have been the worst violators of human rights. India must resist this. And let genuine human rights organisations within our country flourish, instead of those which are in fact terrorist outfits or their supporters. *(February 16, 1992)*

## 11. Alienating the Youth

The Chief Minister of Punjab, Mr. Beant Singh, is a forceful campaigner against militancy and Khalistan as well as against the Akalis of all hues, including the moderates who, in fact, need to be won over. Moreover, Mr. Beant Singh does not think it necessary to seek and get the cooperation of all parties.

Even then he can and does rightly claim improvement in the Punjab situation. But he does not see the danger of this improvement proving temporary unless the fight on the law and order front is accompanied by some other measures.

Nevertheless, it is necessary to emphasise that political initiatives are urgently needed to isolate the militants on a lasting basis. These should include steps to give more powers to all states, including Punjab. Chandigarh should be given to Punjab and Haryana should get more than liberal financial assistance to build its own capital. At the same time, mutually acceptable solutions or ways and means to settle the territorial and river water disputes should be found. Further, Punjabi should get its due in the neighbouring states and in Punjab itself, while Hindi as the link language should be allowed to have its appropriate place in Punjab.

Other political initiatives, too, can and should be taken. It is unfortunate that with some improvement on the law and order front, the Chief Minister is becoming an even bigger votary of the false thesis that the Punjab problem is only a law and order problem. He even forgets that the much greater improvement that was there after Operation Black Thunder did not prove lasting at all.

Nor is this all. Mr. Beant Singh has been correctly emphasising the necessity of removing genuine grievances of the public and providing forums for the same. The practice, however, is quite different. He has not formed consultative committees for different departments even after four months since he came to power. The functioning district-level grievances committees formed during President's rule were wrongly dissolved. This was perhaps one of the first steps taken by the new government in Punjab. New ones were formed only in June and they have not yet started functioning properly.

The Beant Singh government has taken the correct decision to continue the district planning boards as these can help development work if allowed to function properly. For partisan reasons, however, no representation has been given to the opposition parties. They are packed with Congressmen and are sought to be functioned in a partisan manner.

Even when many erstwhile supporters of militants have turned against them, the former remain alienated from the government. An important reason for this alienation is the police excesses against the innocent. And this is the direct result of the way the Punjab police function. I wish to illustrate this point by giving only one example, though one can give many more similar instances.

Tarsem Singh, son of Kartar Singh, and Balbir Singh, son of Kundan Singh, are first cousins. Both are industrial workers and both live in Chheharta. One has four children and the other five. Their wives are sisters. Another sister of their wives is married to Sukhdev Singh of another area. Sukhdev Singh and his brother, Manjeet Singh, have been members of a gang of militants and extortionists. Unlike them, Tarsem Singh and Balbir Singh hold anti-militant views. They are CPM supporters and peaceful citizens. Due to a dispute in the family, Sukhdev Singh and Manjeet Singh and their other gang members have been determined to teach them a lesson by falsely implicating them as their accomplices.

Manjeet Singh was nabbed by the Majitha district police in February, 1989. He falsely told the police that Tarsem Singh had an AK-47 rifle. The house of Tarsem Singh was raided and searched. Nothing incriminating was found, much less any rifle. The family was asked to hand over Tarsem Singh to the police because he was not at home then. The highest authority was told the real facts. I was assured that there would be no torture but a face-to-face confrontation and interrogation. Tarsem surrendered. He was let off after two or three days on March 4 this year. He had been found innocent. However, he had been badly tortured and was in a pretty bad shape. Interestingly, Manjeet Singh, too, was let off.

Towards the end of April the houses of the two cousins were raided again—this time by the Amritsar district police. They had been falsely named as accomplices by an extortionist of the gang of Sukhdev Singh. This extortionist had been nabbed by a young brick-kiln owner and had been handed over to the police. His two accomplices had managed to escape. Instead, Tarsem Singh and Balbir Singh were named. As they were not found at their houses, some other relations of theirs from a village were taken as hostages.

Again, I took up the matter with the authorities. I explained their having been found innocent already. Their surrender was insisted upon and they did surrender on May 2. Once again the assurance of "no torture" was violated. A face-to-face confrontation was promised but it never took place. They were very badly tortured. They were in a bad shape when released on May 5. While in custody one police official had told them, "Why do you go to the higher-ups? You should come to us directly." The meaning of this should be clear.

Both of them told me that if what had been happening to them happened once again, they would become totally unfit to work. Tears flowed down their eyes when they added: "What will happen to our children, our wives and our old parents?"

I wrote to Mr. Beant Singh on May 14. I was informed vide a letter dated June 5 by an officer on special duty with the Chief Minister that my letter had been forwarded to the Home Secretary, Punjab, "for appropriate action." Action followed soon.

On June 10 the Gurdaspur police raided the houses of the two cousins in Chheharta. Balbir Singh was whisked away. As Tarsem Singh was not at home, his brother, Baldev Singh, was taken away to be released after five days. This writer was out of station. A CPM representative, Comrade Mishra, met the I.G. Police (Border Range), and apprised him of the entire background. The I.G. contacted the SSP, Gurdaspur. Manjeet Singh had been nabbed and had named them. He had also told them that on the earlier occasions the police had treated them with kid gloves as I was supporting them. Comrade Mishra was told that Tarsem, too, must surrender. However, he was assured that there would be no torture but only face-to-face questioning. By this time I returned to Amritsar. I, too, took up the matter with the I.G. There was no relenting but the same assurance was given to me also. Due to some misunderstanding there was a delay of one day in Tarsem's surrender. His house was raided again. All the male relatives were whisked away, were treated roughly but were let off when Tarsem surrendered on June 19. While going out of station again I had advised him to get himself medically examined in case he was tortured now.

I met both Balbir Singh and Tarsem Singh on July 2. Both of them were in a much worse position than on the two previous occasions of police torture. I will not give the details of the experience Balbir Singh and Tarsem had while in police custody. It is a harrowing story. But, briefly, here it is:

Barbir Singh was taken to a village where he was severely beaten up for three hours. He was asked to produce Manjeet Singh's weapons which were allegedly with him. Blind-folded, he was taken to another police station on June 12. Again, he was beaten up severely. At 6 p.m. he was taken back to the Kanhuwan police station. The previous treatment was repeated. It was after all this that he was brought face to face with Manjeet who proved a liar, even to the satisfaction of the Gurdaspur police. He was kept there for five or six days.

On June 30 he was brought to Amritsar along with Tarsem and taken to an interrogation centre. He was tied with ropes and hung upside down after which he was given a beating. The question asked was the same: "Where are Manjeet Singh's weapons?" He was brought to the police station, Chheharta, and let off on June 24. He is getting medically treated at his house.

Now about Tarsem. On June 21 he was severely beaten up at the Kanhuwan police station. He was asked to produce Manjeet Singh's weapons which were allegedly with him. The same evening Tarsem was taken to the CIA staff at Gurdaspur. Here he was confronted with Manjeet Singh who proved to have told lies. On June 22 he was taken back to the Kanhuwan police station. On June 23 evening he, too, was taken to the same interrogation centre at Amritsar. Here he was given the same treatment as Balbir Singh had got. He was let off on June 24. He, too, continues to be under medical treatment.

When I met them on July 2, on my return from Delhi, I asked them why they had not got themselves medically examined. They replied: "Our whole mohalla advised us against it. They said if we did that and the police came to know of it, they might nab us again and even liquidate us."

Interestingly, Manjeet Singh had named another relative of his. The police had raided his house but the relative was not at home then. No other effort was made to nab him though he is believed by many to have close links with Manjeet Singh.

No doubt, the police are fighting militancy and have also been making many sacrifices. The Chief Minister and many others have been rightly praising them. It is, however, unwise to keep quiet about the other side of the picture of which one example has already been given.

There is the false theory that any action against the police, even though it involves a serious error of judgement or is motivated by other considerations, will demoralise the force and that will help militancy. The fact is that silence about totally wrong and unjustifiable methods and the excesses committed for extraneous reasons can only bring grist to the mill of the militants. The sooner the Chief Minister realises this, the better it will be for all concerned. I can say without fear of being contradicted that had Tarsem and Balbir been younger or had they not many children and old parents to support, they would have been already in the ranks of the militants. *(July 15, 1992)*

## 12. Misusing the Banner of Human Rights

Those who use the noble banner of human rights to help terrorism stand fully exposed. This is the result of their persistent refusal to condemn in a forthright manner even the most gruesome violations of human rights of men, women and children, including the right to life, by the terrorists. It is time to be explicit and forthright about some other aspects of the matter. The fight against terrorism cannot be conducted as if it were a fight against some ordinary crimes. If terrorism is to be overcome, some violations of human rights and some excesses by security forces are unavoidable. This is clear to everyone who is not a very distant observer of the scene. At the same time, it is essential to take all possible steps to reduce these violations and excesses to the minimum. If proper attention is not paid to this and if the security forces are allowed to run riot on one pretext or another, long-term consequences are bound to be serious for democracy. If police is allowed to do as it pleases in the name of "not demoralising the force". It is bound to get dehumanised more and more. Nor is this all. That will weaken the fight against terrorism. Avoidable excesses and violations of human rights are bound to alienate people—at least sections of them. And let it not be forgotten that the fight against terrorism needs not only the sympathy but also the active support of the people.

Chief Minister Beant Singh, Director General Police and his force have won kudos for the substantial improvement in the Punjab situation. Even those who think that this improvement may not prove stable unless political initiatives are taken to clear the road to a political solution of the Punjab problem do not grudge them this praise. It is, however, a pity that the Chief Minister does not realise the need for curbing police excesses to the maximum possible extent. His repeated denials of excesses can only encourage those who indulge in them.

In the rural areas, people praise the Army. They do not criticise the CRPF. However, they are critical of the Punjab police even when fully recognising the sacrifices being made by it in the fight against terrorism. Recently I toured some rural areas of Amritsar district along with A.B. Bardhan, Secretary, National Council of the CPI. We found almost complete unanimity about not withdrawing the Army for another six months at least. I argued with some that prolonged stay of the Army was not good and some alternative must be there. Quick came the reply: "Reform the police. A reformed Punjab police can be do wonders". Even the police as it is on the whole is doing a good job. However, even the Chief Minister admits that the decisive role has been played by the Army and he is rightly opposed to its immediate withdrawal. One does not know why he does not see the need for reforming the police.

A commonly expressed view in the rural areas is that a section of the Punjab police is out to make maximum money and that the police commits excesses even when they can be easily avoided. These complaints may be exaggerated, but they are not without basis. I have myself come across many such cases and try to get justice for the victims. I will mention only a few out of those which have been brought to my notice only recently.

1. Gurdeep Singh of village Jeobala P.S. Chabhal, police district Tarn Taran, is a work charged employee of the Punjab State Electricity Board. On 23rd July, the police raided the house of his neighbours having

some relationship with him. Among the 4 persons they wanted to take away, one was a 10-year-old child. Gurdeep Singh said to the police: "Why take away this child?" The reply was: "OK, we leave the child, but you come with us". And this was done. The leaders of the PSEB Employees Federation made thorough enquiries. A real brother of Gurdeep Singh was a terrorist but he had been killed more than a year ago. It appeared to them that Gurdeep Singh himself had no links with terrorists. He has four minor children and old parents. The family hardly makes both ends meet. The union leaders took up his case. At one stage family members were given to understand that he would be let off soon. Now, however, they are being told that he was never taken away by the police. I came to know of this case on August 16, 1992 and got details 2-3 days thereafter. I have taken up the matter with the highest police authorities but so far have drawn a blank. The answer is the same, even though there is evidence, including some documents, to prove that he was in police custody. The PSEB Employees Federation (AITUC), known for its contribution to the anti-terrorist struggle, has called for a strike in the area on 27th August to protest against Gurdeep Singh's non-release and refusal of the police to give any information about him.

2. On August 19, one Alvad Bhushan, a Bangla Deshi living in Arjan Nagar, Chheharta, was whisked away by the BSF. On August 21, I was requested by some Punjabis of the area to help find out his whereabouts and to get him released as all their own efforts had failed. I deputed some responsible comrades to check from the area about his antecedents. Next day I was told that he had been living here for more than 15 years, had a valid passport, his two daughters got married here and he was earning his living be selling milk and by working on a spinning wheel given to him or his wife by the Gandhi Ashram and he has four unmarried minor daughters and one 3-year-old son. The thickly populated area vouched that there was no complaint against him. The matter was taken up with the BSF, Amritsar. They had not taken him. Somehow it was found out that he had been taken away by the BSF, Gurdaspur, which had found nothing against him but had handed him over to the police. He was reported to be in police station Dera Baba Nanak. A worker from the area went there. First there was a flat denial, but after some argument he was shown 4-5 Bangla Deshis in the police station. One of them was Alvad. It was then said that information about

him could be given and the question of his release or otherwise could be decided only by the DSP in charge. Despite all efforts all these days it has not been possible for the workers from here to meet the DSP or any higher authority. Nor have I been able to find out anything despite the matter having been taken up with the highest authorities—not even the police version—till the time of writing. Alvad, of course, remains in the police station. A newspaper today carries a report that a case has been registered against him on the basis of some confession.

3. Darshan Singh, s/o Atma Singh, has been living in Kartar Nagar, Chheharta for the last 4-5 years, having migrated from village Mahwa on the border. He does the business of selling sand, etc., and is not very well off. About a year ago a police official, on the ground that there was an opium-related case against him pertaining to the period when he was living in Mahwa, arrested him. It is also alleged that this police official, demanded Rs. 10,000 from him. People of Kartar Nagar intervened. They asserted that Darshan Singh had been living an honest life ever since he came here. He was ultimately let off. About two months ago, the same police official got hold of him in a bazaar and began beating him. The senior police official with him questioned both and then freed Darshan Singh. On August 19, Darshan Singh had gone to Ajnala in Majitha police district. The same police official happened to be there. Darshan Singh and his trolley and tractor were seized. It took the family two days to find out that he and his tractor-trolley were in Civil Lines Amritsar police station. On the request of the residents of the area I took up the case. I told the SSP that people of the area could not say that he had not done anything wrong while in Mahwa but that in Chheharta he had been leading an ordinary simple life. The SSP assured me that he would look into the matter personally. It saved Darshan Singh further harassment and he has also been let off today.

4. Beeru, son of Mohinder Singh, is a young Sikh Jat of 22 years or so. He belongs to village Mehma Pandori P.S. Jandiala in Majitha police district. Mohinder Singh owns only about 2 acres of land. In his village a terrorist family of Amritsar police district has bought a good deal of land which adjoins the land of Mohinder Singh. The village was raided towards the end of July, 1992. Besides some others, Beeru was also taken away by the Amritsar police. After satisfying myself that Beeru was innocent, I took up the matter with the police authorities of Amritsar. It

took some time before I could find out that he had been handed over to Tarn Taran police. The I.G. Police on my request agreed to look into the matter. He was released the next day but he was not in a position to walk. Hardly, two days had passed when police of the Majitha police district raided the house of Mohinder Singh. They took away Beeru. Before that, however, one policeman took pity on the weeping mother and told the family that Beeru would be taken to police station Chowk Mehta. Intervention, protest and pleadings by the village Panchayat which went to Chowk Mehta resulted in Beeru being let off. Two days after that Beeru's old father and his unmarried young sister came to me with a young man who could not walk properly. I already knew the father and the daughter. I had never met the young man before but I knew who he was as soon as I saw him. They had come to seek my advice. The old man said to me: "My other sons are in Calcutta. I think I should let Beeru also to go and join them. He can earn an honest living there as a driver. If he remains with us, he may again be picked up and get the same treatment before they realise that he is innocent . . . . We, the old couple, and our daughter will somehow manage on our own . . . . or, may be you need a driver and can keep him with you!"

The above examples are of different types. The point is that many illegalities could easily be avoided if the functioning of the Punjab police were better, if there was greater coordination within the police and with the public. All suggestions in this connection, however, get no response. It is a pity that the Chief Minister seems unwilling to pay any attention to this aspect of the matter. The fight against terrorism and the inhuman acts committed by the terrorists provide an opportunity to bridge the well known gulf between the police and the people. Unfortunately, this opportunity it is being lost. *(August 6, 1992)*

## 13. Police and Human Rights

The move of the Government of India to constitute a Human Rights Commission which will specially examine violations of human rights of persons in police custody is very timely. Speedy action is needed towards this end. It is also to be hoped that the proposed Commission's composition, powers, etc., will be such as will effectively minimise such violations. Experiences of political and human rights activists of persons wrongly implicated or suspected of unlawful action being tortured or killed in police custody can surely help in evolving a helpful policy.

Since I have for the last decade been actively involved in the fight against terrorism and secessionism in Punjab, I have had a close insight into the police activities. I would like to share my experiences in the sphere of human rights violations by the police, some of which are as grim as the terrorists' doings, and at any rate create hindrance in the fight against terrorism. I give here some instances of personal experiences in this regard, restricting these to Amritsar district during the last two years.

Let me begin with what may appear to be a relatively "mild" police crime. It happened in village Khasa just on the outskirts of Amritsar city. Khasa has a police chowki under the Chheharta police station. A big landlord accused his tractor-driver of having stolen some part of the engine costing a few hundred rupees. The driver had been in service of this landlord for about 10 years and had a clean record. He pleaded innocence. He even offered to make good the loss. The landlord, however, wanted the local police to interrogate him. They complied. Within half an hour of the tractor-driver being taken into custody, he died. The news spread. Hundreds gathered and sat on dharna before the police chowki. It was led by Mr. Jai Karan Singh and other CPI activists. Apart from me, an Additional Deputy Commissioner and a DSP reached the spot.

Consequently, an agreement was arrived at. First, a magisterial enquiry would take place and those found guilty would be prosecuted. Second, post-mortem would be by a board of doctors and not by one doctor. Third, the widow of the deceased would be given some financial help immediately and would finally get the same amount as admissible at that time (Rs. 20,000) to the next of kin of a victim of terrorists. And finally, all the police officials of the Khasa police chowki would be sent to the police lines.

Thereafter, the oral agreement was implemented. The magisterial enquiry took quite a long time. The report was not made public as there is no law as yet requiring the same. However, even though it went against the police, no one was prosecuted. It is stated that those liable to be prosecuted were able to make a deal with the family.

However, within a few days of the above incident, another person died in the same police chowki where he had been sent for interrogation by the Chheharta police. He belonged to Wadala village and was a domestic-cum-shop servant of a rich trader. He was accused of petty theft and was taken into police custody. The incident captured the headlines in the press. The police gave some financial help to the relations of the deceased. Magisterial enquiry proceeded at a leisurely pace. The next of the kin did not pursue it vigorously and it had to be prodded. The enquiry went against the police. However, in this case too no one was prosecuted.

Let me now give a terrorist-related instance of police misdeed. The deceased, who died in the Chheharta police station, belonged to Nanakpura Abadi of the town. It was known that his house was being used by terrorists. He had an enlarged liver and a blow at the sensitive point resulted in his death. The police got the post-mortem done and tried to cremate the dead body.

However, hundreds of people gathered and prevented this. I was present and on my suggestion, a DSP came there with the post-mortem report, and it was found to corroborate the point that injuries on the deceased were inflicted at the sensitive enlarged liver resulting in death.

A magisterial enquiry went against the police but the policeman or men who tortured him were not specified. It was further established that the SHO himself was not in the police station at the relevant time. Two companions of the deceased too had been taken into custody and had witnessed the scene. They, however, had refused to depose out of fear. It became known in the area that not only these eye-witnesses but also the widow had been won over with the help of a substantial amount of money. Had the agitation in this case not been led by the CPI, the pro-terrorist organisations would have succeeded in communalising the atmosphere in the area.

In another instance, a young man died as a result of police torture. He was a Home Guard and belonged to the Purani jail area of Amritsar. He was taken into police custody as he was suspected of belonging to a gang of petty robbers. The suspicion was not ill-founded. After he died as a result of torture in police custody, the police raided his house in the night and took his father to the police station. A deal was made. It was that the deceased would be shown to have been killed by terrorists, which would make the family eligible for a relief package. Also, he would be given an agreed amount in addition.

Early next morning hundreds from the area gathered at the police station and demanded arrest and punishment of the culprits. The father was brought there and was asked to tell the people to give up the agitation. He backed out. A magisterial enquiry started then and there. After two statements, the police objected to the enquiry taking place in my presence. The magistrate decided that the enquiry would be held in his court room. After some days the whole matter was dropped as the father was pressurised and decided to abide by the oral agreement he had originally made.

Here is another case but of a different type—one in which there was no intervention by any section of the local public or by any political party of the village. It happened in Bhakna Kalan. The deceased was a 30-year-old Scheduled Caste labourer. On May 12, 1992, he was taken to the local police chowki in connection with the theft of someone's cycle. He almost died in police custody. The mother came to know of it. She took him to a physician who declared him dead. The police took his dead body to get the post-mortem done. The report was that the death was due to excessive drinking. The deceased has left behind his widow and five minor children.

The mother of the deceased saw me rather late, on July 6. I got the matter enquired into independently and with the help of some very reliable persons. The findings, about which I have no doubt, were: the deceased used to drink a little more than is usual but had no other bad habit. There was no theft. Only a cycle was used for a little while. The man was pushed down the stair-case and was also beaten. He died of the injuries received. The post-mortem was obviously managed.

The case was discussed by me with a sympathetic police officer, besides a formal representation for enquiry. He told me: "I cannot say that your findings are wrong but it is too late to do anything in the matter—either by way of booking any police official or by way of helping the family."

It is hoped that these instances—by no means the worst cases of police violations of human rights—will be of some help to the law-makers and other competent persons to draw some lessons. *(November 5, 1992)*

## 14. Not Only on the Law and Order Front

Terrorism cannot be fought and defeated once for all if it is fought only on the law and order front. At the same time it has to be fought on the law and order front also. It cannot be fought on that front only with the help of laws meant to deal with ordinary crimes. Some violation of human rights in the fight against terrorism seems inevitable. If every possible effort is not made to shun avoidable violations of law and police excesses, the danger is of the police force getting brutalised. A number of examples can be given which go to show that such a danger is very real in Punjab. Below I give just one example the correctness of which I can fully vouch for—having intervened in this case personally.

On 4 January, 1993, in Khadeer Sahib in Amritsar district there was a quarrel between two shopkeepers—Satpal Bawa and Jarnail Singh. This led to some sort of a fight. It was towards evening. Satpal Bawa lodged a complaint with the police soon after the incident, while Jarnail Singh did that next morning.

Jarnail Singh, a member of the CPI, was taken into custody on 5th morning and both his legs were put in "Shikanja" (a torture instrument). No investigation was made as to which party was to blame and to what extent. No action was taken on the complaint of Jarnail Singh, despite his repeated pleas.

On 7th morning, Ajaib Singh and Balwinder Singh (father-in-law and brother-in-law of Jarnail Singh), both of them from Amritsar city, and Swaran Singh Nagoke—a member of the Punjab State Council of the CPI and a top leader of the Khet Mazdoor Sabha, well known in the area—went to the police station Khadeer Sahib. They found Jarnail Singh being beaten with lathis. Balwinder Singh and Ajaib Singh too were given similar beating. Comrade Swaran Singh too would have been given the same treatment but for the intervention of a police official of a neighbouring police station who happened to be there. However, he too was detained in the police station.

Comrade Swaran Singh was let off after a strong protest was lodged. The SHO did not let off the others. He alleged that Jarnail Singh had taken liquor and had beaten up Bawa, causing some injury. However, he conceded that no one had been sent for medical examination. According to reliable reports, some medical certificates were managed subsequently to cover up the illegalities. He chose not to say anything about the illegal custody and the lathi beating given to the father-in-law and brother-in-law who live in Amritsar. They had gone to Khadeer Sahib only after coming to know of the illegal detention of Jarnail Singh.

They were let off only on the 10th late in the evening after the entire matter had been brought to the notice of the higher authorities and they had intervened. They were told that all three had been let off after a compromise. Jarnail Singh, however, was let off only at about 10-30 a.m. on the 11th.

His swollen joints and lathi marks could still be seen. Ajaib Singh could walk only with great difficulty. He and his son were produced before S.P. (H) who expressed his shock and promised to pull up the guilty officials.

The police behaved in the manner in which it did because Jarnail Singh talked about its illegal action in forcing a sarpanch candidate to send a certain number of cement bags from the bazar at his own cost. There was some controversy about it and Jarnail Singh had spoken against the police action. This had been reported to the police. On an earlier occasion the police was made to return an amount of Rs. 360 which they had forcibly taken from Jarnail Singh.

This case had no connection with terrorism. There are cases of many innocents who have been treated much more brutally by the police merely on suspicion or some false reports made because of some personal enmity.

It is time for the government to take effective steps to ensure that avoidable excesses and violation of human rights do not take place.

*(January 12, 1993)*

## 15. Police Excesses Compromise Fight Against Terrorism

It cannot be disputed that for fighting terrorism successfully on the law and order front the police needs to have some special powers—even some extra-legal ones. Equally indisputable is the proposition that if effective measures are not taken to shun avoidable excesses, the police will run riot and will make the life of the ordinary citizens miserable—committing excesses not even remotely connected with the fight against terrorism.

Some very recent examples which I give below on the basis of my own knowledge will amply prove this contention of mine—more than many abstract arguments.

1. In village Gumanpura, police station Chheharta, District Amritsar, a son of a minister in the Punjab Government has a security post in his house. It is manned by policemen and home guards. During the night between the 4th and 5th May 1991, these security men caught hold of a PSEB employee going home on a cycle along with his brother. On discovering that Balkar Singh had some *gur* with him, he was forcibly taken into the house and beaten. The news spread Baba Seetal Singh and some other respectables were forced by people to intervene. When they went to the house of the Minister's son to enquire, Seetal Singh and two others were asked to "come in". Inside, they, Seetal Singh in particular, were given a severe beating. The security men also fired in the air. The police of the Chheharta police station reached the spot, rescued Seetal Singh and others after untying them. Seetal Singh had contested the post of sarpanch against the minister's candidate, but had lost.

Next morning there was a big demonstration at the police station by the people of Gumanpura. It was led by the local CPI leaders. An enquiry and action in accordance with law was promised. Nothing came of it. I took up the matter with the SSP on 11 May 1993 after his return from Chandigarh. The guilty officials were shifted from Gumanpura on 16 May but nothing else was done.

2. In village Khasa Pind P.S. Chheharta there is a powerful unscruplous landlord Kuldip Singh, notorious for his close links with the police. Not very long ago, his tractor driver was taken into custody by the Khasa police at his instance and was tortured to death within half an hour. As a result of the powerful agitation led by the CPI, a case was registered against the guilty policy officials but the landlord himself was not touched. The deceased was suspected of some petty theft.

Recently, Kuldip Singh, and Narinder Singh, son of Dalip Singh, a landowner of the same village, engaged themselves in litigation over the right of possession of some land of the Waqf Board. Knowing that the court case was likely to go against him, Kuldip Singh decided to get the matter "settled" in his favour with the help of his friends in the police.

At about 5 a.m. on 9 May 1993 about 8 policemen accompanied by the driver of Kuldip Singh raided the house of Kuldip Singh and took away Narinder Singh, his son Joga Singh and another family member Harbans Singh. The CPI intervened. Kuldip Singh was called to the police station and was given a shouting. He then revealed that the three persons had been whisked away by the Khalra police at his instance. A police officer at Khalra was earlier at Khasa once and was a pal of Kuldip Singh. Khalra is in Tarn Taran police district. I.G. Police was therefore approached.

Narinder Singh and two others were got released. No less a person than I.G. Police Border Range assured this writer that the law would take its own course against all the guilty persons including policemen. A formal complaint was also lodged. Nothing, however, has happened. Nay, something did happen. Gurnam Singh, a brother of Narinder Singh, and a son of Gurnam Singh were nabbed and whisked away in the early morning of 22 May. The local CPI leaders took up the matter with the higher officers. It was discovered that this time it was the police of Ram Bagh police station of Amritsar police district itself which had acted on the bidding of the son of Kuldip Singh. He as well as the police officials who had acted illegally and wrongly had to take some loud scolding. But that is about all.

3. We had somewhat better luck in another more brutal case. On a minor complaint of a neighbour, 4 police officials led by a sub-inspector raided the house of Shri Kewal Handa, an officer in the Punjab Roadways, and went to his bedroom at the other end of the house without so much as knocking at the door. He and his wife Shakti Handa were told to accompany them to the police station. Shakti Handa asked for the legal basis for this order. She was given a beating, resulting in a number of injuries and the breaking of a tooth. Shri Handa was dragged to the police station. Shakti was asked to go back when people protested. She however insisted on accompanying her husband. At the police station the husband was forced to sign an "apology". The family approached various public men for help to get justice. They narrated to them the entire story and also showed them the medical certificates of Shakti. This writer too intervened on 23 April immediately after his return from Chandigarh. The case was taken up with the SSP. At the instance of a gazetted police officer, one correspondent put out the story that the injuries were self-inflicted and the complaint against the police was false. This of course was challenged. The SSP offered to enquire into the matter himself on 8 May. The truth was established.

Some days later, however, the police and the Handas came to a compromise. The guilty police officials were shifted from the Islamabad police station. An oral apology was tendered to the Handas. An assurance of an adverse entry into the records of the guilty officials was also given.

More instances of this type can be given but that is not necessary. One thing, however, needs to be stated. People do move about on the roads of Amritsar city even long after it is already dark. They do so without any fear of terrorists. However, many have to fork out money to many policemen to avoid being nabbed, taken to police stations and subjected to humiliation. It speaks volumes about the present situation that they do not come forward to complain.

While the fight against terrorism must continue, it is high time to work out an effective strategy to curb police excesses also.

*(May 25, 1993)*

## 16. More on Police Brutality

On 30th October 1993 very early in the morning, a police party brought two "dead bodies" to the Civil Hospital Patti district Amritsar. The two persons were said to have been killed in an encounter. The "dead bodies" were put in the mortuary. A doctor later noticed that one was still alive. He was shifted to a ward. After he regained consciousness and when asked he gave his name as Surjeet Singh, son of Harbhajan Singh of village Valtoha, tehsil Patti, district Amritsar. The doctor was of the opinion that he had a chance to survive if he was shifted to Amritsar.

A message was sent to his family. Before his relations arrived, the SHO Sita Ram of Valtoha police station, having been told of what had happened, rushed to the hospital with some force. He himself was in a dhoti and chappals. Surjeet Singh was forcibly taken away. His dead body was brought back after about $2^1/_2$ hours, was subjected to post-mortem in the hospital and cremated in Patti. The relatives were kept far away and were given the ashes only subsequently.

Two eye-witnesses, CPI local leader Mahabir Singh and advocate Surinder Pal Singh, held consultations and telegrams were sent to the President and Chief Justice of India. Next morning this writer issued a press statement after ascertaining the facts to the extent possible. There was not a shadow of doubt about what has been stated above. It also appeared certain that terrorists used to take shelter in the house of Surjeet Singh, though it is not clear whether he himself was a terrorist. The Supreme Court took *suo moto* notice of the case and is now seized of it.

Be that as it may, the above incident is just one example of the extent of brutalisation of a section of the Punjab police. Two other very recent instances are not in any way connected with the fight against terrorism. One relates to Jandiala, where a number of middle class women and young girls were subjected to brutal beating, humiliation as well as indecencies in the middle of the night after dragging them out of their beds in their night dresses. They belonged to the families of two municipal commissioners who were opposed to the President of the Municipal Committee. It is said that the then SSP Tarn Taran was a friend of the president and the operation was ordered by the SSP to help his friend. The operation was led by an S.P. The Deputy Commissioner offered a public apology. No action, however, has been taken against the S.P. Quite sometime after the incident the SSP was transferred and made in-charge of a full revenue district near Chandigarh. In a way, a reward.

The second incident relates to Hoshiarpur, a district headquarters. A young woman lawyer married a colleague against the wishes of her parents. The father happened to be the Deputy Commissioner enjoying a fairly good reputation, but obviously with a very outdated feudal outlook on inter-caste marriages. The police led by the SSP himself decided to teach the couple, and particularly the husband and his family, a lesson. Only the intervention by the local Bar and the Supreme Court saved them.

It is important to examine how the fight against terrorism has contributed to such brutalisation of a section of the Punjab police so that lessons can be drawn for the future.

There was a time when except for some individual police officers, the Punjab police was not fighting terrorism. It was Rebeiro who first made serious efforts to motivate the police. Later on with a favourable political situation (formation of the Beant Singh government) and given a free hand, K.P.S. Gill brought about a big transformation. However, there was a negative aspect of his outlook and method, which was not taken care of. Motivation was not only on the basis of loyalty to the oath and the uniform and patriotism. It was to a considerable extent also mercenary, and not only on the basis of rewards.

It is undoubtedly true that some violation of human rights is inevitable during the fight against terrorism, especially when terrorists have highly sophisticated weapons and no scruples. War may not be an exact analogy, but it does help to understand the point which is sought to be made. It may also be necessary to let the police exercise some extra-constitutional powers. At the same time it was necessary to ensure that the police was educated to see that avoidable excesses against the innocents were reduced to the minimum, and even in the case of persons not so innocent there were limits not to be crossed. Such an outlook would also require punishing those who committed excesses deliberately and for *mala fide* reasons. This viewpoint was considered not acceptable and total freedom was given to the police. There was a wrong theory that such a policy would lead to demoralisation in the police and hence weaken the fight. Absolute freedom given to the police was bound to lead to some very negative results, for example, brutalisation of a section and a strong feeling in another section that having restored peace, it is the right of the police to rule *de facto* if not *de jure*.

Another factor contributed to this. When terrorists were ruling the roost, they acted against the judiciary also. The judiciary got thoroughly demoralised. In a large number of cases the judges did in the matter of bails, etc. what the terrorists nabbed by the police and produced before them wanted them to do. Much as we admire some recent interventions of the Supreme Court in some cases of police excesses, it has to be noted with regret that neither the High Court nor the Supreme Court in the earlier phase took steps to ensure that the judiciary acted the way it should have, notwithstanding the risks involved even when given maximum security. This resulted in the police resorting to and even being forced to resort to more and more extra-constitutional and illegal methods to deal with the terrorists.

Thirdly, political and public leaders did not play the role they should have, except for the Left to some extent. It has also to be remembered that the Left in Punjab is not a very big force. Most of the Akali leaders talked of "genocide" of Sikhs for ulterior motives. If some of them made an issue of specific cases, these were generally of the terrorists and killers. The Congress-I and the BJP leaders went to the other extreme. Explicitly or implicitly they fully swallowed the thesis that excesses against and even killing of innocents was a part of the price which had to be paid to overcome terrorism. Appreciation of the fight which the police was waging (of course with the very big and invaluable though not publicised support of the Army) and of the sacrifices it had to make combined with criticism of excesses against the innocents, etc., came only from the Left. Again, taking up specific cases and pursuing them with proofs, demanding enquiries and action against the guilty both outside and inside the Assembly, was done only by the Left and especially by the CPI.

The pity is that even now when terrorists have been suppressed to a great extent, no serious efforts are being made to bring about a radical improvement in the functioning of the police. On the other hand, the policy of defending and protecting even those who commit most indefensible acts continues. It is time for public opinion to assert itself in this regard. *(November 10, 1993)*

## 17. The Debate on Immunity for Police Personnel Fighting Terrorism

The unfortunate death of Ajit Singh Sandhu, the former SSP of Tarn Taran in Punjab, has revived in a big way the debate about immunity for police officers who fought terrorism in Punjab. Political overtones and considerations are very much clouding the issues involved. This article is an attempt to give an objective picture of the entire matter.

There were many factors responsible for the rise of terrorism in Punjab, external as well as internal. Terrorism should and could have been controlled and nipped in the bud. If that did not happen and instead it assumed very serious proportions, both the Congress and the Akali leaderships are to blame. For the sake of their vote-bank politics and in their struggle to have an upper hand for power in the state, each tried to play the Bhindranwale card against the other and encouraged terrorism. It was the Congress which brought Bhindranwale into politics. The Akalis took him to the Akal Takht. The Congress rulers allowed modern arms loaded in vehicles with kar sewa banners to be smuggled into the Golden Temple. The Akali Leaders allowed Bhindranwale to convert the Golden Temple into an armed fortress even while declaring that there were no arms at all.

In the initial stages, the police force was not acting against terrorists. Some individual officers were fighting. The police force as a whole was motivated first by Ribeiro and then by Gill. The government, however, not only would not take steps regarding the political aspect. It would not launch a real fight even on the law and order front. It was in fact following a policy of making a deal with the terrorists or a section of them. During a very crucial period, the police was asked to fight the terrorists with their hands tied behind their backs. The order was: "Catch them if you can, but don't shoot to kill them." Also the police would be asked to fight some groups but not the others with whom negotiations had been opened. This helped the terrorists a lot. The Akali leaders, on their part, were helping them by attending the bhogs of the terrorists who got killed, by calling them martyrs, etc.

Nor is this all. For long the SSPs appointed in Amritsar were either cowards or had their sympathies with the terrorists. The wives of some such SSPs would even visit Bhindranwale, bow before him and give him a lot of money. Thus it was that terrorism grew by leaps and bounds.

The judiciary as well as the entire administration got paralysed. Even terrorists who had killed many, when caught and produced in courts, would get bailed out immediately. When a terrorist in jail got bail and when the police would request the jail superintendent to allow him to go out of the main gate so that they could arrest him under some other case already registered against him, in violation of the assurance given he would be allowed to go out from some side gate and at a time different from the one agreed upon. A father would not be willing to give evidence anywhere even if his son had been killed by terrorists before his very eyes. In some parts of Punjab there was no government except that of the terrorists.

A suggestion was made to the government by this writer: The law should be amended to notify Class A terrorists to be called upon to surrender within a specified time, failing which it would be lawful for anyone to catch them alive or dead. Some other suggestions were made by others, as for example, the law should be amended to provide death or life sentences for those who possessed weapons not manufactured in India and who would not surrender them within a specified number of days; summary trials in states other than Punjab, etc. None of these suggestions was accepted.

The policy of making a deal with a section of the terrorists was given up after Beant Singh assumed office. A new policy, which some of us had been demanding, of a no-holds-barred fight on the law and order front was adopted (even though there was no initiative on the political front). However, by then the situation had become so critical that it could not be faced without giving the police extra-constitutional powers as, for example, powers to detain persons beyond the period allowed by law, to kill the killers when caught, etc. DGP Gill, who had earlier failed to control terrorism because he was asked to fight with his hands tied behind his back, was now given unfettered powers—so much so that Chief Minister Beant Singh could not even transfer an SHO.

The decision to wage an all-out fight on the law and order front came at a time when the isolation of terrorists had started growing rapidly. The fearless and selfless campaign of the Left against terrorists, even in their rural strongholds, had contributed towards it. A much bigger "contribution" was made by the terrorists themselves. This is what had happened in Amritsar district. In the first stage, a section of landowning Sikh peasants were sympathetic towards them. In the second stage, this section would say: "The boys are doing bad things but they are doing those for us." Then came the stage when they began saying: "The boys are bad". This stage started when large-scale rapings, forced marriages, etc., began taking place. The army (though not the police) began getting information about the movement of terrorists even in the rural areas. The decision to wage an all-out fight and the growing isolation of the terrorists together enabled the army, the security forces and the Punjab police to control and suppress terrorism in a short time.

In the fight against terrorists all police officers, including the SSP, did not act in the same way. For instance, those in whose houses terrorists got shelter were often taken into custody for questioning. Some officers made a distinction between those who gave shelter to terrorists out of sympathy and with a view to help them, and those who did it out of fear. Some other officers made no distinction between these two categories and gave all of them the usual police treatment.

Even while exercising extra-constitutional powers, some took every possible care to ensure that no innocent person was killed. They did not kill children and old women just to create fear and terror. If as a result of wrong judgement, incorrect information or some *bona fide* mistake some innocent person got killed, the family would be given compensation by the government. But there were some others in the police who cared two hoots for such things. Some indulged in torture and even killing of innocent persons for extraneous reasons—property, etc., and to settle personal scores.

The police force was motivated not only by the appeal to their sense of duty towards the country and of loyalty to their uniform and oath—but was also given monetary motives of more than one type. For instance, at a later stage they were given the freedom to make as much money as possible out of such nabbed terrorists as had been extracting huge amounts as ransom. Some did not take advantage of this. Some did, but only from the terrorists. Some others extracted money by nabbing even petty criminals and threatening to kill them.

Even amongst the SSPs and the SPs there were honest officers (though not many) as well as corrupt ones. The latter category consisted of two kinds. One would let off even terrorists for money, while the other would not spare them in any case.

Here it needs to be mentioned that even the army committed excesses when it was first given the duty of dealing with Punjab terrorism. After that it was given adequate training with the result that during the later period it successfully avoided excesses. No such thing happened with regard to the police. Even different SSPs had different types of conscience. As already stated, there were those who did their best to avoid killing and torturing of innocent persons. There were a few like the one about whom I had once the occasion to discuss with the DGP. I requested the DGP to post him not in the field but at Chandigarh. He was then posted at Batala and earlier at Faridkot. Whenever an incident occurred the suspects would be rounded up, made to lie on the road in broad daylight and beaten up. Parents of many would buy their release. In case of another terrorist incident, many would get the same treatment and thereafter they would join the ranks of terrorists as the only escape route. In my opinion this SSP produced at least as many terrorists as he killed. He once boasted: "What if I get killed by terrorists! I have made enough money even for my grandchildren." This SSP was killed by terrorists. Of course, such was not the general run of police officers, but he was not a rare exception either.

Some police officers made exaggerated and even false claims. For instance, the dreaded terrorist Manochahal was killed by the army while the police wrongly claimed the credit. The role of the army and para-military forces should not be forgotten.

Another digression is unavoidable. This concerns the so-called human rights organisations. With the exception of one or two these were front organisations of the terrorists. They would not condemn the terrorists for their innumerable violations of human rights, for example, forcing men to keep long beards, forcing girls to wear particular types of dresses, forcing newspapers to print their press notes in full and not to print government press notes, raping girls and forcing others to marry them, etc., and above all, violating the most basic and fundamental human right of thousands, that is, the right to life. The leaders of these human rights organisations would say: "We are concerned with only violations of human rights by the state." Nor is that all. They would invariably exaggerate the violation of human rights by the state. At one stage, for instance, there was widespread propaganda inside and outside the country that no Sikh youth above 16 could be found in the villages of Amritsar district. Even dead bodies of illegal Muslim intruders from Pakistan would be declared as bodies of Sikhs. Even a Canadian delegation which was allowed to visit Punjab by the Government of India found this propaganda to be totally false.

It is in this background that the demand for immunity has to be considered to meet the situation arising out of a large number of cases of violations of human rights, etc., filed before the apex court and the High Court of Punjab and Haryana.

There is no doubt that police officers and officials who exercised extra-constitutional powers which they were required to exercise with all necessary precautions and without crossing the limits (that should not have been crossed) must be protected. They should not be punished for unavoidable excesses because some excesses are inevitable in the fight against terrorism just as in war. Ways and means should have been found and should be found even now to protect them. Suitable legal provisions should be possible.

Total immunity, however, is a controversial matter. Apart from the question of constitutional validity, there are other vital considerations. Would it be correct to put a seal of approval on even the worst types of crimes committed by some in the police under the garb of fighting terrorism? Should not certain types of acts be avoided scrupulously even in the fight against terrorism? It is okay to remind Parkash Singh Badal how he dealt with the Naxalites in Punjab, but one should also not forget that two wrongs do not make one right. It is very necessary to ensure that the police does not get demoralised and is able to act if terrorism raises its head again in Punjab. But it should not be forgotten that no police force can fight terrorism without the help and cooperation of the people. The morale of the people too, therefore, has to be kept up.

Judicial paralysis, as we have already noted, helped to create a situation in which the use of extra-constitutional powers became essential. In deciding the cases before them after peace was restored, judges sometimes have tended not to take into account the circumstances which prevailed at the time. In some cases instead of punishing police officers, only compensation can be awarded to those who suffered. Much heavier compensation than for the next of kin of those who died at the hand of terrorists does not send a correct signal.

It needs to be pointed out that families of a number of innocent people who got killed at the hands of the police have not received even a paisa from the government. Ten or twelve such cases were brought to light more than once in the Punjab Vidhan Sabha by Vimla Dang, the then leader of the CPI group in the Assembly, who also agitated on their behalf. These cases were also brought to the notice of the National Commission of Human Rights. In some of these cases, inquiries were held at the insistence of the CPI and the persons killed were found to be innocent. Their families have not been compensated. They have not gone to the apex court because they cannot afford the expenses involved. Those who have gone do include the next of kin of some innocent persons, but many cases concerned the killer-terrorists. In fact, there is a planned move to use the right to go to courts to create an atmosphere favourable to the re-emergence of terrorism. It is my humble opinion that the judiciary should also take this fact into consideration.

Perhaps the state government can appoint an Amnesty Commission which would decide to grant or refuse amnesty and which would also help in the rehabilitation of children of the victims of terrorists killed by the police as well as children of the victims of terrorists in cases in which they have not yet been rehabilitated. Such a commission can also decide on the compensation to be given to the next of kin of innocent persons who got killed by police for whatever reason.

Be that as it may, all political parties should rise above narrow partisan considerations in this connection. They should join together and discuss how best to evolve mutually agreed solutions to the problems and issues which the death of Ajit Singh Sandhu has brought into focus. *(June 21, 1997)*

## 18. The Phenomenon Called K.P.S. Gill

With the restoration of peace (at least for the time being) in Punjab after a horrible period of more than a decade, super-cop K.P.S. Gill became a national hero. There are people anxious to deny Beant Singh any credit. They propagate that peace is entirely due to K.P.S. Gill. Even when his popularity was at its peak, Gill's detractors pointed out ''Gill's failure" to control terrorism during his first stint as Director General of Police, Punjab. They say when it suited the Congress it encouraged terrorism in Punjab. These are half-truths and half-truths are dangerous. It may help see things in proper perspective and to understand the K.P.S. Gill phenomenon, if I narrate my experiences about or with him.

I first heard about Gill when he was entrusted with the job of curbing terrorism in Assam. (A Punjabi Sikh Jat, he belongs to the Assam cadre of the IPS.) A top leader of our Assam Party was all praise for him. Of course, I did not ask him if this was the common understanding of the Party in Assam or his personal opinion. Be that as it may, Gill was certainly and really serious about fighting terrorism. In Punjab on the contrary we had DGPs and SSPs who were more concerned with being on the right side of Bhindranwale than fighting terrorism. One DIG for whom I have considerable regard, once told me, ''It is not the police which is fighting terrorism but only some individual officers''. Rebeiro was the first DGP Punjab who tried hard and honestly to set things right. He did a lot to raise the morale of the police and also to end discord between Punjab police and the para-military forces. At least once in Amritsar, there was exchange of firing between the police and the CRPF. It would be ungrateful to forget the good work done by Rebeiro. In this respect, Gill carried forward the work begun by Rebeiro and achieved great success. He is worshipped in the police by many.

Decisive success could not be achieved either by Rebeiro or by Gill when he took over as the DGP because their hands were tied. Both the Congress-I and the Akalis were trying their best (or ''worst''?) to play the Bhindranwale card against each other. This dirty game was fully exploited by Bhindranwale and the forces backing him. The Government of India wanted to make a deal with a section of the terrorists and also with a section of Akalis. While refusing to take the needed political initiatives, it would not allow even a no-holds-barred fight against terrorists. After some success was achieved, it would call a halt to the fight and go in for negotiations. Every time this strategy proved counter-productive. Terrorists regrouped themselves and the security forces got demoralised. With hands tied, Gill did his best.

Like Rebeiro, Gill and his men kept close contact with such political forces and elements including the Left which they believed to be anti-terrorist. He and his men sought their cooperation. The practice was almost completely given up when the police began to have an upper hand and terrorists were at the receiving end.

Some other aspects of Gill came to light during the earlier period. In a late evening party, a drunken Gill misbehaved with a lady IAS officer. The lady IAS officer decided not to take it lying down. In normal times, there would have been an uproar and Gill might have had to quit. But in the situation which actually prevailed, the lady had to fight a lonely battle in which political parties, women's organisations and the press by and large chose to remain silent. It was not so much out of fear as out of the feeling that Gill was badly needed by Punjab to curb terrorism. A statement issued by Vimla Dang, Punjab Istri Sabha leader, demanding justice for the lady, was printed only by the CPI daily.

After Beant Singh became the Chief Minister, there was a radical change in the policy. While continuing to refuse to take the needed political initiatives, a no-holds-barred fight on the law and order front was decided upon. While Gill was given full powers on that front, the Chief Minister ran a powerful mass propaganda campaign. A newspaper wrote: "There are three real ministers in the state: Gill for Law and Order: Beant Singh for Public Relations and Chatho (chief secretary) for the administration". Even though considerably exaggerated, it had some basis.

Gill did produce results. While the fight was on even some of those who fully supported it, like the writer of these lines, had some apprehensions for the long run. These arose out of the fact that extra-legal powers given to the police began to be used ruthlessly without taking any steps to prevent even clearly avoidable excesses. Any number of persons used to be picked up by the police of one district from another without informing even the boss of the police of the latter. It would take days to locate such persons. People were picked up on the basis of reports given to the police and tortured even though not a few of these reports were later found to be false, which fact could have been easily discovered without any third degree method.

I found some absolutely innocent persons who were tortured not once but four times. Some innocent persons belonging to this category as well as some known anti-terrorist relatives of terrorists died during interrogation. One SSP took out 4 persons from a lock-up and ordered their shooting down to cover up the fact of terrorists having got the better of police in a genuine encounter. As regards one of those, his release next morning had been promised by the SP because this man had been found to be innocent.

One of the incentives given to the police was to take money from those terrorists who had collected lakhs by way of ransom money by keeping hostages. It resulted in threatening to liquidate even small-scale anti-social elements if the amounts demanded were not shelled out by the relatives.

Gill did nothing to stop all this. His theory was twofold: (i) Some price has to be paid in the fight against terrorism, (ii) demoralisation of the police cannot be risked. This was a false thesis. It was necessary not to punish anyone for a *bona fide* error, but it was wrong to spare those who acted *mala fide.* Families of innocent victims were not even compensated.

A police officer in the course of a discussion with me conceded: "We have curbed terrorism. But the methods used were such as to make the future of Punjab and police force both pretty gloomy unless a radical change in the functioning of the Punjab police is brought about. Only Gill Sahib can do that."

K.P.S. Gill started a mass campaign in the form of cultural melas and programmes. Big gatherings took place, but without any decrease in the alienation of rural people from police. A section of police including Gill himself now believed that it was their right to rule Punjab. Nothing else can explain Gill trying to illegally force a Police Commissioner system in Amritsar, Jalandhar, Ludhiana; his unilateral announcement that Punjab commandos would be sent to Assam.

Methods which were used against terrorists have now begun to be used against ordinary people for extraneous reasons. There was the Jandiala Kand in Amritsar district and the Lajpat Nagar Colony Kand in Jalandhar. In the first, women relatives of some Municipal

Commissioner's office were the victims because one SSP wanted to oblige his president friend by forcing Municipal Commissioners to withdraw some writ petitions from the High Court. In Jalandhar, the fault of the women was that they lay down around a plot meant for their children, when many police and civil officers were out to grab it to carve out of it plots for themselves. In either case, no officer really guilty was punished. There is also the famous Valtona case in which some police officials forcibly took away a man who had been left in the hospital as having died in an encounter but who had been found alive. He was shot again and his dead body thereafter was cremated by the police. The SSP concerned was in the first instance inclined not to defend those officials. Gill's orders it seems were to the contrary. Innumerable other examples can be given but that is not necessary.

Once in the course of some enquiry which the Chief Minister had ordered at our instance, someone told the SSP concerned that Gill might not approve of what he had done. His reply was "No worry. For major part of the money he depends upon me."

Yet another police officer said in the course of a discussion, "Many of us realise that a radical change is needed in the functioning of the police. But our DGP now does not seem to have time to provide necessary leadership. Often we find it difficult to contact him." This was during the days when reports were current that Mr. Gill was acting in some films and/or was preparing the ground for a political future.

In this background came his fight for the presidentship of the Hockey Federation. The way he misused the police was no surprise to those who knew their Gill. Note the treatment which the two scribes in Delhi got from Gill's men right in his presence. Nothing could justify that, even if the two were drunk. It is good that Gill has apologised, but it is the big uproar which made him do that.

To be fair to Gill, under his orders policemen and officers in Punjab are being put through study camps in which lectures are delivered on various topics with the object of making the police force more human. Even I was invited to deliver one lecture and answer questions thereafter This is welcome but nothing much will come out of these unless:

1. The job of bringing about a radical reorientation of police functioning together with maintenance of vigil against re-emergence of terrorism is treated as a full-time job.

2. All extra-legal powers given to the police including the power to enact false encounters are withdrawn.

3. Responsibility for illegal and unjustified activities is fixed. Those who are really responsible—howsoever highly placed—must be punished. The practice of finding scapegoats out of the lower ranks, who only carried out orders (when some punishment becomes inescapable) must be given up.

4. Steps are taken to replace third degree methods with scientific methods of investigation.

Maybe K.P.S. Gill does not have the stamina or even the will to do all this. Maybe it is time for him to be given another assignment. After all, a good war-time hero is not necessarily a good peace-time hero. *(September 19, 1997)*

## 19. Purveying Dangerous Falsehood

The book* by the former Director General of Police, Punjab has naturally aroused great interest. All the more because of the danger of recurrence of terrorism in the state.

The book puts forward his thesis that Akalis were mainly, if not solely, responsible for the rise of terrorism and that they backed it fully. It, therefore, ends with a call to the Sikh people to "reject the (Akali) leadership and the institutions" that propagate and perpetuate the false theses that help terrorism.

The book recalls the horrible crimes committed by the terrorists, how they ravaged the countryside and how the most sacred place of worship for Sikhs was "converted into a place of torture and executions" (p. 88). The description is sure to make a powerful impact on the mind of any objective reader. The book also traces the birth and development of the Sikh religion and of the Shiromani Gurdwara Prabandhak Committee (SGPC) through which the Akalis have always been in control of the Golden Temple and many other historic gurdwaras of Sikhs. It also traces the growth and development of the Akali Party. It tellingly makes the point that "the entire spirit of gurdwara politics (of Akalis) militates against the teachings of Gurus" and how this politics as also "selective manipulation of Sikh history" by them helped terrorism. It

*__The Knights of Falsehood__ by K.P.S. Gill, Har-Anand Publications Pvt. Ltd., Delhi, 1997, pp. 142.

also makes out a convincing case that terrorism grossly violated the basic tenets of Sikhism. The greater part of the book is devoted to this. It reveals a deep knowledge of India's supercop about Sikh religion as well as about Akali politics. His political assessments, however, are not free from erroneous views.

On page 66, Gill rightly flays Hindu communalists for their duplicity, for adding more fuel to the fire by persuading a large number of (Hindu) Punjabis to make false declaration about their spoken language confirming "the (false) Akali thesis of Hindu treachery in the minds of the more gullible among the Sikhs". However, Gill seems to believe that all this was a reaction to Sikh communalism and demands like Sikh Homeland of the Akalis. There is no doubt that Hindu communalism on the one hand and Sikh communalism on the other brought much grist to each other's mill but to say that one was (only) a reaction to the other and thus to provide an alibi for it is very wrong. According to Gill, the Akalis were "the first to play the communal card" (p. 70). It is like saying the hen came before the egg or the other way round but it can be very dangerous because it underplays the need for fighting Hindu communalism.

Gill pinpoints some sins of even the moderate Akali leaders. For instance, he writes:

"At one point of time, several leaders 'led' by the moderate Sant Fateh Singh, camped inside the Akal Takht, an unprecedented act (and one that was only to be repeated decades later by Bhindranwale and his gun-toting followers) . . . . " (p. 66).

He reminds the readers how Surjeet Singh Bharnala as the Chief Minister released from jails a large number of terrorists. Without naming Badal he refers to the "burning of the Indian Constitution" by him (p. 92). He could easily give more examples of acts of commission and omission of these Akali leaders. Notwithstanding that, it is wrong to put them at par with the extremist Akali leaders like Tohra or to forget their positive aspects. Badal and Barnala never called upon Sikh youths to buy motorcycles and AK-47s though out of opportunism and/or cowardice they did help terrorism in more than one way. Sant Fateh Singh was the first Akali leader who declared that he wanted a Punjabi Suba purely on linguistic basis and did not care as to whether or not Sikhs would be in a majority in such a Suba. Not to see the important difference between moderate and extremist Akali leaders cannot but lead to serious mistakes in strategy and tactics on the part of secular forces, mistakes which would help only the extremists.

The Akali leadership represents the interests of the Sikh landlords and capitalist farmers above all. It uses the religious card and the gurdwaras to mobilise the Sikh masses behind it by making them believe that its class demands are in fact the demands of the Sikh community. They wanted to use terrorism to pressurise the Congress to agree to the formation of a theorcratic state within, if not outside, India. Gill is no Marxist and has no class approach. He therefore, ascribes the Akali perfidy to their "bigoted mind-set" and has no strategy to offer to fight them politically except on the basis of the "true teachings of Sikh Gurus". And this by itself is not likely to succeed. This should be clear from what Gill himself says about religion. He writes:

"Every great religion of the world has as its fountainhead, a remarkable mystical insight, a remarkable spiritual institution . . . . It is this power that inspires millions to acts of great sacrifice, setting them on the path of selfless service . . . . There is, thus, in the history of every religon, a continuous struggle to harness the immense energies of faith for conflicting ends both good and evil . . . ." Gill approvingly quotes Abdul Karim Soroush: "The clergy earns its living from religion. If your interests are secured through religion, then you will defend your interests first and religion will become secondary."

Gill further says:

"This is the key to understand why religious institutions and those who control them have seldom pursued or promoted truly religious and spiritual ends."

He makes clear his view that "this is true of the religious establishment even in a faith such as Sikhism".

There are a number of references as to how on specific occasions the Congress conduct helped terrorism. He even says:

"It is a well-known and well-documented fact that the flames of terrorism were fanned by Congress-I."

However, there is no deep and detailed analysis of the Congress responsibility which was no less than that of the Akalis. There is no mention of the fact that Bhindranwale was brought into politics by the Congress. It is said that the police was doing so as per the policy of the

Government of India. Gill does not even recall his own experience as the DGP in the first instance. He failed because his hands were tied by the government ("catch them if you can, but don't shoot to kill them") which wanted to make a settlement with the terrorists or a section of them at the cost of the Akalis. This failure to unmask properly the Congress responsibility makes the book one-sided and is therefore not fully convincing.

Except for some references to the ISI, the external factor, which included, besides the Pakistani rulers and NRIs like Ganga Singh Dhillon, the Government of the USA and its allies, is also missing. How the vote-bank politics of the Congress on the one hand and the Akalis on the other helped the terrorists immensely is also not there in detail.

Such secondary factors which helped terrorism in Punjab as excesses including torture and killings committed by a section of the Punjab police find no mention in the book, when the fact is that some police officers produced more terrorists than they killed. Issues brought to the forefront by the suicide of SSP Ajit Singh Sandhu are not touched on deliberately. Obviously, Gill continues to hold the view that to fight terrorism it is necessary to let police torture and kill even innocents and for extraneous reasons. How a demoralised police force was converted into a fighting one is described, but the role of Ribeiro in this is not mentioned at all.

The role played by all political parties including the Congress and the Akalis in foiling the game of terrorists to bring about Hindu-Sikh riots (despite their other sins) and the initiative of the Left in this matter do not find any mention in the book. The fight put up by the Communists and especially by the CPI which was the first to go to even the rural strongholds of terrorists to mobilise the people against them, won tremendous appreciation from the entire country. That, however, finds no place in Gill's book, except for the solitary reference to one defence post of the CPI-M. In fact, Gill has tried to make out that the police alone fought and defeated the terrorists. All political parties have been tarred with the same brush. The thesis put forward by some Akalis that terrorists were overcome by the people alone and that the police had no role in it has been rightly criticised by Gill. However, his own thesis that virtually the police alone is responsible for overcoming terrorism (notwithstanding references to the army and other security forces and brave people, here and there) is equally wrong. This flies in the face of facts and is dangerous. Terrorism cannot be fought without the support of the people.

And to condemn all politicians so that poeple can look for some saviours from the police or the army is most dangerous.

The book, therefore, is not what one would have liked it to be—drawing lessons from the 1978-93 period and using them to prevent the re-emergence of terrorism in Punjab.

It also contains some minor mistakes. For instance: it is not correct that on April 13, 1978, Bhindranwale accompanied the jatha which marched from the Golden Temple to the site of the Nirankari Sammelan and fled from there. The fact is that after having declared that he would lead the jatha and having incited those hearing his harangue, he quietly disappeared and did not even accompany the jatha. Such minor mistakes, however, don't take away the merit of the very well brought out book, subject, of course, to the criticism made above. *(October 11, 1997)*

# CHAPTER VI

# The Left in the Fight Against Terrorism

## 1. Autonomy, Akalis and the Left

Some of the BJP leaders sometimes support or pretend to support the demand for more fiscal powers for the states in India. The fact, however, remains that the erstwhile Jan Sangh and the RSS, which are the backbone of the BJP, have been votaries of a unitary India and opposed to federalism. It is, therefore, understandable that for them the word "autonomy" should be like a red rag to a bull. It is a pity that many a Congress leader too should display the same reaction to this word. Perhaps it will be useful to remind such Congress leaders that the historic August 1942 resolution of the Indian National Congress had visualised the future constitution of free India as "a federal one, with the largest measure of autonomy for the federating units and residuary powers vesting in these units." And in 1946, the Congress reiterated: "The Constituent Assembly shall draw up a Constitution for the Federal Union. This shall consist of an all India Federal Government and Legislature dealing with foreign affairs, defence, communications, fundamental rights, currency, customs and planning as well as such other subjects as on close scrutiny may be found ultimately allied to them. All the remaining powers shall vest in the provinces or units."

It is clear that the Constitution adopted and enforced in India was not quite consistent with the above commitments of the Indian National Congress. In this, three lists of powers were drawn up. The Centre was given power to encroach on the State List and to enlarge its share in the Concurrent List. Financial powers were in the main with the Centre. Moreover, residuary powers vested with the Union and not with the States. Notwithstanding all this, the constitution adopted and enforced was a federal one. It did give a certain measure of autonomy to the states. Even that, however, has been eroded to a considerable extent during the last

32 years. As pointed out by the National Council of the CPI as early as 1978:

"It is the discretionary grants, not assured assistance under the Constitution, which has begun to predominate and constitutes the major share of the total aid (by the Centre to the states), giving the Central Government a powerful leverage for unjustly pressuring and influencing the policies of the states in many fields of the latter's activity. This has caused much resentment in the states, although under the monopoly of one-party power, such resentment has been silenced at the official level". Also: "The arbitrary resort to President's Rule in the states under Article 356, sometimes even for sorting out internal problems of the party in power, the provision for President's assent to certain categories of bills passed by the state legislatures, the power of the Centre to issue directives to states, Centre's control over the All-India Services even when their cadres are under the employment of the states and the sweeping emergency provisions in Part XVIII of the Constitution—all this has enormously contributed to the undermining of the federal principle, and of the powers and autonomy of the states".

Re-assuming the right of the Centre to send para-military or military forces into any state without the state asking for it is another instance of inroads into the limited powers of the States.

This process has helped divisive and separatist forces on the one hand and authoritatrianism on the other. Greater powers and autonomy for the states than they in fact enjoy at present, being demanded by the Left Parties while ensuring a strong Centre at the same time, can go a long way to strengthen the unity of India.

Prime Minister Indira Gandhi, therefore, is not right when she denies the need for having a fresh look at Centre-states relations on the ground that "states already enjoy enough autonomy under the Constitution". (*Indian Express,* November, 19, 1982.)

States need more assured financial resources to be able to discharge the responsibility placed on them by the Constitution in the matter of development needs. At present states do not have adequate resources at their disposal for this. People of different states cannot like the idea of the Centre being allowed to dismiss governments elected by them merely because it does not like them for one reason or another. Peasants of Kerala could not but feel very unhappy and agitated when the Centre permitted import of cocoa, rubber, etc., without consulting Kerala and even when it was quite obvious that it would benefit only the big monopolists and multinational companies, while hitting hard the growers and the agricultural economy of the state. Industrial workers of Bengal could not but feel embittered when, on the advice of the Central Government, the President would not give assent to legislation passed by the West Bengal Vidhan Sabha, the purpose of which was to give them some long-demanded and very justified benefits. Workers of Amritsar did not like the fact that the state government could not take over a mismanaged mill even when it wanted to, because it did not have the powers to do so and because the Central Government would not agree. And is it not scandalous that a state government should not have the power to change the name of a village within its jurisdiction without the permission of the Government of India?

The Akali leaders have been making desperate efforts to convince other Opposition parties in the country that their Anandpur Sahib Resolution makes precisely this demand for more powers for the states and nothing more. If they have failed in this effort, there are quite good and solid reasons for it. The Anandpur Sahib Resolution demands that only five departments—namely, defence, foreign relations, communications, railways and currency—should be under the Centre's control and all the residuary departments should be under the jurisdiction of "New Punjab", which should have the right to frame its own constitution for these departments. In other words, if this resolution were to be accepted, the Centre would not have even the departments of Planning and Customs.

As recently as the third week of November, 1982, Sant Harchand Singh Longowal was asked by B.K. Chum of the *Indian Express* if he was prepared to suitably amend this part of the resolution. He would not go beyond saying: "When there are discussions, we can consider this issue."

In the same interview, published in the November 21, 1982 issue of the *Indian Express*, the Sant went on to reiterate another and even more objectionable aspect of the Anandpur Sahib Resolution. He said: "We cannot give up our political objective which, as the resolution explains, is the pre-eminence of the Khalsa (*Khalsa ji da bol bala*)".

In a desperate effort to overcome its isolation from all other

Opposition parties, the Akali leadership has tried to explain away this demand for Sikh domination in Punjab. Some of the explanations put forward are even contradictory.

Quite some time ago, Gurcharan Singh Tohra said something to the following effect: "If Communists can aspire to rule, that is, to have their domination, what is wrong if Sikhs have the same aspiration?"

The weakness of the argument is quite obvious. A political party wanting to come to power while committed to a secular state is one thing and to demand the political pre-eminence of one religious community is quite another.

Some other Akali spokesmen began to give another argument. According to them, *Khalsa ji da bol bala* was a part of the Sikh religious prayers and nobody had ever taken any objection to it. They asked: Why should a big noise be made now about it? The "noise" was obviously justified, because it was now made a political aim and "New Punjab" was being demanded for this purpose.

The official organ of the Akali Party, *Akali Patrika* (Punjabi daily) came out with yet another explanation on September 7, 1982. It said in its editorial: "The words *Khalsa ji da bol bala* in the Anandpur Sahib Resolution mean the region in which Sikhs would be in a majority and in which it would be possible to safeguard Sikh rights."

This explanation contradicted the assertion made by Sant Longowal that he wanted Punjab with all Punjabi-speaking areas in it and was not worried if that would mean Sikhs becoming a minority in the State. Perhaps he did not really mean it. However, the latest explanation has been given by the Sant himself in the course of the *Indian Express* interview quoted above. Here is what he says:

"The Akali Dal, being the trustee of the Sikhs, also wants its pre-eminence in the same way as the Congress, the Communists, the BJP or any other political party wants for itself. This in effect means gaining power. Why should anybody have any objection if the Akali Dal sets the same political aim as other parties have? The Dal has never said that it wants a separate State or that the Sikhs want secession. In fact, it is the Congress and the Central Government which are separating us from our country. We are being treated as second-class citizens. We want to be assured that we are not second-class citizens."

If the Akalis do not have any aspiration other than to come to power in a secular Punjab in a secular India, why not say so in clear, simple and unambiguous terms to remove all doubts? Why, adopt religious concepts as political aims? Why make the wrong assertion that the Akali Dal is the sole trustee of the Sikhs? And also that Sikhs in India are second-class citizens?

The Sant's words quoted above seem to have a not-so-hidden meaning too. The Sant seems to be saying: "Sikhs will cease to be second-class citizens only in a Punjab in which Sikhs rule through the Akali Dal and only if the Central Legislature and the Central Government have as little power as possible." Let it not be forgotten that the Anandpur Sahib Resolution clearly contains the seeds of "Sikhs are a separate nation" concept.

Akali leaders have been advancing varied arguments in support of their demand for greater autonomy for Punjab. On the one hand, they have been dittoing arguments put forward by the Left. At the same time, they have been making it a Sikh issue by arguing that denial of greater autonomy to Punjab is an act of gross injustice to Sikhs. They have been blowing hot and cold.

In connection with their Morcha, they have put forward some significant arguments which may help to understand the class aims of the Akali "Dharam Yudh" for "greater autonomy."

Akali leaders have been explaining the demand for autonomy to the peasant gatherings on the following lines:

"We grow wheat. Why should its price be fixed by the Centre? Why should we not have the power to do that? Only when we have that power, shall we get justice. When we have autonomy, we can ourselves determine wheat prices. We can then export wheat to other countries at much higher prices. Why should we not have the right to fix wheat prices at the international level if they are higher?"

Poor and lower sections of the middle peasants want only remunerative prices. If the cost of production can be brought down by bringing down the prices of inputs and if manufactured goods can be made available to them at reasonable rates, they may welcome even lower prices for wheat. The capitalist landlords and the rich peasants want profiteering prices. They make no secret of it in informal discussions. They even say: When Tatas and Birlas have the right to raise the prices of their goods as much as possible, then why should we not have the same unlimited right? And this is the clear meaning of the above cited argument of the Akali leaders.

One Akali leader, when asked privately what they would do with all the powers they want, said: "We will put an end to agrarian reforms. We will scrap the Hindu Succession Act. And we will end reservations for Scheduled Castes."

All this should leave little doubt as to whose interests the Akali leaders want to serve and why they want more powers. They cannot be sure that if and when States get more powers, it is they who will exercise these powers and in a manner as will serve the class they represent, if the fight for more powers is for all secular States including secular Punjab in a secular India and if it is conducted as a common struggle of the people with no religious overtones. Kulaks and other landed vested interests are mostly Sikhs in Punjab. Class demands and religious demands get mixed up and that comes in handy.

A section of the Akali leadership, which has also developed considerable industrial interests, seems to be realising that the weapon can prove dangerous too. It can help and has helped the extremists and separatists. But they are too timid to criticise and expose the extremists' ideology, to clearly and sharply demarcate themselves from separatists and fundamentalists, to come out in favour of separation of religion and politics.

They are unable to do this even when they allege with some truth that the ruling Congress-I itself or its factions have been encouraging the extremists for short-term partisan gains.

The Left wants to help the moderates amongst the Akali leaders to gather courage and to adopt and openly stand by a secular outlook. It can do so only if it runs a much bigger campaign than it has done hitherto among the Sikh toiling peasants showing why they, in the interests of the Sikhs themselves, should actively work for separating religion from politics and should actively come out against forces of Sikh separatism and fundamentalism. The policy of moderate Akali leaders to try to use extremists for increasing pressure on the government needs also to be exposed.

All this will remain an important job for the Left in Punjab for quite some time to come, whatever may be the outcome of the negotiations between the Akalis and the Government of India. Like many others, we very much wish that there is a settlement on a principled basis. *(1982)*

## 2. Chheharta: Shining Local Initiative

Chheharta (Amritsar) is much in the news. Various public men are calling upon the people to face and nab the killer gangs of the extremists in the way the unarmed people of Pratap Bazar, Chheharta, did on February 24, 1984. From events in Chheharta, however, many lessons can and should be drawn. We give the main events below.

Some months ago, Dr. Gurdial Singh (a Nirankari) of Ghanupur near Chheharta was killed by extremists in broad daylight at his clinic. The working class of Chheharta observed a half-hour strike in protest. A massive public rally to condemn the murder was held at the centre of Chheharta. Another equally big rally was held right in front of the clinic of Dr. Gurdial Singh. More than 75 per cent of the people attending the latter rally were Sikhs. Besides other things, a call was given that in case of such attacks people should act and take steps to nab the culprits. Both public meetings were called by the CPI.

On another occasion, Chheharta's working class joined the working class of the rest of Amritsar in observing a half-hour protest strike against some other killings. Whenever the situation in the city of Amritsar took a turn for the worse, gate meetings were held in all the mills in Chheharta (as in the rest of Amritsar) by the AITUC unions. Mohalla, hall and public meetings were held by the CPI.

In this background came the call given by the Akali Dal for Punjab Bandh on February 8, 1984. Out of fear and to avoid clashes Hindu shopkeepers of Chheharta closed down their shops. Having been approached by the Akali Party, the managements of the mills in Chheharta approached the Mill Committees of AITUC unions to find out if they would be willing to observe bandh by agreeing to February 8 being declared a weekly holiday. In every mill, the workers turned down the proposal. Only in case of one mill (OCM) the management on its own implemented the proposal. On February 9, workers of all the mills turned up. All the mills started working—except OCM. In case of OCM, workers were not allowed to enter. They dispersed after some time. In all other cases, armed volunteers went to the mills and made the managements close down the mills. The bandh was "complete" as claimed by the Akalis, but it had in fact widened the gulf between Hindus and Sikhs in Chheharta as elsewhere in Punjab.

Then came the call for Punjab Bandh on February 14, 1984, given by the Hindu Suraksha Samiti. Sentiment amongst Hindu middle class, especially youth, was that Hindus too must demonstrate their power, this bandh too must be complete as the one on February 8. Sikhs too must observe it and all methods should be used as on February 8.

All Sikh shopkeepers closed down out of fear and to avoid clashes. Most of the mills were closed as the day was their normal weekly holiday. OCM started working but was forced to close down. Anyone who opened his commercial establishment was made to close down. Youth Congress-I workers were in the forefront. BJP workers helped.

CPI alone had deplored both the bandhs. All other parties had kept a discreet silence. Sant Bhindranwale and the Sikh Students Federation had called for resisting the bandh of February 14. And it was resisted in more than one place—to make some Sikh reopen his shop if he had closed it and to "help" someone else if he wanted to keep open. This happened in Chheharta too.

Once again the bandh was complete but once again it had widened the gulf.

On February 14 local BJP leaders and some Hindu Congress-I leaders announced a closed-door meeting (of Hindus) in a temple the next day. Entry was strictly regulated. The news leaked out that decisions were taken to collect arms, etc, for the defence of the Hindus.

A Sikh meeting had also been called. Besides others, all Sikh shopkeepers of Pratap Bazar were invited. All Sikh Congressmen attended the meeting. Such Sikh shopkeepers as support CPI refused, declaring that they would attend only joint meetings. The meeting was addressed also by representatives of the Sikh Students Federation. Highly provocative, communal and poisonous speeches, even calling for killings, were made. Even a good part of those who attended felt revolted.

The Sikh Students Federation announced "Akhand Path" (continuous recitation of Sikh holy scriptures) near the gate of the OCM Mills (in which a majority of workers are Sikhs). Funds were collected from within the mill. The Akhand Path was started on February 18 and bhog was on February 20. It had been announced in the whole of Chheharta and in the neighbouring villages. The sitting audience at the bhog ceremony was about 150. About the same number of people stood around. Many of the audience were an imported lot.

Highly communal speeches even inciting communal killings were made. A big police force was present. It was ordered to move some distance away. It complied. At least one of the speakers was on the wanted list of the police. Had he and others been arrested, there would not have been any trouble in the area. It is for powers-that-be to explain why the bid to create an atmosphere conducive to killings was not checked.

On February 23 whispers began that extremist killers would strike in Chheharta. It was given out by their sympathisers to help some personal friends. Police was informed by some. On February 24 police was informed again. And on February 24 four killers attacked. One was killed at the site while two were injured.

Four-five young men ran after the killers. Others—both Hindus and Sikhs—followed them. Many from village Wadali Guru too joined. The members of the killers' squad ultimately went into a garden about three kilometres from the place where they had killed one person. The garden was surrounded by the people.

The two armed policemen had been posted very near the site of the incident. A Sikh shopkeeper asked them to act. They ran away saying they would first get instructions from the police station. With them went away two guards at a nearby bank. The police officials posted at Chheharta crossing, however, acted differently. They rushed to the police station. From there the SHO, DSP and other policemen rushed and followed the people chasing the extremists. Ultimately three of the four members of the killers squad were nabbed. One escaped. Two pistols/revolvers were recovered. The news given out by the police about a half-an-hour exchange of firing was exaggerated. The police officers, however, concede that but for the initiative and bravery of the people, the killers would all have escaped. This initiative and bravery of the people should be followed by people elsewhere. The chase had been started before by the young men entirely on their own without any guidance from any leader as none happened to be at the site.

Work of CPI in Chheharta of course was an important factor which contributed to the way the people acted after the killers had attacked. A massive rally had been held on February 17 attended by Hindus and Sikhs from Chheharta as well as by people from a neighbouring (erstwhile) village. On February 22 a hall meeting was held in the area in which the killers attacked on February 24. About 250 filled the hall to capacity, many more than that number stood outside and listened to the speakers. This hall meeting was called by the union of shopkeepers, the Textile Mazdoor Ekta Union and a number of prominent persons with different political views. Speakers too belonged to different parties. CPI workers and Istri Sabha leaders and workers have been holding mohalla meetings both before and after the incident. (Similar meetings and also all-parties meetings are being organised in the rest of Amritsar too on the initiative of CPI workers, AITUC unions and Istri Sabha.)

Shopkeepers observed a protest strike on February 25 also. Funeral of Dharampal, who was killed, was largely attended by the people of Chheharta and Wadali. Prominent among those who attended the funeral were Vimla Dang, General Secretary of Punjab Istri Sabha and Jai Karan Singh, Secretary, Area CPI.

Efforts are on to form an all-parties Peace Committee in Chheharta. Initiative has been taken by CPI. (For Amritsar as a whole an All-Parties Peace Council has already been formed).

Widespread propaganda is being carried on against the dangerous slogan of "retaliation" and against efforts to organise middle-class Hindus and Sikhs in opposing camps. Haryana killings are being condemned equally strongly. *(March 10, 1984)*

## 3. Workers Strike Against Terrorism and Communalism

The working class of Amritsar made history on September 4. Twenty thousand industrial workers and bank employees went on one-day strike. The call was given jointly by AITUC and CITU, the two Left-led trade union organisations. There was no economic demand and no demand even concerning trade union rights. The strike was against separatism, terrorism and communalism of all hues. It was to denounce the recent spurt in terrorist killings not only of industrial workers and political activists but of a number of innocent persons—both Hindus and Sikhs.

It was a strike to declare the determination of the working class to defend the unity of the country and to maintain communal peace and harmony at all costs.

It was a fitting answer to those who accuse the working class of being concerned only with its own standard of living and of unconcern for the future of the country

Interestingly, other trade union organisations including INTUC and BMS had opposed the strike on the ground that it was a political strike. But their members and followers in the mills and factories by and large joined the strike. This for instance happened in the Dayal Bagh Spinning and Weaving Mills and Kapur Mills.

At a massive rally held in Putlighar Chowk, the speakers emphasised: "The battle has to be fought by all patriotic forces, but the working class is called upon to play a leading role in uniting all such forces".

They explained how imperialism is doing all it can to disintegrate India and how bourgeois parties and exploiting classes, for the sake of their narrow economic and political interests, behave in such a manner as brings grist to the mill of the separatists and communalists. They gave concrete instances of how the working class was taking a stand on the basis of justice and national interests.

Among the concrete instances the trade union leaders cited were the following:

To isolate the terrorists, it is necessary to settle the territorial and the river waters disputes. Representatives of exploiting classes allow their spokesmen in different concerned states to take different and opposing stands. The working class alone campaigns for a just solution, keeping in view the national interests and in the spirit of give and take without doing injustice to any state.

Some want release of all Jodhpur detenus. The government is not prepared to release even the innocent ones except as a part of a package deal. The working class demands the immediate and unconditional release of the innocent ones.

Many who condemn the killings in Punjab do not condemn the anti-Sikh riots of Delhi, Kanpur, etc. On the other hand, many who strongly demand punishment for those who organised anti-Sikh riots do not condemn the killings in Punjab. The working class condemns both and demands punishment for the guilty in both the cases. The working class was the first to oppose the theory of revenge and retaliation, holding one entire community responsible for the crimes of some.

Some wrongly accuse the CRP of picking up and killing innocent Sikh youths. Some others seek to whitewash excesses which some in the CRP and also in the Punjab police do commit. The working class has been taking a stand on the basis of facts. It has opposed excesses and sought justice. It has also opposed attempts on the part of some to exploit and exaggerate the excesses with a view to widen the Hindu-Sikh gulf.

Speakers called upon the working class to wage a determined battle against communalism of all kinds and for complete isolation of all those who demand dismemberment of the country and/or theocratic states.

Speakers included Madan Lal Didi (General Secretary, Punjab Committee of the AITUC); Mangat Ram Pasla (General Secretary of the Punjab CITU); Parduman Singh (Secretary, Punjab AITUC); Kishan Singh (CITU); Vijay Mishra (CITU); and Satyapal Dang (Vice-President of the Punjab AITUC).

By a special resolution the rally supported the demands of junior doctors and nurses and called upon the government to settle their strike without further delay.

A number of women attended the rally.

After the rally, a massive peace procession marched to the city—passing through G.T. Road, Bhandari Bridge, Hall Bazaar, Katra Sher Singh, etc. It ended near the Town Hall.

While thousands marched in the procession, thousands watched it with happiness writ large on their faces. *(September 1987)*

## 4. Punjab Naxalites and Fight Against Terrorism

There is considerable confusion about the role which the Naxalites are playing in relation to the present situation in Punjab. There have been allegations made from time to time that many Naxalites have joined the ranks of the Khalistani terrorists. These have been made by Home Minister Buta Singh on the one hand and more than one Akali leader on the other. There is also the fact that quite a few Naxalites have been martyred by the terrorist killers. These include some leading figures like Baldev Singh Mann and Jaimal Singh Padda. Both were shot dead by the terrorists, Mann in 1986 and Padda in March 1988. Charan Singh, a pro-Naxalite headmaster in Amritsar district, a leader of Naxalite-led Bharat Naujwan Sabha in his younger days, was hung from the ceiling of his room and was burnt alive. This was less than a month ago.

It is necessary to remove the prevailing confusion and to examine the role of the Naxalites at length as well as in depth. Let us begin with facts:

Home Minister Buta Singh and some Akali leaders who accused

Naxalites of having joined hands with the Khalistani terrorists were exploiting a partial truth. Even during the days of Jarnail Singh Bhindranwale, some ex-Naxalites had turned into his followers, become active and in some cases even leading members of his killer groups. That some Naxalites who once fought pitched battles against the police during the bus fare struggle along with late Charan Singh later on joined the notorious Khalistan Commando Force, has been admitted by a Naxalite spokesman writing under the pen-name Karnail Singh in the *Hind Samachar* group of papers on January 28, 1988. It will, of course, be useful to examine why a number of one-time Naxalites became Khalistani terrorists. But first about the role of the Naxalite groups themselves—as distinct from ex-Naxalites.

Here is what an admittedly pro-Naxalite journalist wrote on November 16, 1986 in one of the national dailies published from New Delhi:

"Nine out of the 12 Naxalite groups are opposing terrorism and fundamentalism and some of them have even advocated armed resistance along with mass mobilisation. At least three groups have decided to organise armed red guard squads. But nothing practical has been done so far . . . .

"One Naxalite group, not opposed to the terrorist violence the way it should be, brought out a pamphlet last year entitled Programme for the Liberation of Punjabi Nation which in fact was the Programme for Liberation of the Sikh Nation . . . ."

Only four or five, out of the 12 Naxalite groups mentioned by our journalist friend have some pockets of influence in Punjab. And their role has been far from being the same. One group associated with a journal known as *Paigam* has been in fact an all-out supporter of the terrorists in the belief that they are fighting for the liberation of the "Punjabi Nation" from the clutches of the "Brahmanical clique" ruling the Centre.

Some groups were active both in the pre-and post Operation Blue Star period, more or less mobilising people against separatism, against killings and for Hindu-Sikh unity. Some conventions, rallies as well as demonstrations have been held by these groups. The Naxalite-led Punjab Students Union has often joined hands with the CPI-led AISF and the CPI-M-led SFI on the student front against the extremists. The good work done by the well-known pro-Naxalite dramatist Gursharan Singh through his plays before and after Operation Blue Star too has to be noted.

Some of those responsible for the killing of Baldev Singh Mann have been liquidated by his comrades and admirers.

While dramatist Gursharan Singh and Baldev Singh Mann's group have been advocating cooperation with the CPI and the CPI-M, one group known as *Surkh Rekha* (after the name of its journal) in Punjab has been utilising a major part of its energies in ''exposing'' and fighting the CPI. One of its main complaints against the CPI relates to the CPI's refusal to accept its thesis that the Khalistani terrorists have to be fought and defeated by ''armed Communist revolutionaries'' *alone* and it is futile to try to force the state to act against them. It has been fabricating "facts" to slander the CPI. At one stage, whenever a CPI activist was shot dead by the terrorists, *Surkh Rekha* would declare: ''Had he not been killed, he would have joined the Surkh Rekha group of the Naxalites''.

A spokesman of this group would come to attend CPI functions organised to pay homage to martyrs, request time to speak and utilise it to make not much veiled attacks on the CPI. *Surkh Rekha* denounced even Baldev Singh Mann and that too after his martyrdom at the hands of the terrorists.

It would thus be seen that even apart from the ex-Naxalites-turned terrorists, the role of different Naxalite groups in the Punjab crisis has been quite varied.

The challenge of the Punjab situation has brought the CPI and the CPI-M closer to each other, but this has not happened as far as the followers of Naxalite ideology are concerned. Reasons for this need to be examined.

The Naxalite spokesman Karnail Singh referred to above has given an explanation why some of the erstwhile comrades-in-arms of martyr Charan Singh joined a Khalistani terrorist organisation. According to him, this happened because some leaders of their movement had landed themselves into the Right-revisionist deviation and for whom ''arms had become mere showpieces of their drawing-rooms and who had said good-bye to the inter-relationship between the revolutionary mass movement and the armed guerilla struggle''.

This boils down to admitting that some of the youth had been drawn into the fold of Naxalism by the pull of weapons by an adventurist spirit and had become Khalistani terrorists because of ideological political immaturity and because the militant line of liquidating enemies with arms had been discarded.

This is not incorrect, but it does not explain the whole truth. Karnail Singh in his article mentioned one fact which provides another clue to the behaviour of a section of the Naxalites. He writes:

"There was a time when we used to hold night-long meetings to discuss the future of the Naxalite movement and Indian Revolution and hold teachers' union meetings in the Akali Rest House. From the very same place the hit-lists of Communists are now being prepared."

Maybe Naxalites were using the Akal Rest House and other parts of the Golden Temple complex for reasons of safety. However, it is also a fact that a section of the Naxalites in Punjab were taught that Sikhism was the fore-runner and even a more revolutionary ideology than Marxism. Notwithstanding the progressive traditions of Sikhism, this viewpoint was totally wrong, un-Marxist and dangerous. And this may as well explain some of the one-time Naxalites joining the camp of Khalistani terrorists. Partly at least, this would seem to explain the ultra-left Punjabi writer Jaswant Singh Kanwal becoming an enthusiastic supporter and admirer of Khalistani terrorists. He has characterised Simranjit Singh Mann as the Nelson Mandela of Punjab.

(It may be mentioned that Simranjit Singh, an IPS officer had to be shifted from Punjab because of his close links with extremists including Bhindranwale himself. Subsequently, he was dismissed. He was arrested while he was trying to escape to Nepal. He is the President of the Unified Akali Dal, so nominated by the then Akal Takht Jathedar, Prof. Darshan Singh.)

This, however, is not all. There are other ideological cobwebs in the Naxalite thinking because of which some have gone shockingly astray and because of which even the work of the best suffers from weaknesses and sectarianism.

Notwithstanding serious differences between themselves, all Naxalite groups believe that the path to Indian revolution has to be the Chinese path, through the establishment of liberated areas and zones. This has led them to believe that disintegration of India is something to be welcomed. All the Naxalite groups are anti-Soviet to a greater or lesser extent. Some of them still cling to the old Maoist thesis that the USSR is the main enemy of the world revolutionary process and therefore joining hands with US imperialism is not only permissible but necessary. The slogan of "Khalistan" is the slogan for disintegration of India. Khalistanis therefore deserve to be supported especially in view of the fact that their "fight" backed by the US will weaken the Government of India which is said to be a Soviet satellite, and hence the USSR too. At least a few Naxalite groups have let this jaundiced thinking of theirs to blind them even to such a glaring fact that the terrorists are splitting and dividing the toilers on communal lines. Their incorrect view that religion constitutes the main basis for nationhood and that Sikhs are a nation has contributed to derail them. Some, of course, do not put forward this view in such a crude manner. They argue that Punjabi Hindus have repudiated the Punjabi language and culture and, therefore, Sikhs have become the sole champions of the interests of Punjabi nationality. Based on half-truths, this view has the same effect in actual practice.

Any Left group worth the name and which has not gone completely blind will take a stand against all attempts to bring about communal riots and to divide the toiling masses on religious lines. This has helped quite a few of the Naxalite groups to play a positive role in the Punjab crisis, a role which we have already taken note of. Their wrong thinking on certain crucial aspects, however, could not but prevent their full potential coming into the field and could not but result in some weaknesses.

It is not an accident, for instance, that the most consistent fighter against Khalistani terrorists out of the Naxalite groups in Punjab has been the Harval Dast, a group of the late Baldev Singh Mann, and it has not been sectarian in this matter. This group has been the least anti-Soviet and has almost given up even the Naxalite thesis that the USA and the USSR are equally to blame for the situation in Punjab.

Not long ago dramatist Gursharan Singh wrote in his journal *Samita:* "One can understand the concern of the bourgeoisie for unity and integrity of India but why should the Left be agitated about it!" This can perhaps partly explain the lack of continuous campaigning on his part. The failure to realise that disintegration of India will mean a very big blow to the cause of Indian revolution and the world revolutionary process seems a common weakness of all Naxalite groups.

There is another problem which has proved quite a difficult one for the Naxalite groups. The Congress-I does not see any excess being committed by the police and the para-military forces of the state. The Naxalite thinking is that the para-military forces and the police are an essential part of the coercive apparatus of the bourgeois state which has to be overthrown. And therefore it can do only evil and wrong. Instead of extending support to the extent they really and genuinely fight terrorism, and exposing and fighting excesses of all types (opposing also exaggeration of those excesses by the terrorists with a view to exploit the same for strengthening themselves as the CPI has been doing)—some Naxalite groups have lapped up the thesis of state terrorism being responsible for individual terrorism in Punjab—first put forward by an Akali leader. Obviously this provides an alibi for the killer-groups.

Inability to evolve and adopt a correct attitude in this respect is the result of dogmatism and failure to have a clear understanding about the path of the Indian revolution. The *Surkh Rekha* group has resolved the problem by declaring that it is useless to try to force the state to fight terrorism and that the job has to be done by the Communist revolutionaries on their own. They, of course, are not worried by the actual realities and the balance of forces which will make obvious that they are setting an impossible task for the Communist revolutionaries. No wonder this group is the most sectarian and spends a major part of its time in slandering other Left formations, especially the CPI, the strongest amongst them.

Before we end, we will briefly refer to an article of a Delhi-based Punjabi intellectual,* which was reproduced by *Mainstream* in October 1987 from *Economic and Political Weekly*. The author was good enough "to recognise the valour and fortitude of party cadres (of CPI and CPI-M) with many staking their very lives in pursuit of their line." But according to him, those sacrifices were all being wasted. Wrote he:

"Whatever success, real or imaginary, may come the way of this (CPI and CPI-M) political line, it will again leave the objective situation unchanged."

The author accuses them of "a great deal of eclecticism and most pragmatic practice of politics (including praise for CRPF, and exchange

*This refers to Prof. Randhir Singh's article "Punjab: Marxists and Sikh Extremist Movement," reprinted by *Mainstream* in its issue of October 10, 1987.—*Editor*.

of compliments with Rebeiro''. He goes on: ''But essentially they view the struggle against the Sikh extremism and terrorism as part of an overall struggle in 'defence of national unity and integrity', and against 'destabilisation by US imperialism and its allies, etc.'"

We have already dealt with the two different perceptions of relationship between the cause of Indian revolution and the question of unity of India (which undoubtedly has to be unity-in-diversity as CPI and CPI-M have been emphasising again and again while demanding greater autonomy for the states).

As regards ''praising CRPF and exchange of compliments with Rebeiro'', it needs only to be mentioned that the CPI has exposed, opposed and most powerfully fought the excesses by the CRPF and the police. Praise has been showered on Rebeiro by at least one prominent Naxalite.

Coming to the game of imperialism to destabilise and even disintegrate India, many in India for long denied the role of this factor. It is good that now it is recognised by almost all, though some continue to underestimate it. Such friends wrongly accuse the CPI of not seeing or underestimating the internal factors which include the policies of Government of India.

The author of the article referred to above does not recognise the great role the united and organised working class of Punjab has played in preventing Hindu-Sikh riots. Nor would be take note of the role played by the two Communist parties, especially by the CPI, in isolating the terrorists even from the mass base they had developed, by their intensive and extensive mass campaigning throughout the state including the terrorist strongholds in Amritsar district.

Both the CPI and the CPI-M have stood for independent mass campaigning as well as for an all-parties campaign. Obviously, the latter has to be confined to agreed points. Joint platforms must not be utilised to attack each other as that can only disrupt the limited unity. Such unity clearly can and does play a positive role. From their own platform, both the Communist Parties have been exposing and criticising the Congress-I and the Akalis as well as other bourgeois parties for the Punjab mess. These independent campaigns have been on a scale much bigger than the all-parties campaign which regrettably remained confined to a few rallies only. The author in question takes no note of these massive independent campaigns and criticises both the Communist Parties for allegedly covering up the responsibility of various bourgeois parties. It is difficult to come across a cruder example of refusing to see facts as may not fit in with one's preconceived ideas and notions.

One need not be surprised over the opinion voiced by the author about the terrorist-killers. All that he has to say is:

"The extremists with their muddled ideology and practice and the dead-end game of killing and getting killed, advance no cause of theirs, they only play into the hands of the very enemy they claim to be fighting, namely, the Delhi Sarkar, the rulers at Delhi."

According to the author, the correct revolutionary line is represented by some Naxalite groups. He has, in particular, praised Gursharan Singh. Says he:

"A significant recent development in Punjab...has been the coming together, at the initiative of Gursharan Singh, the well-known people's theatre activist, of several revolutionary groups in a Revolutionary Centre and their struggle for a people's politics in Punjab".

Our previous observations in this article should make it clear that we certainly do not grudge praise for these groups for the good work they have done separately as well as together with others. However, we very much wish that our friend, the author of the article in question, had detailed this good work and the "change" it has made "in the objective situation." Had he done this, he would have felt compelled to praise the CPI and the CPI-M much more—instead of telling them they are making futile sacrifices.

It is time that all the Left formations and the intellectuals supporting them shed their mutual prejudices. The situation demands this. Mutual differences should be discussed in a fraternal manner without their being allowed to prevent maximum possible joint action and cooperation amongst all Left forces. *(April 23, 1988)*

## 5. Punjab Communists' Proud Record

Guided and helped by intelligent brains in the USA and the military rulers of Pakistan, the terrorists of Punjab started by killing Nirankaris against whom orthodox Sikhs have a deep prejudice due to the former's belief in a living Guru. Thanks to the Akali Ministry headed by Badal, Nirankaris were virtually denied the right to hold their Satsangs. The pro-Congress Master Akali Dal of Delhi took the same anti-Nirankari stand as Bhindranwale and Akali leaders like Tohra. The CPI alone defended their right to worship in accordance with their religious beliefs, subject of course, to public morality and without offensive attacks on other religions. It could not but incur the displeasure of Bhindranwale and his men.

From indiscriminate killings of Nirankaris, the Bhindranwale-men moved ahead to killings of Hindus as well as Sikhs who dared oppose his line. The Akali leadership decided to play the same Bhindranwale card against the Congress which the Congress-I had been playing to weaken the Akalis in the struggle for power. Bhindranwale became first a parallel and then the only government. No party dared hold any public meeting, especially in certain parts of Punjab. Communists and Communist-led mass organisations, including that of women, did not flinch. Peace marches, public meetings and rallies were held in different parts of the state including the areas dominated by terrorists. Armed volunteers had to guard many of these. The sizeable procession which the CPI brought out in Amritsar within 24 hours of the murder of DIG Atwal, from within the Goden Temple, in which Hindus and Sikhs had participated almost in equal number, was taken note of by leading newspapers and it angered the terrorists. The massive public meeting in Moga Mandi, despite the threats of terrorists, and the subsequent peace march made many, who had decided to migrate, change their minds. And these are not isolated instances. In innumerable villages Sikhs assured safety to Hindus. The Communist Party campaign contributed a great deal towards this.

An important element in the strategy of the terrorists has been to bring about Hindu-Sikh riots. Despite the help rendered to them by Hindu communalists, who advanced the slogan of "revenge" and "retaliation" against the Sikh community, they have not succeeded in this. A good part of the credit for this goes to the Communists and mass organisations led by them. It is the Communists who took initiative for all-party united actions whenever communal tension increased, gave united calls for bandhs to protest against killings. Again and again the organised sections of working class and employees organised demonstrations as did agricultural labourers and women. There were also united strikes by the working class employees. Nor is that all. In Ludhiana, Amritsar,

Gurdaspur and elsewhere Communists physically stood between communally surcharged groups and successfully prevented clashes.

It was not for nothing that Communists were declared as one of their enemies by Amrik Singh, second in command of the Bhindranwale outfit.

Sumeet Singh, Editor of *Preet Lari* and grandson of Gurbux Singh, doyen of Punjabi literature, became the first Communist martyr of Amritsar district at the hands of the terrorists. He was killed on 22nd February, 1984. Sarbjeet Atrey of Gurdaspur district was martyred a few days earlier and Randhir Singh of Faridkot a few weeks later.

Operation Blue Star, for which Bhindranwale on the one hand and Congress -I and the Akalis on the other must bear responsibility, smashed the terrorist headquarters but widened the social base of the terrorists. Anti-Sikh riots in Delhi and elsewhere following the assassination of Indira Gandhi and the refusal on the Government of India to book the VIP culprits helped the terrorists a lot. It was the Communists who tirelessly worked in Delhi, Bihar and elsewhere to protect and save many Sikhs. The Left Front government of West Bengal and the Communists of the state came out with flying colours and won the appreciation of all, including Sikhs all over the country. The Punjab Istri Sabha, in which Communist women work along with many non-Communist progressive women, was perhaps the only state-wide organisation in Punjab to collect and send relief for victims of anti-Sikh riots in Delhi. It was distributed through the National Federation of Indian Women (NFIW). Hindus had contributed as much as Sikhs. Communists (particularly the CPI) alone have run a mass campaign in a number of States for the release of all innocent amongst the Jodhpur detenus, for prosecution of those responsible for anti-Sikh riots in November 1984 and for a political solution of the problem.

The Rajiv-Longowal Accord was arrived at in July 1985. Despite its weaknesses, it could have helped to resolve the territorial and river disputes and deprived the extremists of a weapon they had been using, if all the parties had mobilised the people. Only the Communists did that. All other parties allowed their state units to take opposing stands in the concerned states. Bhajan Lal, helped by the Prime Minister, interpreted it as a victory for Haryana, while the Akalis interpreted it as a victory for Punjab and even themselves. In the face of the opportunism of non-Left parties the Communist campaign could not save the accord. There is, however, much greater realisation now that national level parties must give up this vote-bank, opportunist politics.

From the beginning of 1986, terrorists made a big effort to drive out Hindus from rural areas, particularly of Amritsar and Gurdaspur districts. Everywhere the CPI sought to mobilise people against it. It was in this period that many CPI members were shot dead by terrorists. Amongst them were the State Executive Member, Arjan Singh Mastana and Bibi Guro, a leader of the Istri Sabha—the first woman political worker to be killed by design.

In August and September 1986, the CPI and the CPI-M organised a number of joint rallies in Amritsar district against separatism, extremism, terrorism and communalism in the terrorist strongholds. They got a big response. Killings of many more CPI members, including of Darshan Singh Canadian, one of its tallest leaders, followed these. It was in this period that the CPI-M lost its first cadre, Comrade Avtar Singh, who was martyred on 19 September, 1986, followed by more, including the leaders Chanan Singh Dhoot and Deepak Dhawan. Baldev Singh Mann, a top leader of an anti-terrorist Naxalite group too, was martyred in this period.

Previously, the CPI and the CPI-M and mass organisations led by them, had organised a number of state-wide rallies in different parts of Punjab. In June 1987, the CPI organised a mass contact campaign, the CPI-M following suit. The CPI had covered even the terrorist strongholds. Many more Communists lost their lives following these mass campaigns.

A massive rally organised by the CPI in Delhi, in which a big majority consisted of Sikhs from Punjab, helped the entire country to understand more fully that the terrorists of Punjab did not have the support of the toiling Sikh masses.

It was Communists who, first and in a big way, exposed the game of the Centre to make a deal with the terrorists or a section of them with the help of men like Darshan Singh Ragi, Parkash Singh Badal and Jasbir Singh Rode. Communists also exposed the danger of the Centre making a concession to theocracy in the name of special status for Punjab. Again, Communists alone have been consistently exposing and actively opposing Hindu communalists whose activities, in fact, helped Khalistani extremists. Apart from their own independent as well as joint campaigns, the CPI and CPI-M have been taking the initiative for all-party campaigns on agreed points. While the Congress-I has been denying excesses by the security forces and some others have been exaggerating and exploiting the same, bringing grist to the mill of the terrorists, the Communists have been exposing the excesses and have also been fighting for justice in specific cases.

Following the near fatal attack on S.S. Virk, DIG CRPF from within the Golden Temple, the Government of India was forced to organise Operation Black Thunder in May 1988. This exposed the terrorists, not only as an anti-national group, but also as being ansi-Sikh and anti-Sikhism. This was a most opportune time for all patriotic forces to run a big mass campaign against the misuse of religious places, for separation of religion and politics and for exposing the true nature of terrorism in Punjab and for a political solution. Only the Communists acted. The CPI and CPI-M organised a big state-level convention at Jallandhar followed by district-level joint dharnas. The CPI organised a big mass campaign in towns as well as in rural areas.

The Communists have paid a heavy price. CPI alone has lost 62 comrades in Punjab and 3 in Haryana, including some family members of theirs and such prominent leaders as Malkiat Mahil and Nachhatar Singh. Amongst them was Mangat Singh, who told the terrorists before he was shot dead: "By killing me on 23rd March you are making me not only a martyr but a companion of the great martyr, Bhagat Singh, who was hanged by the British on this very day." The CPI-M has lost about 31, including former MLA Harbans Singh Beeka and Youth leader Gurnam Singh Uppal. The Naxalites have lost more than ten. Notwithstanding heavy losses, the Communists continue the fight for national unity, for communal peace and harmony, for the future of India and the Indian revolution. They do so with the moral, political and material help they get from all over India. Many have foiled the terrorists' efforts to kill them, because they fired first, in the face of which the terrorists ran away and in some cases even got killed or injured.

Apart from the main political fight through mass mobilisation, the Communists are also fighting on other fronts. Communist writers, poets, journalists, dramatists continue to use their pens and art forms to rouse people against terrorism and communalism. Maximum help to the victims of terrorism and internal migrants has been rendered by the CPI, AITUC and, above all, by the Punjab Istri Sabha. This has contributed in a big way to help prevent their communalisation. The relief schemes of the Punjab Istri Sabha, especially its scheme to give stipends to orphaned children of victims of terrorists as also of such innocent persons as became victims of police bullets for one reason or another (such as cross-firing, mistake, over-reaction, etc.), has attracted nation-wide attention. Funds have been collected by units of the NFIW from different states. Individuals, including industrial workers, industrialists, prominent writers, charitable trusts and others, including Indians residing in other countries, have contributed liberally. CPI MP Gurudas Dasgupta donated Rs. six lakhs out of his reward from the government. More than two lakhs have been sent by the Punjab Solidarity Committee, Calcutta headed by Cinema director Mrinal Sen. Punjab Istri Sabha is not a Communist organisation, but Communist women play a very active role in it. Its relief work has helped to keep up morale. It has now set up a broad-based trust which has taken over all its schemes.

With the help of people all over India, Communists will continue to fight separatist-terrorism and communalism on all fronts—on their own as well as jointly with all patriotic forces. They are proud of their share in the fight and are confident that it will play a big role in winning the nation's battle which is being fought on the soil of Punjab, notwithstanding the sacrifices which may have to be made. *(March 6, 1989)*

## 6. In Bhagat Singh's Footsteps

In a ghastly happening on 2 February this year, terrorists including one Piara Singh shot dead Surinder Singh (an Army jawan) and his younger brother, Narinder Singh (a student of Class VIII), sons of ex-sarpanch Deewan Singh, in their village Roopowali in Amritsar district. More ghastly: an announcement was made by the killers that the cremation would not be allowed in the village, that if it was attempted severe punishment would be meted out to the family and those who might want to attend it.

The dead bodies were taken to Seetla Mandir in Amritsar city with the help of the police. It was there that they were consigned to the flames.

Later, in the same village, on 24 July, three "militants" entered the house of Lambardar Ajit Singh at about 10.30 at night. They were Piara Singh, Lakha Jahaj of village Sangrea and Pipla Singh Dholewal. An

Akhand Path of Guru Granth Sahib was going on in the house. Mr. Ajit Singh was asked to come out as one Ajaib Singh wanted to a talk to him. He refused. Ajit Singh and his 22-year-old married son were shot dead. The Granthi stopped the Path and ran away to save his life. Killings in front of Guru Granth Sahib and stopping of the recitation in between constitute a serious sacrilege of the Sikh religion; but this does not matter for some "religious" people.

After committing these killings and sacrileges, the terrorists went to the house of 100-year old Mohan Singh, a veteran Communist and freedom fighter. His grandson Jaswant Singh was sleeping outside his house. He was shot dead.

A note was left according to which Jaswant Singh was killed because he was a "comrade" and because he used to speak against the militants allegedly after taking liquor. The killer gang is also reported to have ordered that cremation would not be allowed in the village.

Mr. Darshan Singh, father of Jawant Singh, went to police station Kathunangal hardly 2½ kilometres away next morning at about 6.45 a.m. The police officials there said that they would not go there at that time as it would be risky. Mr. Darshan Singh was also advised to stay in the police station to avoid the risk of being killed. Darshan Singh, however, did not heed this advice and returned to his village. It was only after 3 hours that the police reached the village.

Much before the arrival of the police, Mr. Lakhwinder Singh (real brother of Jaswant Singh) a young advocate and a leader of the AISF in his student days, had reached the village along with a friend and a others with their weapons

They had rushed to the village from Amritsar City after getting the tragic news. They got the dead bodies ready for being taken for post-mortem. The bodies were brought back to the village after the post-mortem. Cremation was done in the village itself. Prior to the cremation, shots were fired in the air as a warning to those who did not want the cremation to be done in the villag

Nearly 100-year-old Comrade Mohan Singh, being very hard of hearing and fast asleep when his grandson Jaswant Singh was shot dead, did not hear the shots. The family decided not to tell him about the tragedy. Four days after the incident, he asked the child who had gone to his room to give him tea why women of the family were weeping—

which fact he had noted. He was then told the tragic news. About half-an-hour after this Mohan Singh passed away.

Later, the family held intense discussions but decided against migrating from the village.

Yet another facet of Punjab today. Lakha Jahaj and Pipal Singh Dholewal have since been killed by the police in encounters. It is not known whether Piara Singh is alive or he too has been killed. Many announcements of his taking responsibility for killings used to appear in a Punjabi daily published from Jalandhar. For some time now these have not been appearing. What sort of a man is or was this Piara Singh?

He belonged to Roopowali village itself. He had some land dispute with the family of Jaswant Singh. However, this dispute had been settled to his satisfaction. Piara Singh was a jawan in the army. He once went to court to seek divorce from his wife. A compromise however took place. Soon thereafter Piara Singh became an absconder from the army. His wife's parents took away their daughter to their own house. Reports current in the area have it that Piara Singh killed the wife of one of his two brothers because she had refused to respond to his advances. Both his brothers left the village.

Such is the stuff of which at least a section of the "militants" are made of, and such are their deeds and the "respect" they have for the Sikh religion.

Roopowali however has produced not only Piara Singh—the shame of the village. Nor is Mohan Singh the only son of the village of whom they can be proud. Mangat Singh, who was shot dead by terrorists on March 23 this year is another son of the soil. An activist of CPI, 32-year-old Mangat Singh was the President of the Bhatha (brick kiln) workers Union (AITUC). When he was nabbed by the terrorists, he told them: "I am glad that you are going to kill me today—the martyrdom day of Shaheed-e-Azam Bhagat Singh. I am happy that I will be his companion".

*(September 24, 1991)*

## 7. Terrorism and Working Class of Punjab

Punjab does have a few big industrial units/mills in the private as well as public sector. However, by and large industry in Punjab consists of small and middle units. Workers employed in small factories are not easy to organise. Notwithstanding this the trade union movement—which includes unions of workers and employees of Punjab Roadways, Pepsu Roadways, Punjab State Electricity Board, employees of FCI and various Central Government employees and employees of banks, insurance companies, etc., in the state—is very much there and its strength is acknowledged by friends as well as foes. There have been innumerable unit-wise struggles. There have been industry-wise and department-wise general strikes too for economic demands as well as trade union rights. Workers of the state have been participating in a big way in various all India trade unions affiliated to different all India centres. The AITUC and its friendly unions represent the leading and strongest force in Punjab. The AITUC has not been confining its work to economic demands and trade unions rights but has been undertaking other multifarious activities. For instance, it has been in the front ranks in mobilising the working class and employees against communalism. AITUC affiliated unions in Punjab can be proud of the fact that the working class of Punjab has not fallen prey to communalism. Nor is this all, it has made a good contribution in the fight against communalism in the state as a whole. It has been a consistent force for communal peace and harmony. It has had to face communal challenges in different forms.

Soon after independence, the Jan Sangh (predecessor of the Bharatiya Janata Party) and a big section of Hindu Congress leaders carried on very extensive propaganda calling upon all Punjabi speaking Hindus to record Hindi as their mother tongue during the census, instead of Punjabi. The Akali Party, on the other hand, campaigned for the Punjabi language as if it were part of Sikh religion. Thus, in Punjab even the question of language got communalised. Leaders of many AITUC unions campaigned against this and explained to the workers how harmful this totally wrong approach would prove in the long run for Punjab and for the working class itself. They appealed to all Punjabi speaking workers to truthfully get Punjabi recorded as their mother tongue, irrespective of their religion. This campaign had a healthy effect and helped to keep the working class free from tensions on the language question. The Akalis in the beginning demanded a Sikh state and then a Punjabi speaking state with Sikhs constituting at least 60 per cent of its population. Only subsequently Akali leader Sant Fateh Singh made a declaration that he stood for a Punjabi speaking state only on the basis of language. Even he, however, carried on agitation for it from within the Golden Temple. Hindu communal forces and even large sections of the Congress stood for Maha Punjab, to be formed by merging even parts of Delhi and Rajasthan in it. New communal tensions arose and there were even skirmishes. When the present Punjab and Haryana and Himachal were carved out of the erstwhile Punjab, Hindu communalists opposed it in Punjab, which led to some serious incidents. The Punjab working class remained out of all this and remained united. In its strongholds it acted to influence others to maintain communal peace and harmony.

The biggest challenge faced by Punjab in this period was of terrorism based on communalism. Now it was not merely a question of maintaining the unity of the working class and of not letting it be divided communally. The unity of the country itself was threatened because the terrorists demanded another partititon of the India. External as well as internal factors were responsible for the rise of terrorism in Punjab. What led to it assuming dangerous proportions was the fact that both the major political parties of the state, i.e., the Congress and the Akalis, were encouraging communalism to use it against each other. Punjab passed through a long dark period of about 15 years. There were periods when not only villages, but even big towns were absolutely deserted even before sunset. People shut themselves indoors for fear of terrorism. Whole families from a few months old infants to grandparents in their seventies, and including pregnant women, were shot dead. Many trade union leaders, like Nichhatar Singh Dhaliwal, President of Punjab Roadways Union and Vice-President of Punjab State Committee of AITUC, Khet Mazdoor Union leaders like Amolak Singh, Mangal Singh and health department leaders Karam Chand, Tilak Raj and Jaswant Singh with family, etc., were shot dead and Harpal Singh Mohali, Secretary of Punjab AITUC was shot in the neck and maimed for life. There were large scale kidnappings for ransom. There was molestation of women, forcible marriages and rapes. On the other hand, excesses committed by a section of the police for extraneous reasons too were not by any means negligible.

Apart from these, hundreds of kisans and khet mazdoor leaders, intellectuals and others were brutally murdered, e.g., Darshan Singh Canadian, Arjun Singh Mastana, Mohan Mehli, Chanan Singh Dhoot, Sarwan Singh Cheema, Deepak Dhawan and Baldev Singh were killed, amongst others.

In such a situation the working class of Punjab acted with tremendous wisdom and courage. It kept its ranks united.

Serious attempts were made by militants to get the working class to line up behind them. Every conceivable method was used to get their demands conceded by the employers even on the point of the gun, on the one hand, and threats held out to workers, on the other. Workers were asked to discard the Red Flag and adopt the kesari one. Nowhere did they succeed. Even the Sikh workers told them, "Kesari may be the symbol of our religion, but the Red Flag will remain the flag of our unions." The unions of Punjab Roadways, Pepsu Roadways and Punjab State Electricity Board, in which most employees were Sikhs, waged heroic battles for their demands, remained united and stuck to the Red Flag.

In many industrial centres workers took to streets in a very disciplined and organised manner, for national unity, for communal peace, against terrorism, etc. Large numbers of women from working class families too participated. Full throated slogans against terrorism and against demands for Khalistan and Hindu Raj were raised. The slogans coined by Madan Lal Didi, General Secretary of the Punjab Committee of the AITUC—"Na Hindu Raj na Khalistan—jug jug jive Hindustan"—became very popular amongst all sections of the people. The working class of Punjab had another variation of this slogan: "Na Hindu Raj na Khalistan, raj kare mazdoor kisan."

When DIG Atwal was shot dead by terrorists from within the Golden Temple, there was great fear writ large on the face of everyone in Amritsar. It was hours before the police could remove the dead body of the DIG lying just outside the Golden Temple. Everyone wondered what to do next and searched for some ray of hope. Within 24 hours of the incident, a procession consisting of Sikh as well as Hindu workers and some others including women led by AITUC leaders marched through the streets of Amritsar, including those in the vicinity of the Golden Temple. As the procession marched raising appropriate slogans, mincing no words, one could see faces on both sides getting lit up. People saw a ray of hope and felt that sooner or later terrorism would be overcome.

As is well known, terrorism started from Amritsar district. And in this district it became strongest. It was therefore only proper that the working class of Amritsar three days before Operation Blue Star went on a day's general strike against terrorism, for unity and integrity of the country and for communal peace and harmony, organised by AITUC and CITU. A massive rally took place in Putlighar Chowk. Terrorists had a plan to attack. A strong group had gathered in a nearby gurdwara. Police security provided for the rally consisted of one police constable and one home guard, with one stick each. The rally, however, was guarded by armed volunteers of the working class. The "militants" dared not come near it. A massive procession marched and paraded the streets of the city. Such working class processions were taken out in other towns too.

Last but not the least, "militants" made strenous efforts to bring about Hindu-Sikh clashes. They went to the extent of throwing heads of cows before temples. Hindu communalists supplemented their efforts by throwing cigrattes into gurdwaras, etc. The common people of Punjab foiled their games. And in this all parties cooperated. Initiative generally was taken by the Left. In two towns, some small mobs of Hindus and Sikhs stood face to face and were about to clash. It was the AITUC leaders in both places who intervened to prevent the fight.

In villages even unorganised agricultural workers as a class refused to line up behind the terrorists despite threats and killings. Similarly employees of state level unions of PSEB, Punjab Roadways, FCI Paledars, Pepsu Roadways, and Central Government employees as well as employees in banks and insurance companies stuck to their unions and refused to be divided.

Such has been the role of the working class of Punjab in the fight against communalism. I feel certain that in the days to come it will continue to carry forward this tradition. Apart from the danger of communalism, the danger of casteism also faces the country. The working class of Punjab will surely fight against this menace too.

# CHAPTER VII

# Following Correct Policies

## 1. Steps to Defuse Tension

The hukumnama issued from Akal Takht, Amritsar, directing all Sikhs to socially boycott the Nirankaris, has raised some important questions of principle. The democratic movement in the country, especially in Punjab, cannot bypass these questions, except at the risk of grave damage to itself. For a correct analysis of these questions and to find the right answers, it is necessary to go into the background of the present turmoil.

People of different religious faiths have joined the Nirankari sect. However, a majority—perhaps a big majority of the Nirankaris—are from among the Sikhs. The dispute between those who claim to be true followers and custodians of Sikh religious teachings and precepts, on the one hand, and the Nirankaris, on the other, is not a new one. There were clashes even in the nineteen-twenties. There was a feeling among devout Sikhs that the Nirankari Sikhs insulted Sikhism. The Nirankari chiefs used to deliver their sermons sitting in chairs in the presence of Guru Granth Sahib, the holy book of the Sikhs. This is impermissible among devout Sikhs and would be regarded as insult to Guru Granth Sahib.

It is reported that some time around 1950, an understanding was arrived at between the Nirankaris and the then Akali leadership. The Nirankaris decided not to have Guru Granth Sahib in their *satsangs* (religious congregations). This removed an important cause of friction. It is also believed that the then Akali leadership did not want the dispute to go too far. They apprehended that the Nirankaris might declare themselves to be non-Sikhs and this might harm the political interests of the Sikh community as the Akali leadership then perceived them.

There was peace for quite some time. And when differences cropped up, "misunderstandings" were easily removed. That is how it became possible for the Akali Dal candidates for election to the Lok Sabha and the Punjab Assembly to seek the blessings and the support of the Nirankari Baba. During the March 1977 election to Parliament and the June 77 elections to the Punjab Vidhan Sabha, many even of the topmost leaders of the Akali Dal sought the support and blessings of the Nirankari chief. After their success, both extremist and moderate Akalis wrote letters to him praising him in superlative terms.

Inter-marriages between orthodox Sikhs and Nirankari Sikhs too have not been rare. It is no secret in Punjab that at least one Akali Minister is closely related to a Nirankari family in this manner.

During the last two decades or so the Nirankari dispute reappeared. Nirankari gatherings at two or three places were sought to be disrupted by persons believed to belong to a sect known as Akhand Kirtini Jatha of Sant Jarnail Singh, popularly known as Sant Bhindranwale. The Nirankaris held a big protest demonstration before the Punjab Civil Secretariat in Chandigarh. They allege that they did not get any satisfactory response from the state government.

It is in this background that the Amritsar tragedy of April 1978 took place, in which 18 persons lost their lives. A criminal case in this connection is before a court of law. It would, therefore, not be proper to comment on the events of April 13. Certain facts, however, can and need to be stated.

April 13 is Baisakhi day—the birthday of the Khalsa. On this day every year there is a big gathering at Manji Sahib in Amritsar. On this day the Nirankaris also have their Manav Ekta Sammelan. This year they decided to have it at Amritsar, though not for the first time. The site chosen was about three or four kilometres from Manji Sahib. This sammelan was to be preceded by a procession. The authorities gave the necessary permission. The procession passed off peacefully.

Just when the Nirankari procession was marching through the city, speeches were being delivered at the Manji Sahib Dewan. There were at least three very inflammatory speeches. They were delivered in the presence of a cabinet rank Akali minister, who himself made a double-edged speech. This was followed by a meeting.

A jatha of about 200 marched to the site where the Nirankari

Sammelan was to take place. It consisted not of Akalis but of the followers of Sant Bhindranwale. It is claimed that the jatha had gone to make a peaceful and humble request that Sikhism should not be insulted. However, the police FIR itself says that it had traditional arms and had marched with a view to disturbing the Sammelan. The FIR further says that when Nirankaris opened fire, there was firing from the jatha in self-defence—it meant it had at least some guns, maybe one, maybe more.

Admittedly, the jatha was unsuccessfully sought to be stopped by the police when it had reached quite close to the venue of the Nirankari Sammelan.

According to the FIR, the first shot was fired by the Nirankaris. This, of course, is denied by the Nirankaris. There is however, the undisputed fact that 13 of those killed were from the jatha, two or three were Nirankaris and the rest were passers-by. It is believed by many, not without reason, that the Nirankaris had made thorough preparations to "defend" their right to hold their congregation, and to teach a lesson to those who might try to disturb it.

The death of these 13 sent a wave of anger and sorrow amongst the Sikhs. Large sections of the community also began expressing the belief that Nirankaris insult their religion, that their chief occupies a higher seat while Guru Granth Sahib is given a lower place, etc.

The top Akali leaders joined the funeral procession of the thirteen who were declared martyrs in the cause of Sikh religion. The Chief Minister was present at the cremation, though he did not join the procession.

All the political parties, including the Akalis, demanded a judicial enquiry. The Nirankaris, too, made the same demand. The Chief Minister, at that time, hinted that he was thinking of ordering one. Soon, however, he made up his mind otherwise and stuck to his decision which obviously was the result of some rethinking on the part of the entire Akali leadership. This is unfortunate, because a judicial enquiry would have been the correct thing and would have helped considerably to improve the situation.

The events of April 13 were followed by some violent anti-Nirankari demonstrations, as in Patiala, where an Akali legislator was in the lead. It goes to the credit of the moderates within the Akali Dal that they were able to assert themselves and prevent such demonstrations taking place throughout the state. However, extremists have been busy rousing hostility against the Nirankaris and also using the events against Parkash Singh Badal and his leadership of the government. They have been making extremely irresponsible speeches and the government leadership has not been standing up to them. It has, in fact, been succumbing to them.

The Nirankaris have not been allowed to hold their *satsangs* to date. The Nirankari Bhawans are "guarded" by the police. Whenever the Nirankaris try to hold their *satsangs*, armed volunteers of some extremist Sikh organisations appear on the scene and, in the name of preserving law and order, the Nirankaris are dispersed by the police by even using force which, of course, is officially denied.

All the minorities in Punjab, including the Hindus, and even Sikh Harijans, feel insecure. The Janata Party, which in Punjab is mainly the erstwhile Jan Sangh, has lost its urban Hindu following to the Congress-I to a considerable extent.

The CPI took a principled stand from the beginning. Besides being the first in the state to demand a judicial enquiry, it demanded a solution of the problem on the basis of acceptance of two principles: 1. Everyone must have the right to hold and preach his religious views (including the right of worship according to those views); and 2. No one must have the right to abuse or insult any other religious views.

With regard to the allegation that the Nirankaris indulge in abuse and insult of Sikhism—an allegation denied by the Nirankaris—the CPI first called for a meeting of the leaders of the two sides to resolve the dispute. It later proposed that the matter be gone into by some impartial authority. It suggested that an all-parties meeting be called by the Chief Minister and opposed all attempts to rouse hostility on grounds of religious views. It has pointed out that communal divisions suit only the vested interests.

The CPI also took the initiative to call a convention of all secular political parties and forces in the state. Both the Congress parties and forces in the Republican parties responded positively. However, the top leaders of the two Congress parties kept away and sent to the convention only second-rank leaders. Reports in the press that Congress-I and Akalis were having behind-the-scenes contacts may not be altogether baseless. Some of the important ex-Congress Janata Party leaders were keen to attend the convention but were told not to do so. The CPI-M, too, did not join on the plea that both the Congresses had been invited.

The CPI-M has criticised the irresponsible utterances of extremists among the Akalis. On the other hand, it has held the Nirankaris guilty of abusing and insulting Sikh religion and has held that to be the root cause of the trouble.

CPI-M leader Harkishan Singh Surjeet and Akali leader Gurcharan Singh Tohra have also characterised the Nirankaris as a para-military reactionary organisation, getting money from abroad and possibly linked with the CIA. The Nirankaris have been even linked to the Anand Margis. There have also been allegations that the Nirankari doctrine preaches permissiveness in matters of sex.

The Nirankaris have denies these allegations and have declared that theirs is a non-political organisation. Some of their admirers claim that there are progressive features in their views on social life. They claim that the system of simple marriages developed by the Nirankaris is now followed by others. They also point out the sense of equality that prevails among all Nirankaris.

On the other hand, one can point to such Nirankari practices as drinking the water with which the feet of the Nirankari chiefs (including the local chiefs) have been washed. Even the newborn are given this water as a sort of baptism.

All this, however, does not answer the questions: What is the class essence of the Nirankari sect? What is its significance for the class struggle, for the developing democratic movement? Is it really like the Anand Marg? What are its relations with the RSS? Does it play the role of diverting the growing discontent against the exploitative system into harmless channels?

These, no doubt, are important questions. However, these questions can be raised not only in relation to the Nirankaris but also in relation to many other sects, some of which are quite close to the Akali leadership. Moreover, such questions need to be raised at the proper time and in the proper context. To raise these questions in relation to the Nirankaris alone, and in the given context only helps to confuse certain other vital questions of principle—such as the attitude towards differing religious views, the attitude of the state towards religion, and so on.

Let us now come to the hukumnama. It is clear that moderate Akali leaders did not want any hukumnama issued from the Akal Takht, the highest seat of Sikh religion. They, however, could not prevent it. The call in the hukumnama for the social boycott of the Nirankaris has created an awkward situation for the Akali ministers. If they are to obey the hukumnama, can they really carry on the government in accordance with the Indian Constitution? Can they really treat all citizens alike? Can they treat all government employees, including the Nirankaris among them, on an equal footing?

Shiromani Gurudwara Prabhandak Committee chief Gurcharan Singh Tohra, MP, has come to the rescue of the ministers. He has declared that the ministers as ministers will act in accordance with the Indian Constitution, but as private citizens will be bound by the hukumnama. Many doubt if this interpretation will really resolve the dilemma. In one gurdwara the hukumnama was read out by a senior minister of cabinet rank, who also happens to be an aspirant for Chief Ministership. Was it correct on his part to do so? Was he, in doing so, acting only as a private citizen? Had he, at that time ceased to be a minister?

Another minister has declared that he is first a Sikh and only then a minister. What are the implications of this declaration in relation to his duties as a minister? All these questions remain to be answered.

It has been forcefully asserted by the Akali leadership that the hukumnama is an internal matter of the Sikhs and does not concern anyone else. Is the call for social boycott of Nirankaris—Sikhs as well as non-Sikhs—really an internal matter of the Sikhs? According to press reports, on the day after the hukumnama was issued, one Sikh ration depot holder refused to sell sugar or some such thing to someone on the ground that the latter was a Nirankari. Was he right or wrong? And will a devout Sikh be doing the right thing if he were to purchase his levy sugar from his fair price shop if the depot holder happens to be a Nirankari? These, no doubt, are difficult questions, but they cannot be evaded.

The working committee of the Akali Dal has passed a resolution laying down that no non-Sikh has any right to criticise in any manner the hukumnama which, of course, is binding on all Sikhs. It is no secret that during British rule, when the gurdwaras in Punjab were controlled by pro-British mahants, more than one hukumnama was issued declaring anti-British Sikh revolutionaries to be non-Sikhs. Those hukumnamas were also issued from the Akal Takht. How should non-Sikhs as well as Sikhs look upon them? How should these have been looked upon when they were issued? If at that time these hukumnamas were the result of the misuse of the religious authority of the Akal Takht by those who controlled it, why should the present hukumnama, or its desirability, be above discussion either by the Sikhs or by non-Sikhs?

There can thus be no doubt about the stand of the Left and democratic forces on this issue. The call for social boycott is wrong and harmful and is also inconsistent with the principle of secularism. The hukumnama has once again exposed the harmful effects of the Akali theory of religion and politics being inseparable. Left and democratic forces must always stand for keeping religion and politics apart and must not compromise on this matter.

One of the positive features of the situation in Punjab is that both the CPI and the CPI-M have taken correct and more or less the same stand on the question of the hukumnama, notwithstanding some differences on some other aspects of the Akali-Nirankari dispute. The CPI-M, like the CPI, cannot but be keen that communal peace and harmony should be maintained in the state. Neither is supporting the demand for President's rule in the State, which has been raised by the Nirankaris and which is being supported by a section of the Congress-I.

Another positive features in the situation is the good sense of the common people—Sikhs as well as non-Sikhs. This has been the biggest single factor responsible for the situation not being much worse than it is. Criticism of the extremist sections of the Akalis is growing even among the Sikhs. Sections of the Janata Party too have been critical of the hukumnama.

In this situation there can be no doubt that if the CPI and the CPI-M were to act together and rally all democratic forces for resolving the dispute on the basis of correct principles and without being partisan, there will be rapid and radical change for the better. These correct principles can only be as under:

1. The right to hold and preach any religious view, without anyone having the right to abuse or insult others, must be guaranteed. This must include the right to worship.

2. Any attempt to rouse hostility on grounds of religious views must be opposed.

3. Any difference of opinion about insult to any religion by someone must be resolved either through mutual discussion or with the help of some impartial agency acceptable to both sides or in accordance with the relevant provisions of the law.

Above all, the working and toiling people must be mobilised to maintain and strengthen their unity and defeat all those who seek to divide them—consciously or unconsciously—to serve the interests of exploiters. Last, but not the least, men of goodwill who stand for communal peace must be rallied for the cause. *(1978)*

## 2. Warning Signals from Golden Temple

"People are afraid of travelling and roaming about. The future of children in Punjab seems to be dark. As the government is not doing and will not do anything to deal firmly with the bad elements, many people are thinking of leaving Punjab. Sometimes the idea strikes our minds also. Conditions are frightening. Political people usually see all things from the election point of view. Sincere politicians and leaders have a great role to play at this critical juncture. Do you think this desperate condition will improve?"

This truthful description of the Punjab situation is from a letter the writer of this article received some days ago from a non-party, non-political medical practitioner in Amritsar.

Everyone agrees that a political solution of the Punjab problem will be of great help in isolating and putting an end to the nefarious activities of the killer gangs of the extremists.

What is hindering the settlement? It is said to be the question of Chandigarh on the one hand and that of Abohar-Fazilka on the other. And why can this question not be resolved? Electoral considerations have undoubtedly become the main hindrance.

You ask the Prime Minister: "All agree that Chandigarh has to go to Punjab. Abohar and Fazilka have become disputed. Give Chandigarh to Punjab and let the question of Abohar-Fazilka go to a commission along with the question of other disputed areas/villages. The Akalis want this. It will help ensure that the situation in the border state of Punjab does not go out of control at a time when danger from Pakistan and US imperialism is increasing."

One does not have to wait for Indira Gandhi to reply to know her mind. Such a solution will mean her losing Punjab to the Akalis and Haryana to the BJP-Lok Dal combination in the next elections. And this is a price she is not prepared to pay.

You ask BJP leaders and leaders of other parties which matter in

Haryana: "You say you are anxious to see the Punjab problem resolved for the good of the country. Why not assure the Prime Minister that if she gives Chandigarh to Punjab without giving Abohar-Fazilka simultaneously to Haryana, your Haryana units and leaders will support the decision and will not exploit it for electoral purposes by accusing Indira Gandhi of having betrayed Haryana. That will be a great service to the nation."

One can be more than 100 per cent sure they will never agree to this.

You now turn to the Akali leaders and do some plain-speaking to them: "You say that in her Award of 1971 Indira Gandhi herself awarded Chandigarh to Punjab. But is it not a fact that the award was on the basis of a behind-the-scenes agreement you arrived at with her? Had you not agreed to Chandigarh for Punjab and Abohar-Fazilka for Haryana, though it might or might not be simultaneous? Did not the same award which said Chandigarh would go to Punjab also say that Abohar-Fazilka would go to Haryana? Did not the then Chief Minister (Akali leader Gurnam Singh) welcome the award as a victory for your party and order *deep mala*? Is it not a fact that the award could not be implemented because your party made a right-about turn? "In view of all this, why not now agree to Chandigarh as well as the Abohar-Fazilka issue being referred to a commission in the larger interests of the country as well as of Punjab?"

Everyone knows the expected reply, which will not be uttered: "Such a settlement may not enable the Akalis to win the next elections."

For the same reason, the Akalis are not willing to sign an agreement which provides for Chandigarh being divided, though it is known in political circles that some top Akali leaders have suggested to the Prime Minister a 60:40 division of the city.

This example is enough to prove the contention of the medical practitioner whose letter is quoted above.

The lesson is obvious. Let all those for whom national interests come first and electoral fortunes later demand: "Forget about elections. Think of the interests of the nation—its integrity, unity and freedom. No injustice to Punjab, but no injustice to Haryana and Rajasthan also. Act in the spirit of give and take, of mutual accommodation, and settle what remains to be settled."

A political solution will help greatly, but its absence cannot justify failure to do all that is possible to protect the lives and properties of innocent people.

After all it is the first and foremost duty of any civilised government to do that. When Darbara Singh submitted his resignation and Governor B.D. Pandey took over, many had high hopes that the latter would take steps to end the rot in the administration. This has not taken place. Many believe that this failure is the result of the theory in which Governor Pandey seems to believe—that containing the killers cannot be effective till a political settlement is arrived at.

Here are some examples which illustrate the sorry state of the Punjab administration:

1. Soon after the Punjab bandh of February 14, speeches were made at some public functions calling for the killing of Hindus, with the police just listening and watching.

2. Killings are carried out by "outsiders". The locals who guide and help them are more often than not known to the police. Nothing is done against them or about them. The reason given is : lack of instructions from above. Even known killers are not always arrested.

3. There are not a few instances when police officers just looked on or ran away when the extremists indulged in killings. More often than not no action is taken. At least the public are not told if any action is taken.

4. There is a scheme under which rifles are now given to some persons in villages for defence. There have been at least some instances of these being given to known sympathisers of extremists.

5. In some districts of Punjab anyone can purchase a stengun (smuggled from Pakistan) for Rs. 3,000 or more.

6. In Moga there was a peace rally on March 31, organised by the CPI. A group of about twenty persons brandishing sharp-edged weapons came to the venue and told the organisers that Bhindranwale must not be criticised. The police officers present advised the organisers to acquiesce. It is a different matter that the organisers rejected the advice.

7. When some days ago, the Youth jatha proceeding to Hussainiwala to pay homage to Shaheed Bhagat Singh and to pledge to work for national integration was sought to be attacked at Baghapurana by those who claimed to be Bhindranwale's men, Punjab police just looked on. They

were saved first by a Sikh shopkeeper, then by CRP jawans and later by some Communists who had licensed arms.

8. The Municipal Commissioner of Moga told this writer: "Anyone who makes a complaint against any officer at fault gets a threat on phone from the extremists."

9. After the AISSF had been formally banned, at public gatherings, slogans like the following were raised : "*No Hindu, no Hindustan —Le ke rahenge Khalistan*." Among the speakers were leaders known as belonging to the Longowal group of the Akali Dal. This happened at least in Faridkot district.

10. A gazetted police officer justified his failure to act on a particular occasion by saying: "We do not want our son to be killed, as has happened in the case of DSP Bachan Singh of Amritsar (now retired)."

Men belonging to the police do not seem to have been told by Governor Pandey and his advisors that they must be prepared to risk their lives, like the Army jawans. Small wonder then that upright, secular and loyal police (Sikh) officers and men feel demoralised. And let it be said there are many who are neither sympathetic to extremists nor afraid of being on the hit-list. What they need is the right atmosphere around them.

People in Punjab want an early settlement. But they also feel that the job of the Governor and his advisors is to set right the administration to the maximum possible extent and ensure effective steps to protect the lives and properties of the people.

It is anybody's guess to what extent freedom has been given by the Centre to the Governor to act. Maybe, he has no freedom, and he is not to blame. In any case, it is certain that even at the highest level all is not well, to say the least.

To enter or not to enter the Golden Temple has been perhaps the most difficult question facing the Government of India. Sentiments of the Sikhs are being roused by alleging that police entry is imminent. Retaliation in the form of killing of Hindus is being propagated by the extremists.

There is no longer any doubt that the killer gangs have been operating from within the Golden Temple and from premises in the neighbourhood. Armed training is being given at Guru Nanak Niwas. Armed squads have been moving in and out. Squads have fanned out to other districts.

Killers have been taking shelter in these premises. Declarations that killing of Nirankaris will continue till they become Amritdhari Sikhs and convert their bhawans into gurdwaras have been made. A top Akali leader, Jathedar Jiwan Singh, has charged that calls for killing Hindus are given from the neighbourhood of Sant Longowal himself.

Parkash Singh Badal has chosen to maintain absolute silence, whatever his reasons. Sant Longowal has never been a part of the Golden Temple. There is a road between the two which belongs to the Municipal Corporation. When DIG Police Atwal was murdered, everyone expected that the police would enter Guru Nanak Niwas. It did not. Instead, the Home Minister issued an ill-advised "ultimatum". There are reports that the Government of India had to reverse it, because a very high dignitary threatened to resign. Reports are also afloat that Bhindranwale shifted to the Akal Takht on the advice of another bigwig.

The Prime Minister is right when she says that the state has the right to enter any religious place for valid reasons but it must also consider any possible adverse effect of such an exercise. The deep religious and emotional attachment of Sikhs to the Golden Temple cannot be lost sight of.

The question need not have been on the agenda at all, if the government had taken certain other steps (short of entry) to prevent misuse of the Golden Temple by the extremists. Many believe that several such steps can be taken even now. It is for the government to decide.

Democratic forces have a duty to discharge. It is not enough to go on expressing hope that the Akali leadership would take steps to put an end to the misuse of gurdwaras and would demarcate itself completely from the extremists. Big efforts have to be made to mobilise Sikh public opinion for banning entry of all weapons (except kirpans) into the Golden Temple, by the SGPC itself. This is not impossible because already among sections of Sikhs there is revulsion against some of the things being done in the Golden Temple.

Those who claim to speak in the name of the "silent majority", have a big role to play. Their names carry weight. This places a big responsibility on their shoulders. The Hindus among them must go all out to ensure that what happened in Haryana after February 14, 1984, in the name of "revenge", does not happen again there or elsewhere. The Sikhs among them must do all they can to ensure that killings in Punjab are stopped. They can help in a big way if they take steps to rally Sikh opinion for putting an end to misuse of the Golden Temple by the extremists. Let all together work for a political solution on the one hand, and effective steps for protection of lives and properties of the people on the other—in Punjab, Haryana and elsewhere. Let not either of the two be made conditional.

Welcome news is the Government of India's offer to consider amendment to Article 25 to remove any misunderstanding and the Akali response to it by dropping their "Azad Panth Week Programme". This should encourage all democratic, secular and patriotic forces for greater efforts to ensure a peaceful atmosphere and a political solution—the one not conditional on the other. *(March 3, 1984)*

## 3. Some Questions Answered

**1. It is alleged by some that assurances given by Gandhiji and Jawaharlal Nehru to Sikhs were not honoured after India became free. What exactly is the position in this regard?**

Gandhiji had said that free India would have a constitution that would be acceptable to the Sikhs. It cannot be said that this assurance was not honoured. A majority of the Sikh members of the Constituent Assembly which framed India's Constitution voted for it. There is no doubt that the constitution got support of a large majority of the Sikhs.

Jawaharlal Nehru is reported to have said that he would have no objection to the creation of a region in North India in which the Sikhs too would feel the glow of freedom. This was said by Jawaharlal Nehru in 1946, when serious efforts were being made by the Muslim League leadership to win over the Akali leadership to support its demand for the whole of the Punjab going to Pakistan. The Sikh masses were against it. M.A. Jinnah, the Muslim League leader, was making all sorts of promises to the Akali leadership, putting forth all types of baits. It is in this situation that Nehru is reported to have made the observation in question. Its real essence was to assure the Sikhs that they would have as honourable a position in free India as anyone else, including the Hindus. This the Indian Constitution fully guarantees.

Some interpret Nehru's words to mean that he promised a theocratic, Sikh-ruled region within India and wanted Punjab to be such a region.

As is well known, Nehru's whole philosophy and thinking was against the concept of theocracy. If India did not become a Hindu theocratic state when Pakistan became a Muslim state with Islam as its official religion, a good deal of the credit for this goes to Jawaharlal Nehru. He was quite clear that a Hindu India would be against the interests of common Hindus themselves. He could not possibly believe that a theocratic Sikh-ruled region would be in the interests of the common Sikhs.

Maybe Nehru used words which were ambiguous and open to more than one interpretation. One has to take one's stand taking the class realities of today. A Sikh-dominated theocratic Punjab would be a Punjab dominated by Sikh vested interests. The interests of the Sikh masses are inseparable from the interests of the common people of Punjab as a whole. The demand for a theocratic Sikh state in Punjab is as wrong and disruptive as the demand for a "Hindu Rashtra" in India. The former is as anti-Sikh as the latter is anti-Hindu. Both have to be opposed tooth and nail.

**2. Was it not a case of discrimination against the Sikhs when the Government of India did not reorganise Punjab on a linguistic basis even when this had been done in the rest of India?**

It is true that Punjabi Suba and Haryana were formed much later, but that does not prove any discrimination against Sikhs as a religious community. The fact is that the Government of India tried to go back on the commitment made by the Congress that in free India, there would be reorganisation of provinces on a linguistic basis. Everywhere, with the exception of Punjab, this retreat was fought unitedly and the Government of India was forced to form states on a linguistic basis as in Andhra, Maharashtra, Gujarat, etc. In Punjab the issue of linguistic reorganisation and language got mixed up with religion and became communalised. For this, the Akalis are no less to blame than the Hindu communalists. The Government of India which, in fact, wanted to go back on the promise regarding linguistic states was able to resist the demand for a Punjabi-speaking state (and Haryana) for a longer period than elsewhere because of this division.

**3. If Kashmir and Mizoram can have a special status, why not Punjab?**

Let us first take Kashmir. It was a princely state ruled by a Maharaja.

The ruler, a British stooge, was to decide whether Kashmir would join India or Pakistan or become independent. There was a serious move to keep Kashmir out of India and turn it into an anti-India base.

In a very difficult and complicated situation, to defeat the British game Kashmir was given a special status. Otherwise too the position of the two states is not comparable. No one who is not a resident of Jammu and Kashmir can buy land in that state. At one stage this was undoubtedly necessary to safeguard the interests of the people of the state. Did Punjab at any time need such a provision? What is needed in the interests of the country as a whole is that conditions must be created when all States enjoy equal powers, and not to start the reverse process. To some extent at least Kashmir has already moved in the correct direction.

Now about Mizoram. Permission to have trade with some neighbouring countries in local produce under the supervision of the Government of India does not constitute any special status. Nor the assurances that local customary law will not be changed unless the Mizoram Assembly too agrees. Does Punjab stand in need of such assurances?

Last but not the least—one must ask the question: What exactly is the demand of those who want a special status for Punjab? They make no bones about the fact that they want a theocratic state. Neither Kashmir nor Mizoram have been given such status. Nor can any other state in India be allowed to become theocratic.

One thing more. Those who talk of assurances given by Nehru and Gandhi should not forget the solemn assurance given to the nation by the Akali leader Sant Fateh Singh. He had said that they would not demand more powers for Punjab than for the rest of the Indian states.

More powers for states including Punjab—Yes. Special status demanded by some Akali leaders for Punjab—No.

**4. Should the Government of India negotiate with the Damdami Taksal, All India Sikh Students Federation and other extremist groups?**

Any negotiations with any groups which continue to believe in "Khalistan" and which continue killing innocent persons will only strengthen the terrorists. The Congress-I High Command should draw appropriate lessons from the policy it pursued in relation to Bhindranwale and the disastrous results it produced.

**5. What about the demand that all innocent Sikh youths should be released?**

Those who are really innocent should be released without further delay. Some people like Badal, however, characterise every Sikh in jail as innocent. This is as fantastic as the assertion by some others that all Hindus in jail are innocent.

As regards general amnesty, the present is not the appropriate time. It will only add to the strength of the terrorists.

**6. What about Army deserters?**

They do not constitute one category. Some acted under stress of religious sentiments and only deserted. Some killed their officers. There is also the fact that extremist-separatists had created their cells in the Army even before Operation Blue Star. Some of the deserters have made clear only recently that they support the separatist slogan of Khalistan. All these factors have to be kept in view, as also the need for discipline in the Army. There cannot be a uniform policy with regard to all the deserters. The policy pursued by the Government of India with regard to them has satisfied even Akali leaders like Barnala. Badal and Company are using the issue only for their narrow selfish ends. Sometimes Barnala too tends to play their game.

**7. Is Barnala Government sincere in fighting separatists-terrorists?**

It acted against them firmly when "Khalistan" was declared from within the Golden Temple. Barnala has also stood by his declaration that he would not allow Sikh temples to be used for anti-national purposes. The Director General of Police, Shri Ribeiro, has been given freedom to a certain extent at least to deal with the terrorists and he has brought about some improvement in the Punjab police. A blow has been dealt to the terrorists though it would be a serious mistake to underestimate thei strength.

There is however another aspect.

Some of Barnala's ministers continue to help the terrorists. There is also political interference in favour of the terrorists. Fake encounters with the police should be opposed, but some ministers characterise as fake even genuine encounters. Barnala himself seeks to prove that his is a Panthic government, by adopting communally motivated policies. This only widens the Hindu-Sikh gulf and brings grist to the mill of the separatists. Allowing men like Baba Joginder Singh to carry on highly provocative and separatist propaganda will also contribute to the negative aspect of the situation—whatever be the compulsions.

Our attitude towards the Barnala government, therefore, cannot be of general support or general opposition. It has to be decided from issue to issue. However, to bring it down just now may do more harm than good.

**8. Where do we stand as far as Rajiv-Longowal Accord and its implementation in letter and spirit is concerned?**

As far as the letter of the accord is concerned, it is as good as dead insofar as the territorial and surplus water issues are concerned. As far as the spirit in which it was arrived at is concerned, it can be saved only if the gods-that-be in Delhi as well as Punjab and Haryana governments and all political parties and their state units learn to place national interests above their short-term and narrow electoral and partisan interests. Left to themselves, bourgeois parties are unlikely do that. Only strong public opinion can force them. And it is the duty of the Left and also of all other far-sighted patriotic forces to create such public opinion.

*(September 14, 1986)*

## 4. Counter False Propaganda of Terrorists

Terrorists in Punjab would not be able to operate the way they have been doing unless they have the sympathy of at least some sections of the people. Clever propaganda, including untruths, repeated over and over again, is one of their special methods to win this sympathy, apart from exploitation of grievances—genuine as well as imagined.

Only recently, Punjab Police Director General Ribeiro has complained that in some respects at least the police alone has to meet this false propaganda. This implied criticism of the political parties is, in the opinion of this writer, quite well-founded.

It has been propagated on quite a big scale that the para-military forces (and even the police) take away innocent Sikh youths from villages and shoot them down on the Indo-Pak border, declaring them to be infiltrators, terrorists, etc. Not a few Sikhs living in rural areas, at least in the border district of Amritsar, believe this to be true. This falsehood has never been challenged by the main political parties—frontally and in an effective manner—so much so that there are Sikhs who believe that thousands of innocent youths are being done to death in this manner. It was Ribeiro who challenged the terrorists and their friends like Mr. Badal and Mr. Tohra to produce even one name of an innocent Sikh taken away from his village and shot dead. Again, it is Ribeiro who had pointed out that no one has produced any name. Nor is this the only instance.

Not very long ago, the BSF in Gurdaspur district shot dead 10 suspected trained terrorists when they were in the process of crossing over from Pakistan into Indian Punjab. Mr. Parkash Singh Badal and some others immediately alleged that they had been picked up from their villages, taken to the border and shot dead. Some Akali ministers made the same allegation. Facts, however, compelled all these gentlemen to shift their grounds. It was then alleged that the persons shot dead were coming to India to surrender. This version could not explain why they were trying to come to India under cover of night, when many had earlier crossed the border during day and surrendered without any difficulty. It was later on admitted that the persons in question were not only trained terrorists but also were coming with bad intentions. It was now alleged that when discovered, they had raised their hands (or had raised a white shirt) to indicate their desire to surrender, but were still shot dead by the BSF. Assuming this to be true, this is a far cry from the original propaganda mentioned above.

No political party came out against this false propaganda. It was Giani Jagjit Singh, a fearless and respected journalist of Gurdaspur district, who had the courage to puncture the false propaganda through his column in various papers published from Punjab. For his truthful writings he had to pay with his life. He has been shot dead by the terrorists.

Let us refer to another very recent example. One of the dreaded terrorists of Amritsar district, Avtar Singh Brahma, belongs to village Brahmpura. It is no secret that a leader of the "United Akali Dal" hailing from this very village for long was helping and supporting one group of terrorists. Even knowing this fully well, he was not only not arrested but was allowed to go abroad.

He was arrested only a little while ago.

Very recently, Avtar Singh Brahma appeared in the village and using the public address system from a gurdwara indulged in a highly abusive and provocative tirade against the CRPF for about 20 minutes. The CRPF did not act as long as he was there. Later, and after getting reinforcements, they conducted a house-to-house search in a part of the village. During this operation, the CRPF committed some excesses which deserved not only condemnation but also some punishment.

Friends of the terrorists acted promptly to exploit the incident to the maximum possible extent. It was falsely alleged that one copy of Guru Granth Sahib had been burnt and another fired upon. The Hindu communal organisations, on the other hand, denied any excess and painted the CRPF as flawless, etc. Obviously, this posture could only alienate the Sikhs, widen Hindu-Sikh rift and play into the hands of the extremists.

What was required was to put the whole matter in proper perspective on the basis of truth, demand punishment for those responsible for excesses, while exposing the false story about Granth Sahib having been burnt and fired upon as well as the stand of the Hindu communal organisations. Only the CPI has done this. Even some secular parties chose to keep quiet about the false propaganda regarding Guru Granth Sahib. And this could only bring grist to the extremist mill.

More instances of high-powered propaganda designed to create sympathy for the terrorists on the basis of distorted, exaggerated and even fabricated "facts" can be given. That, however, is not necessary. What is necessary is to emphasise the necessity to counter this. It is an essential part of the fight against extremism and terrorism. And political parties committed to national unity and integrity would be failing in their duty if they do not discharge this task—whether out of fear or due to negligence.

The task can be discharged successfully only on the basis of truth and facts. Neither the Punjab police nor the para-military forces consist of angels. In fact, there is much in them which is wrong. Excesses on the one hand, and failure to act on the other, is only to be expected. These must be exposed and criticised with the objective of ensuring that they become better weapons for fighting terrorists. At the same time, it is necessary to expose all false propaganda by the extremists if they have to be isolated.

Recently another aspect of the problem has become a topic of serious discussion. There have been quite a few attempts at jail-break by hardened terrorist-killers. Some have been successful while some could be foiled only at the cost of some lives of the jail staff. It is high time that highly-trained terrorist-killers—when nabbed—are kept in some really high-security jails even outside Punjab. If necessary, they may even be tried inside those jails or the trials may wait till peace is restored in Punjab. This is not a suggestion which one would make under normal circumstances. Even in the abnormal situation which prevails in Punjab and which constitutes a serious threat not only to the unity and integrity of India but to the future of the common people themselves, including Sikhs, this should be applied in as few cases as possible. To those who don't like to entertain any such suggestion on grounds of civil liberties, we only want to say that there can be no absolute rights and freedoms for all in any society under all circumstances. *(January 13, 1987)*

## 5. Negative and Positive Aspects of the Crisis

Extremely serious note needs to be taken of all that happened in the Golden Temple on January 26, 1987 by all those who cherish the unity and integrity of the country.

A so-called "Sarbat Khalsa" had been called by Gurbachan Singh Manochahal, a member of the "Panthic Committee", an extremist outfit.

More than one national flag were burnt and more than one "Khalistani" flags were hoisted. It has been asserted on behalf of the district authorities that this was the handiwork of "some youths" and that "Khalistani" flags were removed on their intervention. One cannot be very sure about it. That, however, it is not the main thing.

One of the resolutions adopted warned of "dire consequences" if those responsible for the assassination of Indira Gandhi were to be hanged. Every intelligent person can understand the dangerous implications of this.

By another resolution, the declaration of "Khalistan" made from within the Golden Temple on April 29, 1986 by the extremists was fully endorsed. Its implications, however, are much more dangerous than that of the 1986 resolution. This for the simple reason that this resolution (as also the one regarding the assassins of Indira Gandhi) had the support and backing of all the five Head Priests officially appointed by the Shiromani Gurdwara Prabandhak Committee (SGPC). Acting Jathedar of Akal Takht, Prof. Darshan Singh, in his speech approvingly quoted the late Sant Bhindranwale in this connection. He had said that the foundation would be laid for Khalistan the day security forces would enter the Golden Temple. It does not have to be mentioned that there were slogans in support of Khalistan and Bhindranwale.

The five new Head Priests had been appointed by the SGPC after sacking the earlier ones, after Gurcharan Singh Tohra had been elected its president defeating the nominees of Akali Dal (Longowal) and after the leadership of the SGPC had been captured by the Tohra-Badal faction of the Akali Party.

These appointments were "approved" by the Sarbat Khalsa. Interestingly, in the case of Prof. Darshan Singh, it was made clear that he would only be "Acting" Jathedar of Akal Takht and that Jasbeer Singh, a nephew of Sant Bhindranwale "remains" the real occupant of the post. Jasbeer was never appointed as such by the SGPC. He was "appointed" by the January 26, 1987 Sarbat Khalsa of the extremists. He was in jail even at that time. Nor is that all.

The supreme position of the Akal Takht Jathedar in the Sikh religion has been circumscribed by two decisions: One, an Advisory Committee has been appointed to advise him; Secondly, the four other Head Priests have been "authorised" to act over the head of and independently of the Akal Takht Jathedar, while the "Panthic Committee" in consultation with the "Other Sikh Organisations" has been given the "power" to overrule all the five Head Priests in certain matters.

In other words, the Panthic Committee, "known to be the brain behind the terrorist-killers has assumed supermacy over the High Priests" (*Indian Express).* It may be noted that almost all the members of this committee are wanted by the police. The SGPC leadership, notwithstanding its great services to the extremists, has been rendered irrelevant.

It is not without significance that Prof. Darshan Singh in his speech called Bhindranwale as "protector of Akal Takht" and warned against "ignoring the importance of the Akal Takht." Obviously, the Panthic Committee did not feel sure of the Professor going whole hog with it and has, therefore, assumed complete supermacy itself.

One shudders to think what would be the consequences if the "Panthic Committee" were allowed to have its way to misuse the Golden Temple the way it would like to. The Amritsar police chief has already given out the numbers of some rooms in the Parikarma of the Golden

Temple in which terrorists are supposed to be living. Some members of the press confirm him, even though privately.

It is good that the Punjab Government has strongly condemned the happenings in the Golden Temple of January 26, 1987. It is also good that the Working Committee of the Akali Dal (Barnala) has expressed its deep concern over the "failure of the SGPC to resist the desecration of the holy complex of the Golden Temple by allowing the anti-Sikh, anti-national and secessionist elements to hold a meeting under the garb of Sarbat Khalsa and to pass resolutions aimed at disrupting the unity of the country and promoting divisive and fissiparous tendencies amongst the Sikhs."

The office-bearers of the SGPC have been asked to assert their authority or quit. One, however, cannot be sure that they will oblige. Nor can one be sure of what the Barnala Akali Dal would do in that case and whether it will give up the policy of appeasement altogether. It has consistently refused to take the position that religion and politics must be separated. Only from this position can extremists be successfully fought politically and isolated completely. The Working Committee has not specifically condemned the Sarbat Khalsa resolution regarding Indira Gandhi's assassins.

Certain other happenings on the eve of the Republic Day also need to be noted:

1. Various extremist organisations have condemned the defensive positions taken by the Indian troops on the Indo-Pak border to meet any threat from Pakistan and have called upon Sikhs not to cooperate with the Indian troops.

2. At 7 p.m. on January 22, 1987, about 10 terrorists entered the only Hindu house in village Bahulian very near police station Ajnala in Amritsar district. They did so by crossing the common wall with the house of a neighbour. One of the four brothers and the young son-in-law of the eldest of the brothers (married only ten months ago) were shot dead. Firing went on for about twenty minutes. The terrorists were on foot. The police station was rung up. No one picked up the phone. The village elders themselves went there to report. It was not yet 8 p.m. All except two officials were reported drunk. The police reached the site at 10 p.m. or perhaps a little before that. A CRPF post is there only one-and-a-half kilometres away. The CRPF reached the site at 10.30 p.m.

The family is thinking of leaving the village. The father of the newly-married young man killed by the terrorists is a retired police official. He is a resident of village Wadala, near Rayya, in the same district. His family too is the only Hindu family in the village. He too is thinking of shifting to Rayya.

The same night, the police raided a house in the area. Three extremists managed to escape after the police had got opened and entered the house. The explanation given for not firing at them by the head of the police party is that it would have resulted in an enquiry against him and his colleagues.

3.(a) On night of the 26th, the extremists hoisted Khalistani flags on top of all the Hindu houses in village Jastarwal Chhina situated very near the above-mentioned village Bahulian. There are about 12 Hindu houses in Jastarwal Chhina.

(b) During the previous night, the CPI flag on the shop of Dr. Beant Singh and the Congress flag on the shop of Raj Kumar Mahesha, both of village Fatehabad, were removed. Kesari flags were hoisted in their places. Comrade Beant Singh on discovering what had happened, removed the kesari flag and re-hoisted the Red Flag. Shri Raj Kumar Mahesha got the CRPF to re-hoist the Congress flag in place of the kesari flag. In the same village, the kesari flag was also hoisted on the building of the government primary school—again in the night. This too was removed by the CRPF.

In this very village, there is a branch of the Punjab National Bank. Four posts of clerks are lying vacant. No new appointee is willing to join duty in this branch, not even a Sikh.

(c) During the same night, a kesari flag was hoisted on the Government High School of village Vain Puain near Fatehabad. We saw it still there on January 28, 1987.

These are some instances of the negative and dangerous situation in Punjab, especially in the border districts of Amritsar and Gurdaspur.

It is necessary to mention some instances which symbolise the positive side.

1. On the day of the Sarbat Khalsa itself, the textile Mazdoor Ekta Union, Amritsar (AITUC) held a massive rally followed by a huge demonstration for Hindu-Sikh unity and against separatism and terrorism as well as against communalism of both hues. It consisted of thousands

of Hindus and Sikhs—almost in equal number. Led by the All India Trade Union Congress President Chaturanan Mishra, MP and AITUC General Secretary Madan Lal Didi, it passed through working class areas as well as some parts of the interior walled portion of the Amritsar city.

2. Ten days before the Sarbat Khalsa, Rayya had seen a 3,000-strong rally, mostly of Sikhs from rural areas, called jointly by six parties (Congress-I, Akali Dal, CPI, CPI-M, BJP, and Janata). It pledged to fight and defeat the imperialist game to destabilise India.

3. Sikh neighbours of the Hindu family in village Bahulian had helped to save the children, who were almost thrown into their houses over the common walls.

4. Some leaders of Congress-I, Akali Dal, CPI, CPI-M and the Desh Bhagat Yadgar Committee have jointly convened a state-level convention in Jalandhar on February 15, 1987 "to discuss such common issues of vital concern as curbing of terrorism and separatism and safeguarding communal peace, amity and national integrity, stopping misuse of all religious places and preserving their sanctity and how to keep religion and the state and religion and politics apart and how to counter the cult of communal hatred, fanaticism and violence by uniting the forces of unity and patriotism and also to discuss implementation of the Punjab Accord."

5. Chief Minister Barnala, according to an uncontradicted press report, had been wanting to transfer the Amritsar SSP, whose firm commitment to fight terrorism is well known, presumably under pressure of his pro-terrorist colleagues. The Director General Police, Rebeiro, is said to have been resisting the move. The SSP, Azhar Alam, has been awarded Padma Shri.

6. This writer along with the district secretary of our Party Harbhajan Singh and some other comrades visited some areas near the Khemkaran border on January 28, 1987. We all felt absolutely certain that the separatists would not get the response they expected from the patriotic Sikhs living in the villages near the border.

The need for providing non-official relief in addition to the relief measures of the government is very much there and will remain so, whether relief is needed for the victims of natural calamities like earthquakes or for the victims of terrorists, communal riots, etc.

Non-official relief can be organised in such a manner as will not only bring succour to those in distress but will also help the forward-looking and patriotic forces. Conversely, it is also possible to organise relief in such a manner as will produce negative results. These propositions are particularly true when the needy are victims not of natural calamities but of social forces. One hundred per cent neutral and purely humanitarian relief work in such cases may not be possible. In any case, it is time to review relief work done in Punjab, Delhi, and other places in connection with the victims of Khalistani terrorists as well as the victims of anti-Sikh riots in Delhi, Kanpur, and elsewhere—official as well as non-official.

This article is an attempt at such a review.

In the beginning, the families (next of kin), of the victims of the terrorists in Punjab were given only Rs. 10,000 for every death. Later on, it was increased to Rs. 20,000, which in most cases remains extremely inadequate—especially when the deceased was the bread-winner of the family. Recently it has been decided that one of the dependents would be given a government job on priority basis, in accordance with the qualifications of the applicant. Another recent decision will be dealt with further down.

In the case of the government employees, their dependents get only what they would have got if death had been natural while in service, the only exception being police personnel.

It needs to be stated that political parties have not taken as much interest as they should have to force the government to give adequate relief.

Now about the non-official relief. Let me start with a specific example. The Congress-I Government led by S. Darbara Singh had resigned after the killings of a number of bus passengers near Dhilwan. President's rule had been promulgated. Some more bus passengers had been killed in a bus near Naushehra Pannuan in Amritsar district. Governor B.D. Pandey had come to Amritsar and had called a meeting of all the parties. At this meeting the Governor said: "Government will help the families of those killed. But if non-official organisations in a position to do so can also help that will indeed be very good."

This writer attended that meeting on behalf of the CPI, along with Comrade Parduman Singh. The Akali leader S. Balwant Singh (present

Finance Minister of Punjab) was also there. Explicitly stating what the Governor was hinting at, this writer, supported by the entire meeting, appealed to Balwant Singh to ensure that those families were given financial assistance by the Shiromani Gurdwara Prabandhak Committee (SGPC). It was stated that financial assistance by the SGPC to the families of the victims (who were all Hindus) would also contribute towards "defeating the objective of the terrorists of widening Hindu-Sikh differences leading to Hindu-Sikh riots." Balwant Singh promised that he would try, but no help was in fact given by the SGPC.

Had the SGPC come forward to help the victims of the terrorists in Punjab in the same way in which it later came forward to help the victims of the anti-Sikh riots in Delhi it would have made a good and positive contribution towards maintaining communal peace and harmony in the state and towards weakening the extremists. It chose not to do so.

Of late, the Hindu Shiv Sena has started helping the families of the victims. On an average, the terrorists are killing one Sikh for every two Hindus in Punjab. The Shiv Sena gives financial help only to the Hindu families.

Non-official relief on a communal basis does not help the fight against extremism and terrorism. It can only weaken the fight, even though it may help the victimised families to some extent.

There are instances of the other type too. At the time of the funeral procession of the BJP leader Harbans Lal Khanna, some Sikhs got killed by the firing resorted to by the CRP. Privately, it was admitted by CRP top officers that this had been a *bona fide* mistake and those who got killed were innocent. The official report, however, was otherwise. The government would not give any financial assistance to the families of the deceased. The SGPC announced financial assistance for all the families because the victims were Sikhs. The Punjab Istri Sabha had been authorised by a charitable trust in Delhi to give financial assistance to such victims as were not being helped by the government. It has helped some poor people who had received bullet injuries at the hands of the terrorists but who were not given any financial assistance by the government. The Punjab Istri Sabha now came forward to help the families of the poor amongst the Sikhs, who died as a result of the CRP firing.

Very good relief work has been done by Left-led and other trade unions of teachers, employees of the Punjab State Electricity Board, railway employees, bank employees, etc. They have collected large amounts on a completely non-communal basis from their members and other employees to help the families of their colleagues killed by the terrorists—all contributed, and irrespective of the community to which victims belonged. This definitely helped not only the families of the victims but also strengthened Hindu-Sikh unity.

Non-official relief work on a scale hitherto unknown has been done to help the families of the victims of the terrorists by the Shaheed Pariwar Fund started by the Hind Samachar group of papers. About this, a little later. Here it needs to be stated that the political parties in the state have hardly paid pay attention to the organisation of non-official relief on a non-communal and united basis.

Let us now come to relief measures for victims of anti-Sikh riots in Delhi and other places.

The government relief announced in the beginning was quite inadequate, as was the case in Punjab. Later on it was increased but it still remained inadequate.

Some new organisations for this specific purpose came up and did good work. Of the established mass organisations and political parties, as far as this writer knows, only the National Federation of Indian Women made collections and did good relief work in some of the worst affected localities, even though on a limited scale.

From Punjab, help was sent in various forms by the SGPC and Akali Party. Funds were also collected by the All-India Sikh Students Federation—an extremist outfit. At quite a few places these were collected without issuing receipts, and not many know what use was made of them. In any case, this was relief on communal lines.

Here and there some new organisations were formed and they did good work on a non-communal basis.

Of the established mass organisations and political parties, only the Punjab Istri Sabha ran a mass campaign to collect funds and clothes for victimised families of anti-Sikh riots. The entire collection was sent to the National Federation of Indian Women. An incident which took place at Chheharta would explain the importance of the work. Some shopkeepers of Pratap Bazar, Chheharta, had met in deputation the local

Istri Sabha leaders and had told them that some boys claiming to be AISSF activists had started collections from the Bazar in the name of relief for victims in Delhi. They were not asking Hindu shopkeepers to contribute. They were not giving any receipts. The deputation requested collection from the Bazars on a non-communal basis. The Istri Sabha leaders were told that all Hindu shopkeepers too were keen to contribute. When the Istri Sabha sent its jatha for collection, it got very good response from one and all.

The Istri Sabha units were helped in a number of places by the trade union workers in this work. However, the positive impact in Punjab itself would have been more if all the political parties had run a big campaign to collect funds for the victims of riots in Delhi, Kanpur, etc., to be disbursed through a similar all-party body in those centres.

Incidentally, quite a few persons asked the Istri Sabha workers: "You are doing good work, but why not do something about the Kanpur victims too?"

The Barnala government immediately after it took power announced a number of relief measures for victims of anti-Sikh riots, who had come and settled down in Punjab. The help announced by the Punjab Government was to be over and above that given by the Delhi administration. Some had doubts about the wisdom of the decision of the Punjab Government. Their argument was that it was the duty of the State administrations concerned to help, that pressure should be put on them to increase the help, that the decision of the Punjab Government would encourage migration and also the feeling that Punjab and not India was the real homeland of the Sikhs.

But the doubts were not expressed vocally. The fact that many undeserving and ineligible persons have got help through fraud too has not been much talked about. What caused much resentment was the fact that the same facilities were not extended to victims of terrorists in Punjab. Obviously this communal discrimination was a part of the effort of Barnala to prove that his government was a Panthic government. This alienated the Hindus, increased Hindu-Sikh differences, which could only help the extremists.

It took the Barnala government more than a year to put the victims of terrorists on a par with the victims of anti-Sikh riots. Additional facilities given to victims of terrorists now include pension for widows at the rate of Rs. 250 per month for three years, provided there is no adult member in the family in a position to support her. Also a house is given if she does not have any in Punjab. Some discrimination remains even now. For instance, seats have been reserved for victims of anti-Sikh riots in medical colleges but not for the victims of terrorists in Punjab.

When many Hindus were forced to migrate from parts of Amritsar and Gurdaspur districts, the question of helping the uprooted families again came up.

We were not in favour of organising relief in a manner as would encourage migration. However, helping these families till they would be in a position to go back was necessary. The Barnala government agreed to open camps for them in towns like Amritsar and Gurdaspur but did not do anything in practice. Nothing was done on a non-communal basis at the non-official level. The Hindu communal organisations exploited the situation to the extent they could. In Delhi, political parties did not move in the matter at all, nor did any class organisations. The administration realised the necessity of doing something a bit late in the day. The result was that the Hindu communal organisations in Delhi were able to exploit the Hindu migrants to incite anti-Sikh incidents on more than one occasion.

This writer has definite reports that in Ghaziabad, Yamuna Nagar, and other places, the migrants were not very much welcome. Their very presence was used to raise rents.

We have narrated these facts to emphasise the great necessity of organising relief on a secular basis.

Earlier in this article we have referred to the relief work being done by the Hind Samachar group of newspapers in the name of Shaheed Pariwar Fund. This group of newspapers was founded by the late Lala Jagat Narain, a veteran freedom-fighter. He was shot dead by the terrorists for his strong opposition to the killings of Nirankaris by the extremists, and to the demand for Khalistan. The Hind Samachar group did have a Hindu communal bias. The Shaheed Pariwar Fund was started by Ramesh Chandra, who took over the editorship after the death of his father, Lala Jagat Narain. Its declared aim was to help the families of the victims of the terrorists. Money poured in a big way but for obvious reasons mostly from Hindus. Ramesh Chandra too was shot dead by the terrorists. His successors—his brother, K. Narendra, and his son—decided to continue the Shaheed Pariwar Fund. It goes to the credit of the Fund that from the very beginning it was made clear that non-Hindu victims of terrorists would be helped on an equal basis and that the Fund would be entirely non-communal. Not only that. Soon after the anti-Sikh riots of November, 1984, it was announced that financial help on the same basis would be given to the victims of anti-Sikh riots. And it has been thus given. The exact amount of financial assistance to be given is decided by a committee members of which belong to the major political parties of Punjab, though they are there in their individual capacities.

What are the lessons that emerge from the above narration?

Firstly, the need for non-official relief as a mass movement is very much there but is not getting adequate attention by the political parties. This writer remembers the massive relief campaign which was organised in India to help the victims of the terrible famine which had broken out in Bengal as a result of the policies pursued by the then British rulers. The fact that we are a free country now does not exclude the need for relief work as a united mass movement.

Secondly, relief work on a communal basis when the unity and integrity of our country is threatened by separatist and communal forces will have negative effects too, though it does help families in distress. On the other hand, relief on a non-communal basis organised on a big scale to help the victims of separatists and of communal violence will definitely strengthen the struggle against the divisive forces.

*(February 7, 1987)*

## 6. Mass Campaigning by Secular Forces: Need of the Hour

The wheel has turned full circle in Punjab. The crisis seems to be heading towards a climax—maybe a big confrontation. A dual trend is emerging, bringing about a new polarisation in the state.

On the one hand, the country faces a grim spectacle. The endorsement of the demand for Khalistan in the so-called Sarbat Khalsa held in the Golden Temple on January 26 in the presence of the five head priests appointed by the SGPC; the resolution of the same Sarbat Khalsa that dire consequences would follow if assassins of Indira Gandhi were hanged; declaration of supremacy of the so-called "Panthic Committee" over the affairs of the Golden Temple and the Akal Takht; the hukumnama disbanding all Akali Dals and setting up of a "United Akali Dal" headed by the well-known extremist Simranjit Singh Mann, its constitution, its aims and the composition of its leading body as laid down by a fiat of the head priests—all these developments make one thing clear. The separatist-extremists and the terrorists have out-manoeuvred the Barnala government and the Government of India both. They have once again succeeded in fully capturing the Golden Temple, but with a difference.

Their grip over the Temple this time is greater than before. They have also the backing of the Singh Sahibans (the High Priests) officially appointed by the SGPC. The latter are more or less allied with the extremist-separatists. In any case, no one is in a position to act independently of them. (Those who had illusions about Professor Darshan Singh should have become wiser by now. Of course, one cannot be very sure; at the time of writing, news comes that the Akal Takht acting chief is himself under threat of being killed by a terrorist faction.)

The extremist-separatists will fully misuse not only the Golden Temple but other gurdwaras also under the Tohra-led Shiromani Gurdwara Prabandhak Committee (SGPC) which has really become irrelevant. The number of these gurdwaras increased by more than 100, thanks to an ordinance which was issued by the Governor of Punjab on the eve of the SGPC elections. The Barnala government, through this ordinance, had placed these gurdwaras under the SGPC directly. The measure has boomeranged.

The people of Punjab had two glimpses during the preceding week of what is likely to happen in the SGPC controlled gurdwaras.

In Mastuana in District Sangrur, the mother of Karamjit Singh, who made an attempt on the life of Prime Minister Rajiv Gandhi, was honoured in the presence of the acting Jathedar of Akal Takht. According to some papers, the acting Jathedar himself honoured her.

There was a conference in support of Khalistan in the historic Dukh Niwaran Gurdwara in Patiala.

There is, however, the other and brighter side of the picture. It is heartening that Mr. Surjit Singh Barnala has refused to resign as the President of the Akali Dal (Longowal) and has also refused to disband it. It is also good that the Punjab Congress-I chief has assured the Barnala government of its full support in all the measures it may take against extremists and terrorists.

All this, however, is not adequate to meet the grave situation. Without any avoidable delay, all the parties and groups which stand for national unity and integrity of India, must arrive at a consensus how best to prevent the Golden Temple from once again becoming the headquarters and guiding centre of Khalistani terrorists. Steps have to be taken to ensure that anti-national activities and propaganda cannot be carried on from places of religious worship.

Government of India is committed to enact an All-India Gurudwara Act. It is necessary to enact another law even before that. This law must ensure that places of worship of no religion are allowed to be used for any political activities—much less activities of an anti-national character.

The Barnala government as well as the Government of India must realise that search for short-cuts will prove counter-productive and dangerous. Policies of appeasement must go and so also the Trojan horses within the government. Short-term interests—electoral or otherwise—must give way to the vital interests of the country. Mr. Barnala must cease claiming to be and acting as the head of a Panthic government.

The battle for separating religion and politics may be difficult but it has to be fought and won. There is no short-cut and there can be no half-way house.

As regards the territorial and river waters disputes, a political solution in the spirit of the Rajiv-Longowal Accord in the larger national interests and in the spirit of give and take must be found. This will not be difficult at all if all political parties place the interests of the nation above their immediate partisan interests.

Above all, the Akali Dal led by Mr. Barnala, and the Punjab Congress-I must give up their fears and inhibitions and must go to the people in a big way—together with Communists and others—for rallying them against separatism and for isolating the terrorists. People have also to be rallied against religious places being turned into centres of political activities. People have to be told that the only guarantee to maintain their sanctity and to ensure that the police, etc., do not have to enter them is to ensure that no one is allowed to misuse them for anti-national purposes.

It is also necessary to briefly deal with the improvements that are necessary in the Punjab Police as well as the para-military forces, especially the CRPF.

Let us recall 1983 and the first 4-5 months of 1984.

Demoralisation in the Punjab Police had set in when Giani Zail Singh as the Home Minister of the Government of India did not want the Punjab Police to act firmly against extremists, only to embarrass his arch rival Darbara Singh. It was also the inevitable result of the more than soft attitude of the gods that ruled Delhi towards Bhindranwale for a long time. Some facts need only to be recalled in this connection. When a loyal-to-his-uniform DIG Police was shot dead from within the Golden Temple, nothing was done to bring the culprits to book. When Mr. Darbara Singh was the Chief Minister and even after Giani Zail Singh had ceased to be the Home Minister, Amritsar had three SSPs appointed on orders from Delhi, who were either in league with Bhindranwale or were afraid of him. A Director General of Police sent from Delhi gave a clean chit to Bhindranwale and also issued oral orders that extremists must not be fired upon in any case. All this could not but demoralise such of the officers as were willing and wanted to fight the menace of terrorism. All this also could not but enable the terrorists to establish strong footholds in the police force.

When CRPF was brought to Punjab, not much attention was paid to properly brief the force regarding the Punjab situation. There was a tendency to regard every Sikh as an extremist or separatist. The CRPF were put up in temples which enabled Hindu communal organisations to inject communal anti-Sikh poison in the force to a considerable extent.

During curfew hours, the Punjab Police would often let off lightly the Sikhs violating the curfew but would beat up the Hindu violators. The CRP would do just the reverse. They would let off the Hindu offenders but would beat up the Sikhs. Of course, this was not a universal phenomenon. But the scale on which it happened was by no means insignificant or negligible. Similarly, sections of Hindus looked upon the CRP as their saviours while sections of Sikhs demanded its withdrawal. Sections of Sikhs wanted only Punjab Police while sections of Hindus wanted only the CRP. Even slogans were coined and shouted on this basis.

In some places, the Communist suggestion of joint squads was implemented. There were good results but there were some virtual clashes too between the men of the Punjab Police and those of the CRP.

Considerable improvement has taken place and the situation is not at all as bad as it used to be. Various factors—policy decisions as well as positive and negative happenings—have contributed towards this improvement.

Mr. Ribeiro's leadership and assertion of his authority to a considerable extent—despite political interference in favour of the terrorists by some of the ministers—has helped some good officers of Punjab Police to go into battle with real zeal and courage. Success achieved by them in arresting or killing a number of hardcore terrorists has improved the image of the Punjab Police. Had Mr. Ribeiro and some of his good officers not underestimated the extremist penetration in the Punjab Police and had Ribeiro received the full backing of the government, the results would have been much better.

As regards the CRP, the need to brief it properly was realised and some steps were taken in that direction. Some companies were replaced too. There is also the fact that the CRP did not always act as it should have. Not a few killings by the terrorists have taken place with the CRP men and even officers standing nearby and not acting. On the other hand, some dreaded terrorists including some who were hated even by the Sikhs of the areas have been arrested or killed in encounters by the Punjab Police as well as by the CRP—working singly as well as jointly. People have also seen sections of para-military forces having the same negative habits as sections of Punjab Police. For instance, this writer some time back told the DC, the SSP as well as the DIG CRP that CRP men in some areas were getting free liquor from boot-leggers and at least some of those who supplied them have also became friendly with them and they are in league with the terrorists too. He was told that this was only a rare phenomenon. That it was not so rare was proved when the terrorists shot dead 4 CRP jawans who were returning from a *dera* after taking liquor.

All such positive and negative developments and the fact that Rebeiro has command of both the Punjab Police and CRP have helped to improve matters to some extent and also the image of both on the whole, whether this is admitted by communal leaders or not. However, it will be a serious mistake to think that everything is now all right. The situation within the Punjab Police is as yet far from satisfactory. Even some of the SSPs are not serious in fighting extremists. There is sympathy for the latter at various levels in sections of the police. Nor has the CRP become completely free from communal bias. Some sections of it do commit excesses too. In many places, it continues to live in the Hindu temples. There have been at least some instances of CRP men inciting retaliation against innocent Sikhs.

There is need for further improvement. And that will be helped if there is exchange of views on the basis of actual experience between the officers of the Punjab Police, the CRP/BSF and the committed leaders of public opinion. Unfortunately, this hardly takes place, especially as far as the para-military forces are concerned.

The strength of the Punjab Police also needs to be increased. Of course care must be taken to keep out extremist elements as also communalists of all hues. It will be good for the Punjab Police itself if the religious minorities in Punjab get better representation in it, without diluting merit and efficiency.

A few words about the army and the situation in Punjab will not be out of place.

It is as clear as daylight that the army cannot solve the problems. It is also clear that frequent use of the army for such purposes is not good for the army itself.

There is no serious demand that Punjab should be handed over to the army. Even the demand for handing over the border districts to the army is not strong: and the demand is wrong.

All this however should not rule out the use of the army by the civil authorities when there is compelling need for the same and only to the extent absolutely necessary—maybe flag marches, maybe patrolling, maybe something else.

It is true that in the period immediately after Operation Blue Star the army committed some excesses in some places. Every excess committed by any force is bad and needs to be condemned and opposed. The army should be no exception. But this cannot rule out the possibility of the situation re-arising where civil authorities have to take army help. It needs also to be stated that there has been deliberate false propaganda grossly exaggerating the excesses committed by the army in Punjab. It can be asserted that:

1. No large-scale atrocities were reported from border areas in the Amritsar district;

2. There was no movement of Sikh youths to Pakistan from border areas in Amritsar district on any abnormal scale;

3. A good number of Sikh youths (a few hundreds) did cross over to Pakistan from Gurdaspur district. Some of them may have done so out of fear of the army even though not having any sympathy for the extremists. But there were others who had links with the extremists and were afraid of being nabbed. There were also Bhindranwale fans who believed that Bhindranwale had not really died in the Golden Temple but had escaped to Pakistan. There were also some who hoped to get substantial financial help and also to be sent to the West.

In the critical situation which is there in Punjab, it is very necessary to see every aspect in correct perspective and not to be taken in by false propaganda of any type from any quarter. It needs to be specially emphasised again that the most important task in Punjab today is mass political campaigning. *(February 13. 1987)*

## 7. Defeat Nefarious Designs of New Priests

It is time to speak frankly, bluntly and without mincing words, as far as the present situation in Punjab is concerned. We owe this to the future of our people including Sikhs.

The meaning of the events which have developed rapidly starting from the so-called Sarbat Khalsa, called by the extremists on Republic Day, 1987 within the Golden Temple, is quite clear. These events were the unfolding of a plan of the extremist-separatists to capture completely the Golden Temple, to bring into existence a ''United Akali Dal'', and a government of this "United Akali Dal", both of which would aid and abet in every possible way the Khalistani terrorists backed by imperialism and the rulers of Pakistan. The plan must have been conceived soon after G.S. Tohra won the election of the SGPC presidentship. Both the Government of Punjab and the Government of India have been taken unawares.

Some may object that the constitution framed by the priests for the United Akali Dal with Simranjit Singh Mann as the President does not declare Khalistan to be its objective. A careful reading will make it clear that the omission is only formal. The purpose of this omission might as well be to save the United Akali Dal sponsored by the priests from being banned.

Others may say: Simranjit Singh Mann is not a hardcore terrorist. He was only carried away by his emotions and was wrongly handled by the government. These gentlemen need to be reminded of one fact. The allegation that he as the SSP of one district helped many extremists to get licences for weapons by pretending that they were Nirankaris was never refuted. There are reasons to believe that he helped to organise one or more killer-squads out of police ranks. He was arrested while trying to escape to Nepal.

The dismissal of the earlier Singh Sahibans, their replacement by persons known for their links with or sympathies for extremists, the resolution of the Sarbat Khalsa in support of Khalistan and the threat of dire consequences if Indira Gandhi's assassins are hanged, declaring a known terrorist-outfit—the Panthic Committee—to be supreme, the way all Akali Dals were ordered to dissolve themselves, the composition of the ordained leadership and the constitution of the United Akali Dal—all these prove our contention that the plan was conceived and sought to be implemented.

The fact that the plan has partly misfired should not make any one complacent. The fight has to be waged both at the administrative and political levels with no holds barred.

It is necessary to remember that the government did not act the way it should have when DIG Atwal was shot dead.

The policy responsible for this failure led to a situation in which the government was forced to undertake an operation which could and should have been avoided.

Today, the grip of the extremists over the Golden Temple is greater than in 1984—for the simple reason that it has the official backing of the SGPC and the "priests". Let all patriotic parties discuss and reach a consensus on how best the terrorists can be prevented from once again making the Golden Temple their centre of operations and an armed fortress.

The Government of India is committed to enact an All-India Gurdwara Act. It is necessary to enact and effectively enforce another law, which must ban politics in places of worship of all religions. It is necessary to emphasise *all* because Hindu communalists, who believe in the theory of revenge and retaliation against innocent Sikhs have made a well-known Hindu temple in Amritsar their headquarters—from where too arms have been distributed. Elsewhere too, religious places have been used by these friends-in-the-garb-of-enemies of the Khalistani terrorists.

At the same time, there is no doubt that the priests have grossly misused the high religious places in which the SGPC executive has put them. Hukumnamas are supposed to be issued when there is a complaint of conduct against a Sikh being anti-Sikh religion, and when the complaint has been found to be correct after hearing the person concerned.

The Akali Party is a political party and large sections of even devout Sikhs do not owe allegiance to it and are even opposed to it. While excommunicating Barnala, Darshan Singh "justified the right of the priests to intervene and interfere in the Akali Dal Affairs." And "since the actual power of the parent Akali Dal had been 'diluted and eroded' by factionalism, it was thought prudent by the five priests 'to merge these factions' to restore the 'strength and authority' of the Party."

Is there any iota of religion in it? Is it not politics, pure and simple? Does it not belie Professor Darshan Singh's claim that the priests had not "over-stepped their religious authority"?

And is their partisanship for those who are Akali followers as against Sikhs who are opposed to the Akali Party not quite clear from this? How can one then accept Darshan Singh's claim that: "We are neutral and not partisan." They have proved that they are not neutral even as between various Akali factions, not to speak of between all Sikhs.

This time they ordered presidents of all Akali factions to resign to make Simranjit Singh Mann the President of the "United Akali Dal". Next time, they may order all Sikhs to join Mann's Dal. Will that also be within their religious authority? Will they ex-communicate all such Sikhs as may refuse to join Mann's Dal?

Obviously, the priests have overplayed their cards. They have helped large sections of Sikhs to realise where mixing of religion and politics can lead to.

Amrinder Singh of the Badal faction has bemoaned: "This was the first time in the last 350 years that Akal Takht's authority had been challenged by the Sikhs."

Amrinder Singh is not right. No devout Sikh has or will challenge the Akal Takht. Even the Hindus have all respect for it. But large sections of Sikhs do see and realise one fact. What comes from the priests in the name of Akal Takht can be good or bad, depending upon what type of persons and Sikhs the priests themselves are. After all, long back, the type of hukumnama which has been issued against Barnala, was once issued against the Sikh Ghadar Babas, those fearless fighters for Indian freedom, of whom every Sikh and every non-Sikh Indian is proud.

Surjeet Singh Barnala has won just praise from various quarters for his courageous stand—even from those who till recently were demanding his dismissal. It is he and his colleagues, who stood by and helped him and who have foiled one part of the extremist game.

A large section of Sikhs, besides others, have come forward to support the position taken by him. This should give him and his colleagues enough courage to give up all efforts for half-way-house positions and compromises. Time has come to take the clear-cut position: supremacy (of Akal Takht) in matters, which are purely religious—yes. Supremacy in matters political and of state—no. In the present times not to keep religion and politics apart can and will prove dangerous.

The point must be realised by devout Sikhs. Those who misuse religion will also mould religion to serve their aims. To allow this misuse of religion for political ends is to endanger the best and the most humanistic traditions of Sikh religion. It is no accident that some claiming to be Sikh religious leaders refuse to condemn killings of even innocent women and children, much less innocent men, but declare those very killers as "martyrs" if they get killed even in very genuine encounters. It is a clear attempt to give a new meaning to Sikh religion, contrary to what Sikhism really stands for. The game cannot be defeated without separating religion and politics.

A massive campaign amongst the people is the need of the hour. The aim should be to mobilise people for:

1. Supporting Barnala's correct position and to help him to go forward so that the policy of appeasement and of half-way-house solutions is given up. These can even lead to virtual surrender.

2. Separation of religion from politics as well as the state—both at the level of the state and at the Centre.

3. Revealing the real face of terrorists and separatists as not only anti-India but anti-Sikh.

4. Exposing Hindu communalists, who preach the theory of "revenge" and "retaliation" in any form and who want India to be a "Hindu nation".

5. Deterrent punishment to those who organise killings of innocent persons. This includes those who organised the anger of the people when Indira Gandhi was assassinated into anti-Sikh riots.

6. Screening of the Jodhpur detenues and release of those who may be found innocent.

7. Making the Centre take meaningful initiative to find the political solution of territorial and river water disputes in the spirit of the Punjab Accord, keeping in view larger national interests, in the spirit of give-and-take and without gross injustice to any state. This will be easy if the big parties place national interests above their immediate electoral or other interests.

Last but not least, the Congress-I as well as the Akali Dal (Longowal) must give up all fears, inhibitions, etc. and join hands with the Left and others and to go to the masses in the rural areas, especially those in which the extremists have developed some bases.

The battle is not easy but it can and will be won. As far as Punjab is concerned, Hindus and Sikhs together can ensure that there is no more division of India. *(February 27, 1987)*

## 8. Mass Mobilisation and New Political Initiatives Needed

It was good that former Punjab Police chief Ribeiro's view has prevailed, at least for the time being.

According to a reliable source Mr. Ribeiro firmly held the view that any negotiations with the terrorist groups—directly or indirectly—at the present would not produce any result except weakening the morale and will of such police officers as are honest and serious in fighting the terrorists. Those in the administration in Chandigarh and New Delhi who held different views in the matter have not overruled him. This indeed is good so far as it goes. This however does not mean that now all is well with the policy being pursued by those who hold the reins of power in New Delhi. Far from it.

Strong measures by the security forces against the terrorists must go hand in hand with a political mass campaign by political parties aimed at weakening the mass base of the terrorists in areas like Tarn Taran sub-division and at countering the false propaganda of the extremists.

If the Congress-I were to put in even half the effort the Communists are putting in, the results will be much bigger. This is so because the Congress-I has a much bigger following amongst Sikh agricultural labourers than the Communists. They as a class are opposed to the aims and methods of the terrorists. Once terror and fear disappear and this class becomes active, poor peasants will also get drawn in and that will make it possible to win over the middle peasants and isolate the landlords and upper sections of rich peasants—the real force behind the extremists. Urban middle class Sikhs too will give up their vacillations. As yet, however, there is no sign that the Congress-I high command and the Congress-I in Punjab have any serious intention to launch such a mass mobilisation campaign.

The Home Minister has more than once ruled out any political initiative till terrorism gets wiped out. One cannot appreciate this position either. Why should such political initiatives be ruled out as will help to isolate the terrorists and thus contribute towards wiping out terrorism? Take for instance the case of the Jodpur detenus.

There is no question of general amnesty, at this stage at least. Those who demand it should not forget the experience of indiscriminate releases ordered by Mr. Barnala on the recommendation of the Bains Committee. At the same time, why should not the innocent among them and those not guilty of serious crimes be released unconditionally? The adamant stand that even innocent persons will be released only as a part of some package deal is neither just nor helpful.

There is also the question of the anti-Sikh riots of November 1984. Mr. Rajiv Gandhi's remark that when a big banyan tree falls there are bound to be tremors, was most unfortunate. The real point was that some Congress-I VIPs, instead of giving a correct lead to the angry people, themselves organised riots or helped the rioters. Their conduct was totally opposite to what Mahatma Gandhi or Nehru would have done or advised. The failure to take any action against them, and the failure to punish any of them or erring police officers will remain a big negative point in the performance record of Mr. Rajiv Gandhi.

Why should he not make some amends now when there is so much talk in the air of big changes in the cabinet as well as in the ruling party? Let the guilty be deprived of the high positions they hold and be made to face the law.

The tragedy is that many who demand punishment for them do not condemn the killings in Punjab, while many who strongly condemn the killings in Punjab believe and in private justify the anti-Sikh riots of November 1984. It is in the Prime Minister's own interest and in the interest of the anti-terrorist fight that he takes steps to clear and retrieve his own position.

Political initiative, here and now, is also needed to resolve the territorial and river waters disputes. It is no use going on paying lip service to the Rajiv-Longowal Accord. Political initiative should be taken to save its spirit.

Let the Prime Minister tell all political parties including his own: "Discuss with your leaders of the concerned state units of your parties. Make up your minds about how the disputes should be resolved. All including the Akali Party should then meet together and arrive at a consensus. No party will then allow any of its state units to oppose this. All parties will campaign for it and all will unitedly oppose any who may choose to try to sabotage the consensus."

There is no doubt that if the big parties for once give priority to national interest instead of to short-term partisan considerations, the disputes will get resolved and that will weaken the terrorists and strengthen the fight against terrorism. *(September 12, 1987)*

## 9. Open Letter to Prime Minister Rajiv Gandhi

Amritsar, March 4, 1988

Dear Prime Minister,

Killings of 34 innocent persons and injuring an equally big number by a group of terrorists in one single operation in Hoshiarpur district has compelled me to write this open letter to you.

Like any other human being with a conscience I am greatly shocked by this most gruesome massacre. And also I am much perturbed, aggrieved and angry at the endless killings of innocent persons and wiping out of entire families.

Like any other patriotic Indian, I am much concerned at the serious threat to the unity and integrity of our great country.

As a Punjabi, I consider it my particular duty to contribute my maximum towards meeting and defeating this threat insofar as this threat comes from some forces within Punjab—even though these are guided, aided and abetted by imperialism and its allies.

As a Communist and a revolutionary, I firmly believe that any success of these forces and any setback to the unity and integrity of India will at the same time be a setback for the Indian revolution and for the world revolutionary process.

I, therefore, wish to do all I can to defeat the forces of terrorism, separatism and communalism of all hues as well as to preserve and strengthen the unity of India. Of course, it can be preserved and strengthened only as unity in diversity. And that requires more powers for the states so that we have a strong Centre as well strong states.

I have no doubt that you and your government too want India to remain united.

The real question is: What is the correct way to keep India united?

I believe that this must be done by having faith in and relying upon the common patriotic and toiling Sikh masses. Together with strong administrative action, including strong action by the security forces, there must be: (a) such political initiatives as will help to isolate the terrorists and to move forward to a political solution of what has come to be known as the Punjab problem; (b) mass campaigning at the grass-roots level against terrorism, separatism, communalism, against misuse of religious places; for separation of religion and politics, etc. These three tasks are equally important. They can and must be carried out simultaneously. I would like to add only one thing. Strong action by the security forces should not rule out civil authorities in Punjab taking the help of the Army to the extent and in the manner considered necessary to prevent killings of innocent persons.

Release of 40 out of the Jodhpur detenues, on being found to be innocent, is welcome. If there are any more innocent ones there, they too should be released. As you know, we have been demanding this for long.

Release of the priests installed by the extremists and known to be firm supporters of the terrorists is, however, an altogether different matter. This reveals the possibility of an altogether different line being pursued instead of the strategy described above.

The policy of appeasing the extremists and attempting to buy peace by striking a deal with them or with a section of them has been followed earlier too. It produces disastrous results. Also, the result of the release of Parkash Singh Badal is there for all to see. What ground is there to believe that the release of these priests too will not prove counter-productive? The apprehension that they may bring even more grist to the mill of the terrorists than Badal cannot be dismissed lightly. I will be too happy if this fear proves wrong.

Please permit me to point out two other important aspects of the situation.

Even if the priests now formally condemn terrorism and killings of innocent persons, there is no guarantee that all the terrorist organisations will act accordingly and stop killings, extortions, etc.

Secondly, it is not a secret that amongst the extremists and terrorists there are two views. One is for "Khalistan" here and now. The other does not consider this to be a practical proposition just now. Those who hold the latter view want some sort of compromise to gain time to be used by them to strengthen their existing cells and create more in the government machinery including the security forces. They need this time all the more in view of the fact that they have started losing support even in areas in which they were able to build some support and win some sympathy.

I hope your government does not fall in any such trap. I know the Indian State is strong enough and if the worst comes to the worst it will guarantee India's unity by handing over Punjab to the Army for a long time. In my opinion, only those who look upon India as a market and not as the motherland can think in these terms. If the unity of India is to be based upon real and genuine unity of her people—notwithstanding their different languages, religions, etc.—the strategy described above must be followed. There must be no appeasement of the terrorists and of separatist forces and even of forces which stand for theocracy. At the same time, what is demanded by the needs of justice must be done unconditionally. For instance, those who organised anti-Sikh riots of November 1984 must be punished.

Such political initiatives as will help resolve the territorial and water disputes without doing gross injustice to any of the concerned states and in the spirit of give and take, keeping in view the overall national interests, must be taken together with strong and effective action against the killer gangs.

In the end, please let me express the hope that the above views of mine will receive the consideration which any citizen of a democratic country is entitled to.

Yours sincerely,
Satya Pal Dang

## 10. Not Vote Bank Politics But People's Intervention

Punjab is witnessing once again several moves and manoeuvres by political forces. The government as well as the Akali Groups—the UAD and the Barnala-led Dal—are active. But the million dollar question is: What happens to the battle against terrorists? Are we serious about fighting decisively the menace of terrorism in Punjab?

The government has given no explanation for not undertaking an operation in the Mand areas of Amritsar, Kapurthala and Ferozepur districts. The successful Operation Black Thunder should have been followed by an operation in the Mand area, whose marshy land and elephant grass are most suitable for the terrorists. Such an operation would have consolidated the gains of Operation Black Thunder. Instead, these gains are being allowed to go waste.

Earlier, the Mand area in Amritsar district was the main centre of activity of the "Khalistani Liberation Force" headed by Avtar Singh Brahma. It has now also become the centre of operation of the "Khalistan Commando Force" headed by the late Labh Singh alias Sukha Sipahi. Moreover, Avtar Singh Brahma has in recent times managed to smuggle many more deadly arms from Pakistan.

In Tarn Taran sub-division of Amritsar district, big groups of terrorists are again moving freely on horses and in cars. They even transport weapons from one place to another by trolleys and trucks.

But—as in December 1987, the security forces seem to have been ordered to lie low again. No wonder terrorists are getting fresh recruits.

The Governor's forming a committee to make recommendations for the development of the Mand area sounds like a big joke. A similar announcement was made some years ago but nothing came of it.

Some argue on behalf of the government that an operation should be undertaken when it is certain that a large number of terrorists would be caught or killed. The argument is fallacious. Nabbing is important but even more important is the task of making it impossible for terrorists to use an area.

Meanwhile, Room No. 18 in the Golden Temple has been allowed to be occupied by men of the Damdami Taksal, of which Bhindranwale was the head when alive.

All this cannot but confirm the suspicion of many that all possible efforts have not been made to fish out weapons which may still be there in various little-known nooks and corners of the huge Golden Temple complex.

The government has since of late been making big claims about various measures being taken against smuggling of weapons from Pakistan. It has not cared to explain why these measures were not taken earlier.

To stem the rot in the police force, Mr. Ribeiro, Mr K.P.S. Gill and some others were inducted. But has the government put on duty on the Indo-Pak border a sufficient number of such officers as will not allow weapons to be smuggled for a consideration, or under pressure of politicians and bureaucrats having links with smugglers? It does not appear so.

What about the Jammu and Kashmir sector of the Indo-Pak border? Who looks after that? Serious apprehensions have been expressed about the situation there. Why does the Government of India not take the people into confidence?

The Centre is not taking the political initiatives which will help isolate the terrorists, like the unconditional release of innocent ones amongst the Jodhpur detenus, punishment of Sajjan Kumar and others guilty of organising the anti-Sikh riots of November 1984, more powers for all states including Punjab and steps to evolve a broad consensus regarding territorial and river waters disputes.

The government has also not yet given up its dangerous policy of trying to make a deal with the terrorists—a policy that has proved counter-productive more than once.

Let us consider the United Akali Dal, which operates today through the SGPC. The SGPC had shown no concern for gaining control of the Golden Temple when it was captured by terrorists. But it is now anxious to obtain full control at the earliest—when its main task should be to cooperate to ensure that the Golden Temple is not recaptured by terrorists for the third time.

The SGPC dismissed Mr. Rode and his fellow priests fearing they would play the political game of the government. The government's efforts to keep them afloat dealt a blow to its claim that it wanted to keep politics out of religious places.

The UAD, on its part, got installed such head priests as would play its political game, just as the Panthic Committee had announced its own set of head priests. The SGPC must, therefore, be judged not by what it says but what it does.

When Mr. Barnala was Chief Minister, his government had positive as well as negative features as far as the fight against terrorism was concerned. A positive act of his was the refusal to dissolve his Akali Dal when ordered to do so by Mr. Darshan Singh Ragi. His stand that the Akal Takht Jathedar, deserving respect as a religious head, had no right to meddle in such matters as formation or dissolution of political parties, strengthened those who wanted religion and politics to be separated. It was an important contribution to the fight against extremism.

But his present decision to tender an apology for this before the Akal Takht Jathedar is a power game of the same type as that played by other parties. In any case, in the long run, it will not prove helpful in the fight against extremism.

The political gains of Operation Black Thunder were much more than the mere nabbing of about 10 per cent of the terrorists. The terrorists stood exposed as anti-social elements who had not hesitated to commit the worst kind of sacrilege within the most sacred Harminder Sahib, who had converted the Golden Temple premises into a torture house and graveyard for many Amritdhari Sikhs, including women. They also stood exposed as cowards. Never before in Sikh history were there rival sets of head priests.

Even those who had developed a soft corner for the terrorists were shocked. The leaders of the terrorists acted promptly to overcome their serious setback not only by indulging in large-scale killings to demonstrate their strength, but by acting on the propaganda front too.

One line taken was that the terrorists inside the Temple were government agents and not genuine "militants". The Panthic Committee has owned them as genuine "militants" but has argued that at times, it is better to surrender.

The urgent issue confronting us today is how to put an early end to the killings. That demands active intervention by the people against the politics of vote banks. The Left has a leading role to play and its historic duty to discharge. *(July 20, 1988)*

## 11. A Strategy with People

The million-dollar question is: how serious are the powers-that-be about fighting terrorism in Punjab? Ground realities in this benighted state give cause for apprehension on this score.

Till very recently, the Prime Minister and the Home Minister were trying to create the impression that the problem was almost resolved. The terrorists have made these claims look ridiculous by unleashing a spate of bomb blasts, attacks on the railways and kidnappings for ransom, injuring and killing a large number of people. Terrorism cannot be fought without the cooperation of the people, and creating illusions about the situation is dangerous. Even now, the media do not faithfully depict the grim situation in the border districts of Punjab.

A very large number of kidnappings and extortions have gone unreported even though they have taken place in broad daylight. As for the terrorists' attacks on the press—such as their attempts to force closure of the *Hind Samachar* group of papers and the Communist Party of India daily *Nawan Zamana*—by killing newspaper agents and hawkers—they have succeeded to some extent. Some villages in Amritsar get no newspapers, because after one hawker is killed, no one else is willing to take up the job. Again, there are villages and small towns which get only those papers which the terrorists do not disapprove of.

According to the report of a responsible journalist, the population of village Verka (now part of the Amritsar Municipal Corporation area) has trebled as a result of migration from rural areas, mostly of Sikhs.

The authorities do not seem to have any idea of the terrorists' strategy. Therefore, they often draw the wrong conclusions. For instance, when the terrorists feel they are getting more and more isolated, they suspend communal killings on a mass scale and stop murdering women and children. The government then rushes to the conclusion that the situation has improved.

There has been legitimate criticism of the government for its failure to take timely initiatives which would help bring about a political solution. Moreover, even at the administrative level, the government is not doing its best. And it is unfortunate that the term 'administrative level' is usually understood to refer to security forces.

The judiciary in Punjab has been paralysed by the terrorists. Even those who have killed dozens of people are moving about scot-free. If the government were to tell the people how many convictions it has obtained, the number would be shockingly insignificant. The Punjab Governor's security adviser Julio Ribeiro did take steps to improve the morale of the police and ensure better coordination between the Punjab Police and the Central Reserve Police Force (CRPF). Nothing of this kind has been done in relation to the judiciary.

School education in many rural areas of Amritsar district and of Batala sub-division of Gurdaspur district has been defunct for a long time. Many schools are without teachers because terrorists have made schools their special targets. School graduates cannot even write two sentences. Only well-off parents have shifted their children to expensive, so-called public schools in towns. Not even once, despite repeated pleas, has the government discussed the matter with anti-terrorist mass organisations of students and teachers. The same holds good for some institutions of higher learning which have come to be dominated by the terrorists. There is no policy to counter this menace.

For similar reasons, many public health centres in the rural areas of Amritsar district have stopped functioning.

The Punjab State Electricity Board (PSEB) has done good work in providing relief to the families of employees who became victims of terrorist violence. However, from the viewpoint of ensuring security, its record has been equally dismal, although PSEB offices, like schools, have been special targets of the terrorists.

One reason for the failure of the administration in dealing with the situation is the absence of a well-thought-out policy for postings to key positions. Often, at crucial points, officers who have neither the desire nor the will to fight terrorism get posted. There is no dearth of good officers but when it comes to postings, it is 'connections' in Delhi that count more than anything else.

The record of the security forces too is far from satisfactory. Some police officers who sincerely want to fight terrorism don't understand the importance of public cooperation. Their ruthless methods alienate people in the rural areas. In fact, it is the victims of such police excesses who are swelling the terrorists' ranks. Corruption is rampant. There have been instances when terrorists are said to have bought their freedom.

Another cause for concern is the increased smuggling of sophisticated arms from across the border. The weapons our security forces are equipped with are antiquated compared with those the extremists possess. For instance, while every section of a CRPF battalion should have at least one light machine gun, this gun is not issued even in an area like the Tarn Taran sub-division.

As for the Mand operation, said to have been going on from the first week of August this year, the success achieved is being exaggerated. There are also some intriguing aspects about this operation.

A thoroughgoing operation to make it impossible for the terrorists to function from the Mand area should have been undertaken immediately after Operation Black Thunder of May 1988. But that was not done. Then came the rains in July and August, giving the administration the excuse that no operation in the Mand area could be successful in the monsoons.

The topography of the Mand area makes the participation of the army in any operation of the kind envisaged imperative. The Mand area comprises three contiguous districts. To be really successful, the operation has to cover the entire area. This would require a large number of boats and even helicopters.

Some CRPF officers concede in private that the army is necessary. Others assert that it is not. Recently, several CRPF posts have been removed from some badly-affected areas and deployed for the Mand operation. Such a move could have a disastrous impact on the areas from where the CRPF posts were removed, and may even force large-scale migration. Thus, one fails to understand why army help was not obtained in the first place.

A majority of Sikhs never supported the demand for Khalistan and the means adopted by the terrorists to achieve it. However, despite this, the terrorists were able to build a mass base in Amritsar district and parts of Gurdaspur district. Even this base has been gradually eroded with the various misdeeds committed by the terrorists inside the Golden Temple complex being exposed during Operation Black Thunder.

The real face of the extremists emerged when they killed innocent Sikhs, including women and children, kidnapped people for ransom, abused women sexually and relied more and more on anti-social elements. The Communists were alone in campaigning in the terrorists' rural strongholds and have paid a heavy price for it.

There was a time when most of those who provided shelter to the terrorists did so out of sympathy. Now most of them do it out of fear. It will, however, be wrong to overlook the fact that in two or three districts there is still a little sympathy for the extremists.

But for police excesses, the process of isolation of the terrorists would have been more rapid. There are many examples of Sikhs having risked and even sacrificed their lives to save Hindus. These have been widely reported in the press and helped defeat the efforts of the terrorists to bring about Hindu-Sikh riots. As yet, however, mass resistance has not become widespread. Fear of gun-toting terrorists, the communication gap between the government and the peasantry and inadequate mass campaigning by secular forces in areas where it is needed most are some factors which have contributed to this state of affairs.

While fundamentalism has lost much of its appeal, new gurdwaras continue to be constructed and kar seva vehicles are still being used to transport weapons, etc. The administration does not seem to be aware of this.

There is no doubt that recruitment into the terrorists' ranks continues. However, the number of those who are persuaded by the appeal of religiosity has considerably decreased, though it has not disappeared altogether. The sources of recruitment now are: (a) youths who are attracted by kar seva and made party to committing some heinous crime, which forces them to remain with the terrorists; (b) those who, unable to find gainful employment, are lured by the terrorists by the promise of good money; (c) those who are forced to join because the lives of their family members are threatened; and (d) those who are looking for a way to escape from police excesses and to wreak vengeance.

The success of the security forces in recent months in nabbing and killing a number of terrorists has created the impression that the government has given up the policy of making a deal with the extremists. This, however, is not true. Attempts are being made to strike a deal with the Bhindranwale family, a section of the Damdami Taksal and a section of Akali leadership not known for moderation. This would perhaps explain the government's soft attitude towards terrorists owing allegiance to the Bhindranwale family. Here are two examples.

The death anniversary of Avtar Singh Brahma, the leader of one of the most dreaded terrorist outfits, was observed in his village on July 22, 1989. About 2,000 persons attended the function, including the general secretary of the Unified Akali Dal (Mann) Ranjit Singh Brahmpura.

The speeches were quite provocative. Siropas were presented to honour terrorists killed in encounters. Brahma was posthumously honoured with the Hari Singh Nalwa Award. Not a single policeman was present at the function. (Brahma's group used to operate from the Mand area and not from the Golden Temple. That is why the Mand operation was not undertaken immediately after Operation Black Thunder.)

One of the killers of Professor Ravinder Singh Ravi of Patiala University was a university student. Soon after the professor's death, his killer was murdered by a rival terrorist gang. Now, the university has set up a committee to build a grand memorial for this student. The Governor of Punjab is the Chancellor of the university, and the secretary to the Punjab government's department of education is the chairman of the committee.

This will shock many people but the explanation is not hard to find. The student killer belonged to a group which owes allegiance to Jasbir Singh Rode, whose press conference in Amritsar jail last year was organised by the district authorities when the Governor was present in Amritsar. Unfortunately, most Akali leaders and some other Opposition leaders too, wittingly or otherwise, continue to aid the terrorists.

*(September 12, 1989)*

## 12. Combine Political Initiatives with Fight Against Terrorism

The all-party meeting regarding the Punjab problem and the joint appeal issued by it is a positive development, notwithstanding the absence of the Akali Dal (Mann) and the Akali Dal (Badal) and the jarring note struck by the Congress. The fervent appeal made to all concerned, and to the people in general, to help restore peace and for a new approach, is bound to have some effect.

The meeting rightly welcomed the Prime Minister's visit to Amritsar, the setting up of a cabinet sub-committee and the convening of the all-party meeting. Its demand for "speedy steps to secure conviction of the guilty persons in respect to the anti-Sikh riots of November 1984", likely to be accepted by the National Front government, is of great significance as that will be much more than merely a good gesture. It will help considerably to isolate the terrorists. Of course, more political initiatives will have to be taken, especially in the matter of giving more powers to all States, including Punjab, and regarding territorial and river-water disputes. Future all-party meetings will have to try to evolve national consensus on these issues. That will be possible if these steps are preceded by adequate spadework.

The joint appeal is also welcome because it seeks to point out the weaknesses in the policy pursued by the government so far, even though this is done by implication and without criticising the government even indirectly.

The joint appeal rightly calls for an end to police excesses and for action against those who have resorted to extortion of money and harassed the people. At the same time it warns that "nothing should be done to demoralise those who have remained loyal to their duty, and combated terrorism even at the risk of their lives".

The fact is that serious efforts have been on for quite some time to demoralise such officers and to get them replaced by those who either are sympathetic to the extremists or lack the will to fight them. The government must rebuff those efforts without further delay.

Perhaps the central point of the appeal is that along with every possible effort to find a political solution, there must be no let-up in the fight against the terrorists. Wrong signals sent to the authorities in Punjab and to the security forces by the government must be withdrawn.

The appeal does not mention the fact that the Golden Temple has been taken over by the terrorists. The omission is sought to be made good by the call contained in it that "firm steps must be taken to ensure that places of religious worship are not misused".

Such steps are needed on an urgent basis.

The appeal also correctly points out the danger of fresh migration. It is good that action has been demanded to guarantee security to students in hostels and colleges and normal functioning of the educational institutions. It is because of absence of such action that students belonging to the minority community and even Sikh students with trimmed beards had to leave hostels, and vacations in all professional colleges in the state have had to be preponed.

In short, the appeal welcomes the right steps taken by the new government but does not fail to point out the weaknesses in its policy—even though indirectly—and has demanded rectification.

The absence of the Mann group is clearly due to the fact that

Mr. Simranjit Singh Mann has not yet decided whether to oppose the terrorists or to go along with them to a very great extent. We will be happy if Mr. Mann decides to adopt the former path though that is doubtful. So far Mr. Mann has been going along with the extremists except in one respect. He demands virtual Khalistan within India while those who fought his electoral battle want a fully independent sovereign Khalistan. Some of the preconditions announced for participation are simply impossible and these have been dictated by the extremists.

Whatever Mr. Badal may say, it is no secret that the Akali Dal (Badal) kept out because the Mann group kept out. One wishes that Mr. Badal picks up some courage to adopt an independent and constructive line as has been done by Mr. Barnala.

As regard the Congress attitude, the less said the better. I had occasion to meet one member of the Congress team for the all-party meeting. From the discussions I had with him, it became clear to me that the team would not adopt a constructive attitude with the objective of restoring peace and resolving the problem. It was clear to me that the Congress high command had decided to continue to play partisan politics even with bleeding Punjab. Press reports of the all-party meeting's proceedings have confirmed my assessment.

The objection that an already prepared draft was placed before the meeting was childish, to say the least. I understand that other parties went to the extent of suggesting the formation of a drafting committee to amend and change the draft to make it acceptable to all. The Congress did not agree to this.

One objection of the Congress was that the draft did not make any reference to the slogans of Khalistan and Anandpur resolution. The firm declaration in the joint statement that a political solution would have to be within the framework of India's Constitution and national unity clearly ruled out Khalistan, while strong and explicit emphasis on secularism would rule out agreeing to any theocratic state in India—i.e. Anandpur resolution. Objection was thus only for the sake of objection.

Some say that the real reason why the Congress did not want to be party to any joint statement was: while they did not want prosecution of those guilty of the November 1984 riots, they could not say so openly. But leaders of the Congress in Punjab had been making this demand. As regards reference to police excesses, even ex-Prime Minister Rajiv Gandhi had himself admitted these more than once. Possibly the Congress team did not like the demand for repeal of the 59th Amendment to the Constitution. But then it is reliably understood that others were willing to drop it.

It was also argued by the Congress team that no statement or resolution would serve any useful purpose when the Akali Dal (Mann) and the Akali Dal (Badal) were not present. Their absence was unfortunate and efforts would no doubt be made to draw them in. However, no party or group should be allowed to veto all efforts to restore peace in Punjab and to find a political solution.

Clearly the Congress was playing a dog-in-the-manger policy—quite contrary to Rajiv Gandhi's announcement that the Congress as Opposition would play a constructive role. One can only hope that there would be some rethinking and the Congress would start treating Punjab as a national issue and not an issue to be used for partisan advantage.

*(December 21, 1989)*

## 13. Role of the National Front Government

The National Front government had taken some correct steps on the political front as far as the fight against terrorism in Punjab is concerned. Their real value was that they could and still can help to isolate the terrorists, to weaken their mass base. Unfortunately, the powers-that-be nursed the illusion that these steps would make the terrorists and their spokesmen and supporters respond positively and stop killings, kidnappings, etc. This obviously reflected their extremely inadequate understanding of the Punjab problem and the real nature of terrorism in Punjab and all the forces and factors responsible for it. The fight against the terrorists to improve law and order was slowed down because of this faulty understanding and the situation has worsened rapidly. Nor is this all. As in the days of Rajiv Gandhi, the fight against terrorism continues to be neglected on many other fronts.

First and foremost is the propaganda front. Through his speeches and statements, Simranjit Singh Mann has been carrying on very extensive and widespread propaganda aimed at bringing grist to the mill of the terrorists. Others like Rajinder Singh Mehta (organizing secretary, AISSF) and Dhanna Singh (a Panthic Committee member), both released in December 1989 together with quite a few others like Manjit Singh of

AISSF (released a few weeks before the elections) have been campaigning for Khalistan and terrorism. Amarjeet Singh Chawla of the AISSF has joined them in this immediately on his being bailed out a few days ago. Nothing is being done by the government to counter this type of propaganda through the mass media or otherwise. Neither the Governor and his advisors nor the top bureaucrats seem to be aware of the need to do this.

One technique to carry on their propaganda, evolved by the terrorist organisation, is to hold "Samagams" and to issue advertisements in some widely circulated Punjabi papers, announcing their dates, etc. These are for the bhog or Akhand Path in memory of the "martyrs" or to observe their death anniversaries. Terrorists who get killed by the security forces are described as "martyrs", "Shaheedi Samagams" are held to observe their death anniversaries and to honour them.

Highly provocative speeches are made at these Samagams. One aim of these is to get new recruits. Invariably, advertisements which precede these Samagams eulogise Bhindranwale and call upon the people to join in large numbers to pledge to continue the fight started by him. More often than not, every such advertisement includes a photograph of Bhindranwale along with that of the "martyr" for whom the Samagam is being advertised.

*Ajeet*, published from Jalandhar has the largest circulation of all Punjabi dailies. It had five such advertisements on February 2, 1990, three on February 3, four on February 4, one on February 5, one on February 9 and four on February 10. These are of different sizes. Some are quite big. And some appeared on the front page. Some relate to more than one "martyr" in each case. Also, there are more than one advertisement for one and the same "martyr". Either they are repeats, or they are issued by different (terrorist) organisations. Many of these are in the names of such top terrorists as Gurbachan Singh Manochahal for whose capture government has announced big cash prizes—even one lakh each in some cases.

Some newspapers carry in full long press notes issued by terrorist organisations. These press notes give the number of terrorists who attended their meetings. Names of most dreaded and most wanted terrorists are specifically mentioned. They demand the release of killers of General Vaidya and also of all other terrorists in custody. They announce that police officers as per lists prepared will be shot dead. Eulogisation of Bhindranwale and calls to carry on his battle and demand for Khalistan are of course there. A press note printed in *Ajeet* of February 7, contains the following:

"Atrocities are being committed on Sikhs in the Ferozepore jail . . . . Bhai Nishan Singh has warned the newly recruited jail wardens that they and their families would be wiped out unless they quit their jobs within a week. Militants have been deputed to take action against officers under whose supervision atrocities are committed. Bhai Nishan Singh asked Sikh youngmen in the Home Guards and in the police to leave their jobs and to join their forces (i.e., the terrorist forces.) He offered them one lakh rupees as advance in each case if they were in government forces for the sake of money . . . . Panchayats have been asked to look after the comforts of Singhs detained in jails."

The formation of new terrorist organisations is also announced.

Of course, all of us are proud of the freedom of the press in our country. But our Constitution also provides for reasonable restrictions on all such freedoms in the interest of society as a whole. However, let us leave that alone. There is no sign of any strategy or policy of the government to counter such nefarious propaganda. Next to nothing was done by the previous government and next to nothing is being done by the present government even to counter the technique of providing alibis for killings by terrorists by attributing every terrorist killing to RAW, I.B., Black Cats, vigilance groups set up by Congress-I etc. Even killings of Congressmen are being attributed to Congress-I groups and of men and officers of the security forces to government agencies, and even by such intelligent persons as Simranjit Singh Mann.

Not only are provocative and inciting speeches delivered at these "shaheedi samagams". Siropas are also offered to families of "martyrs". "Shaheedi samagams" are not always held in gurdwaras. They are being held also in government-aided and even in government educational institutions. For instance, one such Samagam was held on February 5 in the Lyallpore Khalsa College Jalandhar. Another was held on February 7 in the ITI College in Hoshiarpore—a government institution. There is no policy decision as to whether or not government and government-aided educational institutions should be allowed to be used for anti-national secessionist propaganda based on communalism.

The heads of some government educational institutions and even of some universities have been helping the extremists directly or indirectly. Never has the government shown any anxiety over this. In any case, if it ever felt any anxiety, no concrete action has ever followed from it.

It is no secret at all that the judiciary in Punjab has been totally paralysed by the terrorists. More often than not killers when nabbed and produced before courts get bails immediately or before long. If a son gets killed by the terrorists before the very eyes of his father, the father would not have the courage to appear as a witness. Moreover, generally judges and trying magistrates are not willing to convict any terrorists. Over years there have been hardly any convictions. Hardly anything has been done by the government to overcome the state of paralysis of the judiciary in Punjab—except that financial assistance for families was increased to one lakh after a judge was shot dead. Some security was also provided to serving judges. No security however is provided to them as yet after their retirement, even though they may have tried some hardened killers.

Examples from some other fields of life can also be given. However, what has been stated above is enough to emphasise that the fight against terrorism has to be fought simultaneously on the political and the administrative fronts. And the administrative front does not mean only the law and order front as many seem to think. *(February 11, 1990)*

## 14. Open Letter to Prime Minister V.P. Singh

Amritsar, February 26, 1990

Dear Prime Minister,

By the time this letter reaches your hands (I hope it does), elections in 8 states would have been over and all the results declared. People all over the country would be anxiously waiting for some initiatives from you and your government in connection with the Punjab problem.

The main features of the situation in Punjab are as under:

1. The situation which began worsening during elections to the Lok Sabha continued to worsen further after the National Front government assumed power, even though it took some correct steps on the political front. This happened because of the instructions issued, which meant asking the security forces to go slow and asking the officers to fight terrorists with their hands tied behind their backs. The other reason is that the fight is not being waged against terrorism on all fronts.

Just now the situation is extremely alarming and may soon become uncontrollable.

2. Terrorist strategy just now is manifold and extremely clever.

(a) There is the steeply stepped up attack on the security forces.

(b) More killings, many more kidnappings for ransom, sale of hostages by one group to another, a very big increase in the ransom amounts demanded, a big increase in extortions, etc.

(c) New measures to break emotional links of sections of the Sikhs with the country. Aim of orders to managements and teachers of schools not to teach Hindi (which is a second language in government schools) is an instance of this.

(d) A "social reform movement" on the point of the gun is sought to be started to neutralise the negative effects of their other actions, which include even molesting of young girls, acting in collusion with a section of the police, etc.

For instance, orders are being issued that marriage parties must not consist of more than 11 in one case. Copying must not be allowed during examinations. Those who sell harmful drugs like heroin will be finished off.

3. There has been a serious split in the ranks of the terrorists. Mutual killings have increased.

4. The "Rail roko programme" announced by the Manjit Group of the AISSF for February 22, 1990 proved a total failure. Perhaps one factor that contributed to this failure was the increased mutual infighting of the extremists. It is not without significance, however, that the government changed in time its original strategy of not running most of the railways. Of greater significance is the fact that the "Rail roko programme" was a total fiasco despite the support extended to it by the Mann group of Akalis. It should provide some food for thought to those in your government who keep on harping that "Mann is the best bet".

5. The much advertised and publicised "Shaheedi Conference" announced to be held in the Punjab Agricultural University, Ludhiana on February 22, 1990 did not take place because of more than one reason, including tactful handling by the new Vice-Chancellor. The "Shaheedi Conference" announced to be held in the Khalsa College, Amritsar on March 2, 1990 has been postponed.

Failure on the part of your government to evolve a correct strategy taking into account all the above negative and positive aspects of the situation will prove disastrous.

A correct strategy requires action on various fronts simultaneously.

1. No-holds-barred fight against terrorists by police must be allowed, while taking steps to prevent excesses against innocent people.

2. Terrorists must be fought on all fronts of administration, including the propaganda front, educational front, judicial front, etc.

3. Political steps already announced, including punishment of those guilty of anti-Sikh riots of November 1984 must be implemented promptly and immediately.

4. Immediate steps must be initiated to give substantially more powers to all states including Punjab. This will not weaken but strengthen India's unity. This will also help to isolate those who want nothing less than Khalistan within India *a la* Anandpur Sahib resolution in the name of greater autonomy.

5. An all-parties meeting must be held at the earliest in which broadest possible national consensus must be sought to be built regarding the territorial and rivers waters disputes. In this connection, I suggest the following:

(a) Leaders of the Janata Dal (especially Shri Devi Lal), leaders of the Congress-I and the BJP in Haryana should in national interests agree to transfer Chandigarh to Punjab without any condition. I am confident if they do, people of Chandigarh will also agree in the greater interest of the motherland. Centre must build an equally beautiful capital for Haryana.

(b) All other territorial disputes between Punjab, Haryana and Rajasthan should be referred to a high-powered judicial tribunal. The tribunal should be asked to decide all the claims and counter-claims keeping in view over-all national interests, the need to prevent gross injustice to any state and also all other relevant factors. All parties must pledge beforehand to abide by the verdict of the tribunal.

(c) Disputes regarding surplus waters of Ravi and Beas should be referred to the Supreme Court, whose decisions must be final.

If, unfortunately, a broad national consensus is not reached on the above lines, your government should proceed to enforce the above on its own—as it is or with some minor amendments.

6. Suitable economic measures must also be taken.

7. Our Constitution recognises the separate *religious* identity of the Sikhs. The propaganda that Sikhs in India are treated as second class citizens is utterly false. Even then, those who claim to be "Sikh leaders" may be asked in the all-parties meeting what steps would ensure removal of any feeling of injustice—genuine or make-believe—to Sikhs as a religious minority in India. Suitable measures not inconsistent with the basic framework of the Indian Constitution may be agreed to. At the same time, suitable measures must be taken to remove similar apprehensions of the minority Hindu community in Punjab.

I am sure, Mr. Prime Minister, that if your government acts promptly and effectively on the above lines, it will greatly help to isolate, to weaken and to contain terrorism in Punjab. It will become possible to hold elections to the Punjab Assembly which will mean a really democratic process and not a travesty and parody of the same.

Interests of the people of Punjab—Sikhs as well as Hindus—and of our great country demand this. This in my opinion is also the call of patriotism.*

With regards,

Yours sincerely,
Satya Pal Dang

## 15. Learning From Past Mistakes

There are wrong notions about some important aspects of the Punjab situation which need to be corrected. Many people, for instance, believe that the situation in Punjab has been continuously worsening, especially whenever there was President's rule. But facts reveal a different scenario.

Let us go back to pre-Blue Star days. Bhindranwale had not yet shifted to the Akal Takht. He was in Guru Nanak Niwas, a building outside the Golden Temple proper. DIG police Atwal was shot dead by terrorists from within the Golden Temple. Everybody in Amritsar and the rest of Punjab, including Sikhs in general, was certain that Bhindranwale would be sent to jail. This was what the then Chief Minister, Darbara Singh, recommended.

The proposal was, however, shot down by Indira Gandhi. The Congress-I game of using the Bhindranwale card had not yet been played

*The author sent copies of this letter to Rajiv Gandhi, Leader of Opposition in Parliament; Lal Kishan Advani, President, BJP; Indrajit Gupta, M.P. and Harkishan Singh Surjeet, Member Polit Bureau, CPI-M.

out. The Akali leadership too wanted to use the Bhindranwale card. The Sant was allowed to make the holy Akal Takht his headquarters and convert the Golden Temple into an armed fortress and the main operational centre of the terrorists. The consequences for Punjab of the political games of the Congress and the Akalis are well known.

The Rajiv-Longowal Accord was signed in July 1985. It helped to improve the situation. But it was clear that it would be extremely difficult to implement it. We know from hindsight that before holding elections to the assembly to restore popular government, all parties should have jointly run a powerful mass campaign calling upon the people of Punjab and Haryana and also Rajasthan to accept the accord in the national interests, instead of the non-Left parties allowing their state units to put conflicting interpretations on it and thus make its implementation much more difficult.

Few will deny today that the Barnala government which took power was not an unmixed blessing. Mr. Barnala spoke against terrorism. At the same time, he closed his eyes when some of his ministers allowed their official cars to be used by dreaded terrorists to kill people. It was in this period that migration started in a big way. All in all, there was once again a worsening of the situation.

The timing of the dismissal of the Barnala government was decided keeping in view the Haryana elections, although it did not help the Congress. The first major anti-terrorist mass campaign was organised by the CPI soon after the dismissal of the Barnala government, with good results. This would not have been possible if the government had continued in office.

By October 1987, the security forces gained the upper hand though the backbone of the terrorists was not broken. Killings came down. Instead of taking correct political initiatives while continuing the offensive on the law and order front, the fight was called off and an attempt was made to make a deal with a section of the terrorists with the help of a part of the Akali leadership. The terrorists made use of this development to regroup themselves and opened a big offensive from January, 1988. Under President's rule, there was thus considerable improvement first, but rapid deterioration followed.

Operation Black Thunder of May 1988 also took place under President's rule. It dealt a big blow to the terrorists. It also isolated them considerably. But instead of going forward to an operation in the Mand area and taking correct political steps, the fight was once again called off in the hope of making a deal with a section of terrorists with the help of Mr. Jasbir Singh Rode.

When this failed, the fight was resumed. The result was that by September-October 1989, the terrorists were again at the receiving end. Then came the elections to the Lok Sabha. Mr. Ray let the terrorists have a field day. They emerged stronger and also spread to new areas. The National Front government that entered the scene thereafter took some correct political initiatives. Even though half-hearted, these had a positive effect. However, in the uncalled for hope of being able to solve the Punjab problem with the help of Mr. Simranjit Singh Mann, the NF government and the Governor appointed by it called off the fight against the terrorists. The situation worsened rapidly.

The moral is obvious. Terrorism in Punjab can be fought successfully only if the fight is carried on consistently and simultaneously on all fronts, including political and administrative. Secondly, any attempt to make a deal with a section of the terrorists before their backbone is broken will be counter-productive. Thirdly, popular rule by itself may not prove helpful but may even make things worse if wrong policies are pursued.

Recently, many Akali leaders have started emphasising that the problem in Punjab is really a Sikh problem. It needs to be remembered that the green revolution in Punjab had led to the emergence of a powerful class of capitalist farmers and rich peasants. They want to rule Punjab. Since the overwhelming majority of them are Sikhs, it helps them to clothe their demands, aspirations and ambitions as those of the Sikhs in general.

The communal card suits them to increase their mass base. Hence the demand for special status for Sikhs, for a Sikh theocratic state, maybe within India. Obviously such a demand cannot be conceded, for that can only strengthen the forces which want India to become a Hindu theocratic state and strengthen the demand for secession of Kashmir. The Anandpur Sahib resolution, even while not demanding complete secession, can therefore pave the way for a disintegration of the country.

At the same time, false propaganda of Akali leaders that Sikhs are second class citizens of India must be met by declaration of willingness to take adequate steps to remove fears of the Sikh community, even though the fears may not be well-founded.

Many wonder why with rare exceptions Akali leaders refuse to condemn the terrorists, why even when they deplore killings, they do it in a manner which adds grist to the mill of the terrorists. Partly, it is an attempt to use the terrorist card. Partly, it is due to fear. While all sections of Akali leaders should not be tarred with the same brush, it would be a big mistake to rely on them to bring peace in Punjab. The need now is a no-holds-barred fight against the terrorists while avoiding excesses against innocents. This has to be combined with correct political initiatives covering such matters as more powers for states, the future of Chandigarh, territorial and river water disputes, and prosecution of VIP culprits of anti-Sikh riots of November 1984. *(June 11, 1990)*

## 16. Strengthen Counter-Terrorism

The kidnapping of the Romanian diplomat, Mr. Liviu Radu in New Delhi is not an isolated development. It represents a serious setback to the official measures to tackle terrorism in Punjab.

The Punjab policy of the Rao government suffers from the complete absence of any political initiative when such initiatives are badly required. Nevertheless, unlike the V.P. Singh government, it has not stopped fighting the terrorists. In fact, the drive against the terrorists has been stepped up. This is evident from the large number of terrorists, including the most wanted by the police, killed or nabbed.

This is not to suggest, however, that the terrorists have been totally demoralised. Rather, they have been getting good results from their counter-offensive against the police. If the terrorists succeed in their efforts to demoralise the police, the situation in Punjab will further worsen.

The terrorists have stepped up their offensive against the entire police force. They have killed quite a large number of the police forces recently, including a S.P. They are also killing relations of police personnel including the very old, children and women. During the last one month, about 100—and perhaps more—relations of policemen have been killed.

The kidnapping of the Romanian diplomat on October 9 is the first incident of its kind involving the Punjab terrorists. Apparently, the act is linked with their abortive attempts to kill the former Punjab DGP, Mr. Ribeiro. The first attempt was made on his life when he was still the DGP of Punjab. He had a narrow escape. The second attempt was made in Romania where he serves as our Ambassador. He has survived the attempt again. The kidnapping of Mr. Radu under the very nose of the government cannot but send strong signals that those who wage a serious fight against terrorists will not be spared, besides demoralising the police greatly.

**Big Increases:** The government has announced big increases in relief admissible to the survivors of relatives of police personnel killed. It has also announced some steps to provide security to the families of police personnel. The effect of all these measures is yet not clear. But what we require is a strategy to bridge the gulf between the police and the people and to isolate the terrorists to the maximum possible extent.

Some terrorist outfits have formally opposed the killings of family members of policemen. But such killings do continue. While parties which have been fighting terrorism have condemned the killings, all Akali factions have chosen to maintain silence.

No doubt, a section of the police has been committing excesses and has been minting money by harassing innocents, and a small section of them even help the terrorists. Such misdeeds of the police have to be exposed and fought. But that can be no excuse for letting the terrorists demoralise the sections of the police who are fighting terrorism. Needless to say, this fight against terrorism has to be combined with political initiatives to produce good results.

To let the terrorists demoralise the police force completely will prove disastrous not only for Punjab but for the country as a whole. The responsibility is of the government as well as of all political parties. The government must evolve a strategy to protect foreign citizens in India as well as envoys of other countries.

Worse, the terrorists have stepped up the killings of innocent persons and especially of policemen in some other states, particularly in U.P. Terrorists have not started spreading to other states only recently. Indeed, they started building their *addas* and bases in a number of other states long ago. Only, they are not carrying out terrorist acts. A similar strategy has been followed within Punjab too. For instance, Mohali has long been a base for terrorists. But they started open attacks only recently.

This strategy of the terrorists must be considered not only by the government to evolve a counter-strategy, but also by the national political parties. The government must act not only when terrorist acts take place on a big scale as in parts of U.P. now, but nip them in the bud. It is the duty of political parties to fight terrorism and separatism outside Punjab, Assam and Kashmir. That would require cooperation among the political parties and co-ordination with counter-terrorist forces in Punjab and outside.

Lastly, we need to take note of the pressure being exerted to entrust the kar seva to complete the construction of Akal Takht to Damdami Taksal. The fact that the Akal Takht is still incomplete is painful not only for the Sikhs, but for all. While all would like it to be completed in the shortest possible time, there is the danger of kar seva being exploited by the terrorists if carried out under the auspices of the Damdami Taksal. *(October 18, 1991)*

## 17. Return to Democracy

Democracy stands restored in Punjab. After a spell of 57 months of President's rule, elections were held on February 19, 1992 and an elected government has assumed office. However, it is democracy of a sort. The poll was the lowest ever. It was especially low in the rural areas. Elections were held under the shadow of the gun. Those out to sabotage elections could not create much trouble at the booths.

However, despite the presence of the army and para-military forces besides the police, there was widespread fear and terror because of threats held out to those who would dare become polling agents, vote, etc. The main reason for the low poll was this terror created by the terrorist outfits. The boycott call by two main Akali factions also had some effect. Although one Akali faction did take part in the elections, it fared poorly, and of the two main parties in Punjab, the Congress has won a record majority in the Assembly on the basis of a really much smaller mass base while the Akali party has a mere 3 seats in a House of 117. Despite all these and perhaps some other limitations, we have a popular government in place of bureaucratic rule under which people have been living since long. Will this help to resolve the Punjab problem and restore peace?

In theory, any popular rule is better than the rule of bureaucracy. In actual practice, however, democracy may or may not prove effective in dealing with the scourge of terrorism. The Congress government of Punjab led by the late S. Darbara Singh had a popular mandate. And yet it proved a failure in this respect. As the situation worsened, he was made to quit by the Congress government at the Centre. No tears were shed by anyone in Punjab when President's rule was imposed after he resigned. In fact, there was a sigh of relief. It was a democratic government pursuing wrong policies determined by vote-bank politics and not keeping in view the interests of the nation and the people. In 1985 the formation of a popular government with Barnala as the Chief Minister raised great hopes. Barnala had acted boldly when he refused to dissolve his Akali Dal on orders of the then Akal Takht Jathedar. At the same time, one needs to recall that his government tried to fight terrorism and separatism on its own grounds by trying to prove that it was a Panthic government. This proved counter-productive. Not only were official cars of some of the ministers used by terrorists to kill people, about 75 per cent of those released from jails rejoined or joined the ranks of the terrorists immediately after they were set free. The so-called social reform movement reached its peak during the Barnala government—though it was on the decline when the democratically elected Government of India dismissed it with the hope that it would help the Congress during the elections in Haryana.

What do these instances show? A bureaucratic rule is unable to tackle the problem of terrorism because it relies only on bullets and does not/cannot tackle the root cause because of which terrorism gets its mass base. On the other hand, a democratically elected government, undoubtedly in a better position to find a political solution to the problem, cannot succeed unless it pursues correct policies and is not motivated by narrow partisan considerations. The experience of Assam too has the same lesson though the situation is not exactly alike. It is not necessary to go into the details.

The new popular government of Punjab despite the narrow nature of its mandate can help to solve the Punjab problem and substantially contain terrorism in the state provided it and the Government of India give up vote-bank politics atleast in relation to Punjab.

First and foremost, while framing its policies it must keep in view the need of seeking cooperation of all sections of the people. Its record majority in the Assembly must not blind it to the ground realities.

Priority must be given to very badly needed political initiatives—what have come to be known as the political package. The people of Punjab must be convinced that the state (as also other states) will be given more powers and that India will become more federal than it is today—with a strong Centre as well as states. This will weaken the slogans of theocracy and separatism. Chandigarh should be given to Punjab while Haryana should be given generous help to build its own capital. This will not in any way do any injustice to Haryana because it would be able to claim the Hindi-speaking areas in Punjab just as Punjab will be able to claim Punjabi-speaking areas in Haryana through a high powered commission which should be appointed to decide the entire territorial dispute. Its terms of reference can be such as will be acceptable to both the states. Its composition should be such as will make it impossible for any government to manipulate it. A mutual agreement regarding river waters dispute should be attempted. Failing that, the dispute should be referred to the Supreme Court even while continuing efforts are made for an agreed solution. The dispute regarding the Cauvery waters has amply proved that an agreed solution is the best and real solution. The Government of India must convince people through deeds that it is serious in prosecuting the VIP culprits of the 1984 anti-Sikh riots. Punjabi should get rightful place in Haryana, Delhi and Himachal. These and such other measures, taken unilaterally if necessary, will not change the Pak-backed terrorists or the anti-India forces in Pakistan. But they will help considerably to isolate them and to weaken still further their base.

Fight on the law and order front must continue and must not be slackened as killings are likely to be stepped up by terrorists. Along with that, excesses by the police must be reduced to the minimum. Excesses committed for extraneous reasons (for making money, etc.) must be severely dealt with. The theory that action against the culprits will demoralise the force is a false one and must be discarded. Officers and ranks who have been loyal to their uniforms and oath, who have fought terrorists and suffered heavily must be rewarded. Pressure to victimise such officers will be there from not a few legislators—MLAs and MPs. Quite a few have links with the terrorists. Pressure to let off certain killer-terrorists will also be there which too must be resisted. Effective steps must be taken to remove the feeling that people have to suffer not only at the hands of terrorists but also at the hands of the police.

Terrorists have a much better strategy on the propaganda front than the government. This weakness must be overcome. The government needs to have policies for fighting the terrorists on various administrative fronts other than the law and order front. For instance, nothing has been done to overcome the paralysis of the judiciary. Some jails have become universities of terrorism. Adequate attention is not being paid to metal roads necessary for operation of security forces. There are other administrative fronts also.

Along with all this, a mass campaign on agreed issues needs to be built up on as broad a basis as possible. The government must act to strengthen the public distribution system to give some relief to the people on the price front. Corruption must be reduced. That is not going to be easy. There is a view that unless the new Chief Minister acts strongly and firmly, corruption may increase. An effective machinery to remove grievances of the public must be evolved. There should be a minister for removal of grievances with no other charge. His integrity and determination must be above doubt. There should be a state level grievances committee with this minister as chairman and all parties represented in it. Every district should have a grievances officer and district grievances committees should be made more effective. There should be greater devolution of powers. Adequate attention must be paid to give justice to women and scheduled castes.

If really correct policies are followed with determination, the government will achieve positive results, earning the gratitude of the people of the whole country. *(March 1, 1992)*

## 18. Punjab Government's Wilful Ignorance

The Punjab government claims improvement in the situation in the state. In support of this claim, it says the number of terrorists being killed has increased considerably. And they include several important terrorists. Some have started surrendering. The number of innocent persons being killed has gone down, as also of the security personnel.

Certain areas, previously hotbeds of terrorism, have not seen any killing for quite some time now. New recruitment into the ranks of terrorists has slowed down considerably in some areas, if not all over the state. The Chief Minister is not allowing even Congress ministers to pressurise police officers to release terrorists when nabbed. There is the instance in which Beant Singh is said to have upheld the position taken by the SSP against a minister's demand for the release of a terrorist related to him.

A warning has to be sounded against likely mistakes and even blunders because of this conception of improvement in the situation. Some people in the seats of power in New Delhi and Chandigarh want the withdrawal of the army, notwithstanding the fact that the Punjab terrorists retain the capacity to make big strikes.

Secondly, there is the danger of continued refusal to take steps to minimise police excesses against the innocents. The phenomenon of *mala fide* excesses to extort money has been highlighted several times, including in the media. Some other negative aspects, which are widespread, have not been taken adequate notice of. Quite a few innocents get nabbed on the basis of false reports made against them out of enmity. Except rarely, this is discovered only after these innocents have got a good dose of the usual police medicine. When persons are nabbed after midnight knocks, their relatives go from pillar to post to find out where they have been taken. Persons are nabbed from one district by policemen of another district and even the SSP of the latter police district is not informed about it.

Such counter-productive methods can easily be remedied and even done away with. However, no attention has been paid to this aspect by the Beant Singh government. It is worth recalling that what happened in Behla in Tarn Taran district is the direct result of this attitude. In this village, the police, supported by the army, claimed to have killed nine terrorists after an encounter lasting 28 hours. It now seems that four or five of them were innocent persons who had been pushed into the house by the police as human shields. The refusal to recognise this and to announce at least the usual relief package for the families of the innocent has only boosted the morale of pro-terrorist outfits. It is time the government paid adequate attention to the question of police excesses and the methods employed by the guardians of the law.

There are other more serious dangers arising out of the feeling that the situation is improving. It appears that the mistaken tendency to regard the Punjab problem as only a law and order problem is getting strengthened. The realisation of the urgent need for political initiatives is weakening. The wrong view that the problem can be solved through law and order measures alone seems to be growing.

The government persistently fails to recognise the need to win over the moderates amongst the Akalis. Secondly, there is the danger of another behind-the-scenes attempt being made to seek to 'resolve' the problem by striking a deal with a section of terrorists.

It is useful, in the present context, to recall what happened after Operation Black Thunder. At no other time was the isolation of terrorists greater. At no other time were they more down and out. What was needed was to continue the fight on the law and order front while simultaneously undertaking the much-needed political initiatives. Together these steps would have paved the way for a political solution within the framework of Centre-state relations. Instead, the government took no political initiatives, and made an attempt to strike a deal with a section of the terrorists. The results, as we all know, were disastrous. Let the same story not be repeated now. *(June 30, 1992)*

## 19. How to Consolidate Gains?

Only those who have the habit of observing facts not as they are but as they fit in with their preconceived ideas can refuse to note and welcome the substantial improvement in the situation in Punjab. In fact, it is time to understand the factors which have led to this and also to draw appropriate lessons. That will help the anti-militant forces not only in Punjab but also in other affected parts of the country.

It is now admitted by all that notwithstanding the external and internal factors favouring the growth of separatist militancy in Punjab, this phenomenon would not have assumed the serious proportions it did but for the vote-bank politics of the Congress, the Akali Dals and certain other parties. The main culprits, without doubt, were the Congress and the Akalis. One brought Bhindranwale into politics while the other helped him to entrench his forces in the holy Akal Takht—as part of their game to pull down each other. Unlike the Congress, the major Akali factions have not learnt any lesson from the disastrous consequences of this game. The common people must make them learn and change or repudiate them.

The present substantial improvement is the result of an all-out fight on the law and order front. This has proved wrong all those who believed that no improvement at all was possible without a political solution. At the same time, it has to be noted that as a result of the fight on the law and order front, improvements did take place earlier too during President's rule. However, every time these proved short-lived.

The improvement was considerable immediately after Operation Black Thunder in May, 1988. Some of us are on record as having warned that it would prove short-lived unless the fight was continued and was combined with mass public information campaign and political initiatives leading to advance in reaching a political solution of the pending issues. In order that the militant outfits did not again recoup, we had also demanded an operation in the Mand area. Top police and CRPF officers also warned that calling off the fight till the backbone of militancy was broken would prove counter-productive.

The Government of India, however, followed a different course. The fight on the law and order front was much slowed down and efforts were made to make a deal with a section of the militants—those led by Jasbir Singh Rode and Avtar Singh Brahma. The result was disastrous. The same story was repeated when Mr. V.P. Singh became the Prime Minister—the attempt being to make a deal with Mr. Simranjit Singh Mann. Mr. Chandra Shekhar too began negotiations with Mr. Mann and others but did not make the mistake of calling off the fight on the law and order front.

The bid to make a deal with a section of the militants, however, has been given up at least for the time being by the government of Mr. Narasimha Rao and, in Chandigarh, by Mr. Beant Singh. This policy change has paid dividends. The lesson is that negotiations at a wrong time and attempts to reach agreements when the situation is not ripe, especially by calling off the fight against the militants, are bound to prove counter-productive. This also explains why the Punjab police chief, Mr. K.P.S. Gill, has been able to produce such results now as could not be produced by him earlier.

It would be wrong to think that the substantial improvement achieved is the result only of the fight on the law and order front. Mr. Beant Singh has combined this fight with a mass campaign. True, it would have been much better if this mass campaign was a multi-party drive. Also true, that it is the government in the name of the Congress which went to the people and not the Congress organisation which had not dared go to rural areas when it was not in power. However, the fact remains that the mass contact campaign launched by Mr. Beant Singh played a positive role.

The fact that the militants had managed to isolate themselves considerably by their misdeeds and crimes (including crimes against women) was another factor which played a positive role.

It was a serious mistake on the part of the main Akali factions to boycott the elections. This mistake, however, has proved a blessing in disguise. One shudders to think of what would have been the scene if the Akalis had participated in the elections and a Badal-led government had been formed, whose first action would have been to order release of all the militants, including the notorious killers, and to call off the fight on the law and order front.

However, the picture today is not all rosy. In the first place, excesses continue against innocent people for one reason or another. They may now be less for money-making and more because of false reports against the innocent for teaching lessons to some and also because of extremely faulty police methods of interrogation. Neither Mr. K.P.S. Gill nor Mr. Beant Singh seems to be very serious about avoiding at least the avoidable excesses. The result is that alienation continues. Not long ago I saw on TV policemen being taught at the police training school at Phillaur how to fight militants and how not to, so that militants, and not policemen, became victims. I was happy, but I wished policemen were also taught why and how excesses against innocent people could and must be avoided. Every such excess must be exposed, opposed and fought in the interests of justice to the people and of the anti-militancy fight itself.

What has been stated does not mean that sections of the police are not making money. The fact, not widely known as yet, is that policemen have been told that they can extort as much money as they like from militants and extortionists. And many are doing this in a big way. In the process, even those guilty of petty crimes and their families are being made to suffer much. Of course, money is extracted from many innocent persons too. It is also suspected that police officers of a particular level have been given the authority to order liquidation of any anti-social element if in their opinion he is incorrigible, even though not a killer. If such a policy is not reviewed immediately, it will have serious negative consequences. The police force, already notorious for third-degree methods, will become still more brutalised, to say the least.

I continue to differ with the view of the Punjab Chief Minister that the problem in the State is only of a law and order variety. If sooner or later the political initiative is not taken, clearing the way for political solutions, and if alienation is not overcome, militancy will not end, though it may not be very much visible. We will face the problem again.

Let us not shut our eyes to the fact that in one form or another militant propaganda continues. And not a few Akali leaders—though not all—continue to bring grist to its mill. The sooner the needed political initiative is taken, the better it will be. At the same time, it does need to be emphasised that steps to make India more federal than it is today—a strong Centre as also strong states—occupy a very important position. Correct political steps in relation to Punjab will also help fight militancy, fundamentalism and the rising danger of communalism in the country as a whole.

*(November 9, 1992)*

## 20. Why Beant Singh Failed to Condemn Babri Masjid Demolition

A few days before the two-day Session of the Punjab Assembly held on 21-22 December, 1992 a high powered CPI deputation led by State Secretary Comrade Avtar Singh Malhotra had met S. Beant Singh. Besides other things the deputation pleaded with the Chief Minister that the Assembly should adopt a resolution regarding the demolition of the Babri Masjid in Ayodhya and subsequent developments. These included destruction of two places of worship and a good deal of property in Malerkotla in Punjab. The Chief Minister was non-committal. The request was repeated on behalf of the CPI group in the Assembly. Again there was no definite reply.

On the initiative of the CPI group, a joint adjournment motion to discuss the situation arising out of the Babri Masjid demolition was given notice of by MLAs belonging to BSP, CPI, IPP and Janata Dal for 21 December. The Speaker disallowed it. However, the signatories as also the CPI-M MLA were able to speak on the issue. The leader of the CPI group Vimla Dang made a pointed suggestion that the Chief Minister should move a resolution in the Assembly.

During his reply, the Chief Minister said that the Congress legislature party in its meeting held that very morning had adopted a resolution condemning the demolition. He went on to say that he did not want to hurt anyone in Punjab because of the specific situation in the state—

indicating thereby his opposition to the Assembly adopting a resolution, which the BJP would oppose.

The Chief Minister was not explicit about what was in his mind. However, it was informally given out that as the BJP was cooperating with the government in the fight against terrorism in Punjab, it would not be wise to annoy it, as it would be if the Assembly were to adopt a resolution regarding the Babri Masjid demolition and the situation arising out of that. Perhaps for the same reason, the Chief Minister in his reply to BJP's demand for the release of persons arrested in Punjab after some organisations were banned, told BJP MLAs that only about 100 persons had been arrested in Punjab and most of even these had been released on bail.

This attitude of the Chief Minister has caused considerable anxiety amongst the secular forces in the state.

It is true that the BJP has been opposing terrorism in Punjab and as in case of other parties many of its activists have been killed by terrorists. It is also true that at the time of Hindu-Sikh tension in the past it used to cooperate with others for Hindu-Sikh unity. At the same time it never gave up its right to criticise other parties and it did criticise some of them day in and day out. Other parties too had the same right and exercised it too off and on. The BJP's opposition to terrorism in Punjab is no argument for soft-pedalling the issue of Babri Masjid demolition when it has shaken the very foundation of our democratic and secular system, as well as the rule of law. Nor is that all. Demolition of Babri Masjid has brought grist to the mill of Khalistani terrorists of Punjab. They argue: "Today it is a masjid. Tomorrow it can be a gurdwara. No religious minority is safe in India". If this argument is to be refuted convincingly, people of Punjab need openly to come out against the ruthless drive of the Sangh Parivar to capture political power by exploiting the Hindu religion and then to establish a Hindu theocratic state. Not to do that is a short-sighted policy.

Even otherwise, the Sangh Parivar has been bringing grist to the mill of separatists in Punjab even while opposing them. The RSS slogan of making India a Hindu Rashtra and the BJP's insistence that Indian nationhood must be synonymous with Hindutva cannot but help the case for Khalistan. Secondly, the Sangh Parivar denies the independent religious identity of Sikhism. It propagates that Sikhism is not a separate religion, but only a part of Hinduism. This provides an argument to Khalistanis: "If Sikhs remain in India, they will get absorbed by Hindus. For the sake of our religion, we must have Khalistan".

Cooperation of the BJP to the extent it helps fight against terrorism and separatism can be welcome but for the sake of this fight itself the right to criticise and oppose many positions and acts of the BJP cannot be given up.

Beant Singh has taken the position that the Punjab problem is only a law and order problem. For a long time this was also the position of the BJP. Perhaps this partly explains Beant Singh's softness for this Hindu communal party which is responsible for a much more dangerous situation for the country as a whole than the Punjab terrorists have been able to create. Many have also the feeling that motivated by vote-bank politics, Beant Singh does not want to confront the BJP brand of Hindutva. It is not without significance that the Congress-I in Amritsar was made to back out of an agreement for a joint Congress-I, CPI, CPI-M, Janata Dal campaign even when the Prime Minister was talking of the need for a joint front of and campaign by all secular parties against communalism. This again is a short-sighted policy and will prove counter-productive—just as the policy of Giani Zail Singh as Chief Minister, Punjab *vis-a-vis* the Akalis only helped the latter, instead of weakening them.

Another recent pronouncement of Chief Minister Beant Singh should cause worry to all those who want to save secularism in India. *The Tribune* of 27 December 1992 reported his speech at Jor Mela at length. According to the report: "Mr Beant Singh ridiculed the Akalis for discovering a new fondness for the Muslims in the wake of the demolition of the Babri Mosque. The act of vandalism at Ayodhya was no doubt condemnable. But how could one forget one's history? Was it not a fact that Aurangzeb had seized power after killing his brothers and imprisoning his father, Shahjahan? Was it not a fact that Guru Teg Bahadur had sacrificed his life to safeguard Kashmiri Pandits and Hindu religion from the tryranny of the Mughal emperor. Was it not a true that Guru Gobind Singh spent a lifetime fighting the Mughals? His two sons, in whose memory today's fair was being held, had been entombed alive by the same rulers."

The mixing of half-truths with truths and thus equating all Muslims with some tyrannical (Muslim) kings can only please and help the BJP and its controlling authority—the RSS, for whom no Muslim can be a true Indian unless he gets Hinduised. Such pronouncements make one doubt whether Beant Singh is serious in his condemnation of the demolition of the Babri Masjid.

The relentless fight waged by K.P.S. Gill, Director General Police, Punjab against terrorists has brought about a big change for the better in the situation. Due credit for this must be given to Beant Singh, who has given him a free hand and who has not called off the fight after some success for making a deal with a section of the terrorists as was done more than once in the past. Punjab, however, is not yet out of the woods. Terrorism has been suppressed to a great extent but has not been uprooted. Refusal to take the needed political initiatives and softness in actual practice for the BJP even at the time of a grave peril for the whole country because of it, will prove harmful in the long run even from the viewpoint of Punjab in isolation. S. Beant Singh must do some serious rethinking.

*(January 2, 1993)*

## 21. Credit to Masses for Normalcy

Congressmen claim the entire credit for the big improvement in the Punjab situation for their party and for Chief Minister Beant Singh. The uncharitable critics of the Congress reply back: "The Congress brought Sant Bhindranwale into politics and encouraged terrorism when that suited its narrow partisan ends. It could have controlled terrorism much earlier if it wanted to."

Akali leader Parkash Singh Badal asserts: "The present peace in Punjab is only a lull before the storm." Obviously, he would feel vindicated if terrorism raises its head again and is able to claim innocent lives if only to disprove the Congress claim.

BJP leaders are of the view that the entire credit for the improvement should go to Mr. K.P.S. Gill, the Director General of Police. The super-cop, no doubt, is an experienced fighter against terrorism, but the fact remains that he was the police boss in Punjab earlier too—when the situation could not be controlled.

There are others who say: "It is the popular government which has made all the difference. If President's rule had been done away with by holding elections much earlier as demanded by us, Punjab would not have suffered the way it has." These friends conveniently forget that it was under a popular government that the situation in Punjab began to worsen rapidly. And that nobody shed any tears when the popular government headed by Darbara Singh was made to quit and when President's rule was imposed. They also overlook the obvious fact that the boycott of elections by the Akalis has proved a blessing in disguise.

Be that as it may, what has been stated above highlights the need for a really objective analysis of factors that have brought about a sea-change in the Punjab situation, instead of playing the game of claiming and denying credit.

First, it needs to be recalled that improvement in Punjab took place earlier too and more than once, even though it was short-lived—for instance, immediately after Operation Black Thunder. Improvement was the result of a successful fight on the law and order front. It was short-lived because of the wrong policy then being pursued.

After some improvement was recorded, the political leadership would order the fight to be called off or slowed down. It would then try to make a deal with a section of the terrorists. Warnings by the Left that such a strategy would prove counterproductive were not heeded but invariably they proved correct. Credit must go to Mr. Beant Singh for adopting the new strategy of a no-holds-barred fight till the backbone of terrorism is broken. It also needs to be recalled that a section of the Left at least had been demanding and campaigning for such a strategy since long.

Second, terrorism cannot operate without some mass base. And it cannot be fought without combining the fight on the law and order front with mass political campaigning. It has to be recognised that Mr. Beant Singh has done tremendous mass political campaigning during the past one year. Its importance does not get negated by the fact that most Congress leaders would not move out of their drawing-rooms before Mr. Beant Singh took over as Chief Minister.

During that extremely difficult period, it is only the Left, the two Communist parties, which dared do mass campaigning in the rural areas and paid heavily for that. That campaigning by the Left paid dividends now when Mr. Beant Singh went to the people even though as Chief Minister.

Third, the above two factors came into play at a time when terrorists stood isolated to a great extent. Towards this end, of all political parties, the two Communist parties had contributed most by their propaganda and campaign. However, terrorists themselves had contributed most towards this. They had managed to isolate themselves as a result of their misdeeds like large scale extortion and more particularly their misbehaviour towards women, including forcible marriages and rape. Also, even those families were not spared which were sympathetic to them and had been helping them. Their misdeeds were overlooked for some time but by the time Mr. Beant Singh took power even their supporters had become thoroughly fed up with them, especially in Amritsar district. When people in the rural areas found that the security forces this time meant business, they started helping them.

Fourth, the army played a significant role in containing terrorism. It must be said to the credit of the army posted in Punjab that it won the hearts and support of the people, including the Sikh peasantry. Scrupulously avoiding excesses against the innocent and the common people (except rarely), it did many things to help them.

Last but not the least, about the role of the police. There was a time when a greater section of the Punjab police was either neutral or was helping the terrorists—either out of fear or out of sympathy. For sometime now, the Punjab police has been waging an all-out fight against terrorism. Various factors are responsible for this transformation.

First, as long as it appeared that terrorist leaders would or could come into power in Punjab as a result of a compromise, only a few police officers or jawans would fight them whole-heartedly and with enthusiasm. A basic change in this respect as already noted came with Mr. Beant Singh. Mr. K.P.S. Gill, therefore, cannot be blamed for his earlier "failure".

Second, really good work to uplift the morale of a demoralised police force was done first by Mr. Ribeiro and then by Mr. Gill. A small band of police officers had helped them in this task. To forget the role of Mr. Ribeiro and his close colleagues would be an act of ingratitude. Not to do that does not mean not appreciating fully the good job done by Mr. Gill.

Third, for whatever reasons, a change in the tactics of terrorists too helped. Earlier, they were concentrating their attack on the para-military forces and were pretending to be friendly with the Punjab police. At some stage, they began a big attack on the Punjab police too—killing even the family members, including children of policemen. This in a way left no alternative for the Punjab police but to wage an all-out fight against terrorists.

We have spoken of the army and of the Punjab police. The big role played by para-military forces—the CRPF and the BSF must also be noted. This role deserves greater appreciation by the government than is there. For proper coordination between the para-military forces and the Punjab police, Mr. Ribeiro did really good work.

Changes in the international situation have also helped to some extent. A detailed analysis of this aspect is not possible in this short article.

Various factors responsible for the improvement in the Punjab situation have been examined. The two Communist parties, the most consistent fighters against terrorism, took time to note the improvement when it began to take place. This happened because they had held the strong belief that without the needed political steps and initiatives, no substantial improvement would be possible. It cannot be said that they have been proved fully wrong. There are political, economic and psychological issues which the terrorists can still exploit. If these problems are not resolved, the possibility of terrorism re-emerging remains very much there. The Director General of Police is quite off the mark when he says that there is no politics involved behind terrorism in Punjab and it is the handiwork of "some young men gone mad".

There is another factor which can help in the re-emergence of terrorism. This is the fact of police excesses and the way the Punjab police functions. No doubt, some excesses are unavoidable in the fight against terrorism. This is fully realised by the people. However, there are two aspects because of which alienation remains.

One, hardly anything is being done to end avoidable excesses and to improve the functioning of the police. Two, in cases in which innocent persons become victims, their families are often not given the help they should get. In fact, even all the avoidable excesses are sought to be justified by a false theory that these represent the necessary price to be paid to overcome terrorism.

How one wishes that Mr. Gill had an open mind or that Mr. Beant Singh could bring about the necessary change in his outlook. As things stand, every police officer—good or bad—has full freedom to act the way he likes. And a "subtle" propaganda campaign has started against those who dare raise the question of excesses but who cannot be attacked openly. Such a situation is not good for the health of democracy in Punjab. *(April 24, 1993)*

## 22. Punjab Intellectuals Question the Past

The observance of the anniversary of Operation Blue Star this year was an extremely low-key performance, with most Akali leaders keeping mum over the episode which almost shook the nation nine years ago.

Only the SGPC chief Tohra called for holding "Akhand Paths" to observe the anniversary, while the remaining Akali leaders allowed the occasion to pass off as if unnoticed.

There were no shrill demands for apology from the Government of India. On the other hand, a number of pro-Akali intellectuals put the Akalis on par with the government and claimed that both owed an apology for the happenings connected with Operation Blue Star . Such comments from pro-Akali intellectuals are noteworthy, as these confirm that there is a wind of change in Punjab following the success of punitive drive against the terrorists. The fear of the gun having vanished, an atmosphere has been generated in which an objective assessment of past mistakes is possible.

It has always been our opinion that Operation Blue Star could and should have been avoided. If it did take place, the reason was that the Government of India as well as the Akali leadership were obsessed with trying to play the Bhindranwale card against each other for the sake of their narrow partisan political ends.

First and foremost, responsibility for Operation Blue Star has to be borne by late Bhindranwale and his advisors, who in complete violation of the sanctity of the Golden Temple, converted it into a stronghold of terrorists and one of the main centres of their operations. The Congress-I controlling the government in New Delhi and Punjab on the one hand, and the Akali leadership controlling the SGPC (and thus the management of the Golden Temple) on the other, have to share responsibility, because both of them allowed Bhindranwale to do what he did. Each was hoping that it would play its game against the other, not realising that Bhindranwale and the forces behind him were using both for their own game. In one sense Akali responsibility is greater because they provided political and ideological arguments for separatism and even terrorism. In another sense the Congress responsibility is more because it ran the government.

Be that as it may, to demand an apology from the government alone is to provide an alibi for converting places of religious worship into operating centres of terrorism, resulting also in sacrilege of religion itself. For the most unfortunate event which should never have taken place the Akalis and the Congress both need to apologise not only to the Sikhs, but to the nation as a whole. It needs to be stressed here that when the operation actually took place, it could not be on the lines of the operation executed later, "Black Thunder". The "military situations" inside the Golden Temple on the two occasions were entirely and qualitatively different. Some Leftists had previously demanded not only an apology from the government alone but also the prosecution of army officers who carried out the orders of the government. It is to be hoped that they too would do some rethinking.

There is one aspect of the operation which the government should explain. Even when considered unavoidable, why was it undertaken on the martyrdom day of Guru Arjan Dev? For this the government alone may have to apologise, if an apology is to be offered.

Rethinking should be there about some other matters too. For long there was much talk about "Sikh psyche". Some retaliated by asking: "What about the Hindu psyche"? That apart, entry of the army into the Golden Temple could not but cause great pain to all decent persons, but more so to the entire Sikh community. Notwithstanding this, the degree of anger was not the same in districts like Sangrur as in Amritsar. Within Amritsar district the reaction of Scheduled Caste Sikhs was quite different from that of landowning Sikh Jats—though the former too were unhappy. Some surveys carried out soon after Operation Blue Star revealed that a minority of Sikhs held the view that though unfortunate and painful, it had become necessary.

I would like to share another fact with the readers. Once an Akali leader (later on shot dead by terrorists) had said during an informal discussion: "When we talk of Sikh psyche, we mean Sikh Jat psyche". In fact, on certain issues the entire Sikh community may react exactly in the same way. On certain other issues (even apparently religious issues) even the reaction of Sikh landlords on the one hand, and Sikh poor peasants on the other, may not be the same, and may even be opposite of each other. This is even more true of Hindus on Hindu religious issues.

There is another issue which needs some rethinking. Sikhs have played a glorious role in India's struggle for freedom. Their recognition of this and paying tributes for this fact is quite right, natural and just. However, some began proclaiming that India owes her freedom only to the Sikhs. Some went a step ahead and said that Khalistan being demanded by them should have the same proportion of total Indian territory as the proportion of sacrifices made by the Sikhs for winning independence. And what amounted to insulting the memory of the thoroughly secular patriots of the Ghadar Party and the prisoners in Andaman jails, they would count them religion-wise.

It will be good for the country and all its people, irrespective of their religion, if it is remembered that in the freedom struggle as a whole every community—Hindus, Muslims, Sikhs, Parsis and others, played a notable part, though at some stage one community may have played a bigger role and at some other stage some other community may have done so.

The entire country is proud of the Ghadar Babas and of those who suffered great hardships in the Andaman jails. But while we eulogise the sacrifices of the Ghadar heroes, we must also remember the 15,000 Santhals who were slaughtered during the 1855 uprising by the British imperialists. There was a revolt by Hindu and Muslim Sepoys at Vellore near Madras in 1805. "The British Commander Colonel Gillespie sentenced the ring leaders to death and strongly suppressed the Vellore Mutiny".

And should we not remember the countless martyrs of India's first war of independence, that is 1857? One should also take note of what the British historian Kaye wrote: "Infuriated English troops bayonetted women, infants and even old parents. Sikh migrants in the hired ship Kamagata Maru when forced to return from Canada fought a heroic battle with the British at Budge Budge. About 40 of them lost their lives. Along with this there is also the fact that many young revolutionary Muslims left India and set up a liberated government in a distant tract. It was against them the government started the Silk letter conspiracy case."

And should we not remember along with the Hindustan Socialist Republican Army of Sardar Bhagat Singh and Chandra Shekhar Azad, the Chittagong Armoury Raiders of Bengal led by Surya Sen, the Moplah Revolt in South Malabar and the Hindu Garhwali troops led by Chandra Singh Garhwali who refused to fire at the Muslim Pathan crowd, and the Meerut Conspiracy Case? One can go on and on right up to the Quit India Movement of 1942 and the Azad Hind Fauj. What happened during the trial of INA officers and during the revolt in the Royal Indian Navy? The lesson is clear and obvious. For India's freedom countless people belonging to all communities made great sacrifices and became martyrs. Let no one be allowed to use their names and their religions for communal slogans and demands, for splitting India and for establishing theocratic states. *(June 14, 1993)*

## 23. We Are Punjabis But Indians Too!

Akalis stand for a Sikh theocratic state in Punjab while the RSS which controls the BJP wants India to be a Hindu theocratic state. The BJP is more dangerous than the Akalis. However, I have no hesitation in rejecting outright Jathedar Tohra's attack on Prime Minister Vajpayee for not conceding "Punjab's demands".

Tohra is angry that Chandigarh has not been given to Punjab. He forgets that his is a regional party while that of the Prime Minister is a national one. The Communists in Punjab, Haryana and Chandigarh take one and the same stand, that is, the City Beautiful should go to Punjab. But like other national parties the BJP in Punjab wants it for Punjab; in Haryana it says it may be given to Punjab if Punjab gives Abohar and Fazilka to Haryana; and the BJP in Chandigarh wants it to remain a Union Territory. If Vajpayee does what Tohra wants him to do, he will have to face a revolt in the BJP in Haryana as well as in the UT. Also, there will be every possibility of once again the people of Punjab and Haryana finding themselves confronting each other. And that will only complicate the problem more. There is another aspect to the matter. The Akali leaders have been demanding that the views of the people of Udham Singh Nagar district of UP be ascertained on whether it should go to the proposed Uttaranchal State or should remain in UP. In the situation as it obtains today, the Prime Minister cannot but ask the Akali leaders whether they are willing to ascertain the views of the people of Chandigarh.

Everyone knows that the overwhelming majority will be for Chandigarh remaining a Union Territory.

Tohra also wants the Punjabi-speaking areas wrongly given to Haryana to be transferred to Punjab. The Jathedar knows that some Hindi-speaking areas too were wrongly included in Punjab. These include the highly fertile area of Abohar and Fazilka. The argument that one village breaks its contiguity with Haryana and therefore Punjab has a right over it will not carry conviction. Moreover, its culture is akin more to Rajasthan than Haryana. And there is contiguity also. What if Rajasthan demands it? Ground realities, however, would favour the status quo. Ethnic composition of the areas in question has changed to a considerable extent. In any case, it is my view that because of various considerations, including economic compulsions, people of the areas in question want to remain where they are.

The Akali leader also wants the Prime Minister to decide the dispute about surplus river waters as per their dictates. No national party can accept their thesis on this issue. Even though the rivers may be originating in Himachal, they are said to be "Punjab rivers" of which "not a drop of water will be given to any other state". Even previous agreements reached long ago are sought to scrapped. They also want that the dispute be decided as per the riparian principle. Like many others, I too want India to be more federal than it is today. However, India is one country and not a federation of 24 or so countries. The riparian principle is applicable between countries and not states of a country like India. In our case, the river basin principle may be much more relevant.

I would like to remind the Akalis that their stand till the mid-eighties or so was quite different. They, like us, wanted greater share out of the water which had been agreed upon for erstwhile Punjab than was given by two unjust awards of the Government of India. They for long did not take the position that neither Haryana nor Rajasthan can claim any share. They did not dispute till recently the shares of Rajasthan, Delhi and J&K. The stand which the Akalis are now taking was first taken by the Khalistani terrorist organisations. Let them realise that they are not in good company when they talk of "not a drop of water", etc. For short-sighted opportunistic reasons, the Congress in Punjab too has taken the same stand as the Akalis. Its counterparts in Haryana and Rajasthan are sure to oppose this stand strongly.

Last but not the least: territorial and river waters inter-state disputes should be resolved in a peaceful atmosphere through negotiations on a just basis and in the spirit of give and take without doing injustice to any state but not losing sight of national interests either. The fact that the BJP is in power at the Centre and all the concerned states is a helpful factor. The criticism of some Akali leaders that the BJP Prime Minister is not trying to make use of this is valid.

If such a settlement proves impossible, the dispute should be referred to the Supreme Court to be decided by judges not belonging to the states involved. There should be a firm commitment that no agitation will be launched against the decision of the Supreme Court. During the pendency, all parties should campaign amongst the people for acceptance of the Supreme Court decision. Experience has proved that agitations and counter-agitations do not help. They make the solution even more difficult.

I am proud of being a Punjabi. Like other Punjabi Communists, I strongly opposed those who wanted Punjabi Hindus to wrongly declare Hindi as their mother tongue. I also opposed the Akalis treating Punjabi language as a part of Sikh religion, thereby bringing grist to the mill of Hindu communalists. Let all Punjabis be proud of being so. However, let no Punjabi forget even for a moment that we are Indians too. A national outlook is absolutely necessary if territorial and river waters disputes are to be resolved without breaking heads. Incidentally, Punjab is not going to be a loser, even if the disputes take some more time before a solution is found.

*(October 10, 1998)*

# Conclusion

Peace was restored in Punjab almost fully by the end of 1993, i.e. within less than two years after the Beant Singh government took power after many years of Presidential rule. Many friends ask me two questions: 1. How is it that terrorism in Punjab was overcome in a very short period, relatively speaking? 2. Is terrorism likely to re-emerge in Punjab?

There were many factors—both external and internal—for the rise of terrorism in Punjab. Genuine or imagined grievances of the Sikh community provided one of the important internal factors. Another very important internal factor was that both the major political parties in Punjab, i.e. the Congress and the Akalis, pursued for long the policy of trying to use Bhindranwale and terrorism as a weapon to gain an upper hand for their narrow political objectives.

As a part of this game both the Congress and the Akalis tried for long to use Bhindranwale against each other. The Congress government at the Centre and the administration in Punjab pursued a policy of making a deal with Bhindranwale terrorists or a group of terrorists. The Akalis were trying all along to use Bhindranwale terrorism as their stick to beat the government with. This enabled the terrorists to use both the parties and thus grow stronger themselves. As far as the government was concerned, no serious attempt was a made for long to fight terrorism either on the law and order front or on the political front, when it was necessary to wage a relentless fight against this menace.

This suicidal policy was reversed soon after Beant Singh came to power in 1992. Whether the credit for this should go to Beant Singh or to the then Prime Minister P.V. Narsimha Rao or to both is immaterial. A relentless no-holds-barred fight was waged by the Beant Singh government against the terrorists through K.P.S. Gill, who was given a free hand. Luckily, this happened at a time when the terrorists had managed to isolate themselves to a great extent by their misdeeds—especially by indulging in forcible marriages, kidnappings, rapes of young girls and so on. Even those who had sympathies with them earlier now began providing information about them to the army and in some cases even to the police. It is this which produced quick results. And this answers the first question. The results would have been even better if care had been taken to avoid police excesses and if the unscrupulous amongst the police officials had not been given freedom to make money for themselves.

As regards the second question, a basic proposition has to be kept in mind—the need to fight terrorism on both the political as well as the law and order front. Beant Singh denied that terrorism in Punjab had any political aspect. He kept on repeating that it was *only* a law and order problem. The fact that the political aspect has not been attended to creates the possibility of the re-emergence of terrorism in Punjab. It is not necessary to deal here with all the political problems which were exploited by the terrorists. We may, however, mention only one question—that of Centre-state relations. The need is for India to become more federal than it is today. Till this happens the Akali leaders will be able to rally some sections for a theocratic Punjab—either within India but with a very weak Centre, or a sovereign Sikh state. Other grievances—genuine as well as imagined—too will continue to be exploited. Disputes regarding Chandigarh and some Punjabi-speaking areas being in Haryana and some Hindi-speaking areas being in Punjab can be resolved easily. People are no longer very much bothered about them. All out efforts must be made to resolve the river waters disputes amicably. In case of failure to arrive at an agreed solution, the matter may be referred to the Supreme Court with all parties pledging to accept its verdict. There should not be any agitation on this question.

Of course, terrorism needs some sort of mass base. Its mass base in Punjab has shrunk very much, but it would be wrong to think that it does not or cannot have any. It goes without saying that in the changed circumstances terrorism cannot re-emerge in the same form and on the same scale. But that there is a danger of its re-emergence can be seen from the following.

Many top leaders of the terrorists are still functioning from other countries, including Pakistan. Some of them visit Punjab off and on. Many "boys" are living in their own villages, and will act at the "proper" time. We must not forget that Chief Minister Beant Singh himself fell a martyr at the hands of terrorists. Some incidents took place before, and even after, Parkash Singh Badal became Chief Minister of Punjab. Not all of them are insignificant. The rulers of Pakistan are becoming more active in fuelling Khalistani terrorism to make their game in Kashmir easier. The head of the recently set up Pakistan Gurdwara Prabandhak Committee, who is a retired chief of the ISI, has openly declared his determination to use gurdwaras in Pakistan with a view to bring about

India's disintegration. Neither Nawaz Sharif nor his army bosses contradicted him. Nursing illusions about US imperialism as a result of whatever criticism it has made of Pakistan in relation to the invasion of Kargil can prove dangerous. The basic aim of the US Government remains to control Kashmir in its own interests.

The factional fight that has broken out between Parkash Singh Badal and Gurcharan Singh Tohra factions of the Akalis cannot but help terrorism in Punjab to re-emerge. It has been a lifelong ambition of Jathedar Tohra to become the Chief Minister of Punjab. He opened his attack immediately after the Akali candidate in an assembly by-election lost from Adampur, a traditionally Akali constituency. Tohra asked Badal to step down from the presidentship of the Akali Party.

Badal had plans to organise the tercentenary celebrations of the birth of the Khalsa on behalf of the Punjab Government in order to draw the maximum political and factional advantage. Tohra would have liked the job to be left to the SGPC of which he was then the President, with similar motives, with the government helping only by providing the infrastructure. The proper thing would have been to set up a committee for the purpose. It should have consisted of representatives of the SGPC and should have included Sikh religious personalities and even some Sikh political leaders, but in their individual capacity. The state should have helped in providing for essential civic amenities and infrastructure facilities. A major part of the celebrations should have been a massive campaign on issues like the caste system. From Guru Nanak to Guru Gobind Singh, all the Sikh Gurus fought against the caste system. But what is the actual situation amongst the Sikhs today? In a very large number of villages in Punjab Scheduled Caste Sikhs have separate gurdwaras and are required to have separate *shamshan bhumis* to cremate their dead. A Sikh Scheduled Caste young man can marry a young Jat Sikh girl only if both are ready to risk their lives. Not to speak of any campaign, the issue was hardly mentioned anywhere. After all, Sikh landlords stand to gain if poor peasants and agricultural labourers can be kept divided, making use of caste differences.

What is most dangerous is the fact that both Tohra and Badal have been misusing the sacred institution of the Akal Takht for their narrow political and factional interests. Once again there are rival claimants to the Akal Takht jathedarship. They have aligned themselves with Badal and Tohra respectively. Tohra declares openly that the Akal Takht Jathedar must be supreme even in the political field and that his political hukumnamas too are bindings on all Sikhs. Badal also says that politics and religion cannot be separated. Nor is that all. He stands for a Sikh theocratic state within India with a very weak Centre. He has been claiming that his government is a Panthic government and in actual practice he has been functioning his government as if Sikhism is the official religion of Punjab. (The BJP does not object, because the Akalis do not object to their working for a Hindu Rashtra as dictated by the RSS, by taking steps to Hinduise India. Also, the BJP is, after all, the junior partner.) Badal therefore seeks to fight Tohra on the latter's ground. He does not demand that the Akal Takht Jathedar should not dabble in politics, that politics and religion must be separated. He got his own man appointed as the Akal Takht Jathedar and deposed Ranjit Singh, who according to Tohra, is the real jathedar. It is futile to expect Parkash Singh Badal to call for a debate amongst the Sikhs on whether such institutions as hukumnamas and Sarbat Khalsa have any relevance today, and whether they should be misused more for wrong ends than used for good. Such a debate is very necessary today. Except for those who do not want to learn any lesson from the long and terrible years of terrorism, all will realise that such a situation can help terrorism to re-emerge in one form or another—even though Badal and his government may not want that. The difference between Badal and Tohra has to be noted and taken into account by all progressives. However, its limitation too must not be lost sight of, if the re-emergence of terrorism has to be prevented by rousing the people against it and by ensuring that the government continues to act firmly.

Last but not the least, we must not be carried away by Tohra's declarations that his Akali Dal stands for the unity and integrity of India, nor the declaration of Simranjit Singh Mann that he will not raise the issue of Khalistan "during elections". Electoral compulsions may lead to some more sweet-sounding declarations. But let us not forget that Mann had made a similar declaration before the previous elections. Then he had made clear that this was only to bypass constitutional hurdles for candidates demanding India's disintegration. For obvious reasons, he has chosen to maintain a discreet silence. Let us not judge anyone by the declarations they make now, keeping in view the coming elections. Let us judge all by their deeds hitherto. All should be happy if there is a change for the better in any party or leader. But let us not decide our line of action on the basis of wishful thinking.

*(June 26, 1999)*

## Appendix-I

## Some Prominent Persons Killed by Khalistani Terrorists

**Author's Note: This is not a complete list.**

| S. N. | Name | Date on which Killed |
|---|---|---|
| 1. | Nirankari Chief Baba Gurbachan Singh | April 4, 1980 |
| 2. | Lala Jagat Narain, Chief Editor, *Hind Samachar* group of papers | November 9, 1981 |
| 3. | Sarbjit Arri, prominent leader of government teachers, Gurdaspur | February 22, 1984 |
| 4. | Harbans Lal Khanna, BJP leader and former MLA | April 2, 1984 |
| 5. | Dr. Vishwa Nath Tiwari of Punjab University, MP, Chandigarh | April 3, 1984 |
| 6. | Sukhraj Khaddar (CPI-ML), Editor, *Chingari* Gurdaspur | April 11, 1984 |
| 7. | Sumit Singh alias Shammi, Editor, *Preet Lari* | April 22, 1984 |
| 8. | Giani Partap Singh, former head priest of Akal Takht | May 10, 1984 |
| 9. | Romesh Chander, Editor, *Hind Samachar* group, son of Lala Jagat Narain | May 12, 1984 |
| 10. | Principal O.P. Bagga, ex-MLA | June 2, 1984 |
| 11. | Bhisham Prakash, Congress leader of Khanna | May 1, 1985 |
| 12. | Ch. Balbir Singh, well-known socialist leader of Punjab, Hoshiarpur | May 10, 1985 |
| 13. | Sant Harchand Singh Longowal, Akali leader | August 20, 1985 |
| 14. | Arjun Singh Mastana, prominent CPI leader | March 27, 1986 |
| 15. | Khet Mazdoor leader (CPI) Ajit Ram, along with his 8-year old son Babla | July 3, 1986 |
| 16. | Bibi Guro, Istri Sabha and CPI activist, her husband Babu Ram and brother-in-law Parswarth Ram (old freedom fighter and CPI activist who gave shelter to Subhas Bose when he escaped from India) | August 8, 1986 |
| 17. | Darshan Singh Canadian, member National Council and former secretary, Punjab CPI | September 25, 1986 |
| 18. | Baldev Singh Mann, CPI-ML leader | September 26, 1986 |
| 19. | Joginder Pal Pandey, Congress leader and former minister | January 19, 1987 |
| 20. | Chanan Singh Dhoot, veteran CPI-M leader | February 16, 1987 |
| 21. | Sukhdev Singh, son of prominent Akali leader Jiwan Singh Umranangal | May 8, 1987 |
| 22. | Deepak Dhawan, youth leader of CPI-M | May 19, 1987 |
| 23. | Gurnam Singh Uppal, President, Punjab unit of Democratic Youth Federation of India | July 3, 1987 |
| 24. | Harnam Singh Jhumra, famous freedom fighter and CPI leader, shot on June 26 and died on | July 6, 1987 |
| 25. | Capt. Pritam Singh, freedom fighter and former INA member | July 8, 1987 |
| 26. | Swaran Singh Sohal, member Amritsar district committee of CPI, his wife Surinder Kaur, | |

| | | |
|---|---|---|
| | his mother Datto, daughter Rupinder (12), agricultural helper Hira Singh (15) | July 21/22, 1987 |
| 27. | Bhupinderjit Singh, member Punjab State Council, CPI | November 11, 1987 |
| 28. | Ch. Jagat Ram, Vice-President Punjab Congress, former minister | January 5, 1988 |
| 29. | Dasaundha Singh, member Amritsar District Council, CPI | March 1, 1988 |
| 30. | Jaimal Singh Padda, CPI-ML leader, Editor, *Hirawal Dasta* | March 17, 1988 |
| 31. | Avtar Singh Pash, well-known revolutionary poet, and Hans Raj, Jalandhar | March 23, 1988 |
| 32. | Khushdev Singh, advocate, Gurpreet Kaur and Gurdip Singh (The House of Haryana State Council Secretary, CPI, Dr. Harnam Singh was attacked by a gang of terrorists. The family fought back heroically. Dr. Harnam Singh lost his son, daughter-in-law and a nephew. Two relatives were injured and a terrorist was also killed) | April 9, 1988 |
| 33. | Harbans Singh Beeka, CPI-M leader, Jalandhar | May 13, 1988 |
| 34. | Malkiat Chand Mohli, member CPI State Council | May 23, 1988 |
| 35. | Hit Abhilashi, BJP leader and former minister | September 19, 1988 |
| 36. | Nachhattar Dhaliwal, member CPI State Council, Vice-President Punjab State AITUC | October 21, 1988 |
| 37. | Rajinder Kaur, daughter of late Akali leader Master Tara Singh, Editor, *Sant Sipahi* | February 5, 1989 |
| 38. | Gurmail Singh Hoojan, member Punjab State Council, CPI | May 14, 1989 |
| 39. | Dr. Ravinder Ravi, professor in Punjab University and general secretary, Kendri Punjabi Lekhak Sabha | May 18, 1989 |
| 40. | Dalip Singh, CPI-M leader and President District Kisan Sabha along with 6 family members including two infant grand-daughters | May 20, 1989 |
| 41. | Sohan Singh Dhesi, CPI-M, secretary DYFI, Punjab | September 18, 1989 |
| 42. | Gursewak Singh, UCPI | January 11, 1990 |
| 43. | Jaswant Singh, CPI, President Trade Union Council | January 25, 1990 |
| 44. | Sarbjit Singh Bhittewad, Secretary, Amritsar District CPI-ML | May 3, 1990 |
| 45. | Balwant Singh, Akali leader and former Punjab finance minister | July 10, 1990 |
| 46. | Fauja Singh, member District Council, CPI | July 23, 1990 |
| 47. | Vijay Kumar, CPI-M leader, along with his gunman Hari Singh | September 29, 1990 |
| 48. | Sat Pal Duggal, member Gurdaspur District Council, CPI | December 18, 1990 |
| 49. | Dhanwant Kaur, CPI-M, leader of Janwadi Istri Sabha, along with her son | September, 1990 |
| 50. | Jagdish Chander, secretary District Committee CPI-M, Ropar | January 24, 1991 |

| | | |
|---|---|---|
| 51. | Satwant Kaur w/o late Jaswant Singh (see No. 43 above), Balwant Singh, his younger brother and youth leader CPI, Paramjit Kaur w/o Balwant Singh of CPI and Sukhwant Singh, CPI-M, brother of late Jaswant Singh and his wife Paramjit Kaur (Also 3 security guards; in all 11 persons including 3 children were shot dead.) | May 16, 1991 |
| 52. | Brij Bhushan Mehra, Congress, former Speaker, Punjab Vidhan Sabha | June 3, 1991 |
| 53. | Amolak Singh, CPI State Council member and top leader of agricultural workers | June 7, 1991 |
| 54. | Swaran Singh Cheema, ex-MLA, CPI-M | November 4, 1991 |
| 55. | Harpal Khokhar, President Punjab unit of DYFI | January 25, 1992 |
| 56. | Beant Singh, Chief Minister of Punjab | August 31, 1995 |

# Appendix-II

## Brutal Mass Killings by Khalistani Terrorists

**Author's Note : For the following material I am indebted to the book *The Bleeding Punjab — A Report to the Nation* edited by Amolakh Singh and Jaspal Jassi. As the editors say, this is not an exhaustive list and there have been many more incidents. For instance on March 11, 1992, 15 engineers from outside Punjab were killed by terrorists. They were working on a project in Sangrur district and had come from different states: Haryana, UP, Maharashtra, Madhya Pradesh and Kerala. The list, however, will show the extent of the indiscriminate mass killings of innocent people by those who professed to be fighting for Khalistan.**

| **Year and Date** | **Place** | **Nature of Incident** |
|---|---|---|
| Oct. 1983 | Dhilwan | 6 Hindu bus passengers killed. |
| Oct. 21, 1983 | Gobindgarh | Massacre of rail passengers. |
| Sept. 12, 1984 | Batala | 8 Hindu bus passengers killed. |
| June 22, 1984 | Irish Sea | Air India Boeing 747 blasted by bomb; all 329 passengers killed. |
| February, 1986 | Nakodar | 15 persons killed and many injured in indiscriminate firing. |
| March 6, 1986 | Kapurthala | Many innocent persons killed in indiscriminate firing. |
| March 28, 1986 | Ludhiana | 13 Hindus killed in indiscriminate firing. |
| March 29, 1986 | Mallian (Jalandhar) | 20 innocent labourers killed. |
| July 25, 1986 | Muktasar | 15 Hindu bus passengers gunned down. |
| Oct. 31, 1986 | Ludhiana | 8 migrant and local Hindu industrial worker gunned down on Daba Road. |
| Nov. 30, 1986 | Khudda | 24 Hindu bus passengers gunned down. |
| July, 1987 | Lalru Fatehabad | 80 bus passengers killed in three Haryana Roadways buses. |
| Aug. 6, 1987 | Jgadev Kalan (Majitha) | 13 Hindus gunned down. |
| Sept. 28, 1987 | Alawalpur (Jalandhar) | 5 killed and 8 injured in firing near Geeta Bhawan. |
| Oct. 20, 1987 | Delhi | 12 persons shot dead at various places on *Diwali* day. |
| Jan. 15, 1988 | Dhadial Nijhran (Near Batala) | 8 members of a family, including 2 women and 3 children killed. |
| Feb. 19, 1988 | | Bombs exploded by Babbar Khalsa at Gurdaspur, Hoshiarpur and Patiala. 12 persons killed, over 50 injured. |
| March 2, 1988 | Bhaian (Verowal) | 8 members of a family killed. |
| March 3, 1988 | Kahri Sahri (Hoshiarpur) | 35 person shot dead, 50 injured in indiscriminate firing at a festival gathering. |
| March 31, 1988 | Theh Rajbah (Patti) | 18 members of a Rajput family shot dead in village Theh Rajbah under police station Harike. |

| | | |
|---|---|---|
| April 2, 1988 | Ramgarh (Amritsar) | 6 persons massacred in this village under police station Gharinda. 18 more person killed in other parts of Punjab. |
| May 15, 1988 | | 40 persons gunned down, 10 injured in different incidents at Samana, Patiala, Jalandhar and Mukerian. |
| May 16, 1988 | | 26 killed (3 members of a family, 3 bus passengers and 20 others) in Amritsar, Ludhiana, Jalandhar and Gurdaspur. |
| May 17, 1988 | Kharar | 35 labourers killed. |
| May 24, 1988 | Dhaliwal (Nakodar) | 6 members of a family massacred. |
| June 19, 1988 | Kurukshetra | 15 persons blown to pieces when a bomb exploded at a TV shop during the telecast of TV serial "Ramayana". |
| June 25, 1988 | Moga | 26 RSS volunteers killed, 22 injured in an indiscriminate firing in Nehru Park. |
| Sept. 7, 1988 | Rure Aasal | 15 rail passengers killed, 25 injured at Rure Aasal railway station near Khem Karan. |
| Nov. 1, 1988 | Pathankot | Many killed and injured in a bomb blast in a Jammu-bound bus. |
| Nov. 1988 | Majaat | 32 migrant labourers working on SYL Canal gunned down. |
| Nov. 3, 1988 | Sufianwala | 11 bus passengers killed by a BTFK gang from a Dera Nanal bound bus. All killed were Hindus. |
| Nov. 4, 1988 | Lodhuwal (Ludhiana) | 19 labourers shot dead at government seed farm Lodhuwal. |
| Nov. 1988 | Batala | 25 persons killed in a bomb blast in Chakkri Bazar. |
| | Sirhind | Indiscriminate firing in bazar, many killed. |
| | Pathankot | Bomb blast near a tempo overloaded with passengers. Many including a woman killed. |
| Nov. 22, 1988 | Kaithal (Haryana) | 25 persons massacred, 37 others injured. |
| Nov. 22, 1988 | Batala | 22 persons killed, many injured in indiscriminate firing in bazar on eve of Guru Nanak's birthday. |
| Dec. 1988 | Makhu | 7 Hindu passengers kidnapped from a Chandigarh bound bus and killed. |
| Dec. 7, 1988 | Gujran | 5 members of a marriage party killed in indiscriminate firing on Zeera-Makhu Road. |
| May 21, 1989 | Chakk Kania | 7 members of a family, including a CPI-M member Dalip Singh massacred. |
| | Bagga Kalan | 4 members of a family killed. |
| Aug. 27, 1989 | Kabarwala (Abohar) | Dozens shot dead in indiscriminate firing for 50 minutes on a train at Kabarwala station. |
| Oct. 5, 1989 | Kandhwala (Fazilka) | 5 members of a family shot dead. |
| Nov. 1989 | Patiala | 19 Hindu students massacred in Thapar Engineering College. They had come from other states to participate in a youth festival. |
| Jan. 19, 1990 | Bahmanwal (Majitha) | 8 including 6 Hindus massacred. |
| March 7, 1999 | Abohar | 32 shot dead in indiscriminate firing in a crowded bazar. |

| | | |
|---|---|---|
| March 19, 1990 | Talwandi Bhai | 14 persons shot dead. |
| | Chandigarh | 6 persons killed, 27 injured in a bomb blast. |
| | Nawan Shahar | 11 persons killed in a bomb blast. |
| April 3, 1990 | Batala | 36 persons killed in a bomb blast. |
| April 19, 1990 | Pathankot | 15 passengers killed, 40 injured in a bomb blast in a bus. |
| May 28, 1990 | Ferozepur | 13 Bihari labourers shot dead. |
| May 30, 1990 | Talwandi Bhai | 10 persons massacred. |
| June 4, 1990 | Patiala | 8 including 6 children killed and 30 injured in a bomb explosion. |
| July 15, 1990 | Taredan | 8 members of a family gunned down in village Tarendan under Mamdot police station. |
| July 30, 1990 | Bidar (Karnataka) | 35 killed, 30 injured in abomb explosion in a local cinema hall. |
| Aug. 8, 1990 | Ludhiana | 9 gunned down in indiscriminate firing. |
| May 5, 1990 | Batala | 9 Hindu passengers shot dead in a Batala-Jalandhar bus. |
| Nov. 9, 1990 | Batala | 5 Hindus shot dead after forcing them to alight from vehicles on Batala-Pathankot Highway. |
| Nov. 12, 1990 | Kothe Lal Singh (Bathinda) | 8 Hindus killed by KCF (Zafarwal) gang. |
| Nov. 15, 1990 | Ferozepur | 7 Hindu passengers of a Ferozpur-Dharamkot bus shot dead. |
| Nov. 17, 1990 | Kilianwali | 11 RSS workers killed in indiscriminate firing on morning assembly. |
| Nov. 20, 1990 | Amritsar | 12 killed in a massacre. |
| Nov. 22, 1990 | Chandigarh | 16 Hindus killed after forcing them to alight from two buses near Parhol. |
| Nov. 24, 1990 | Patti | 5 Hindus shot dead. |
| Nov. 25, 1990 | Jalandhar | 15 shot dead in indiscriminate firing. |
| Nov. 26, 1990 | Ludhiana | 5 members of a Hindu family shot dead on Daba Road. |
| Dec. 13, 1990 | Sedeke | 5 Hindu passengers shot dead in Sedeke village near Guru Harsahai. |
| Jan. 8, 1991 | Gill | 14 Hindus Kidnapped from different places shot dead at village Gill near Ludhiana. |
| March 22, 1991 | Chandigarh | 30 employees of Punjab Tractors Ltd. Foundry, all Hindus, shot dead. |
| April 9, 1991 | Sewewala | 18 activits shot dead and 22 injured in indiscriminate firing on a gathering. |
| June 15, 1991 | Baddowal Kila Raipur | 75 train passengers shot dead by KLF. |
| Nov. 17, 1991 | Sirsa | 16 persons, all Hindus, shot dead. |
| Nov. 9, 1991 | Faridkot | 7 family members shot dead in a village in Faridkot district. |
| Nov. 17, 1991 | Rudarpur (UP) | 12 persons shot dead. |
| Dec. 19, 1991 | Ludhiana | 12 killed in a bomb blast in Bharat Nagar Chowk. |
| Dec. 26, 1991 | Sohian | 32 rail passengers shot dead at Sohian railway crossing in Ludhiana district. |

| | | |
|---|---|---|
| Jan. 8, 1992 | Kharar, Kup Kalan | 21 industrial workers shot dead. |
| Jan. 15, 1992 | Dhanaula | 5 electricity employees gunned down at grid station. |
| Jan. 17, 1992 | Samana | 7 persons killed in a bomb blast. |
| March 10-20, 1992 | Samana | 75 persons gunned down in 4 separate incidents, factory workers from outside the state at Ghabadan, others in indiscriminate shootouts twice in Ludhiana and once in Ahmedgarh. |
| June 25, 1992 | Kila Raipur | 9 Hindus gunned down. |
| July 13, 1992 | Bassian | 7 Hindus gunned down. |
| July 13, 1992 | Bathinda | 7 Hindus (5 sweepers and 2 migrant workers) gunned down. |
| May 2, 1992 | Kadarvaad | 7 members of a family of 8 killed in village Kadarvaad, poilce station Majitha. |
| May 3, 1992 | Sadarpur (Haryana) | 10 persons killed, 3 injured in village Sadarpur, district Karnal. |